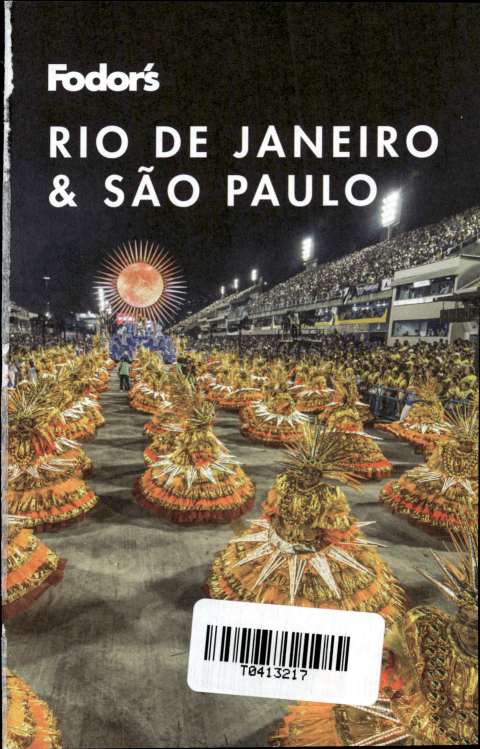

TOP REASONS TO GO

★ **Rich culture:** Brazil is a vibrant blend of cultures, reflected in its stunning architecture, diverse cuisine, and laid-back lifestyle.

★ **Carnival like no other:** From dazzling parades to countless free street parties, there's a celebration in every corner.

★ **Incredible food:** Indulge in fresh tropical fruits, tapioca, açaí, and the world's finest churrasco (barbecue).

★ **Breathtaking nature:** From idyllic beaches and lush rainforests to dramatic mountains, Brazil's landscapes make you feel like you're visiting multiple countries in one trip.

Welcome to Rio de Janeiro & São Paulo

There's a local saying that "God is Brazilian," and it's hard to disagree when you witness the country's breathtaking wonders—some of the world's most beautiful beaches, vast rainforests, and stunning mountains. Yet, Brazil's greatest treasure is its people. Beyond the image of a joyful and friendly nation, Brazil is, at its core, a land shaped by a powerful history of resilience and resistance, built by the diverse peoples who have contributed to its unique identity.

With more than 4,745 miles (7,637 km) of coastline, Brazil is home to iconic beaches like Copacabana and Ipanema. But the country offers far more than sun and sand. It's also home to São Paulo, Latin America's largest city—a true cultural melting pot filled with global influences. São Paulo is famous for its world-class restaurants, renowned museums, dynamic street art, and impressive skyline.

Planning an itinerary for a vast country like Brazil can be overwhelming. While it's impossible to cover everything in one visit, focusing on Rio de Janeiro and São Paulo will give you an authentic taste of Brazil's culture, energy, and diverse landscapes.

In Rio, explore its iconic beaches and lively atmosphere, while São Paulo offers the urban experience with landmarks like Avenida Paulista. Don't miss the chance to savor national dishes paired with a refreshing caipirinha. Renting a car unlocks even more possibilities, allowing you to discover São Paulo's unexpected coastal gems and Rio's charming mountain towns—once a favorite getaway for Brazil's imperial family.

Plan for at least one week to see the main highlights of Rio and São Paulo. However, two weeks is ideal to explore at a relaxed pace, visit nearby cities, and truly enjoy the experience.

One of the magical aspects of Brazil is how dramatically the landscapes change after just a short drive. If you're renting a car, be aware of speed limits: 30 km/h (18 mph) in cities, 60 km/h (37 mph) on multilane avenues, and 80 km/h (50 mph) on highways for light vehicles. Road conditions are generally good, but traffic can be heavy during holidays and summer months. São Paulo and Rio are particularly known for congestion, so it's often best to rely on public transportation or taxis within the cities. As you plan your trip, reconfirm that places are still open and let us know when we need to make updates at ✉ *corrections@fodors.com*.

Contents

1 EXPERIENCE RIO DE JANEIRO AND SÃO PAULO 8

22 Ultimate Experiences 10
What's Where 18
Brazil Today 20
What to Eat in Rio de Janeiro and São Paulo 22
What to Drink in Rio de Janeiro and São Paulo 24
Best Beaches of Rio de Janeiro 26
Best Beaches Outside of São Paulo 28
What to Buy in Rio de Janeiro and São Paulo 30
Best Museums of Rio de Janeiro and São Paulo 32
History You Can See 34
What to Read and Watch ... 36

2 TRAVEL SMART 39

Know Before You Go 40
Getting Here and Around ... 42
Essentials 47
Best Tours 63
Helpful Brazilian Phrases ... 64
Great Itineraries 66
On the Calendar 70

3 RIO DE JANEIRO 73

Welcome to Rio de Janeiro 74
Carnival 76
Planning 79
Centro 87
Catete and Glória 98
Flamengo and Botafogo ... 100
Urca 105
Copacabana 106
Leme 116
Santa Teresa and Lapa 117
Ipanema and Leblon 124
São Conrado and Barra da Tijuca 138
West of Downtown 143
Inland Zona Sul 148

4 SIDE TRIPS FROM RIO 153

Welcome to Side Trips from Rio 154
Planning 157
Niterói 161
Arraial do Cabo 164
Búzios 166
Petrópolis 172
Angra dos Reis 175
Ilha Grande 177
Paraty 182

5 SÃO PAULO ... 189

- Welcome to São Paulo 190
- Parque Ibirapuera 192
- Planning 195
- Centro 202
- Avenida Paulista, Bela Vista, and Bixiga 213
- Vila Madalena and Pinheiros 223
- Parque Ibirapuera 227
- Itaim Bibi 230
- Liberdade 233
- Vila Olímpia and Brooklin .. 235
- Barra Funda 237
- Jardins 239
- Greater São Paulo 245

6 SIDE TRIPS FROM SÃO PAULO ... 249

- Welcome to Side Trips from São Paulo 250
- Planning 253
- Santos 254
- São Sebastião 258
- Ilhabela 261
- Ubatuba 265
- Águas de São Pedro 268
- Campos do Jordão 268
- Serra Negra 274
- Embu 276
- Santana de Parnaíba 278

INDEX ... 280

MAPS

- Rio de Janeiro Metro Network 82
- Centro 88–89
- Flamengo, Botafogo, and Urca 102–103
- Copacabana and Leme 108–109
- Santa Teresa and Lapa 118
- Ipanema and Leblon .. 126–127
- West of Downtown and Inland Zona Sul .. 146–147
- Costa do Sol 161
- Costa Verde 184
- Centro 204
- Avenida Paulista, Bela Vista, and Bixiga 214
- Vila Madalena and Pinheiros 224
- Parque Ibirapuera 228
- Itaim Bibi 231
- Jardins 240
- Inland 256
- The North Coast 259

About Our Writers

The beaches of Rio de Janeiro are amazing, but Ilha Grande is worth the trip outside of the city.

Leticia Davino has worked as a translator and interpreter, fluent in English and Spanish, which has given her the opportunity to meet people and explore cultures around the world. With a degree in international relations, she has always been fascinated by the differences and similarities between peoples, which led her to live in cities such as Dublin and New York. However, her true passion has always been São Paulo, her hometown, which she considers one of the best places on the planet.

Having visited over 40 countries, Leticia believes that travel experiences are transformative and enrich the lives of those who live them. This passion for exploring the world inspired her to open her own travel agency, with the goal of helping others realize their dream of discovering new destinations and cultures. Through her Instagram (@ledavino), she shares her own adventures and offers a unique perspective on the daily life of a true travel enthusiast, always encouraging her followers to embark on their own journeys of discovery and learning.

She is thrilled to be able to showcase and share a little of the city where she was raised, and all that it can offer and surprise. She knows the tourism potential that São Paulo and Brazil as a whole have, and feels excited to see more and more people showing interest in her beloved country.

Luana Ferreira holds a degree in journalism and has over 15 years of experience in the field, writing about a wide variety of topics for outlets such as BBC, Al Jazeera, and *Food & Wine*. She speaks Portuguese—her mother language—and is fluent in English and Spanish, which enables her to conduct interviews, research, and write in these languages. Luana is also an experienced travel

Avenida Paulista is the main drag in Sao Paulo, attracting tourists and locals alike for shopping and museum hopping.

journalist, having visited dozens of countries in recent years. However, none of them seem as surprising to her as her home country, Brazil. She is passionate about the nuances of this complex place and, of course, firmly believes there's no place in the world like Rio, though she insists there's no better place to eat than São Paulo.

Luana takes pride in her deep knowledge of the many facets of these two cities, going far beyond the typical clichés, and she helps people discover these destinations beyond the obvious. She shares her travel tips from around the world on Instagram: @luanaferreiratravelwriter.

Gabriela Godoi holds a degree in journalism and has over 10 years of experience in the tourism field. She has worked in public relations for tourism industry members, such as Hyatt Hotels, Visit Tampa Bay, Saint-Martin, Ethiopian Airlines, and local hotels and associations in Brazil. She speaks Portuguese—her mother language—and is fluent in English and has an intermediate level of knowledge of Spanish and French. Her passion for tourism started long ago, when she was planning her first trips alone and met some other travelers in associations like Couchsurfing. Gabriela became a representative for her hometown—Rio de Janeiro—on its website, organizing events and providing updates on what is new and hot in the "Wonderful City". She is also passionate about the main party of her city, Carnaval, and tries to keep the flame lit all year long, going to the samba schools and other Carnaval-related events. She has just started an Instagram profile to gather her tips: @gabimeguia.

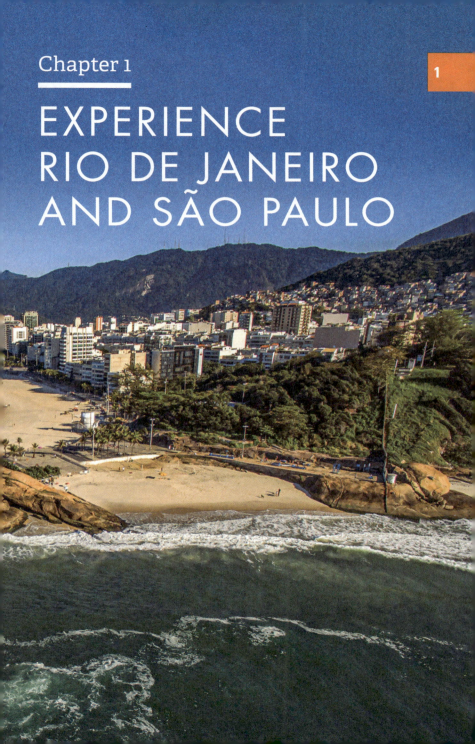

Chapter 1

EXPERIENCE RIO DE JANEIRO AND SÃO PAULO

22 ULTIMATE EXPERIENCES

Rio de Janeiro and São Paulo offer terrific experiences that should be on every traveler's list. Here are Fodor's top picks for a memorable trip.

1 Sugarloaf Mountain

To reach the peak of Sugarloaf Mountain, choose between the cable car ride or the hiking trail. For an unforgettable experience, plan to visit on a Sunday afternoon to enjoy a traditional samba. *(Ch. 3)*

2 Paraty
Visit the UNESCO World Heritage Site to discover a well-preserved Portuguese colonial town. Paraty is a cultural hub and is surrounded by pristine beaches. *(Ch. 4)*

3 Carnival in Rio
Whether enjoying the over 450 street *blocos* or the famous Carnival parade at Sapucaí, experiencing the Greatest Show On Earth should be on everyone's bucket list. *(Ch. 3)*

4 Copacabana and Ipanema Beaches

Visiting two of the world's most famous beaches and blending with locals sunbathing or playing sports by the beach makes you feel almost like a *Carioca*. *(Ch. 3)*

5 Brazilian Beats

The vibrant music scene goes from enjoying a traditional Roda de Samba to discovering rhythms such as the funk carioca, brega funk recifense, forró, and piseiro. *(Ch. 3)*

6 Museu de Arte de São Paulo

MASP offers an unparalleled cultural experience with its striking modernist architecture and one of the most impressive collections of Western art in the Southern Hemisphere. *(Ch. 5)*

7 Soccer Matches

Soccer is the country's second religion. Watching a major team playing in a stadium along with thousands of fans is unforgettable. *(Ch. 3,5)*

8 Ilhabela

This tropical paradise has over 40 pristine beaches surrounded by lush rainforests, making it a dream destination for nature lovers and adventure seekers alike. *(Ch. 6)*

9 Buzios

Driving a few hours from Rio, enjoy this upscale town with unspoiled beaches, top restaurants, and great nightlife. *(Ch. 4)*

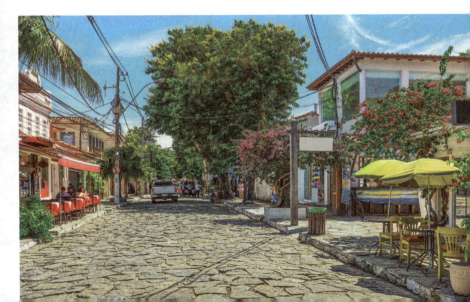

10 Markets in São Paulo

São Paulo's markets, like the iconic Mercado Municipal, offer a lively mix of fresh produce, exotic spices, and gourmet delights, making them a foodie paradise. *(Ch. 5)*

11 Brazilian Food and Drink

The cuisine here is influenced by varying cultures. Make sure to try *pão de queijo* (cheese bread) and *feijoada*, paired with a caipirinha or fruit juices. *(Ch. 3-6)*

12 São Paulo Nightlife

From the bohemian bars at Vila Madalena to upscale clubs scattered along the city, the party here never ends. *(Ch. 5)*

13 Beco de Batman

It is famous for its ever-evolving street art, transforming alleyways into an open-air gallery. *(Ch. 5)*

14 Christ the Redeemer Statue

When visiting Rio for the first time, this is a mandatory stop. Visit early in the morning to avoid the crowds and check the weather conditions before visiting. *(Ch. 3)*

15 Coffee in São Paulo
Brazil is famous for its coffee beans and São Paulo has several specialized shops to enjoy them. *(Ch. 5)*

16 Ilha Grande
This tropical paradise is known for its beaches and lush nature, ideal for hiking and snorkeling. *(Ch. 4)*

17 Liberdade
This neighborhood is celebrated for its rich Japanese heritage, bustling markets, and authentic Asian cuisine. *(Ch. 5)*

18 Rua Oscar Freire
This chic shopping destination is renowned for its luxury boutiques, trendy cafés, and sophisticated restaurants. *(Ch. 5)*

19 Sidewalk Cafes in Rio de Janeiro

Enjoy Rio's laid-back vibe while sipping a refreshing drink and watching the city's vibrant street life. *(Ch. 3)*

20 Afro-Brazilian Culture

The influence is everywhere. Music, dance, religion, cuisine, language, and traditions are deeply rooted in African heritage. *(Ch. 3-6)*

21 Praia do Arpoador

It's a favorite spot among Cariocas and tourists to watch the sunset and swim in the emerald waters. *(Ch. 3)*

22 Autódromo de Interlagos— Grand Prix do Brasil

Home to the electrifying Brazilian Grand Prix, this is a must-visit for its rich motorsport history, thrilling high-speed corners, and passionate fan energy. *(Ch. 5)*

WHAT'S WHERE

1 Rio de Janeiro. Rio does justice to the title of Marvelous City. Nestled between lush mountains and the Atlantic Ocean, it boasts one of the most stunning natural settings in the world. Known for its fantastic beaches, iconic landmarks like Sugarloaf Mountain and Christ the Redeemer, and vibrant city life, Rio is a blend of breathtaking landscapes and rich culture.

2 Costa do Sol. Heading north of Rio de Janeiro, the Costa do Sol (Sun Coast) is a paradise of unspoiled beaches, turquoise waters, and charming coastal towns. Here you can choose to visit places like the fancy Búzios or the paradisaic Arraial do Cabo—each town offers the perfect scape for sunseekers and nature lovers alike.

3 Costa Verde. Stretching from Itaguaí (Rio de Janeiro) to Santo (São Paulo), the Costa Verde (Green Coast) is a lush, tropical paradise perfect for adventure. This region is famous for its emerald forests, crystal-clear waters, and islands like Ilha Grande, which makes it a haven for eco-tourism.

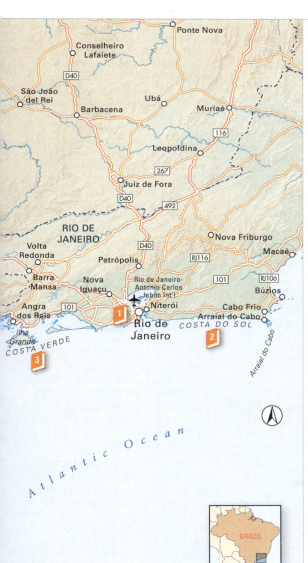

4 São Paulo. As Brazil's largest city, São Paulo is a bustling metropolis renowned for its cosmopolitan culture, world-class dining, and vibrant arts scene. Known among Brazilians as the Stone Jungle, the city is located in southeastern Brazil and it is a hub of innovation and history, surrounded by architectural landmarks and green spaces that reflect its dynamic character.

5 Coast of São Paulo. São Paulo's coastline is a treasure trove of sandy beaches, small fishing villages, and thriving marine life. From the historic port city of Santos to the idyllic beaches of Ubatuba, this region offers everything from relaxation to famous beach parties.

6 Inland São Paulo. Offering a contrast to the Stone Jungle in the capital, inland São Paulo reveals a different side of the state, with rolling hills, coffee plantations, and charming colonial towns like Santa da Parnaíba. The region is perfect for exploring Brazil's cultural roots and enjoying a romantic getaway within the mountains.

Brazil Today

Brazil is immensely diverse—socially, culturally, racially, economically—and rife with profound contradictions that are not always evident at first. All this makes for a complex nation that eludes easy definitions—but is fascinating to discover.

CULTURE

Brazil is often described as the land of samba, Carnival, soccer, and beaches. If you ask locals, they usually define their home country as a land of contrasts—this undeniable truth is reflected in its landscape, where massive favelas and upscale neighborhoods coexist side-by-side. Yet the contrast goes beyond the socioeconomic aspect, as the country with the world's largest number of Catholics—over 100 million—also hosts the world's largest Carnival celebrations, when the country stops for five days and millions of people take over the streets to party.

Brazilians are mostly warm and outgoing, and public displays of affection are natural among friends, family, and couples. On the other hand, Brazilians can be surprisingly conservative in certain aspects; views on marriage, politics, and religion are just a few examples.

Brazil's culture is shaped by approximately 300 Indigenous ethnic groups, over four million enslaved Africans, Portuguese and Spanish colonizers, Italians, German, Japanese, and Arabic immigrants. Their influences can be noticed in the language, accents, gastronomy, music, architecture, and religion. Despite their importance to Brazilian society, Indigenous groups and Black peoples' issues are often overlooked.

POLITICS

Brazil's political landscape is ever-evolving. After more than two decades of military dictatorship, Brazilians regained the right to elect their president in 1989. Fernando Collor won that election but was impeached in 1992. In the last decade, political polarization deepened, culminating in the election of Jair Bolsonaro, a far-right politician who governed from 2019 to 2022. In 2022, he was defeated by Luiz Inácio Lula da Silva, now serving his third presidential term. Lula had previously led Brazil during an economic boom in the 2010s but was later imprisoned for 18 months on corruption charges. In 2019, the Supreme Court annulled his case, citing procedural errors, leading to his release. The Supreme Electoral Court has since banned Bolsonaro from running for office for eight years, effective until 2030.

To this day, the country remains deeply polarized, and the tension extends beyond elections. Despite being a democracy, Brazil cannot take its democratic stability for granted, as its institutions have recently had to resist threats such as the infamous events of January 8 and the plot to assassinate Lula before his 2023 inauguration. Brasilia—the country's capital and political heart—serves as a backdrop for protests and significant historical events, but São Paulo and Rio also have significant roles.

ECONOMY

After years of economic instability and hyperinflation in the 1980s and 1990s, Brazil's economy experienced significant growth, driven by high global demand for its key commodities. The 2000s and early 2010s were marked by rapid social progress, with around 35 million Brazilians lifting themselves out of poverty, contributing to the expansion of a new middle class. However, starting in 2014, Brazil faced its worst recession in decades, compounded by political crises, corruption scandals, and plummeting commodity prices. Recovery efforts post-pandemic have been mixed, with the country grappling with inflation, high unemployment, and public debt. Despite these challenges, Brazil remains one of the world's largest agricultural producers and an important player in global trade. In 2024, GDP is expected to grow by 1.7%.

RELIGION

Numbers can lead one to think Brazil is simply a Christian country, but syncretism is the best way to describe its complexity. The country is indeed the world's largest Catholic population, with over 100 million worshippers, approximately 50% of its population. The scenario is expected to change in a few years, thanks to the rise of Evangelical churches, which represent 30% of the Brazilian population. Evangelical churches are becoming more popular in poor communities, but they also reach upper-scale boroughs and strongly influence politics with their evangelical bloc.

Yet, as with many aspects of Brazil, the reality of religion is far more complex. Brazil's multicultural heritage has led to unique expressions of Christianity, frequently blended with other beliefs. Afro-Brazilian religious practices are perhaps the most notable example. Enslaved Africans, forbidden from practicing their traditional religions, fused their *orixás*, or deities, with Catholic saints. This syncretism allowed them to honor their gods secretly under the guise of Catholic worship. Today, Afro-Brazilian religions like Candomblé and Umbanda remain influential, though often marginalized. While Brazil's constitution guarantees freedom of religion, there is still societal prejudice against these faiths.

SPORTS

Soccer is Brazil's second religion. Soccer has a special place in Brazilian culture, with the country producing legendary players like Pelé, Ronaldo, and winning five FIFA World Cups, more than any other nation. The excitement around the sport is palpable during matches, especially during tournaments like the World Cup or local derbies. One of the best icebreakers in the country is asking about the latest match, especially if it involve teams like Flamengo and Corinthians.

Brazilians follow their favorite sports: soccer, volleyball, and Formula One. Their love for sports can also be seen on the beach, where people are always playing beach volleyball and its variations or *frescobol*, a rack sport created in Brazil.

What to Eat in Rio de Janeiro and São Paulo

MOQUECA
Moqueca is a traditional seafood stew made with fish, shrimp, or other seafood, cooked in a flavorful broth made from coconut milk, tomatoes, onions, and spices. The dish is known for its bright and aromatic flavors, reflecting Afro-Brazilian cuisine's influences.

FEIJOADA
Brazil's national dish, feijoada, is a hearty black bean stew with pork (such as sausages and ribs). It's often served with rice, collard greens, orange slices, and *farofa* (toasted cassava flour mixture). It's typically enjoyed on weekends and at casual get togethers.

BRAZILIAN CHURRASCO
Churrasco is deeply rooted in Brazilian tradition, and there are all-you-can-eat *churrascarias* (steakhouses) everywhere. Most beloved cuts include *picanha* (rump cap), *cupim* (beef hump), *maminha* (tri-tip), and chicken heart.

BOTECO'S FOOD
Comida de boteco (Boteco food) refers to the casual, flavorful dishes typically served in botecos—informal, neighborhood bars or pubs in Brazil. Popular choices include *bolinho de feijoada* (a snack prepared with feijoada), *coxinha* (deep-fried pastries filled with shredded chicken), and kebabs.

JAPANESE FOOD AT LIBERDADE
Liberdade is a neighborhood in São Paulo known for being one of the world's largest Japanese communities. The area is home to many Japanese dining options, from sushi bars and ramen shops to izakayas (Japanese pubs), street food, and bakeries. You can enjoy everything from sushi and sashimi to tempura and udon noodles.

AÇAÍ
Açaí is a small, dark purple fruit primarily found in the Amazon rainforest. It's become a Brazilian favorite—especially on hot days. The most common way to enjoy it in São Paulo and Rio is by asking for *açaí na tigela* (açaí in a bowl). The fruit is blended into a thick, smooth, frozen puree.

FRESH FRUITS
Common fruits such as watermelon, pineapple, banana, papaya, and mango are often sweeter here and can be found year-round in markets and sold by street vendors. You can take advantage of Brazilian biodiversity and discover fruits like cashew fruit, guava, jaboticaba, and sugar apple.

TRADITIONAL BRAZILIAN BREAKFAST
A Brazilian breakfast features a combination of items that reflect the country's traditions. The day often starts with a *pingado* (coffee and milk), grilled bread, fresh fruits (such as papaya and bananas), pão de queijo (cheese bread), and *tapioca* (a type of pancake made from tapioca flour).

BRAZILIAN DESSERTS
Brazilians have a sweet tooth, and you can expect to indulge yourself with treats prepared with lots of condensed milk. The most traditional ones include *brigadeiro*, round chocolate truffles made from condensed milk, cocoa powder butter, and coated with chocolate sprinkles and *pudim de leite*, a creamy caramel flan made from condensed milk.

MORTADELLA SANDWICH AT MERCADO MUNICIPAL
The *sanduíche de mortadela* (mortadella sandwich) at Mercado Municipal in São Paulo is a renowned gastronomic experience and is considered an informal cultural heritage dish. Two slices of bread are filled with many layers of Ceratti mortadella and a layer of melted cheese.

What to Drink in Rio de Janeiro and São Paulo

MANY CAIPIRINHA FLAVORS
Caipirinha is Brazil's signature drink, often prepared with *cachaça* (a spirit made with fermented sugar cane), lime, sugar, and ice. The strong taste of cachaça is perfect when paired with citric fruits, and you can try different flavors, including passion fruit, strawberries, and cashew fruit.

FRESH JUICE
In Brazil, *sucos naturais* or *da fruta* (fresh juices) are typically made directly from the fruit rather than concentrate or pre-packaged mixes, so they are free of preservatives. Many *suco* parlors in Rio and São Paulo sell flavors such as orange, soursop, passion fruit, and a mix of orange, beet, and carrots, which is famous among locals for boosting tanning. Before making your order, always clarify whether you want them to add sugar.

COLD MATE TEA
On Rio's famous beaches like Copacabana and Ipanema, you'll find vendors walking along the shore carrying large coolers filled with cold *Chá Mate*, usually sweetened and often mixed with lemon juice (*mate com limão*).

CACHAÇA
While Cachaça is widely known as the base for the Caipirinha, many Brazilians also enjoy sipping it neat, especially premium aged cachaças that offer a more refined tasting experience. Some people prefer to drink it with a few ice cubes, which can slightly mellow the flavor without diluting it too much.

AÇAÍ AND CUPUAÇU SHAKE
You can have a taste of the Amazon in Rio and São Paulo by trying açaí and *cupuaçu*. While açaí is thicker and more earthy, cupuaçu is creamy and tropical, with a sweet and tangy flavor.

CAFÉ PINGADO
Brazil is the world's largest coffee producer, so it's no surprise that people drink it a lot during the day. The traditional *cafézinho* (little coffee) is a small, strong, and usually sweetened cup of coffee served any time of the day.

Caldo de cana

BRAZILIAN BEER
The country's most popular type of beer is Pilsen, a light and refreshing lager that pairs well with Brazil's warm climate. These beers are typically mild, easy to drink, and have a lower alcohol content, making them perfect for social gatherings and scorching days at the beach. Traditionally, Brazilians love their beer to be as cold as possible, and they often call the beverage *gelada* (cold). Brazilians' favorite national brands are Bohemia, Original, Skol, and Brahma.

CALDO DE CANA
Caldo de cana, also known as sugarcane juice, is a popular drink in Brazil. It's made by extracting the juice from fresh sugarcane stalks using a machine. The result is a pale green liquid that's naturally sweet and packed with nutrients. The juice has a slightly grassy undertone, characteristic of the sugarcane plant. You can find it easily at street markets—where it's a favorite along with a *pastel*—beaches, juice bars, and roadside stalls.

GUARANÁ SODA
Guaraná soda is made from the guaraná berry, a fruit from the Amazon, and its taste is often described as a mix between ginger ale and apple soda with a hint of berry flavor. It's sweet, refreshing, and slightly fruity. The flavor is distinct but not overpowering, making it a favorite among many Brazilians. The most famous brands are Guaraná Antarctica and Kuat and they are available everywhere.

Best Beaches of Rio de Janeiro

BARRA DA TIJUCA
The city's longest beach stretches nearly 11 miles, from the western end of Joatinga Beach all the way to Recreio dos Bandeirantes. It offers wide, open spaces with plenty of room for sunbathing, playing sports, or simply enjoying the view.

COPACABANA
Copacabana Beach is world-renowned and has been a symbol of Rio's lifestyle for decades. Its 2.5-mile-long stretch of sand framed by a dramatic backdrop has hosted international events, including concerts and New Year's Eve celebrations. The beach is a melting pot of people. You'll find a mix of Cariocas, tourists from around the world, families, young people, and celebrities. It's a popular spot for playing beach soccer and *frescobol* (a type of paddleball game).
Amenities: food and drink; lifeguards; showers, toilets.
Best for: walking; sports; swimming.

IPANEMA
Ipanema is a more sophisticated cousin to Copacabana. It's known for its fashionable crowd, upscale surroundings, and a certain bohemian vibe. The beach is famous for its stunning sunset views, with the Dois Irmãos (Two Brothers) mountains on the backdrop. The stretch at Posto 7, near the Arpoador, is the favorite spot for surfers; Posto 8 and 9 are the most popular among the LGBTQI+ community and artists, and Posto 10 is ideal for sports.
Amenities: food and drink; lifeguards; showers; toilets.
Best for: surfing; walking; sports; sunset.

ARPOADOR
Arpoador is situated between Copacabana and Ipanema. It's easily accessible from both neighborhoods and is marked by a large rock formation that extends into the ocean, known as Pedra do Arpoador, where people gather to watch the sunset and sunrise. The beach is one of the most famous surfing spots, ideal for beginner and experienced surfers. The beach often hosts surfing competitions, and it's not uncommon to see surfers hitting the waves at all times of the day.
Amenities: food and drink; lifeguards; showers; toilets.
Best for: surfing; sunset; sunrise.

RESERVA
Located between Barra da Tijuca and Recreio dos Bandeirantes, two popular neighborhoods in the western zone of Rio de Janeiro. Reserva Beach is part of a protected environmental area, surrounded by lush vegetation, sand dunes, and the Marapendi Lagoon. It is a less-developed beach and a popular spot for surfing, stand-up paddle, and kite surfing.
Amenities: food and drink; lifeguards; showers; toilets.
Best for: surfing.

Best Beaches Outside of São Paulo

Maresias, São Sebastião

JUQUEHY BEACH, SÃO SEBASTIÃO

Juquehy Beach strikes a perfect balance between laid-back and sophisticated, which makes it a favorite among families, couples, and those looking for a relaxing escape. The beach is well-preserved, with a natural and somewhat exclusive feel. The calm waters make it ideal for swimming, and the surrounding nature provides a picturesque setting perfect for unwinding. Juquehy is 52 km (32 miles) from downtown São Sebastião, and you can reach it by bus L21 or L22 (R$2). **Amenities:** food and drink; toilets. **Best for:** biking; football; beach soccer.

MARESIAS, SÃO SEBASTIÃO

Located 27 km (16 miles) from São Sebastião center, this beach is famous for its lively atmosphere and vibrant nightlife. Maresias is a hot spot for surfers and young crowds drawn to its consistent waves and trendy beach clubs. The stunning coastline is surrounded by lush mountains, making it

Praia de Castelhanos, Ilhabela

Experience Rio de Janeiro and São Paulo

BEST BEACHES OUTSIDE OF SÃO PAULO

popular among families during the daytime. Beyond the surf, Maresias offers a variety of restaurants, bars, and shops. The easiest way to get there is by taking the bus 5505 (R$4.50). **Amenities:** food and drink; toilets; shops. **Best for:** nightlife; surfing; beach soccer.

PRAIA DE CASTELHANOS, ILHABELA

Praia de Castelhanos is a remote location that gives a sense you have the place all to yourself, especially on the weekdays. It's the perfect escape from the bustling Ilhabela, but it's often busy from December through Carnival and public holidays. Castelhanos is located on the eastern side of Ilhabela, approximately 22 km (13 miles) from the island's main village. If you are into off-road tours, the most popular way to get to this beach is by booking a 4x4 tour (R$130). You can also discover secluded beaches nearby by scheduling a half-day boat tour with local agencies (R$350). **Amenities:** food and drinks; toilets. **Best for:** hiking; off-road.

ILHA DAS COUVES, UBATUBA

Ilha das Couves is a small, breathtaking, undeveloped island located off the coast of Ubatuba, about 26 km (16 miles) from the town center. Accessible by a short boat ride (R$70), the island is a true tropical paradise, known for its crystal-clear waters and prime scuba-diving spot. The island's two main beaches are ideal for swimming and snorkeling, as the waters teem with colorful fish. **Amenities:** none. **Best for:** scuba diving; snorkeling; swimming.

FÉLIX BEACH, UBATUBA

Praia do Félix is a stunning beach located 220 km (354 miles) from São Paulo and 17 km (27 miles) from Ubatuba's downtown. Nestled within the lush Atlantic Forest of Ubatuba, it blends calm waters on one side with gentle waves on the other. The secluded beach becomes packed during holidays and weekends when *paulistanos* flock to its vast stretch of sand. The easiest way to get there is by bus 18 Picinguaba Divisa (R$5) from Ubatuba. You can also drive along the BR 101 Rio-Santos toward Rio de Janeiro, Felix Beach, which is at kilometer 33.

What to Buy in Rio de Janeiro and São Paulo

BRAZILIAN CHOCOLATES
Chocolate fans can indulge with local brands in Rio and São Paulo. Check for brands such as Dengo (R$69), produced exclusively with Brazilian cacao and using ingredients such as nuts, spices, and fruits such as lemon, cajá, and jackfruit.

OFFICIAL SOCCER JERSEYS
Few countries are as passionate about soccer as Brazilians. The iconic yellow jersey holds historical significance and is a great souvenir. The official jerseys can be purchased in official CBF shops (R$350) and sport stores.

SWIMSUIT
Brazil has a strong beach culture, so it's not surprising that they have stylish, high-quality swimwear. From the iconic Brazilian bikini with its distinctive cuts to more conservative options, there's something for everyone.

HAVAIANAS
Havaianas sandals are a Brazilian trademark and are much cheaper when purchased in the brand's home country (R$50). There are several Havaianas official shops, and they have expanded their product range to include a variety of accessories, including purses and bags (R$75). The pouches are made from rubber or silicone, reflecting the brand's signature flip-flop material, and are perfect for carrying essentials like your phone, keys, and wallet.

GROUND COFFEE
Brazil is the world's largest coffee producer, and the country's coffee industry has a rich history. Its beans are celebrated for their smooth, well-balanced flavor profiles with notes of chocolate, nuts, and fruit, which makes it an excellent souvenir. Although the best ground coffee isn't in supermarkets, you can find premium brands such as Orfeu, Santa Monica, Black Tucano, and Baggio in specialized shops.

BRAZILIAN SPARKLING WINE
The country isn't often associated with wine, but its sparkling wine is gaining recognition thanks to its unique terroir in southern Brazil. Sparkling wines such as Conde de Foucauld Brut Branco, Séries by Salton Moscatel, and Ponto Nevo have international recognition and are affordable options for those who want to start discovering Brazilian sparkling wines. They can be easily found in supermarkets and restaurants.

GEMSTONE JEWELRY
There is no better place to purchase authentic gemstone jewelry than Rio and São Paulo. Brazil is renowned for its rich deposits of high-quality gemstones, and the country is one of the world's largest producers of gems like tourmalines, topaz, and aquamarine. Both cities are home to jewelry retailers such as H. Stern, Manoel Bernardes, and Vivara. You can also find unpolished gemstones in several shops.

LOCAL TOILETRIES
Brazilian toiletries often feature ingredients that reflect the country's rich biodiversity. You can find a range of perfumes, moisturizers, soaps, and oils produced with ingredients sourced from local flora, such as Amazonian extracts and indigenous plant oils, known for their beneficial properties. Natura is famous for its collections using scents such as Brazilian nuts, açaí, and passion fruit.

PHOTOGRAPHY BOOKS
If you want to have a visual memory of Brazilian cultural diversity, buying a photography book is an option that can capture everything from the Amazon rainforest to urban life. Thanks to his social work and powerful black-and-white images, Sebastião Salgado is Brazil's most celebrated photographer. You can also find photo books such as *The Art Book Brasil—Fotografia*, featuring the work of several photographers.

CACHAÇA
Cachaça is Brazil's national spirit, made from fermented sugarcane juice. It is the key ingredient in the country's famous cocktail, the caipirinha. Buying cachaça directly from Brazil ensures that you're getting an authentic product with a rich history and cultural significance.

Best Museums of Rio de Janeiro and São Paulo

PINACOTECA DO ESTADO DE SÃO PAULO
The Pinacoteca do Estado de São Paulo—or just Pinacoteca—is one of Brazil's most important art museums. Its collection focuses primarily on Brazilian art, with works ranging from the 19th century to contemporary pieces.

MUSEUM OF THE PORTUGUESE LANGUAGE
How about a whole museum dedicated to the Portuguese language? The Museu da Língua Portuguesa is an interactive museum exploring Brazil's mother language's evolution, diversity, and richness.

MUSEU DA ARTE DE SÃO PAULO (MASP)
The Museu de Arte de São Paulo (MASP) is one of Brazil's most important cultural institutions. Located on the iconic Avenida Paulista, MASP is renowned for being home to one of Latin America's most diverse collections of Western art.

MUSEU DO FUTEBOL
The Museu do Futebol is an interactive museum dedicated to soccer's history in Brazil. The museum pays homage to Brazil's football legends, such as Pelé, Garrincha, Zico, and Romário, showcasing their careers, achievements, and contributions to the sport.

MUSEUM OF JAPANESE IMMIGRATION
São Paulo is home to one of the world's largest Japanese communities, and the Museum of Japanese Immigration offers a look at this community from the early 20th century to the present day. It provides insights into the challenges faced by these immigrants and their contributions to Brazilian society through a vast collection of artifacts, documents, photographs, and personal items donated by families.

MUSEUM OF TOMORROW
The Museu do Amanhã (Museum of Tomorrow) describes itself as a new type of science museum. Located in Rio, it focuses on exploring issues related to the future of our planet and humanity, combining science, technology, and art in innovative ways. It offers a range of interactive exhibits that engage visitors in discussions about climate change, technology, urban planning, and sustainability.

BEST MUSEUMS OF RIO DE JANEIRO AND SÃO PAULO

CENTRO CULTURAL BANCO DO BRASIL (CCBB)

The Centro Cultural Banco do Brasil (CCBB) in Rio de Janeiro is one of Brazil's most renowned cultural centers. Located in the heart of Rio's historic downtown, the CCBB Rio de Janeiro is known for its high-quality art exhibitions.

MUSEU CARMEN MIRANDA

Carmen Miranda is arguably Brazil's first international star and the museum dives into the history of this vibrant singer and actress. The museum provides a detailed look at Carmen Miranda's life and career, celebrating her as a major cultural figure. Miranda was known for popularizing Brazilian music and dance internationally, and the museum offers insight into her legacy by showcasing a collection of memorabilia, costumes, and personal items associated with Miranda.

HISTORICAL MUSEUM OF THE ARMY AND COPACABANA FORT

The museum is dedicated to the history of the Brazilian Army and military fortifications, particularly focusing on the role of the Copacabana Fort in Brazil's military history. The fort itself is an important historical site dating back to the late 19th century, and the museum's exhibits cover a broad range of military and historical topics. The museum also provides a unique setting for its exhibits and offers stunning views of Copacabana.

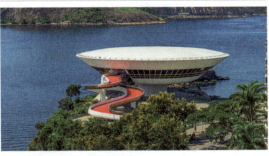

RIO MUSEUM OF ART (MAR)

The Museu de Arte do Rio (MAR), or Museum of Art of Rio, is located in the city's downtown area—a few minutes from the Museu do Amanhã—and is dedicated to showcasing Brazilian and international art while also focusing on the cultural and historical context of Rio de Janeiro.

History You Can See

Walking the streets of Rio de Janeiro and São Paulo is also a journey through Brazil's history. Both cities have been part of significant moments in the country's past, especially after the arrival of the Portuguese royal family in 1808. To this day, it's possible to find colonial-era landmarks and remains of progress of the coffee boom phase. Each building stands as a testament to pivotal moments in Brazil's history, reflecting the influences of indigenous traditions, European colonization, and the country's journey to independence and industrialization.

ARCOS DA LAPA (LAPA ARCHES)

Today, the Arcos da Lapa serve as a backdrop to Rio's most bohemian borough, which is famous for its nightlife, samba clubs, and colonial buildings. The arches are among the most photographed places in the city and have appeared in countless movies, popular soap operas, and series. Yet, the landmark is also a glimpse into the city's past. The 42 arches were originally built in the mid-18th century as an aqueduct to supply water to the city. Later, in the early 20th century, the aqueduct was repurposed as a viaduct for the iconic Santa Teresa tram, further cementing its role in Rio's cultural narrative.

PAÇO IMPERIAL (IMPERIAL PALACE)

When the Portuguese Royal family moved to Rio in 1808, the now fancy areas by the beach didn't catch their attention. They decided to set the Paço Imperial (Imperial Palace) in the center, where the 18th-century building is still standing and is a testament to Rio's imperial grandeur. Later, it became the hub of political decisions during the Empire of Brazil, hosting critical events like the signing of the Lei Áurea (Golden Law) that abolished slavery in 1888. Today, the beautifully restored building serves as a cultural center featuring art exhibitions, performances, and historical artifacts.

MUSEU HISTÓRICO NACIONAL (NATIONAL HISTORICAL MUSEUM)

The Museu Histórico Nacional is a treasure trove of Brazilian history, located near Praça Mauá. Established in 1922, it occupies a site that was originally a 17th-century fort, linking the museum itself to the city's military past. The extensive collection includes artifacts from Brazil's indigenous cultures, colonial times, and the republican era, offering visitors a comprehensive journey through the nation's history. Highlights include the royal carriages of the Portuguese court, historical maps, and items related to Brazil's independence. It's a must-visit destination for history buffs, thanks to its interactive exhibits, and it features a lovely courtyard.

REAL GABINETE PORTUGUÊS DE LEITURA (ROYAL PORTUGUESE READING ROOM)

The Real Gabinete Português de Leitura is often mentioned as one of the world's most impressive libraries. This masterpiece of neo-Manueline architecture was built in 1837 by Portuguese immigrants serving as a tribute to Portuguese heritage. Its ornate interior features towering wooden bookshelves, intricate carvings, and a magnificent skylight, making it one of the most beautiful libraries in the world. Housing over 350,000 volumes, including rare manuscripts and first editions, it is a haven for literature lovers. Beyond its breathtaking design, the reading room symbolizes the enduring cultural ties between Brazil and Portugal.

CEMITÉRIO SÃO JOÃO BATISTA (SÃO JOÃO BATISTA CEMETERY)

Founded in 1852, Cemitério São João Batista is a place where history and art merge. This sprawling necropolis in Rio offers a unique window into the lives of Brazil's most influential figures. Among the notable individuals buried here are former presidents, writers like Machado de Assis, and iconic musicians such as Tom Jobim. The cemetery is also renowned for its elaborate tombs and mausoleums, which showcase various architectural styles, from neoclassical to art deco. Wandering through its peaceful paths, visitors can reflect on the cultural, political, and artistic legacies that shaped Brazil.

PÁTIO DO COLÉGIO

In the heart of São Paulo's bustling center, the Pátio do Colégio offers a tranquil escape with its peaceful courtyard. The place is arguably the city's most important landmark, as it's where São Paulo was founded in 1554 by Jesuit priests José de Anchieta and Manuel da Nóbrega. Yet, this is not the original construction but a replica of the 16th original church that now serves as a museum. It offers visitors an in-depth look at São Paulo's early days and its development from a small Jesuit mission to a sprawling metropolis. The adjacent church retains its historical charm and still holds mass five times a week.

MUSEU DO IPIRANGA (INDEPENDENCE MUSEUM)

The Museu do Ipiranga, officially known as the Museu Paulista, is a landmark of Brazilian history, standing at the site where Emperor Dom Pedro I proclaimed the country's independence on September 7, 1822. The museum showcases an extensive collection of artifacts, documents, and artworks that narrate Brazil's journey to sovereignty. The surrounding Independence Park, with its beautifully landscaped gardens and fountains, complements the museum's grandeur. The Monument to Independence, located nearby, houses the tomb of Dom Pedro I. After extensive renovations, the museum reopened in 2022, offering modern exhibits while preserving its historical and architectural legacy.

ESTAÇÃO DA LUZ (LUZ STATION)

Estação da Luz, inaugurated in 1901, is an iconic landmark that symbolizes São Paulo's transformation during the coffee boom. This railway station was the central hub for exporting coffee from São Paulo's interior to the Port of Santos, fueling the city's economic rise. Designed by British architects, its architecture blends Victorian elegance with Brazilian flair. Today, it serves as both a transportation hub and a cultural destination, housing the Museum of the Portuguese Language. The museum celebrates the richness of the Portuguese language through interactive exhibits and is a must-visit for history and language enthusiasts alike.

TEATRO MUNICIPAL DE SÃO PAULO

Opened in 1911, the Teatro Municipal de São Paulo is a masterpiece of eclectic architecture, influenced by European styles. Built during the coffee boom, the theater became a cultural beacon for the city's elite. It gained historical significance as the stage for the 1922 Modern Art Week, an event that marked the beginning of modernism in Brazilian art and literature. Visitors can admire its opulent interiors, with gilded details, marble staircases, and crystal chandeliers. The theater continues to host operas, ballets, and concerts, blending its historical legacy with contemporary cultural offerings. The best way to not miss any detail is to hire a guided tour.

What to Read and Watch

DOM CASMURRO BY MACHADO DE ASSIS

Machado de Assis is considered Brazil's best author not just for the quality of his work but for how his writing elevated Brazilian literature to the world stage. Dom Casmurro is often labeled as his masterpiece as it explores themes of love, jealousy, and memory through the unreliable narration of Bento Santiago, or "Dom Casmurro." The novel revolves around his obsessive suspicion that his wife, Capitu, was unfaithful to him with his best friend, Escobar. Today, there is still a debate about whether Capitu was genuinely guilty or if Bento was paranoid.

CHILD OF THE DARK BY CAROLINA MARIA DE JESUS

Carolina Maria de Jesus is a powerful narrator using her real-life diary to register the harsh reality of a *favela* in São Paulo in the 1950s. Carolina, a Black single mother and waste picker, details her daily struggles with poverty, hunger, and marginalization, offering a raw and unfiltered look at the lives of Brazil's urban poor. Through her vivid and emotional prose, she sheds light on systemic inequalities while also portraying her own resilience, dignity, and desire for a better life. Intellectuals celebrated the book during the 1960s; it was later forgotten and has regained popularity in the last few years.

CAPTAINS OF THE SAND BY JORGE AMADO

Jorge Amado is one of Brazil's most prolific writers, and Captains of the Sand is one of his finest works. The story follows a group of street children, known as the "Captains of the Sand," who survive through theft and cunning. The group is led by Pedro Bala, a courageous and charismatic boy who dreams of a better future. Each gang member has a unique backstory, and through their adventures, Amado explores themes of friendship, loyalty, resilience, and the struggle for dignity. The novel delves into the social conditions that drove these children to crime, criticizing the indifference of society and the lack of opportunities.

NEMESIS: ONE MAN AND THE BATTLE FOR RIO BY MISHA GLENNY

Misha Glenny dives into the complex world of organized crime in Rio. The book centers on the rise and fall of Antônio Francisco Bonfim Lopes, better known as Nem, one of Rio's most notorious drug lords and the leader of the Rocinha favela. The investigation explains how Nem, a humble working man, turned into one of the most feared figures in Rio's criminal underworld. The book traces his journey as he navigates the brutal realities of drug trafficking, violence, and the deep-rooted corruption that connects the world of crime with law enforcement, politicians, and the wealthy elite. The book also paints a broader picture of the socioeconomic conditions in Rio's favelas beyond the sensationalism of crime stories.

BRAZIL: A BIOGRAPHY BY HELOISA MURGEL STARLING AND LILIA MORITZ SCHWARCZ

This book offers a sweeping narrative that spans over five centuries, from the arrival of the Portuguese in 1500 to the modern-day challenges facing the country. Schwarcz and Starling, both renowned Brazilian historians, present a portrait of Brazil's complex identity. The book showcases key events and figures that shaped the nation, including colonial exploitation, the impact of slavery, independence, the monarchy, the military dictatorship, and the country's ongoing struggles with corruption, inequality, and social justice. It also explores Brazil's rich cultural heritage, from Carnival to samba, offering insights into how art, music, and literature reflect and shape national identity.

CITY OF GOD, DIRECTED BY FERNANDO MEIRELLES

City of God is based on the novel by Paulo Lins, which draws from real events to depict the rise of organized crime in the Cidade de Deus favela in Rio de Janeiro from the 1960s to the 1980s. The story is told through the eyes of Rocket (Buscapé), a young boy who dreams of becoming a photographer amidst the violence and chaos around him. Through Rocket's perspective, the film follows the lives of several characters, particularly Li'l Zé, a ruthless gang leader whose thirst for power drives much of the violence in the community. The film's kinetic style, dynamic camera work, and nonlinear storytelling create an intense and immersive experience that pulls viewers into the world of the characters. The cast, composed mainly of nonprofessional actors from Rio's favelas, adds to the film's authenticity, bringing a sense of urgency and realism to their performances.

VALE O ESCRITO, DIRECTED BY FELIPE AWI

Vale o Escrito is a documentary series that dives into the world of *jogo do bicho* (animal game), an illegal lottery in Brazil that has been deeply ingrained in the country's culture for over a century. A handful of families rule the multimillionaire business, and the series shows never-before-revealed details about fraudulent schemes, and how the criminal groups expanded their power and linked the game with Carnival. They are also connected with several brutal crimes in Rio, and each episode shares details of the private lives of crime bosses and their descendants, who often inherit the business.

CENTRAL STATION, DIRECTED BY WALTER SALES

This critically acclaimed Brazilian drama tells the moving story of an unexpected bond between an older woman and a young boy. The film is set in Rio de Janeiro and follows Dora, a bitter former schoolteacher who works at the bustling Central Station writing letters for illiterate clients. One day, Dora encounters Josué, a young boy whose mother is tragically killed in a traffic accident right outside the station. Reluctantly, Dora takes Josué under her wing, and together, they embark on a journey across Brazil in search of his estranged father. This journey takes them through Brazil's vast and varied landscapes, highlighting the country's social contrasts and the resilience of its people. Fernanda Montenegro, who plays Dora, earned an Academy Award nomination for Best Actress for her performance.

THE SECOND MOTHER, DIRECTED BY ANNA MUYLAERT

The Second Mother centers on Val, a live-in housekeeper working for a wealthy family in São Paulo. Val has spent years working for the same family, caring for their home and children while maintaining a distant relationship with her daughter, who lives in a different part of the country. The film's narrative shifts when Val's daughter, Jéssica, comes to São Paulo to take an entrance exam for university. Jéssica's visit challenges the existing social boundaries and expectations, prompting Val to reconsider her role and her sacrifices. The film is a powerful commentary on social inequality and the rigid class structures in Brazil.

Chapter 2
TRAVEL SMART

Updated by
Luana Ferreira

★ **CAPITAL:**
Brasilia

POPULATION:
216.4 million

LANGUAGE:
Portuguese

$ CURRENCY:
Brazilian Real

COUNTRY CODE:
+55

⚠ EMERGENCIES:
190 (Military Police)
192 (Ambulance)
193 (Firefighters)
199 (Civil Defense)

🚗 DRIVING:
Right

⚡ ELECTRICITY:
110V or 220V
(Depending on the region)

🕐 TIME:
2 hours ahead New York

🌐 WEB RESOURCES:
www.climatempo.com.br;
www.visitbrazil.com;
www.gov.br/mre

Know Before You Go

COVID AND VACCINATION
Brazil does not have mandatory vaccination requirements for entry, including for COVID-19. However, the Brazilian Ministry of Health strongly recommends that travelers are up-to-date on certain immunizations for their safety.

LEARN SOME PORTUGUESE
Portuguese is the official language of Brazil, so learning even a few basics before traveling can make your trip much smoother. A recent survey found that only about 20% of Brazilians have any knowledge of English, which can make communication a bit challenging. However, many travel agencies provide English-speaking guides, and Brazilians are famous for their hospitality. They'll often rely on Google Translate or gestures to help visitors. Even so, locals truly appreciate it when foreigners make an effort to speak their language. You don't have to become fluent, but simple phrases like *obrigado* (thank you) and *por favor* (please) can go a long way.

VISA REQUIREMENTS
As of 2023, the Brazilian government has reintroduced the requirement for e-visas for travelers from the United States, Canada, and Australia due to reciprocity policies. Although initially planned for earlier implementation, this change will officially take effect in April 2025. Tourists and business travelers can apply for the e-visa online through the VFS eVisa (Electronic Visa) platform (🌐 *visa.vfsglobal.com/ago/en/bra*), eliminating the need to visit a consulate in person; the document is valid for 90 days. This is the only official platform. As the visa requirements rules have changed on a regular basis, it's important to double-check before planning your trip.

DOWNLOAD WHATSAPP
Will Cathcart, head of WhatsApp, famously called Brazil "the country of WhatsApp," and for good reason: over 90% of Brazilians use it as their primary messaging app. The Meta app has overshadowed other messaging apps and it's an essential tool for communicating with shops, travel agencies, and local services. Most businesses are more effective using the app than answering the phone—they are quick to respond or inform when they are available online. Be prepared to receive lots of stickers during conversations, as Brazilians use them to make chats more playful and fun.

SEASONS ARE OPPOSITE TO THE NORTHERN HEMISPHERE
In Brazil, the seasons are reversed compared to the Northern Hemisphere, as the country lies mainly in the Southern Hemisphere. Summer spans December to March, bringing hot and humid weather, particularly in coastal and tropical regions like Rio de Janeiro, Salvador, and the Amazon. Temperatures can exceed 30°C (86°F), with frequent rain in some areas. Winter, from June to August, is milder than in many Northern Hemisphere countries but can still be chilly in São Paulo and Rio. In southern cities like Curitiba, Porto Alegre, and Gramado, or mountain destinations like Petrópolis and Campos do Jordão, temperatures may drop below 10°C (50°F).

CARNIVAL STOPS THE COUNTRY
Brazilians take Carnival seriously—the country essentially pauses for five days of festivities. Carnival occurs 40 days before Easter, usually in February or early March, and is officially celebrated from Friday to Wednesday. During this time, banks and most businesses are closed, and services are hard to find. Each state has its own Carnival traditions, but travelers should expect higher prices and

large crowds. Those who aren't partying often use the holiday to travel within the country, making it the most expensive period of the year. Planning ahead is crucial, as streets are often closed, making it hard to find transportation. Staying near metro stations in cities like Rio and São Paulo is the most convenient option.

SAFETY

While Brazil offers unforgettable experiences, safety can be a concern. Before booking accommodations, check reviews to ensure the area is secure. When in Rio, stay in the Zona Sul boroughs instead of center. In general, it's safe to explore on foot, but theft and robbery are common worries, even for locals. It's fine to carry your phone, but use it discreetly, especially outdoors. In São Paulo, avoid using your phone while in traffic and travel with the windows closed. Leave valuables such as jewelry and watches at home, and at the beach, always keep your belongings within sight.

AVOID TOURIST TRAPS

Brazilians are friendly, but tourists should watch out for common scams. Vendors often charge higher prices to foreigners, so research average costs before purchasing services or items (e.g., street food or beach chair rentals). Don't hesitate if you have a Brazilian friend who can ask for the prices. When using a credit card, verify the total before completing the transaction and when making a deal, it's preferable to have details written down. In Salvador, avoid accepting "welcome gifts" like wrist ribbons or body painting; these often come with unexpected fees and vendors quickly become coercive.

LOCAL ETIQUETTE

Brazilians are famously warm and expressive, often showing affection even in public. It's common to see them treating new acquaintances like longtime friends after just a few minutes of conversation, and this friendly attitude is frequently extended to foreigners as well. In informal settings, don't be surprised if someone greets you with a hug or a pat on the back. In more formal environments, handshakes are standard, but kisses on the cheek (usually two or three, depending on the region) are also common, especially between women or between men and women. Keep in mind that punctuality is often flexible in Brazil; locals might arrive 10 to 15 minutes late for appointments, so plan accordingly to avoid frustration.

GETTING AROUND

Public transportation in Brazil is generally reliable and widely available, especially in major cities like Rio de Janeiro and São Paulo. Buses and metro systems are excellent options for navigating these bustling cities while avoiding traffic. For smaller towns and less urbanized areas, buses are often the most cost-effective choice and can connect you to a wide range of destinations. Ride-hailing apps like Uber and 99 are popular and operate nationwide, offering a convenient and often safer alternative to traditional taxis. If you do opt for a taxi, be cautious— verify the route to ensure the driver isn't taking a detour or overcharging. Planning your transportation in advance can save time and money.

Getting Here and Around

Only 12.4% of Brazil's highway network is paved, which has a significant impact on travel conditions. Road quality varies greatly across the country, and while trains are available in some regions, they are far from sufficient to cover Brazil's vast territory. For short distances, cars and buses remain the most popular modes of transportation. Bus quality depends on the company, with executive buses typically offering a more comfortable experience, though delays are common. Air travel is a faster alternative for long distances, but domestic flights often come with high ticket prices.

 Air

It's especially important to plan your itinerary carefully in a country as big as Brazil. Book as far in advance as possible, particularly for weekend travel. Planes tend to fill up on Friday, especially to or from popular destinations like Rio and São Paulo. To check prices and make online flight reservations, see individual airline sites, like ⊕ *voegol.com.br*, ⊕ *voeazul.com.br*, and ⊕ *latam.com*. Avoid purchasing tickets from third parties and choose direct flights.

The majority of direct flights to Brazil fly to São Paulo's Guarulhos International Airport or Rio's Aeroporto do Galeão. There are direct flights to both cities departing from New York, Miami, Orlando, Atlanta, and Dallas. When flying direct to Brazil, the flights last up to 10 hours. The shortest flight departs from Miami, taking 7 hours and 45 minutes to arrive in Brasilia (Brazil's capital). Direct flights from New York City take 9½ hours to Rio and São Paulo.

Reconfirm flights within Brazil, even if you have a ticket and a reservation, as flights tend to operate at full capacity.

The Brazilian government doesn't have a departure tax, which is charged by airlines when the tickets are purchased and sent to the airport administration.

Miami, New York, Orlando, and Toronto are the major North American gateways for flights to Brazil. United Airlines flies nonstop from Houston, Newark, and Chicago; American Airlines has direct service from Dallas, Miami, and New York; and Delta offers nonstop service from Atlanta and New York. Air Canada has nonstop service between Toronto and São Paulo.

LATAM Airlines flies nonstop from Miami, Orlando, New York, Los Angeles to São Paulo and Rio. GOL covers several American cities, including New York, Miami, Atlanta, Los Angeles, Las Vegas, Detroit, Austin, and Chicago. The Colombian airline Avianca flies from Washington Dulles International Airport in Virginia to São Paulo, with a brief stopover in Bogotá.

AIRPORTS

São Paulo–Guarulhos International Airport (GRU): This is the main international airport in São Paulo, handling most of the international flights. It is located in the Guarulhos area, approximately 25 kilometers (15 miles) from downtown São Paulo. The traffic to the city is often intense.

Congonhas Airport (CGH): This is the primary domestic airport in São Paulo, handling mainly flights within Brazil. It is located closer to the city center, around 8 kilometers (5 miles) south of downtown.

Viracopos International Airport (VCP): Officially known as Campinas International Airport, this is another important airport serving the São Paulo metropolitan area. Located in the city of Campinas, about 100 kilometers (62 miles) from São Paulo, it primarily handles both domestic and international flights.

Rio de Janeiro–Galeão International Airport (GIG): Officially named Rio de Janeiro–Antonio Carlos Jobim International Airport, this is the main international airport in Rio. It handles the majority of international flights and is located about 20 kilometers (12 miles) from downtown Rio de Janeiro. GIG serves as the primary gateway for travelers arriving in the city from abroad.

Santos Dumont Airport (SDU): This is a smaller airport primarily handling domestic flights. Located closer to downtown Rio de Janeiro (approximately 2 kilometers or 1 mile), it is mainly used for flights to other Brazilian cities, such as São Paulo, Brasília, and Belo Horizonte. Santos Dumont is known for its convenient location, making it a popular choice for domestic travelers.

AIRPORT TRANSFERS

In the major hubs, airport transfers are offered between airports: in São Paulo between Guarulhos and Congonhas, and in Rio de Janeiro between Galeão and Santos Dumond. This type of service is not common outside of Rio and São Paulo; most other Brazilian cities have only one commercial airport.

There's regular jet service within the country between all major and most medium-size cities. Remote areas are also accessible—as long as you don't mind small planes. Domestic airlines include LATAM, Azul, and GOL, a reliable airline with routes covering most major and medium-size Brazilian cities. The flight from Rio to São Paulo is one hour.

AIR PASSES

If you reside outside Brazil, you're eligible to purchase air passes from GOL and Azul, which can save you hundreds of dollars if you plan to travel to multiple cities. The options have been reduced after COVID-19, but you can purchase multiple types of passes through Miami-based travel agency and tour operator Brol (⊕ *www.brol.com*). Prices start around USD $505 (plus tax), and you must purchase your pass before you enter Brazil. Passes that include flights between Brazil and other South American countries are also available.

Bus

The nation's *ônibus* (bus) network is affordable, comprehensive, and efficient—compensating for the lack of trains and the high cost of air travel. Every major city can be reached by bus, as can most small to medium-size communities.

The quality of buses in Brazil is good; in many cases better than in the United States. The number of stops at roadside cafés depends on the length of the journey. Usually, buses stop at large outlets with food services, and souvenir and magazine stalls.

Lengthy bus trips can involve travel over some poorly maintained highways, a fact of life in Brazil. When traveling by bus, bring water, toilet paper or tissues, and an additional top layer of clothing (handy if it gets cold or to use as a pillow). Travel light, dress comfortably, and keep a close watch on your belongings—especially in bus stations. If your bus stops at a roadside café, take your belongings with you.

When buying a ticket, you'll be asked whether you want the *ônibus convencional*, the simplest option; the *ônibus executivo*, which gets you air-conditioning, coffee, water, a sandwich, more space between seats, and a pillow and blanket; or the *ônibus-leito*, where you have all the facilities of an executive bus plus a seat that reclines completely. If you're over 5 feet 10 inches (1.8 meters),

Getting Here and Around

it's prudent to buy the most expensive ticket and try for front-row seats, which usually provide more space.

Most buses used for long trips are modern and comfortable, usually with bathrooms and air-conditioning. Note that regular buses used for shorter hauls may be labeled "*ar condicionado*" ("air-conditioned") but often are not.

Bus fares are substantially cheaper than in North America or Europe. Sometimes competing companies serve the same routes, so it can pay to shop around.

Tickets are sold at bus company offices, at city bus terminals, in some travel agencies, and online. Larger cities may have different terminals for buses to multiple destinations, and some small towns may not have a terminal at all (you're usually picked up and dropped off at the line's office, invariably in a central location). While credit cards are now accepted in most places, it's still best to bring cash, especially if you're traveling outside of the major city centers. Reservations or advance-ticket purchases generally aren't necessary except for trips to resort areas during high season—particularly on weekends—or during major holidays (Christmas, Carnival, etc.) and school-break periods (July and December/January). In general, arrive at bus stations early, particularly for peak-season travel.

If time is not an issue, traveling among Brazil and Argentina, Uruguay, Chile, Peru, or other neighboring countries is a good idea. It's inexpensive, and you can enjoy the landscapes.

To ensure that your destination is understood, write it down on a piece of paper and present it to bus or taxi drivers, most of whom don't speak English.

 Car

Traveling by car is recommended if you meet the following criteria: you're not pressed for time, you enjoy driving even in places you do not know well, and you do not want to be limited by airline or bus schedules. Traveling by car is reasonably safe in most areas, especially if you avoid driving at night, and it is a wonderful way to see the country and access lesser-known areas.

Driving can be chaotic in cities like São Paulo and Rio. In the countryside, the usually rough roads, lack of clearly marked signs, and language differences can make driving a challenge. Further, the cost of renting can be steep. All that said, certain areas are most enjoyable when explored on your own in a car: the beach areas of Búzios and the Costa Verde (near Rio) and the North Shore beaches outside São Paulo, to name a few.

If you are feeling at all unsure, don't forget that hiring a car with a driver gives you almost the same level of flexibility with none of the stress of driving in an unfamiliar country. You could hire a car and driver through your hotel concierge, or make a deal with a taxi driver for extended sightseeing at a long-term rate. Often drivers charge a set hourly rate, regardless of the distance traveled. You'll have to pay cash—don't pay 100% of the amount in advance—but you may actually spend less than you would for a rental car.

CAR RENTAL

Rates are sometimes—but not always—better if you book in advance or reserve through a rental agency's website. Although international car rental agencies have better service and maintenance track records than local firms (they also provide better breakdown assistance), your best bet at getting a good rate is to rent on arrival, particularly from local companies. But reserve ahead if you plan to rent during a holiday period or at a particularly popular destination, or need a specific type of car (an SUV or a van). You can contact local agencies through their websites in advance. At many airports, agencies are open 24 hours.

When you reserve a car, ask about cancellation penalties, taxes, drop-off charges (if you're planning to pick up the car in one city and leave it in another), and surcharges (for being under or over a certain age, for additional drivers, or for driving across state or country borders or beyond a specific distance from your point of rental). All these things can add substantially to your costs. Request car seats and extras such as a GPS when you book.

Some common-sense tips: Always give the rental car a once-over to make sure the headlights, jack, and tires (including the spare) are in working condition. Taking pictures or filming the vehicle at the shop is recommended. Before you set out, establish an itinerary and ask about gas stations. Be sure to plan your daily driving distance conservatively and don't drive after dark.

Make sure that a confirmed reservation guarantees you a car. Agencies sometimes overbook, particularly for busy weekends and holiday periods.

CAR-RENTAL INSURANCE

Car insurance is not compulsory when renting a car, but if you have plans to drive in more than one city we strongly recommend buying car insurance, given the bad conditions of Brazilian roads in some states and the risk of accidents. Most car rental companies offer an optional insurance against robbery and accidents. Minimum age for renting a car is 21, but some companies require foreign clients to be at least 25 or charge extra for those under 26.

If you own a car, your personal auto insurance may cover a rental to some degree, though not all policies protect you abroad; always read your policy's fine print. If you don't have auto insurance, then seriously consider buying the collision- or loss-damage waiver (CDW or LDW) from the car rental company, which eliminates your liability for damage to the car.

Some credit cards offer CDW coverage, but it's usually supplemental to your own insurance and rarely covers SUVs, minivans, luxury models, and the like. If your coverage is secondary, you may still be liable for loss-of-use costs from the car rental company. But no credit card insurance is valid unless you use that card for all transactions, from reserving to paying the final bill. All companies exclude car rental in some countries, so be sure to find out about the destination to which you are traveling.

■ TIP→ **Diners Club offers primary CDW coverage on all rentals reserved and paid for with the card. This means that Diners Club's company—not your own car insurance—pays in case of an accident. It doesn't mean your car insurance company won't raise your rates once it discovers you had an accident.**

Some rental agencies require you to purchase CDW coverage; many will even include it in quoted rates. All will strongly encourage you to buy CDW—possibly implying that it's required—so be sure to ask about such things before renting. In most cases it's cheaper to add a supplemental CDW plan to your comprehensive

Getting Here and Around

travel insurance policy than to purchase it from a rental company. That said, you don't want to pay for a supplement if you're required to buy insurance from the rental company. Another possibility is to purchase insurance through a third-party provider, which can cost significantly less than coverage offered by car rental companies.

Train

Brazil has an outdated and insufficient rail network, the smallest of any of the world's large nations. Although there are commuter rails to destinations around major cities, don't plan on taking passenger trains between major cities. There's one exception: the Serra Verde Express from Curitiba to Paranaguá, in the southern state of Paraná, is a fabulous ride with spectacular vistas of ravines, mountains, and waterfalls from bridges and viaducts.

Public Transportation

SÃO PAULO METRO

The São Paulo Metro (Metrô de São Paulo) is a lifeline for millions of residents and visitors navigating Brazil's largest city. With a sprawling network of over 90 interconnected lines, the metro system plays a crucial role in alleviating São Paulo's infamous traffic, offering a fast, reliable, and affordable way to move through the metropolis.

The São Paulo Metro consists of six main lines (Lines 1 through 15), each identified by distinct colors and numbers. It covers over 100 kilometers (62 miles) of track—not enough for the country's largest city, so stations are often crowded, especially during rush hours. The lines are complemented by an extensive network of commuter trains and buses.

The metro runs from 4:40 am to midnight. Line 1 (Blue) connects the north and south, passing through important areas like Sé Station, a central hub. Line 4 (Yellow) is known for its modern trains and automation; this line links key commercial and residential districts. Line 15 (Silver) is a monorail system serving the city's eastern outskirts.

Users can pay R$5 per ride or purchase the Bilhete Único, which can be requested by accessing the SPTRans website.

RIO DE JANEIRO METRO

The Rio de Janeiro Metro (MetrôRio) makes exploring the city much easier, especially during major events such as Carnival, when most streets are blocked. While smaller than São Paulo's system, Rio's metro is an excellent choice for locals and tourists alike, connecting major neighborhoods and attractions with ease.

The Rio Metro features three main lines. Line 1 (Orange): Runs from General Osório in Ipanema to Uruguai, serving the southern and central parts of the city. Line 2 (Green): Connects Pavuna in the north to Botafogo, intersecting with Line 1 at key points. Line 4 (Yellow): Extends from Ipanema to Jardim Oceânico, providing access to the bustling Barra da Tijuca area.

It has around 41 stations and over 58 kilometers (36 miles) of track and runs from 5 am to midnight Monday through Saturday and from 7 am to 11 pm on Mondays. MetroRio has one of the country's most expensive rates, charging R$7.50 per ride.

Essentials

🏃 Activities

Brazil is a very sports-centric country. With vast and diverse environments, Rio has an endless list of sports activities along with the urban landscape. Beach volleyball, surfing, and stand-up paddleboarding dominate the coastline, while soccer, or *futebol*, is the main frenzy within the country. Past hosts of the 2014 FIFA World Cup and the 2016 Olympics show the importance and influence sports have in Brazilian culture. Maybe it's the environment or maybe the culture, but participating in organized sports isn't usually a huge part of a Paulistano's regime. An exception is soccer, which you will see being played in most parks, either on full fields, half-size arenas, or even sandy courts, every weekend and on weeknights. Basketball and volleyball also have loyal, if smaller, followings at parks and SESC centers around the city.

🧭 Addresses

Finding addresses in Brazil can be frustrating, as streets often have more than one name and numbers are sometimes assigned haphazardly. In some places street numbering doesn't enjoy the wide popularity it has achieved elsewhere. Hence, you may find the notation "s/n," meaning *sem número* (without number). In rural areas and small towns, there may only be directions to a place rather than a formal address (i.e., street and number). Often such areas do not have official addresses.

In Portuguese *avenida* (avenue), *rua* (street), and *travessa* (lane) are abbreviated (as *Av.*, *R.*, and *Trv.* or *Tr.*), while *estrada* (highway) often isn't abbreviated, and *alameda* (alley) is abbreviated (as *Al.*). Street numbers follow street names. Eight-digit postal codes (CEP) are widely used.

In some written addresses you might see other abbreviations. For example, an address might read, "R. Presidente Faria 221-4°, s. 413, 90160-091 Porto Alegre, RS," which translates to 221 Rua Presidente Faria, 4th floor, Room 413 ("s." is short for *sala*), postal code 90160-091, in the city of Porto Alegre, in the state of Rio Grande do Sul. You might also see *andar* (floor) or *edifício* (building).

The abbreviations for Brazilian states are: Acre (AC); Alagoas (AL); Amapá (AP); Amazonas (AM); Bahia (BA); Ceará (CE); Distrito Federal (Federal District, aka Brasília; DF); Espírito Santo (ES); Goiás (GO); Maranhão (MA); Minas Gerais (MG); Mato Grosso do Sul (MS); Mato Grosso (MT); Pará (PA); Paraíba (PB); Paraná (PR); Pernambuco (PE); Piauí (PI); Rio de Janeiro (RJ); Rio Grande do Norte (RN); Rio Grande do Sul (RS); Rondonia (RO); Roraima (RR); Santa Catarina (SC); São Paulo (SP); Sergipe (SE), Tocantins (TO).

🍴 Dining

Food in Brazil is delicious, inexpensive (especially compared with North America and Europe), and bountiful. Portions are huge and presentation is tasteful. A lot of restaurants prepare plates for two people. When you order, be sure to ask if one plate will suffice—or even better, glance around to see the size of portions at other tables.

In major cities the variety of eateries is staggering: restaurants of all sizes and categories, snack bars, and fast-food outlets line downtown streets and fight for

Essentials

space in shopping malls. Pricing systems vary from open menus to buffets where you weigh your plate. In São Paulo, for example, Italian eateries—whose risottos rival those of Bologna—sit beside Pan-Asian restaurants, which, like the chicest spots in North America and Europe, serve everything from Thai *satay* to sushi. In addition, there are excellent Portuguese, Chinese, Japanese, Lebanese, and Spanish restaurants.

Outside the cities you find primarily typical, low-cost Brazilian meals that consist simply of *feijão preto* (black beans) and *arroz* (rice) served with beef, chicken, or fish. Manioc, a root vegetable that's used in a variety of ways, and beef are adored everywhere.

Many Brazilian dishes are adaptations of Portuguese specialties. Fish stews called *caldeiradas* and beef stews called *cozidos* (a wide variety of vegetables boiled with different cuts of beef and pork) are popular, as is *bacalhau*, salt cod cooked in sauce or grilled. *Salgados* (literally, "salteds") are appetizers or snacks served in sit-down restaurants as well as at stand-up *lanchonetes* (luncheonettes). Brazil's national dish is feijoada (a stew of black beans, sausage, pork, and beef), which is often served with rice, shredded kale, orange slices, and manioc flour or meal—called farofa if it's coarsely ground, *farinha* if finely ground—that has been fried with onions, oil, and egg.

One of the most avid national passions is the churrascaria , where meats are roasted on spits over an open fire, usually *rodízio* style. Rodízio means "going around," and waiters circulate nonstop carrying skewers laden with charbroiled hunks of beef, pork, and chicken, which are sliced onto your plate with ritualistic ardor. For a set price you get all the meat and side dishes you can eat. Starve yourself a little before going to a rodízio place. Then you can sample everything on offer.

At the other end of the spectrum, vegetarians can sometimes find Brazil's meat-centric culture challenging, especially outside of larger cities. Increasingly, though, salads and vegetarian options are offered at nicer restaurants in areas catering to foodies, tourists, and those with more international tastes. You'll also find salads at buffet restaurants, called *quilos,* found throughout Brazil.

Brazilian *doces* (desserts), particularly those of Bahia, are very sweet, and many are descendants of the egg-based custards and puddings of Portugal and France. *Cocada* is shredded coconut caked with sugar; *quindim* is a small tart made from egg yolks and coconut; *doce de banana* (or any other fruit) is banana cooked in sugar; *ambrosia* is a lumpy milk-and-sugar pudding.

Coffee is served black and strong with sugar in demitasse cups and is called *cafezinho.* (Requests for *descafeinado* [decaf] are met with a firm shake of the head "no," a blank stare, or outright amusement.) Coffee taken with milk is called *café com leite.* Bottled water (*agua mineral*) is sold carbonated or plain (*com gás* and *sem gás,* respectively).

PAYING

Credit cards are widely accepted at restaurants in major cities. In the countryside all but the smallest establishments generally accept credit cards as well, but check before you order. Smaller, family-run restaurants are sometimes cash-only. Gratuity is 10% of the total sum, and it's usually included in the bill. The tip is always optional; if you weren't happy with the service, you can ask for it to be removed from your bill.

⇨ *For more tip guidelines, see Tipping.*

RESERVATIONS AND DRESS

Appropriate dress for dinner in Brazil can vary dramatically. As a general rule, dress more formally for expensive restaurants. In most restaurants dress is casual.

Regardless of where you are, it's a good idea to make a reservation if you can. We only mention them specifically when reservations are essential (there's no other way you'll ever get a table) or when they're not accepted. For popular restaurants, book as far ahead as you can (often 30 days), and reconfirm as soon as you arrive. (Large parties should always call ahead to check the reservations policy.) We mention dress only when men are required to wear a jacket or a jacket and tie.

MEALS AND MEALTIMES

It's hard to find breakfast (café da manhã) outside a hotel restaurant, but in bakeries (padarias) you can always find something breakfast-like. At lunch (almoço) and dinner (jantar) portions are large. Often a single dish will easily feed two people; no one will be the least bit surprised if you order one entrée and ask for two plates. In addition some restaurants automatically bring a couvert (an appetizer course of such items as bread, cheese, pâté, olives, quail eggs, and the like). You'll be charged extra for this, and you're perfectly within your rights to send it back if you don't want it.

Mealtimes vary according to locale. In Rio and São Paulo, lunch and dinner are served later than in the United States. In restaurants lunch usually starts around noon and can last until 3. Dinner is always eaten after 7 and in many cases not until 10.

■ TIP→ **Unless otherwise noted, the restaurants listed in this guide are open daily for lunch and dinner.**

DINING PRICE RANGES

⇨ *Restaurant prices are the average cost of a main course at dinner or, if dinner is not served, at lunch. Reviews in this book have been shortened; for full reviews, visit Fodors.com.*

What It Costs in Reais			
$	$$	$$$	$$$$
AT DINNER			
under R$50	R$50–R$130	R$131–R$200	over R$200

WINES, BEER, AND SPIRITS

The national drink is the *caipirinha*, made of crushed lime, sugar, and *pinga* or *cachaça* (sugarcane liquor). When whipped with crushed ice, fruit juices, and condensed milk, the pinga/cachaça becomes a *batida*. A *caipivodka*, or *caipiroska*, is the same cocktail with vodka instead of cachaça. Most bars also make both drinks using a fruit other than lime, such as kiwi and *maracujá* (passion fruit). Brazil has many brands of bottled beer. In general, though, Brazilians prefer draft beer, called *chopp*, which is sold in bars and restaurants. Be sure to try the carbonated soft drink *Guaraná*, made using the Amazonian fruit of the same name. It's extremely popular in Brazil.

🌐 Embassies and Consulates

U.S. CONSULATE GENERAL IN RIO DE JANEIRO
✉ *Av. Pres. Wilson, 147, Centro* ☎ *21/3823-2000*

U.S. CONSULATE GENERAL IN SÃO PAULO
✉ *R. Henri Dunant, 500, Santo Amaro* ☎ *11/3250-5000*

Essentials

EMBASSY OF THE UNITED STATES, BRASÍLIA
✉ *St. de Embaixadas Sul 801 - Asa Sul, Brasília* ☏ *61/3312–7000*

U.S. CONSULATE IN RECIFE
✉ *R. Gonçalves Maia, 163, Soledade, Recife* ☏ *81/3416–3050*

⊕ Health and Safety

The major health risk in Brazil is traveler's diarrhea, caused by eating contaminated fruit or vegetables or drinking contaminated water. So watch what you eat—on and off the beaten path—and choose industrially packaged beverages when you can. Using ice in city restaurants is usually safe. Order tropical juices only from places that appear clean and reliable.

If you have problems, mild cases of traveler's diarrhea may respond to over-the-counter medications like Imodium (known generically as loperamide) or Pepto-Bismol (not as strong), both of which can be purchased at a *farmácia* (pharmacy). Drink plenty of purified water or *chá* (tea)—*camomila* (chamomile) is a good folk remedy, as is dissolving a tablespoon of cornstarch in a mix of lime juice and water. In severe cases rehydrate yourself with a salt–sugar solution: ½ teaspoon sal (salt) and 4 tablespoons *açúcar* (sugar) per quart of agua (water). If you can't keep fluids down, seek medical help immediately.

The SUS is Brazil's public healthcare system, providing free access to medical services for locals and visitors alike. Services include emergency care, consultations, hospitalizations, and vaccinations. In case of emergencies, head to the closest UPA (Unidade de Pronto Atendimento), a 24-hour emergency care facility in Brazil, part of the country's public healthcare system. UPAs serve as an intermediary between basic health units (UBS) and hospitals.

Any person, regardless of nationality or residency status, has the right to emergency care in Brazil through the SUS. If you're visiting and need urgent medical attention, public hospitals and clinics will treat you free of charge. You must present your passport or CPF.

English-speaking medical assistance in Brazil is rare. If the language is a barrier, you can also try to contact your consulate or embassy. Private clinics and hospitals are available in most cities.

Although there has been a real effort to crack down on tourist-related crime, particularly in Rio, petty street thievery is still prevalent in urban areas, especially in places around tourist hotels, restaurants, and discos. By day the countryside is safe.

Note that Brazilian law requires everyone to have official identification with them at all times. Carry a copy of your passport's data page and of the Brazilian visa stamp (leave the actual passport in the hotel safe).

For many English-speaking tourists in Brazil, standing out like a sore thumb is unavoidable. But there are some precautions you should take:

■ Don't bring anything you can't stand to lose.

■ Don't wear expensive jewelry or watches—stories of thieves yanking chains or earrings off travelers aren't uncommon.

■ Make sure your camera is in your bag when you're not taking pictures. Don't carry lots of cash.

- Don't let a camera hang around your neck while you wander around. Keep it in a secure camera bag, preferably one with a chain or wire embedded in the strap.

- Carry backpacks on your front; thieves can slit your backpack and run away with its contents before you notice. Be attentive while walking around and when riding on buses.

- Don't let your purse just dangle from your shoulder; always hold on to it with your hand for added security. If you cross the strap over your body, you run the risk of being dragged with your bag if you're mugged.

- Distribute your cash and any valuables (including credit cards and passport) between a deep front pocket, an inside jacket or vest pocket, and a hidden money belt. (If you use a money belt, carry some cash in your purse or wallet so you don't have to reach for the hidden pouch in public.)

- Keep your hand on your wallet if you're in a crowd or on a crowded bus or boat. Do not keep it in your back pocket.

- Keep car windows rolled up and car doors locked at all times in cities; elsewhere, roll up windows and lock doors whenever you leave your car.

- Park in designated parking lots if possible.

- Never leave valuables visible in a car, even in an attended parking lot: take them inside with you whenever possible, or lock them in the trunk.

- Padlock your luggage.

- Talk with locals or your hotel staff about crime in the area. They'll be able to tell you if it's safe to walk around after dark and what to avoid.

- Never walk in a narrow space between a building and a car parked on the street close to it; this is a prime hiding spot for thieves.

- Do not walk in parks or on the beach at night.

- Never leave a drink unattended in a club or bar: scams involving date-rape drugs have been reported in the past few years, targeting both men and women.

- Never leave your belongings unattended anywhere, especially at the beach.

- If you're traveling by bus or boat, or just walking in crowded areas, carabiners come in handy for clipping your bag or other items to a luggage rack, your belt loops, or any other ingenious place to provide extra security.

- If your hotel room has a safe, use it, even if it's an extra charge. If your room doesn't have one, ask the manager to put your valuables in the hotel safe and ask him or her to sign a list of what you are storing there.

- If you're involved in an altercation with a mugger, immediately surrender your possessions and walk away quickly.

If the worst happens and you want to make a police report, be prepared to wait hours for an English-speaking officer and to see justice done. Many people prefer not to make a police report unless their passport is stolen, but this will depend on the area and on the police officer you talk to. If your credit card is stolen, call your credit card company.

⇨ *(Credit Cards in Money, above)*

Essentials

Most tourist-related crimes occur in busy public areas: beaches, sidewalks or plazas, and bus stations (and on buses, too). In these settings pickpockets, usually young children, work in groups. One or more will try to distract you while another grabs a wallet, bag, or camera. Beware of children who suddenly thrust themselves in front of you to ask for money or who offer to shine your shoes. Another member of the gang may strike from behind, grab whatever valuable is available, and disappear in the crowd. It's best not to protest while being mugged. Those on the take are sometimes armed or will tell you that their backup is, and although they're often quite young, they can be dangerous.

On the other hand, some of these children are only looking for handouts; 50 centavos is an average amount to give. Usually these kids will show up when you park your car on a street and will ask to "take care of your car" so that nothing happens to it; that's why they expect to be paid. We strongly recommend that you give a few cents to these kids, especially in São Paulo, otherwise they might damage your car. Depending on the neighborhood, however, these so-called *guardadores de carros* (car guardians) charge much more, from R$1 to R$10. An alternative to this is to park in paid parking lots, which can be more expensive, but much safer.

■ **TIP→ Distribute your cash, credit cards, IDs, and other valuables among a deep front pocket, an inside jacket or vest pocket, and a hidden money pouch. Don't reach for the money pouch once you're in public.**

SAFETY TIPS FOR WOMEN

Although women are gradually assuming a more important role in the nation's job force, machismo is still a strong part of Brazilian culture. You should have no fear of traveling unaccompanied, but you should still take a few precautions. Ask your hotel staff about safety tips, such as areas that are safe to walk alone or reliable taxi companies. When it comes to clothing, Brazil is far from being conservative, but some specific places require modesty, especially churches, temples, or other sacred places.

Depending on the place and the time of day, it might be dangerous for a woman to be by herself (in a bar late at night, for example). Brazilian men are said to have an insurmountable urge to flirt, and that has been our personal experience. This can be either fun or inconvenient, and it's up to you to decide whether you give them attention or not.

Shaking hands with men, talking to them by yourself, and even kissing cheeks lightly as a greeting are not considered taboos. However, when you greet men for the first time, be on your guard, as some Brazilian men take advantage of the "kissing greeting" to be closer to you (this doesn't mean, however, that they will attack you). Avoid eye contact with unsavory individuals. If such a person approaches you, discourage him by politely but firmly saying, "*Por favor, me dê licença*" (pohr fah-vohr, meh day lee-sehn-see-ah), which means "Excuse me, please," and then walk away with resolve.

Hermail and Journeywoman are two websites specifically for women traveling alone or with other women.

DIVERS' ALERT

Do not fly within 24 hours of scuba diving. Neophyte divers should have a complete physical exam before undertaking a dive. If you have travel insurance that covers evacuations, make sure your policy applies to scuba-related injuries, as not all companies provide this coverage.

HEATSTROKE

Heatstroke and heat prostration are common though easily preventable maladies throughout Brazil. The symptoms for either can vary but always start with headaches, nausea, and dizziness. If ignored, these symptoms can worsen until you require medical attention. In hot weather be sure to rehydrate regularly, wear loose lightweight clothing, and avoid overexerting yourself.

INFECTIOUS DISEASES AND VIRUSES

Meningococcal meningitis and typhoid fever are common in certain areas of Brazil—and not only in remote areas like the Amazon. Meningitis has been a problem around São Paulo in recent years. Dengue fever, chikungunya, yellow fever, and malaria—all caused by mosquito bites—are common in Brazil or in certain areas of Brazil. They are usually only a problem in the Amazon, but dengue and chikungunya can affect urban areas and malaria is sometimes found in urban peripheries. Yellow fever is generally only found in rural areas, but a 2017 outbreak of the virus in states where it generally isn't found caused concern that the urban variety could return. Zika, another mosquito-borne disease, has also become a concern since a 2015–2016 epidemic, mostly in the country's northeast. Most travelers to Brazil return home unscathed, but you should talk with your doctor (at least six weeks prior to traveling) about what precautions to take, particularly if you're pregnant, traveling with children, or have a chronic illness. It's also a good idea to check the CDC or World Health Organization websites for health alerts.

If you get sick weeks, months, or in rare cases, years after your trip, make sure your doctor administers blood tests for tropical diseases.

OVER-THE-COUNTER REMEDIES

Aspirin is *aspirina*; Tylenol (acetaminophen; paracetamol) is pronounced *tee-luh-nawl*. Advil (ibuprofen) is ah-jee-viu.

■ **TIP→ If you travel a lot internationally—particularly to developing nations—refer to the CDC's Health Information for International Travel (aka Traveler's Health Yellow Book). Info from it is posted on the CDC website (wwwnc.cdc.gov/travel).**

Vaccinations against hepatitis A and B, meningitis, typhoid, and yellow fever are highly recommended. Consult your doctor about whether to get a rabies vaccination. Check with the CDC's International Travelers' Hotline if you plan to visit remote regions or stay for more than six weeks.

For travel anywhere in Brazil, it's recommended that you have updated vaccines for diphtheria, tetanus, and polio. Children must additionally have current inoculations against measles, mumps, and rubella.

Internet access is widespread, and Wi-Fi is often available in Rio and São Paulo. Many hotels have in-room access to Wi-Fi. 4G access in big cities like São Paulo and Rio is common, but check with your local provider to find a plan that mitigates the often-steep roaming charges. Switching your device from cellular data to Wi-Fi whenever it is available should save you money.

Be discreet about carrying laptops, smartphones, and other obvious displays of wealth, which can make you a target of thieves. Conceal your laptop in a generic bag and keep it close to you at all times.

Essentials

🛏 Lodging

All hotels in Rio and São Paulo have bathrooms in their rooms. The simplest type of accommodations usually consists of a bed, TV, table, a little fridge, a telephone, and a bathroom with a shower. In luxury hotels you'll also generally have cable TV, and a bathroom with a bathtub and shower. Hotels listed with EMBRATUR, Brazil's national tourism board, are rated using stars. Staff training is a big part of the rating, but it's not a perfect system, since stars are awarded based on the number of amenities rather than their quality.

If you ask for a double room, you'll get a room for two people, but you're not guaranteed a double mattress. If you'd like to avoid twin beds, ask for a *cama de casal* (couple's bed).

■ **TIP→ For top hotels in Rio during Carnival, you must make reservations a year in advance.**

Carnival, the year's principal festival, takes place during the four days preceding Ash Wednesday. Hotel rates rise by at least 30% for Carnival. Not as well-known outside Brazil but equally impressive is Rio's New Year's Eve celebration. More than a million people gather along Copacabana Beach for a massive fireworks display and to honor the sea goddess Iemanjá. To ensure a room, book at least six months in advance.

Most hotels and other lodgings require you to give your credit card details before they will confirm your reservation. However you book, get confirmation in writing and have a copy of it handy when you check in.

Be sure you understand the hotel's cancellation policy. Some places allow you to cancel without any kind of penalty—even if you prepaid to secure a discounted rate—if you cancel at least 24 hours in advance. Others require you to cancel a week in advance or penalize you the cost of one night. Small inns and bed-and-breakfasts are most likely to require you to cancel far in advance. Most hotels allow children under a certain age to stay in their parents' room at no extra charge, but others charge for them as extra adults; find out the cutoff age for discounts.

BED AND BREAKFASTS

B&Bs in Brazil are comfortable, friendly, and offer a modicum of privacy. They're a nice option if you're looking for something a little more intimate than a hotel. Websites like Booking.com and Decolar.com are great resources.

Airbnb is another option that has become a popular choice in Brazil. You can look up listings of short-term lets and small B&Bs that locals post on the site. Usually the rates are a fraction of other accommodations.

FAZENDAS

Another accommodations option is to stay on a *fazenda* (farm), or *hotel fazenda*, where you can experience a rural environment. They are ideal for families with kids, as most have adventure sports and programs for children. Some farms in the state of São Paulo date back to colonial times, when they were famous Brazilian coffee farms.

POUSADAS

If you want the facilities of a hotel plus the family environment of an apartment, but at a lower cost, a *pousada* is a good option. Cheaper than hotels and farms, pousadas are simple inns. They usually offer breakfast and have swimming pools, parking lots, air-conditioning and/or fans, TVs, refrigerators, and common areas such as bars, laundry, and living rooms. Some have a common kitchen for guests who prefer to cook their own meals.

PRICES

⇨ *Prices are for a standard double room in high season. Reviews in the book have been shortened; for full reviews, visit Fodors.com.*

What It Costs in Reais			
$	$$	$$$	$$$$
FOR TWO PEOPLE			
under R$150	R$150–R$300	R$301–R$500	over R$500

💲 Money

Brazil's unit of currency is the real (R$; plural: reais). One real is 100 *centavos* (cents). There are notes worth 5, 10, 20, 50, 100, and 200 reais, together with coins worth 5, 10, 25, and 50 centavos and 1 real. Outside major cities, changing money in Brazil becomes more challenging. When leaving a large city for a smaller town, bring enough cash for your trip.

At this writing, the real is at about R$6.13 to the U.S. dollar.

PRICES

Brasília, Rio, and São Paulo tend to be the most expensive cities. In other capitals, things tend to be much cheaper compared to these cities. You're also likely to find things cheaper in the countryside. The average price of a cup of coffee, for example, is R$9 (1.55¢) in Brazil. However, depending on where you are, prices can be higher.

Top hotels in Rio and São Paulo go for more than $180 a night, and meals can—but do not have to—cost as much. Outside Brazil's two largest cities and Brasília, prices for food and lodging tend to drop considerably. Self-service restaurants where you pay by weight (per kilo, about 2.2 pounds) are inexpensive alternatives everywhere, though be sure to choose carefully among them. A considerable advantage of self-service restaurants is that you don't need to know the names of the foods, which is especially helpful for those who don't speak Portuguese.

Taxis can be pricey, and prices vary enormously from one city to another—not only because price tables may be different, but also (and mainly) because of traffic. In São Paulo, for example, expect to pay more, as you're going to spend more time inside the taxi, due to traffic. City buses, subways, and long-distance buses are all inexpensive; plane fares aren't. If you're price-conscious and want to travel by plane within Brazil book well in advance.

Prices here are given for adults. Substantially reduced fees are almost always available for children, students, and senior citizens.

ATMS AND BANKS

Even if a currency exchange booth has a sign promising no commission, rest assured that there's some kind of huge, hidden fee. And as for rates, you're almost always better off getting foreign currency at an ATM or exchanging money at a bank.

■ **TIP→ If you're withdrawing money from an ATM in Brazil you can use a six-digit PIN, but if you're paying at a store, restaurant, etc. with your credit card it has to be four digits.**

Essentials

Where Should I Stay?

	NEIGHBORHOOD VIBE	PROS	CONS
Copacabana & Ipanema	Most popular choice among travelers that plan to stay in a hotel overlooking Brazil's most famous beaches.	Beach with a lively boardwalk; wide range of accommodations.	Some areas can feel less safe at night, so caution is advised.
Leblon	One of Rio's most affluent neighborhoods.	Ideal for families or couples seeking tranquility.	High prices for accommodation.
Santa Teresa	This bohemian neighborhood is full of charm and historic mansions.	Artistic atmosphere; stunning views of Rio's skyline.	Not close to the beaches; limited public transportation.
Botafogo	A more residential area overlooking Sugarloaf Mountain.	Public transport connections; affordable accommodations.	No major beaches; the nearby beach is unsuitable for swimming.
Flamengo	Located near the city center, it's a predominantly residential area that gives a glimpse of what everyday life in Rio looks like.	Green spaces for walking and cycling; affordable accommodations and dining options.	The beach nearby is not swimmable; quieter lifestyle.
Avenida Paulista	São Paulo's most iconic avenue.	Central location with excellent public transport connections.	Busy and noisy, especially during weekdays and rush hours.
Vila Mariana	A blend of residential vibe, cultural attractions, and facilities.	Access to Ibirapuera Park; good public transportation.	Traffic jams; high prices.
Vila Madalena	Known as São Paulo's bohemian and artistic hub and street art; galleries; and bars abound.	Beco do Batman; live music venues; eclectic dining scene.	Can get noisy at night, especially near the main bar streets.
Jardins	Travelers seeking an upscale neighborhood shouldn't hesitate to stay at Jardins, São Paulo's fanciest borough.	High-end boutiques and Michelin-starred restaurants.	One of the most expensive areas in São Paulo.
Itaim Bibi	A modern, business-oriented neighborhood known for its skyscrapers, upscale hotels, and trendy restaurants.	High-end hotels; upscale dining and nightlife options.	Less cultural or historical charm.

Item	Average Cost
Cup of coffee	R$9
Glass of wine	R$25
Glass of beer	R$15
Sandwich	R$25
1-mile taxi ride	R$5.50
Museum admission	R$20

Nearly all the nation's major banks have ATMs, known in Brazil as *caixas eletrônicos,* for which you must use a card with a credit card logo. MasterCard/Cirrus holders can withdraw at Banco Itau, Banco do Brasil, HSBC, and Banco24horas ATMs. Visa holders can use Bradesco ATMs and those at Banco do Brasil. American Express cardholders can make withdrawals at most Bradesco ATMs marked "24 horas." To be on the safe side, carry a variety of cards. For your card to function in some ATMs, you may need to hit a screen command (perhaps, *estrangeiro* or *inglês*) if you are a foreign client.

Banks are, with a few exceptions, open weekdays 10 to 4. Avoid using ATMs alone and at night, and use ATMs in busy, highly visible locations whenever possible.

Nightlife

Rio de Janeiro and São Paulo maintain their lively atmospheres 24/7. Despite their geographical proximity, the two cities have completely distinct lifestyles, which is evident in how they embrace the night. While Rio is synonymous with rodas de samba, baile funk, and beachside revelry, São Paulo takes pride in its cosmopolitan vibe, boasting countless clubs and bars.

In Rio de Janeiro, nightlife often feels like an extension of the city's daytime culture—it's not uncommon to see young people transitioning from the beach to a nearby bar. The streets of Copacabana and Ipanema are bustling with people of all ages enjoying the *botecos* or simply hanging out on the sidewalks. Galetos, Pavão Azul, and Belmonte are among the favorite spots for Cariocas. Unsurprisingly, Rio offers the best *rodas de samba*. This rhythm is most prominent in Lapa, Rio's bohemian neighborhood, where you can plan a bar-hopping adventure to catch samba performances and maybe even learn some of the more elaborate steps. To enjoy samba like a local, visit Pedra do Sal (from Friday to Monday starting at 6 pm), an open-air, free event, or Samba do Trabalhador, every Monday from 4:30 pm to 9:30 pm. These rodas de samba are located outside the Zona Sul, so exercising some caution is advised. The Mirante do Arvrão Bar offers a unique view of Rio by night and hosts some of the city's best parties. Located in Vidigal, a pacified favela, Arvrão has become a popular hub among tourists and locals alike. Heading west to Barra da Tijuca, the nightlife takes on a more upscale atmosphere. For a bohemian twist, Santa Teresa is the place to be: its hilltop streets are filled with bars featuring live jazz and samba.

São Paulo's nightlife reflects its multicultural atmosphere, with each neighborhood offering a different experience. Paulistanos often enjoy sharing a litrão (a 1-liter bottle of beer) in a boteco, a no-frills bar. These can be found in every neighborhood and start to get busy after working hours. Vila Madalena, the city's creative heart, is famous for spots like Boteco São Bento and Olívio Bar. The neighborhood is also home to Beco do Batman, a renowned street art alley surrounded by casual bars and live music

Essentials

venues. For a more polished nightlife experience, Itaim Bibi and Jardins have a reputation for sophistication. Here, you'll find cocktail bars, fine dining establishments, and exclusive clubs. Itaim Bibi's rooftop lounges, such as Skye Bar at the Unique Hotel, offer stunning skyline views and expertly crafted drinks, while the Jardins district features elegant wine bars and refined social hubs that cater to São Paulo's cosmopolitan crowd. Centro, São Paulo's downtown area, welcomes everyone. Its historical buildings serve as a backdrop for an alternative nightlife scene, making it a haven for underground electronic music enthusiasts. Meanwhile, Liberdade, the Japanese district, offers karaoke bars and izakayas, reflecting the area's rich cultural heritage.

Packing

For sightseeing, casual clothing and good walking shoes are appropriate; most restaurants don't require formal attire. For beach vacations, bring lightweight sportswear, a bathing suit, a beach cover-up, a sun hat, and waterproof sunscreen that is at least SPF 30. A sarong or a light cotton blanket makes a handy beach towel, picnic blanket, and cushion for hard seats, among other things.

If you're going to Rio in summer (December, January, and February), dress more informally and feel free to wear flip-flops (thongs) all day—and don't forget your sunglasses. São Paulo, which has lower temperatures, tends to be more formal and more conservative when it comes to clothing (sometimes even Brazilians are shocked by the way people in Rio dress). In both cities it's always a good idea to have some nice outfits for going out at night.

Passports and Visas

At this writing, passports are required for citizens—even infants—of the United States but they don't need a visa to enter Brazil for tourism, business, or transit purposes. Starting April 10, 2025, U.S. citizens will be required to obtain a visa to enter Brazil. The Brazilian government will offer an e-visa option for qualified applicants, which can be obtained through the official Brazilian government-authorized website.

PASSPORTS

Carry your passport or a copy with you at all times. Make two photocopies of the data page (one for someone at home and another for you, carried separately from your passport).

If your passport is lost or stolen, first call the police—having the police report can make replacement easier—and then call your embassy. You'll get a temporary Emergency Travel Document that will need to be replaced once you return home. Fees vary according to how fast you need the passport; in some cases the fee covers your permanent replacement as well. The new document will not have your entry stamps; ask if your embassy takes care of this, or whether it's your responsibility to get the necessary immigration authorization.

VISAS

Go to the website for the Brazilian embassy or consulate nearest you for the most up-to-date visa information. At this writing, a tourist visa will become mandatory for Americans in April 2025 for US$80.90 and will be valid for 10 years. Apply at ⊕ *www.brazil.vfsevisa.com*.

General Requirements for Brazil

Passport	Must be valid for six months after date of arrival.
Visa	Required for Americans (US$160 or US$44.24 for e-visa).
Vaccinations	Needed in some areas: yellow fever and diphtheria. Recommended for all travelers but not mandatory: hepatitis A and B, typhoid, meningitis, tetanus, polio.
Driving	Driver's license with Portuguese translation or international driver's license required; CDW is compulsory on car rentals and will be included in the quoted price.
Departure Tax	Approximately R$250 (US$74).

Performing Arts

THEATERS AND VENUES

Auditório Ibirapuera: Located in the famous Ibirapuera Park, this venue offers an eclectic program ranging from orchestral performances to contemporary music and experimental theater. Its open-air design integrates the park's natural beauty with world-class performances.

Cidade das Artes: Located in Barra da Tijuca, this modern complex is a hub for music, theater, and dance. It frequently hosts large-scale productions, including concerts by the Brazilian Symphony Orchestra and touring international acts. ⊕ www.cidadedasartes.rio.rj.gov.br.

Theatro Municipal de Rio de Janeiro: One of the city's most iconic landmarks, this place is a must-visit for lovers of classical music, opera, and ballet. Inspired by the Paris Opera House, it hosts performances by the Brazilian Symphony Orchestra and guest artists from around the world. ⊕ www.theatromunicipal.rj.gov.br.

Theatro Municipal de São Paulo: This is one of Brazil's most prestigious venues for opera, ballet, and classical music. It regularly features performances by the São Paulo Municipal Symphony Orchestra and Ballet Company. ⊕ www.theatromunicipal.org.br.

SESC São Paulo: SESC is a cultural institution with venues across the city offering diverse performing arts programming. From affordable theater productions to experimental dance and live music, SESC's calendar endorses the Brazilian culture. Notable locations include SESC Pompeia and SESC Vila Mariana. ⊕ www.sescsp.org.br

SAMBA AND LOCAL PERFORMANCES

Pedra do Sal: Although informal, the samba rodas here are living examples of performance art, showcasing the energy and passion of Rio's music scene.

Samba Schools: Most samba schools open their rehearsal spaces to visitors, which starts in September.

BALLET AND DANCE

Deborah Colker Dance Company: Renowned internationally, this contemporary dance company blends athleticism and artistry in its productions. Performances often take place at venues like the Cidade das Artes.

São Paulo Dance Company: São Paulo Dance Company showcases both classic and contemporary works. Performances are held at various theaters, including the Theatro Municipal and Teatro Sérgio Cardoso.

Essentials

MUSIC AND EXPERIMENTAL ARTS

Experimental Theater: São Paulo's avant-garde theater scene is thriving, with groups like Grupo Tapa and Teatro Oficina presenting thought-provoking works in unconventional spaces.

Sala São Paulo: Housed in a restored railway station, Sala São Paulo is the home of the São Paulo State Symphony Orchestra (OSESP). Its stunning acoustics and diverse programming make it a highlight for classical music enthusiasts.

Shopping

With no fewer than 54 shopping malls, São Paulo holds the title of Brazil's top consumer city and is the best place to shop. These establishments attract thousands of visitors daily, whether for shopping, entertainment like movies, dining, or simply strolling—a common hobby among Brazilians. High-end malls, such as Cidade Jardim, boast enviable structures and beautiful views. Other malls cater to the needs of workers in commercial centers and communities in the suburbs, providing entertainment and convenience. From luxurious venues to popular suburban hubs, São Paulo's shopping scene offers something for everyone.

Taxes

Sales tax is included in the prices shown on goods in stores but listed separately on the bottom of your receipt. Hotel, meal, and car rental taxes are usually tacked on in addition to the costs shown on menus and brochures. At this writing, hotel taxes are roughly 15%, and car rental taxes 12%.

Brazil doesn't charge departure taxes on international flights, but some taxes are included in the tickets. These typically include the International Boarding Tax (Taxa de Embarque Internacional) and other related charges.

Telephones

The country code for Brazil is 55. When dialing a Brazilian number from abroad, dial the international access code of your home country, the Brazilian country code, the two-digit area code (drop the initial 0 if there is one), and the local number.

If you want to call from your hotel, remember long-distance calls within Brazil are expensive, and hotels add a surcharge.

There's a wide choice of long-distance companies: Tim, Vivo, and Claro are the most popular. Hence, to make direct-dial long-distance calls, you must find out which companies serve the area from which you're calling and then get their access codes—the staff at your hotel can help. (Some hotels have already made the choice for you, so you may not need an access code when calling from the hotel itself.) For long-distance calls within Brazil, dial 0 + the access code + the area code and number. To call Rio, for example, dial 0, then the company code, then 21 (Rio's area code), and then the number.

International calls from Brazil are extremely expensive. Hotels also add a surcharge, increasing this cost even more. Calls can be made from public phone booths with a prepaid phone card.

For international calls, dial 00 + phone company code + the country code + the area code and number.

AT&T and Sprint operators are also accessible from Brazil; get the local access codes before you leave home.

Big cities in Brazil have 4G Internet available to anyone with a smartphone. Roaming charges can be extremely high, however, so make sure to check rates with your provider before arriving in Brazil. Your provider may offer international data plans and should be able to provide details on connectivity. It's a good idea to use local Wi-Fi when available and to make international calls with services like Skype, Viber, or WhatsApp.

If you will be making many local calls and will be in the country for a few weeks, consider buying a new SIM card (note that your provider may have to unlock your phone for you), and signing up for a pay-as-you-go plan. You'll then have a local number and can make calls at local rates. Be aware that as a nonBrazilian you must show proof of citizenship (such as a passport) to buy a SIM card, which costs around R$10. Note that you'll use up the credit on your SIM card more quickly when calling numbers in a Brazilian state other than the one in which you purchased the card. Many travelers buy a new SIM card in each state they visit. If you plan on visiting rural areas, find out from locals which mobile phone provider works best in the area before buying your SIM card. There are often several available, but one or two providers tend to get better coverage because of tower locations, especially in Amazonas.

Tipping

Wages can be paltry in Brazil, so a little generosity in tipping can go a long way. Tipping in dollars is not recommended. Large hotels that receive lots of international guests are the exception. Some restaurants add an optional 10% service charge onto the check. If there's no service charge, you can leave as much as you want, but 15% is a good amount. In deluxe hotels tip porters R$5 per bag, chambermaids R$5 per day, and bellhops R$10 for room and valet service. Tips for doormen and concierges vary, depending on the services provided. A good tip is around R$30, with the average at about R$20. For moderate and inexpensive hotels, tips tend to be minimal.

In general, you don't tip taxi drivers. If a service station attendant does anything beyond filling up the gas tank, leave him a small tip of some spare change. Tipping in bars and cafés follows the rules of restaurants, although at outdoor bars Brazilians rarely leave a gratuity if they have had only a soft drink or a beer. At airports and at train and bus stations, tip the last porter who puts your bags into the cab (R$2 per bag at airports, R$1 per bag at bus and train stations).

Visitor Information

Embratur. (⊕ *www.visitbrasil.com*), Brazil's national tourism organization, doesn't have offices overseas, though its website is helpful.

Cities and towns throughout Brazil have local tourist boards, and some state capitals also have state tourism offices.

ONLINE RESOURCES

News site *The Brazilian Report* (*brazilian.report*) has articles and a podcast on everything going on in Brazil, as well as a guide to the country's politics, culture, and social issues. The online magazine *Brazzil (www.brazzil.com)* and Internet newspaper the *Rio Times Online (www.*

Essentials

riotimesonline.com) have interesting English-language articles on culture and politics. Brazil's biggest national newspaper, *Folha de S.Paulo,* (⊕ *www1.folha.uol.com.br/internacional/en)* also publishes its content in English and Spanish on the international version of its site.

📅 When to Go

Defining the period during which you travel to Rio de Janeiro and São Paulo is essential to setting a budget and being prepared for the weather. São Paulo is famous for having four seasons in one day, so always bring a coat with you even if the day is sunny.

Low season in Rio and São Paulo runs from May to September, coinciding with Brazil's winter months. During this time, temperatures are mild, ranging from 18°C to 25°C (64°F to 77°F) in Rio and slightly cooler in São Paulo, averaging 13°C to 23°C (55°F to 73°F). Days are often cloudy, but rainfall isn't usually an issue—unless you plan on going to the beach. It's a great time to explore the cities' cultural attractions. For travelers looking to save, the low season is ideal as flights and accommodations are generally more affordable.

Shoulder season: Spans March to April and October to November, offers a balance between favorable weather and reasonable costs. These transitional months feature warm temperatures, ranging from 22°C to 30°C (72°F to 86°F) in Rio and 17°C to 27°C (63°F to 81°F) in São Paulo. Rainfall is moderate, especially in São Paulo during October and November, but overall, the climate is pleasant. Costs for flights and accommodations are moderate, making this period a sweet spot for budget-conscious travelers who want to avoid the peak-season crowds. In Rio, the weather remains ideal for beachgoers, while both cities offer manageable crowds at attractions and cultural sites.

High season: Runs from December to February, encompassing Brazil's summer and major holidays like Christmas, New Year, and Carnival. This is the most expensive time to visit both cities, as demand for flights and accommodations skyrockets. In Rio, temperatures soar, reaching 40°C (104°F) on some days, while São Paulo sees a more moderate range of 20°C to 30°C (68°F to 86°F). Humidity is high, with sporadic afternoon showers, particularly in Rio. The high season is defined by its vibrant atmosphere, with iconic events like Rio's New Year's Eve celebrations on Copacabana Beach and the world-famous Carnival, which draws millions of revelers. Book well in advance.

Best Tours

ADVENTURE TOURS

Aventura Turismo. This tourism operator conducts six-hour Jeep tours that head into Serra da Bocaina National Park, crossing rivers and visiting fantastic waterfalls, with stops for swimming in natural pools, hiking through rainforest, and even visiting sugarcane rum distilleries (complete with tastings). Aventura Turismo also runs boat trips, adventure sports excursions, and motorbike trips. ✉ *Av. Dom Pedro I, 444, Centro Histórico* ☎ *24/99995–7041* ⊕ *www.agenciaaventuraturismo.com.br* 🖃 *From R$100.*

Rio Xtreme. Rio Xtreme offers group and private adventure tours and activities in Rio de Janeiro State. The friendly, English-speaking guides and instructors can take you scuba diving in Cabo Frio or ziplining, hiking, and rafting in the jungle that surrounds Rio.

■ **TIP→ Booking inquiries are best made via the website, email or WhatsApp.** ⊕ *www.rioxtreme.com* 🖃 *From R$290.*

BIKE TOURS

Baja Bikes. This 3-hour tour of Rio de Janeiro's landmarks, including its most famous beaches like Copacabana and Ipanema. Perfect for first-time visitors, this tour allows you to see numerous highlights in just a few hours, making it an efficient way to explore the city. ✉ *Rio de Janeiro* ☎ *646/252–199 WhatsApp* ⊕ *www.bajabikes.eu/en/rio-de-janeiro-sightseeing/.*

Sampa Bikes. Several bike tours are available to explore São Paulo, including one that covers approximately 20 kilometers through the city's streets. Sampa Bikers organizes several biking events during the year. Participants are accompanied by experienced guides, and part of the proceeds is directed toward purchasing bicycles for those in need. ✉ *São Paulo* ☎ *11/5517–7733, 11/98585–9559 WhatsApp* ⊕ *sampabikers.com.br/.*

BUS TOURS

Rio Samba Bus City Tour. This panoramic musical city tour passes by Rio's most important landmarks from the comfort of an open-top bus. Unlike other touristic buses, the experience is enhanced by musical performances during the tour. For travelers who have only a short time in Rio, this option is ideal as it stops at places such as the historic center and famous beaches. ☎ *21/3083–4554 WhatsApp* ⊕ *www.riosambabus.com.br.*

WALKING TOURS

Rio Free Walking Tour. Expert English-speaking guides lead free tours through Centro, Copacabana, and Rio's downtown dock area each weekday. Rain or shine, the guides will take you on a three-hour morning stroll (tours start between 9:30 and 10:30 am), explaining the history of downtown Rio's major buildings, streets, statues, and monuments. The walk is followed by lunch at a pay-by-weight buffet restaurant. There's no need to book in advance, just look out for the yellow-shirted guides. Although there's no charge, tips are welcomed. ✉ *Rio de Janeiro* ☎ *21/98600–2593* ⊕ *www.riofreewalkingtour.com* 🖃 *Free.*

SP Free Walking Tours. To explore the city's historic center or the gleaming towers and old mansions around Avenida Paulista, join one of the free, English-language group tours run by this outfitter. Tours are around three hours long; check their site for a full weekly schedule and meeting points. ✉ *São Paulo* ⊕ *www.saopaulofreewalkingtour.com.*

Helpful Brazilian Phrases

BASICS

Hello	Oi	Oy
Yes/No	SIM/NÃO	seem / now
Please	Por favor	pohr fah-vohr
Thank you	Obrigado	oh-bree-gah-doo
You're welcome	Bem-vindo	deh nah-dah
I'm sorry (apology)	Desculpe	des-kool-peh
Sorry (Excuse Me)	Com Licença	kohm lee-sen-sah
Good morning	Bom dia	bohn jee-ah
Good day	Bom dia	bohn jee-ah
Good evening	Boa noite	boh-ah noh-ee-chee
Goodbye	Tchau	Chow
Mr. (Sir)	Senhor	sen-yor
Mrs.	Senhora	sen-yor-ah
Miss	Senhorita	sen-yor-ee-tah
Pleased to meet you	Prazer conhecer você	Prah-zehr koh-nyeh-sehr voh-seh
How are you?	Como você está?	koh-moo voh-seh es-tah

NUMBERS

one-half	metade	meh-tah-jee
one	um	oom
two	Dois	doys
three	Três	trehs
four	Quatro	kwah-troh
five	Cinco	seen-coh
six	seis	says
seven	Sete	seh-chee
eight	Oito	oy-toh
nine	Nove	noh-vee
ten	Dez	dehs
eleven	Onze	ohn-zee
twelve	Doze	doh-zee
thirteen	Treze	treh-zee
fourteen	Catorze	kah-tor-zee
fifteen	Quinze	keen-zee
sixteen	Dezesseis	deh-zeh-says
seventeen	Dezessete	deh-zeh-seh-chee
eighteen	Dezoito	deh-zoy-toh
nineteen	Dezenove	deh-zeh-noh-vee
twenty	Vinte	veen-chee
twenty-one	Vinte e um	veen-chee oom
thirty	Trinta	treen-tah
forty	quarenta	kwah-ren-tah
fifty	Cinquenta	seen-kwen-tah
sixty	Sessenta	seh-sen-tah
seventy	Setenta	seh-ten-tah
eighty	Oitenta	oy-ten-tah
ninety	Noventa	noh-ven-tah
one hundred	cem	sen
one thousand	Um Mil	Oom mee-oo
one million	Um milhão	oom meel-yown

COLORS

black	Preto	Preh-too
blue	Branco	A-zool
brown	Marrom	Mah-hohm
green	Verde	Ver-jee
orange	Laranja	La-rahn-ja
red	Vermelho	Ver-meh-lyo
white	Branco	Brahn-ko
yellow	Amarelo	Ah-mah-reh-lo

DAYS OF THE WEEK

Sunday	Domingo	Doh-mee-n-go
Monday	Segunda	Seh-goon-dah
Tuesday	Terça	Tehr-sah
Wednesday	Quarta	Kwar-tah
Thursday	Quinta	Keen-tah
Friday	Sexta	Seh-shtah
Saturday	Sábado	SAH-bah-doo

MONTHS

January	Janeiro	jah-NAY-roh
February	Fevereiro	feh-veh-RAY-roh
March	Março	MAR-soo
April	Abril	ah-BREE-oo
May	Maio	MY-oh
June	Junho	JOO-nyoh
July	Julho	JOO-lyoh
August	Agosto	ah-GOHS-too
September	Setembro	seh-TEM-broo
October	Outubro	ow-TOO-broo
November	Novembro	no-VAIM-broo
December	Dezembro	deh-ZEM-broo

USEFUL WORDS AND PHRASES

Do you speak English?	Você fala inglês?	voh-SEH FAH-lah een-GLAYS?
I don't speak [Language].	Eu não falo português.	eh-oo NOW fah-loh pohr-too-GAYS
I don't understand.	Eu não entendo	eh-oo NOW en-TEHN-doo
I don't know.	Eu não sei	eh-oo NOW say
I understand.	Eu entendo	eh-oo en-TEHN-doo
I'm American.	Eu sou americano	eh-oo so ah-meh-ree-KAH-noo
I'm British.	Eu sou britânico	eh-oo so bree-TAH-nee-koo
What's your name?	Qual o seu nome?	kwow oo SEH-oo NOH-mee?
My name is …	Meu nome é…	meh-oo NOH-mee eh
What time is it?	Que horas são?	keh OH-rahz sow?
How?	Como?	COH-moo
When?	Quando?	KWAN-doo
Yesterday	Ontem	ON-tem
Today	Hoje	OH-zhee

Travel Smart — HELPFUL BRAZILIAN PHRASES

English	Portuguese	Pronunciation
Tomorrow	amanhã	ah-mahn-YAH
This morning	Essa manhã	EH-sah mahn-YAH
Afternoon	Essa tarde	EH-sah TAR-jee
Tonight	Essa noite	EH-sah NOY-chee
What?	Por que?	pohr KEH
What is it?	O que é isso?	oo KEH eh EE-soo?
Why?	Por que?	pohr KEH
Who?	Quem?	KAYN
Where is …	Onde é…	OHN-jee eh
… the train station?	A estação de trem?	ah es-tah-SOWN jee TREHM
… the subway station?	A estação de metrô?	ah es-tah-SOWN jee meh-TROH?
… the bus stop?	O ponto de ônibus?	oo PON-too jee OH-nee-boos
… the airport?	O aeroporto?	oo ah-eh-roh-POR-too?
… the post office?	O correio?	oo coh-HAY-oo?
… the bank?	O banco?	oo BAHN-coo
… the hotel?	O hotel?	oo oh-TEL
… the museum?	O museu?	oo moo-ZAY-oo
… the hospital?	O hospital?	oo os-pee-TAHL
… the elevator?	O elevador?	oo eh-leh-vah-DOR
Where are the restrooms?	Onde são os banheiros?	OHN-jee sow ooz bahn-YAY-rooz
Here/there	Aqui/Lá	ah-KEE / LAH
Left/right	Esquerda/Direita	ehs-KEHR-dah / jee-RAY-tah
Is it near/far?	é perto/longe?	eh PEHR-too / LOHN-zhee
I'd like …	Eu gostaria	eh-oo gohs-TAH-ree-ah
… a room	De um quarto	jee oon KWAR-too
… the key	Da chave	dah SHAH-vee
… a newspaper	Um jornal	oon zhohr-NOW
… a stamp	De um selo	jee oon SEH-loh
I'd like to buy …	Eu gostaria de comprar	eh-oo gohs-TAH-ree-ah jee koom-PRAHR
… a city map	Um mapa da cidade	oon MAH-pah dah see-DAH-jee
… a road map	Um guia de ruas	oon GEE-ah jee HOO-ahz
… a magaine	Uma revista	oo-mah heh-VEE-stah
… envelopes	Envelopes	en-veh-LOH-peez
… writing paper	Papel de carta	pah-PEHL jee KAR-tah
… a postcard	Um cartão postal	oon kahr-TOWN pohs-TAHL
… a ticket	Um bilhete	oon bee-LYEH-chee
How much is it?	Quanto isso custa?	KWAN-too EE-soo KOOS-tah
It's expensive/cheap	Isso é caro/barato?	EE-soo eh KAH-roo / bah-RAH-too
A little/a lot	Um pouco/muito.	oon POH-coo / MOY-too
More/less	Mais/menos	myze / MEH-noos
Enough/too (much)	Suficiente/demais	soo-fee-see-EHN-chee / jee-MY-see
I am ill/sick	Eu estou mal/doente	eh-oo eh-STOH MAHL / doh-EN-che
Call a doctor	Chame um médico	SHAH-mee oon MEH-jee-coo
Help!	Ajuda	ah-ZHOO-dah
Stop!	Pare!	PAH-ree!

DINING OUT

English	Portuguese	Pronunciation
A bottle of …	Uma garrafa de…	oo-mah gah-HAH-fah jee
A cup of …	um copo de..	oon COH-poo jee
A glass of …	Uma taça de..	oo-mah TAH-sah jee
Beer	Cerveja	sehr-VAY-zha
Bill/check	A conta	ah COHN-tah
Bread	Pão	pown
Breakfast	café da manhã	kah-FEH dah mahn-YAH
Butter	Manteiga	mahn-TAY-gah
Cocktail/aperitif	Coquetel/aperitivo	cohk-TEHL / ah-peh-ree-CHEE-voo
Coffee	café	kah-FEH
Dinner	Jantar	zhahn-TAR
Fixed-price menu	Menu de preço fixo	meh-NOO jee PREH-soo FEEK-soo
Fork	Garfo	GAR-foo
I am vegetarian/ I don't eat meat	Eu sou vegetariano/ eu não como carne	eh-oo so veh-zheh-tah-ree-AH-noo / eh-oo NOW COH-moo KAR-nee
I cannot eat …	Eu não posso comer…	eh-oo NOW POH-soo coh-MEHER
I'd like to order…	Eu gostaria de pedir..	eh-oo gohs-TAH-ree-ah jee peh-DEER
Is service included?	O serviço está incluso?	oo sehr-VEE-soo eh-STAH een-KLOO-zoo
I'm hungry/thirsty	Eu estou com fome/sede	eh-oo eh-STOH cohng FOH-mee / SEH-je
It's good/bad	Está bom/ruim	eh-STAH bohn / hoo-EEN
It's hot/cold	Está quente/frio	eh-STAH KEN-chee / FREE-oo
Knife	Faca	FAH-kaH
Lunch	Almoço	ahl-MOH-soo
Menu	Cardápio (menu also used)	kahr-DAH-pee-oo
Napkin	Guardanapo	gwar-dah-NAH-poo
Pepper	Pimenta	pee-MEN-tah)
Plate	Prato	PRAH-too

Great Itineraries

Introduction to Rio, 6 Days

DAY 1: EXPLORE THE BEACHES AND THE BARS

Shake off your jet lag and satisfy your curiosity for the iconic Rio you're heard about in so many songs by heading straight to **Ipanema Beach.** Before hitting the beach, order a tasty, blended glass of açaí from any of the nearby juice bars. Fortified by the Amazonian berry's many vitamins and antioxidants, take a stroll and watch the show. On the city's beaches, you'll find the most spectacularly proportioned bodies and equally spectacular views. When you've had enough sun, surf, and sightseeing, make your way to Leblon for a tasty bite of *bolinho de bacalhau* (small cod cake)—or any other seafood dish on the menu at one of the restaurants that we recommend. A sunset visit to **Pão de Açucar** is a lovely way to end your first day.

Logistics: Be careful with Rio's strong undertow and waves. Bring only the bare minimum of belongings to the beach, and make sure someone from your group keeps an eye on them if you take a dip.

DAY 2: ENJOY BIRD'S-EYE VIEWS FROM CORCOVADA

Regardless of how you chose to end your first night, wake up early on Day 2 to see gorgeous views of the city from **Corcovado.** It's also a good idea if you want to avoid both the haze and throngs of sightseers who set upon the peak as the day wears on. Next, spend the afternoon in Santa Teresa, taking the *bonde* (Rio's last trolly) or leisurely walking the narrow, cobblestone streets lined with beautiful, Portuguese-style homes. Stop by **Bar do Arnaudo** for a hearty late lunch, or **Cultivar Brasil** for a fortifying coffee and the best *pão de queijo* in town. If you still have enough energy, make a night of it in Lapa.

Logistics: Check the weather to make sure the Christ statue will not be above the clouds. Wear comfortable shoes for hiking.

DAY 3: THE CITY AS IT LIVES AND BREATHES

Wandering around Centro is a lovely way to spend your third day, stopping by the **Theatro Municipal** and exploring the various plazas and churches. The ornate **Confeitaria Colombo** is one of the oldest eateries in Rio and it's a nice place for a tea break. Order the lavish afternoon teas if you really want to treat yourself. If you missed Lapa by night, see it by day by taking a stroll down here—be sure to check out the colorful *Escadaria Selaron* and the gigantic, whitewashed *Arcos da Lapa*. Or, if you have an itch for sand between your toes, head down to Copacabana, where you can either sunbathe or simply walk its 4-km (2.5-mile) promenade.

DAY 4: SHOP TILL YOU DROP

If your final day falls on a weekend, Ipanema's **Feira Hippie** takes place on Sunday and is well worth a gander. Local arts and crafts, handmade clothes, and accessories are on offer alongside mass-produced tourist souvenirs. There is more outdoor shopping along Avenida Atlântica and at the Feira Nordestina, also known as the Feira de São Cristóvão, which runs from Friday at 10 am through Sunday at 8 pm. The fair, which celebrates Northeastern Brazilian food and culture, features live *forro*music and feels like a vast nightclub after midnight on Saturdays. If it's raining, popping into the Rio Sul mall is a good option.

DAYS 5–6 (OPTION 1): BRIGITTE BARDOT'S BÚZIOS

Just over two hours from Rio, the old fishing village of **Búzios** has some wonderful beaches (Azeda and Azedinha are particularly quiet and perfect for a romantic afternoon). If you can swing the sometimes hefty price tag, stay at the **Casas Brancas**—it's a delicious spot for doing absolutely nothing and feeling wonderful about it. For those with a little less money to burn, the Galápagos Inn has a lovely view of the sea and sunset, and even has bar service at the beach. Don't miss the statue of Brigitte Bardot on the Orla Bardot along the water near downtown. When hunger strikes, **Cigalon** is one of the finest restaurants in town; make sure to have a meal on its seductive veranda that overlooks the beach. If you're on a budget, just off the Rua das Pedras is the pay-per-kilo restaurant Buzin, which also serves churrasco. Its casual, welcoming atmosphere is perfect for those who want to keep their weekend away from Rio as unpretentious as possible. There are plenty of activities to keep you busy in Búzios, such as surfing lessons or windsurfing. For those who want to be on the water but don't want to paddle, take a three-hour catamaran around the peninsula from Orla Bardot.

Logistics: Búzios is about 175 km (110 miles) northeast of Rio. The trip is much more pleasant if you rent a car. Driving in Rio de Janeiro State isn't difficult but do be mindful of other drivers. You'll be thankful you have a car if you want to find some of the more idyllic beaches in the area.

DAYS 5–6 (OPTION 2): THE UNSPOILED ISLAND OF ILHA GRANDE

Ilha Grande once provided refuge for pirates, and was the first point of entry for many enslaved people brought here from Africa. Now, it's known for its lovely, somewhat unspoiled beaches. The island is a nature-lover's dream, and getting there is easier than it once was thanks to collective transfer services, which include hotel pickup, minibus, and schooner boat from Conceição de Jacareí or Angra dos Reis. Once there, we recommend using **Vila do Abraão**—the island's only real town—as a starting point for your beach explorations. There are no roads and no private cars on the island, so try to travel light, bring comfortable shoes, and expect to walk a lot. Hire a local boatman who can take you to a quiet, pristine beach or an even more remote islet. Don't miss the shockingly clear waters of Abraãozinho beach, accessible only by foot (about 25 minutes from Vila do Abraão) or by boat.

Logistics: The quickest and most cost-effective way to reach the island is by organized transfer. You'll be whizzed along in a comfy minivan to the small town of Conceição de Jacareí, around two hours' drive from Rio, before taking a schooner boat (around 45 minutes) to the island's main settlement. The island has bountiful trekking opportunities, although taxi boats are on hand to whisk less energetic visitors to the best beaches.

Introduction to São Paulo, 6 days

DAY 1: GETTING TO KNOW THE CITY

Those who set out to explore this vast, packed Brazilian metropolis will be well rewarded for their efforts. Top-flight restaurants, hip nightclubs, and excellent museums and galleries make São Paulo Brazil's cultural reference point, while architecture buffs can marvel at some impressive examples of grand colonial architecture.

International flights will bring you in through Guarulhos, which is actually a sister city to mega-city São Paulo. Budget at least an hour of travel time—double

Great Itineraries

that if it's rush hour—to get to your lodgings in the center of São Paulo. Once you get yourself somewhat situated—always difficult in this sprawling megalopolis—find your way to the top of **Avenida Paulista** (where it meets Consolação) and begin a walk down the long blocks of this busy business artery. You'll pass one international bank after another, interspersed with the occasional multinational corporation, until you reach the inimitable and easily identifiable **Museu de Arte de São Paulo (MASP),** designed by the late Oscar Niemeyer. Right across the street is **Trianon Park,** a surprisingly peaceful jungle in the midst of all the traffic and concrete of Paulista. If you continue down Paulista to Brigadeiro, you can either walk or catch a bus into Bixiga and lunch at one of the charming Italian cantinas on 13 de Maio.

DAY 2: THE ARCHITECTURE OF SÃO PAULO

São Paulo is the financial heart of the country, and architecturally, it shows. Try exploring the city's structures by starting with the old: search for the elegant **Theatro Municipal** first. From there, the iconic **Edifício Martinelli** shouldn't be hard to pick out of the modernist skyline. The spectacular view over the valley on Anhangabaú makes for a great photo opportunity. Another treasure is the **Centro Cultural Banco do Brasil.** The building itself is a small marvel and it often has world-class exhibits within its marbled walls. From there, the **Praça da Sé** is not far, and the massive Cathedral is certainly worth a peek inside. Take a seat on one of the Praça's benches to watch a veritable cross section of Paulistano life go by. Just two metro stops away at República, you can see perhaps the most iconic São Paulo skyscraper, Niemeyer's **Edifício Copan.** It's just down the street from the Edifício Itália, which was once the city's tallest building. In the waning daylight hours, make your way to the vaulted roofs of São Paulo **Estação da Luz,** a bustling train station. Finish the day by walking to the nearby top-notch **Pinacoteca** art museum and resting in its elegant tree-lined grounds.

DAY 3: SÃO PAULO'S BOUTIQUES

Fashionistas from all over the continent flock to São Paulo for the clothes, shoes, fashion shows, and accessories. In fact, shopping is a tourist attraction in its own right. Rub elbows with São Paulo's rich and fabulously dressed by doing a little clothing shopping at the western end of **Rua Oscar Freire** (where it meets Rebouças). Here you can find some of Brazil's most famous designer collections, as well as a good sampling of international names. Sustenance for shopping can be found at popular sandwich shop and snack bar Frevo. With your new outfits, you may want to sample São Paulo's famous nightlife. Make your way to **Vila Madalena** or **Pinheiros,** both lively nighttime neighborhoods lined with bars and restaurants. Catch a live performance of bossa nova or samba at happy hour at Grazie a Dio.

DAY 4: A JUNGLE WITHIN THE CITY

When you need a break from the urban jungle, surround yourself with lush greens at **Ibirapuera Park.** It's crowded on the weekends—great for people-watching—and doesn't see too much foot traffic during the week. Follow the path to Marquise Ibirapuera, which connects several buildings, including the **Museu de Arte Moderna (MAM)** and the **Pavilhão da Bienal,** the site of São Paulo Fashion

Week. Also worth visiting is the polygonal **Oca,** built by Oscar Niemeyer, who, along with Roberto Burle Marx, helped design the park itself. The nursery in Ibirapuera is a charming visit, and the staff will be able to point you to the park's most exotic trees, such as glorious wide-limbed banyans. Take some time to explore the outskirts of the city—surrounding **Parque Ibirapuera** has some of the most expensive mansions and apartment buildings in Latin America. Make your way to the lively **Liberdade** neighborhood to catch the Saturday street food festival or to dine at its many sushi and yakisoba restaurants.

DAYS 5–6 (OPTION 1): EMBU DAS ARTES

Embu is a small Portuguese colonial-era town of churches and antiques shops, handicrafts fairs, and furniture makers. It makes a relaxing alternative to the nonstop urban pulse of cosmopolitan São Paulo. Visit the **Igreja Nossa Senhora do Rosario,** built in 1690, then check out the **Canto das Artes** for mosaics and furniture. If you need a break, relax at Os Girassóis Restaurante e Choperia over a nice frosty beer. Devote some of your visit to understanding why Embu is also called Land of the Arts. Explore the Open Arts fair, which occupies all the central areas of the city and specializes in historical and colonial art. It is open Saturday, Sunday, and holidays. Be aware that the Embu is a popular destination and can get crowded.

Logistics: Embu is a mere 27 km (17 miles) west of São Paulo. You can catch a bus at the Terminal Bandeira close to metro Anhangabaú or at Tietê bus station. Once there, it's easily navigable by foot.

DAYS 5–6 (OPTION 2): ILHABELA

Ilhabela is the largest sea island in the country and will hit the spot if you're in the mood for pure relaxation. There are two small towns on the island. One is where the locals live; the other is where most of the hotels, restaurants, and stores are located and, hence, the tourists as well. Be aware that during the winter months most businesses that cater to travelers, including restaurants, are open only on weekends. When you arrive, head straight for **Praia Grande** for your first taste of the shore, and at night, **Praia do Curral** will satisfy all your restaurant and bar needs. Ilhabela is a sportsman and sportswoman's paradise; there is plenty of boating, sailing, hiking, scuba diving, and surfing (both of the board and wind variety) available. Scuba divers have several 19th- and early-20th-century wrecks to explore—this region has the most wrecks of any area off Brazil's coast—and hikers can set off on the numerous inland trails, many of which lead to a waterfall (the island has more than 300). Be aware: not all sport options are available on all parts of the island.

Logistics: Ilhabela is a 7-km (5-mile) boat ride from São Sebastião. The boat leaves every 30 minutes from 6 am to midnight and hourly during the night. It should take about 15 minutes. The coastal town São Sebastião itself is easily reached by bus from the Tietê bus station. If you want to navigate easily around the island, you can rent a car on the mainland (not available on the island itself), then transfer it by ferry.

On the Calendar

February

Carnival. Brazilians often say that the year truly begins only after Carnival. The festival is celebrated in every corner of Brazil, but the most famous parades are in Rio and São Paulo. Carnival's dates are movable, tied to the Christian calendar, falling 47 days before Easter. Typically occurring in February or March, the celebration is described as the "greatest show on earth." In Rio, the famous parades at the Sambodromo showcase samba schools on Sunday and Monday, competing with elaborate floats and costumes. In São Paulo, the parades happen on Friday and Saturday. Street parties, known as *blocos* take over the streets. Every year, the cities release the official calendar with the time and location of each *bloco*. ⊕ *www.riocarnaval.com, www.sasp.com/br*

April

Comida di Buteco. Paulistanos are passionate about their boteco dishes. The snacks served in casual bars have a special place in the city's culture, and they're celebrated at the Comida di Buteco festival. Bars must create a unique dish that highlights local flavors, using specified ingredients or themes provided by the organizers each year. Visitors can taste the dishes at various bars and vote on their favorites, judging on criteria such as taste, creativity, and service. The festival lasts for a few weeks and it's an excellent opportunity for locals and tourists to explore São Paulo's neighborhoods. ⊕ *www.comidadibuteco.com.br*

May

Lollapalooza. Lollapalooza São Paulo is one of Brazil's biggest music festivals, drawing international and local artists across genres like rock, pop, hip-hop, and electronic. Held annually at the Interlagos Racetrack, it spans multiple days and features several stages, offering an immersive musical experience. Beyond music, the festival includes food trucks, art installations, and interactive spaces. ⊕ *www.lollapaloozabr.com*

Virada Cultural. São Paulo has a dynamic cultural spirit year-round and the Virada Cultural in São Paulo is a 24-hour cultural festival that celebrates the city's culture. Held annually, it turns the city into a vibrant hub of creativity with performances, exhibitions, and workshops in public spaces, museums, and theaters. Events are free, attracting diverse crowds and showcasing local and international talent. ⊕ *www.viradacultural.prefeitura.sp.gov.br*

June

São Paulo LGBTQI+ Parade. The event is held annually on Avenida Paulista and is one of the largest Pride parades in the world, attracting thousands of participants. Known for its vibrant atmosphere, it features colorful floats, music, and performances that celebrate diversity and equality. Beyond the festivities, the parade carries a powerful message of LGBTQI+ rights and visibility.

Bienal do Livro. São Paulo hosts one of the most prestigious book fairs in Latin America. Held every two years, it brings together publishers, authors, and readers from across the globe at the São Paulo Expo. The event features book launches, author signings, interactive panels, and cultural activities suitable for all ages. ⊕ *www.bienaldolivrosp.com.br*

September

Rock in Rio. Rock in Rio is Brazil's most famous festival, happening every two years. First held in 1985, it has grown into a global event, with editions in Lisbon, Madrid, and Las Vegas. The Rio edition happens over multiple days at Cidade do Rock. The event has welcomed national and international artists across genres like rock, pop, EDM, and more. Beyond music, the festival offers attractions like amusement rides, interactive spaces, and gourmet food courts, creating a fully immersive experience. ⊕ *www.rockinrio.com*

ArtRio. ArtRio is a premier art fair held annually in Rio de Janeiro. It showcases Brazilian and international galleries and connects artists, collectors, and art enthusiasts. Held in iconic venues such as Marina da Glória, another plus of ArtRio is having breathtaking views of Rio. ⊕ *www.artrio.com*

October

Flip. The Festival de Literatura de Paraty (Flip) is a renowned literary festival held annually in Paraty. The event has become a global hub for literature, attracting acclaimed authors from around the world. The event offers panels, readings, book signings, and workshops in various historical venues in the city. ⊕ *www.flip.org.br*

Rio de Janeiro International Film Festival. Held annually, the festival features a diverse lineup of films, including premieres, documentaries, feature films, and shorts, screened in iconic venues like Cine Odeon and cultural centers across the city. ⊕ *www.festivaldorio.com.br/en/*

Mostra Internacional de Cinema de São Paulo. Spanning multiple venues, including iconic cinemas and cultural institutions, the event is known for fostering dialogue between filmmakers and audiences through Q&A sessions, workshops, and debates. With competitive and noncompetitive sections, the Mostra celebrates both emerging talents and acclaimed directors. ⊕ *www.mostra.org*

November

São Paulo Grand Prix. The event is part of the Formula 1 World Championship held annually at Interlagos. This Grand Prix de São Paulo has been a staple in the F1 calendar, often playing a decisive role in the championship outcomes. ⊕ *www.f1saopaulo.com.br*

Chapter 3

RIO DE JANEIRO

3

Updated by
Gabriela Godoi

WELCOME TO RIO DE JANEIRO

TOP REASONS TO GO

★ **Mix of nature and city:** The city has both beautiful nature, especially in the beaches, and remarkable architecture.

★ **Carioca happiness:** The people from Rio (no matter if they are natives or moved there) are very proud of their city, and they will do everything to make you a fan as well.

★ **Perfect weather all year round:** Even winter in Rio de Janeiro can be beach time, as the perfect tropical weather guarantees sun throughout the whole year.

★ **Home of the biggest party on Earth:** Come for the biggest parties you will ever experience: New Year's Eve or Carnival. In both, you will enjoy the tropical summer, the beaches, and Rio happiness.

1 Centro. The city's historic and commercial heart.

2 Catete and Gloria. Traditional areas with cultural landmarks.

3 Flamengo and Botafogo. Affordable, local vibes with stunning views.

4 Urca. A tranquil neighborhood near Sugarloaf Mountain.

5 Copacabana. Iconic beaches and lively nightlife.

6 Leme. A quieter extension of Copacabana.

7 Santa Teresa and Lapa. Bohemian charm and vibrant nightlife.

8 Ipanema and Leblon. Chic beaches, upscale dining, and shopping.

9 Sao Conrado and Barra de Tijuca. Modern neighborhoods with pristine beaches.

10 West of Downtown. Emerging cultural hubs like Gamboa, historical sites like São Cristóvão, and cultural heart of Rio like Tijuca.

11 Inland Zona Sul. Residential areas but also with good dinning spots like Jardim Botânico and Gávea.

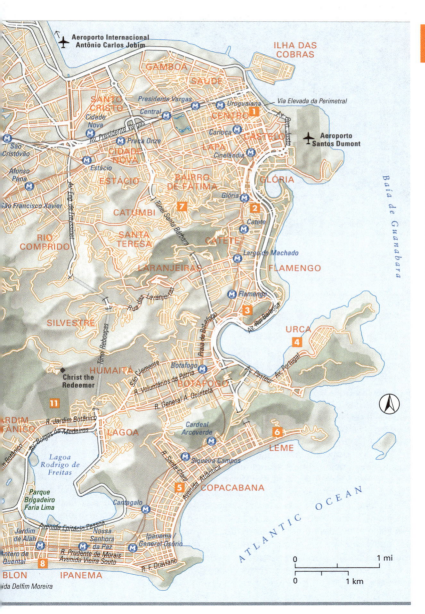

CARNIVAL

The mesmerizing and bright floats of Rio Carnival.

More than just a party, Carnival is a state of mind for the people of Rio. The festive atmosphere, combined with the organization of an event that stops the city from growing in population and still takes place annually, shows all the creativity and dedication of the people of Rio.

Organization is the key word for those who want to experience Rio during this period. Check the correct dates for the event, make a budget, and start by choosing your accommodation. Staying close to the beaches and subway stations helps save time traveling around the city. The free street parades (*blocos*) take place all over the city, but the samba school parades take place in the city center, with two subway stations close to the event. The second step is to organize your itinerary. Set aside a few days before or after the main dates of Carnival for traditional tourism and to visit the city's tourist attractions. During the carnival days, the city gets so crowded that the tourist attractions also get very crowded. Alternate the party with relaxing on the beach to recharge your batteries.

CHILDREN'S PARADE

The children have their parade day, on the Friday after Carnival, where they parade in groups formed by the main schools. Admission to the grandstands on this day is free. The children's parade can be a good addition to the program for those who want to experience Rio's Carnival but are scared off by the high prices during this period and would prefer to attend the winners parade (on the following weekend).

SAMBADROME PARADES

In 2025, the Sambadrome will change its schedule, with an extra night of parades for the special group. Tickets are sold in the second half of the previous year and will now be valid for any of the sectors, except the tourist sector. The passport gives access to the three nights of the special group parade (Sunday, Monday, and Tuesday of Carnival). It can be purchased online at the partner website Ticketmaster Brasil (🌐 *www.ticketmaster.com.br*).

Other groups perform at the Sambadrome, hoping to one day parade on the special group nights. The advantage of watching the second division parade, on the Friday and Saturday of Carnival, is that you pay a lower ticket price and still see a show that reflects the culture of Rio and Brazil.

On Ash Wednesday, the best schools are announced when the envelopes containing the scores given by the judges on the parade days are opened. The six schools return to the Sambadrome on the Saturday after Carnival, presenting a summary of the best of the parades.

PARTY IN THE STREET EVERYWHERE

Blocos are groups of friends or neighbors who get together around a theme

People travel from all over the world to see the largest Carnival on earth.

or situation to make music. The phenomenon has been growing throughout the city and today it is difficult to say which is the best one to participate in.

Every year the city hall accredits the bloco and authorizes their parade, at a specific location and date. This information is published about a month before Carnival on the Riotur (🌐 *riotur.rio/en/welcome*)(Tourism authority) website and app, making it easier to find the closest event.

The most famous or traditional blocos usually perform in the city center or at Aterro do Flamengo, which are large areas where a crowd can gather. But sometimes, that small group near your hotel can be much more fun. The main tip for surviving a bloco is to wear comfortable clothes (don't forget to wear your bathing suit underneath so that you can end up taking a dip), a money belt with change and a card (prepaid ones are better, since you can limit the amount available), sunscreen, water, and comfortable shoes. If you are lucky, you will spend many hours under the sun and standing.

Eat well before going out, with light foods such as sandwiches and fruit. Choose drinks sealed in cans or plastic bottles and don't overdo it with alcohol.

The traditional costumes worn represent the strong Afro-Brazilian culture.

Rio de Janeiro, affectionately known as the Marvelous City, is a destination that captivates visitors with its unique blend of breathtaking natural beauty, vibrant culture, and infectious energy. This Brazilian metropolis offers an unparalleled experience for all types of travelers.

Rio's lush nature is a spectacle in itself. With nearly 73 km (45 mi) of stunning beaches, including the world-famous Copacabana and Ipanema, the city invites moments of relaxation and fun by the sea. Tijuca National Park, a vast urban rainforest, provides exciting trails and refreshing waterfalls for nature lovers. For a breathtaking panoramic view, don't miss visiting Christ the Redeemer atop Corcovado Mountain and Sugarloaf Mountain.

Rio's cultural richness is as diverse as its landscape. Explore the charming Santa Teresa neighborhood, with its colonial architecture and bohemian atmosphere. Visit the Rio Art Museum (MAR) and the Museum of Tomorrow for a dose of contemporary art and science. The vibrant street art in the Olympic Boulevard offers a glimpse of Carioca urban creativity.

Rio's culinary scene is a feast for the senses. From upscale restaurants to street markets, there are options for all tastes. Be sure to try local specialties like *pastel* (savory pastry), *feijoada* (bean and pork stew), and *bolinho de bacalhau* (codfish cakes). From south zone to downtown and up on the north, you will find a good variety of dishes.

Rio pulsates with rhythm and music. Carnival is undoubtedly the pinnacle of this cultural expression, but the city offers musical experiences year-round. Visit Lapa to enjoy samba and choro performances in historic venues like Carioca da Gema. For bossa nova lovers, a stroll through Ipanema is a must. In Tijuca, you can dress like a samba dancer all year and try a few steps of dance.

Cariocas are known for their hospitality and warmth. Don't hesitate to chat with locals—they're often eager to share their favorite places and insider tips. This interaction can transform your trip, offering unique perspectives on the city.

While Rio has its peak seasons, it's a destination that enchants at any time of year. Each month offers unique experiences, from New Year's Eve celebrations on Copacabana Beach to the Rio Film Festival in October. The city also hosts international sporting events and major concerts throughout the year.

With an open mind and a smile on your face, you'll be ready to absorb the Carioca spirit and enjoy everything Rio de Janeiro has to offer. Prepare for an unforgettable experience in this city that truly deserves the title of Marvelous.

Planning

Activities

Simply put, Rio de Janeiro is mad for sports. Though much of the frenzy centers on soccer, other sports—among them volleyball, basketball, beach soccer, beach volleyball, and *futevôlei* (a soccer-volleyball hybrid)—are taken extremely seriously. Invigorated by the success of the 2014 FIFA World Cup and the 2016 Olympics, facilities and funding have improved across the city and Rio is more sports-focused than ever. In addition to the vast sums spent to renovate existing and create new sports facilities and an Olympic village in the city's West Zone, significant investments are being made to upgrade the public transportation system.

SURFING

Surfing remains hugely popular in Rio, and stand-up paddleboarding is a current trend—kiosks offer stand-up paddleboards and classes all along the Zona Sul beaches. Kite surfing is growing rapidly, too, with several schools opening on Barra beachfront and out of town toward Cabo Frio.

Getting Here and Around

Rio's shuttle system currently extends from the Zona Norte to Ipanema, with shuttles to areas west of the final stop. The Metro system, extended to Barra da Tijuca in 2016, is a convenient and quick way to get around town and avoid the city's often troublesome traffic jams. Within Ipanema and Copacabana, it's easy to get around on foot, but some attractions are far apart, so a taxi might be in order. Ride share apps like Uber are widely used in Rio and are a safe way to move around.

After dark you should always take a taxi if you're venturing into unexplored territory. Cabs are yellow and easy to hail on every main street. Public buses are cheap and cover every inch of the city, but can be difficult to figure out if you don't speak Portuguese. If you decide to visit downtown, VLT (light vehicle) is a good way to move from Praça Mauá and Novo Rio bus station to Santos Dumont airport.

AIR

Nearly three dozen airlines regularly serve Rio, but most flights from North America stop first in São Paulo. Several international carriers offer Rio–São Paulo flights.

All international flights and most domestic flights arrive and depart from the Aeroporto Internacional Antônio Carlos Jobim (⊕ *www.riogaleao.com*), also known as Galeão (GIG). The airport is about 40 minutes northwest of the beach area and most of Rio's hotels. Taxis are plentiful and operate on a fixed-fare basis (those outside the arrivals area are cheaper than those from kiosks inside). Comfortable, spacious, air-conditioned buses leave the airport for Centro, the Zona Sul, and Barra da Tijuca. A special bus line connects the international airport with the local main bus station, if you want to reach other cities in Rio state. Aeroporto Santos Dumont (SDU) (⊕ *www.aeroportosantosdumont.net*), 20 minutes from the beaches and within walking distance of Centro, is served by the Rio–São Paulo air shuttle and other domestic flights. Both airports have lounges for people waiting for rideshare apps.

Most visitors arrive at Rio International Airport, about a 40-minute car ride from the tourist destinations. The speediest way to reach Centro and the Zona Sul is to take a taxi. Prices are steep, however. Expect to pay up to R$130 to reach Copacabana, and slightly more to Ipanema and Leblon. There are taxi booths in the arrivals area, and passengers pay a set fare in advance, though drivers may charge extra if you have lots of luggage. Also trustworthy are the white radio taxis parked in front of arrivals; these metered vehicles cost an average of 20% less than the airport taxis. You can also call an app car using your own mobile phone and meet the driver at their lounge, following the signs in the hall.

Comfortable, air-conditioned buses run by Real (marked Real Premium) park curbside outside the arrivals lounge. There is plenty of luggage storage space, and staff will safely stow your luggage beneath the bus. The buses (R$24.85) make the hour-long trip from Galeão to the Zona Sul, following the beachfront drives and stopping at major hotels along the way. If your hotel is inland, the driver will let you off at the nearest corner. Buses operate from 5:30 am to 11:45 pm. If you feel more adventurous or have more time until you reach your accommodation, a second bus option is taking the BRT options. This one is called BRT Expresso, and costs R$15 with a nonstop ride from the airport to the Terminal Gentileza, right next to the Novo Rio bus station, in buses with room for luggage. From there, you can reach downtown with VLT (R$ 4.30) and then to the subway (R$ 7.50).

BUS

Long-distance and international buses leave from and arrive at the Rodoviária Novo Rio (⊕ *www.novorio.com.br*). Any local bus marked "rodoviária" will take you to the station. You can buy tickets at the depot or, for some destinations, from travel agents. To buy online you will need a CPF (Brazilian Social Security) number. A staff member at your hotel may be able to help you with online purchases.

Rio's urban buses are cheap, frequent, and generally safe to use, but do not show cameras or wallets, and do not wear expensive-looking clothes or jewelry. Wear backpacks on your front, and avoid getting on or off the bus in deserted areas. Most of them have air-conditioning. Local buses have a fixed price (R$4.30), and can take you anywhere you want to go. Route maps aren't available, but local tourist offices have route lists for the most popular sights. Enter buses at the front, pay the attendant, and pass through a turnstile. Have your fare in hand when you board to avoid flashing bills or your wallet. When you want to get off, pull the overhead cord and the driver will pause at the next designated stop; exit from the rear of the bus. You can also buy the card at metro stations and add credits depending on the number of days and the number of bus trips you will take. The card can also be used on the VLT, subway, and ferries.

There are also two comfortable, privately run, and air-conditioned lines that connect the International Airport (Galeão) to Barra da Tijuca or Leblon (through downtown and South Zone). These vehicles, which look like highway buses, stop at designated bus stops; expect to pay around three times the price of the regular bus.

CAR

The Carioca style of driving is passionate to the point of abandon: speeding is de rigueur, traffic jams are common, the streets aren't well-marked, and red lights are often ignored by drivers. Although there are parking areas along the beachfront boulevards, finding a spot can be a real problem. If you do choose to drive, exercise extreme caution, wear seat belts at all times, and keep the doors locked.

Car rentals can be arranged through hotels, agencies, or online sites like ⊕ *www.rentcars.com.br*, which tend to offer the best value. While international companies such as Hertz and Avis are present, the best customer service can be found at local agency Movida, which has affiliates in the international and domestic airports and Copacabana. Rental costs range from R$110–R$800 a day.

Turismo Clássico Travel (⊕ *www.classicdmctravel.com*) can arrange for a driver to get you around the city, with or without an English-speaking guide. Clássico's owners, Liliana and Vera, speak English, and each has more than 20 years of experience in organizing transportation. They also lead sightseeing tours.

SUBWAY

Metrô Rio (⊕ *www.metrorio.com.br*), the subway system, is clean, relatively safe, and efficient, but it's not comprehensive. Line 1 covers the Zona Sul, with 20 stops between Tijuca and Ipanema. Line 2 goes from the Zona Norte neighborhood of Pavuna to Botafogo in South Zone (Zona Sul). Line 4 was extended in time for the 2016 Olympics and now stretches through São Conrado to Jardim Ocêanico in Barra da Tijuca. Reaching sights distant from metro stations can be a challenge, especially in summer, when beach traffic increases. Tourism offices and some metro stations have maps.

Trains operate daily between 5 am and midnight except on Sunday and holidays, when they run between 7 am and 11 pm. A single metro ticket costs R$7.50, but it is quicker and easier to use a prepay card, or you can tap your credit or debit card (Mastercard, Visa, or Elo) or mobile phone with a wallet app. Machines at each metro station allow passengers to buy and load up cards from R$7.50 to the value of their choice. Although there are no financial savings, you'll avoid queues and hassle each time you take the subway.

TAXI

Taxis are plentiful in Rio, and in most parts of the city you can easily flag one down on the street. Yellow taxis have meters that start at a set price and have two rates. The "1" rate applies to fares before 8 pm, and the "2" rate applies to fares after 8 pm, on Sunday, on holidays, throughout December, in the neighborhoods of São Conrado and Barra da Tijuca, and when climbing steep hills, such as those in Santa Teresa. Drivers are required to post a chart noting the current fares on the inside of the left rear window. CentralTaxi has a fare calculator on its website that will give you a general idea of what the fare from one destination to another might be.

■ **TIP→ Taxi drivers may be reluctant to make the steep climb to Santa Teresa, so if you are heading here wait until you are already inside the taxi before stating your destination, and stand your ground—by law drivers cannot refuse to take you here.**

Radio taxis and several companies that routinely serve hotels (and whose drivers often speak English) are also options. They charge 30% more than other taxis but are reliable and usually air-conditioned. Other cabs working with the hotels also charge more, normally a fixed fee that you should agree on before you leave. Reliable radio cab companies include Coopacarioca (⊕ *www.cooparioca.com.br*) and Coopatur (☏ *21/3885–1000*).

Most Carioca cabbies are pleasant, but there are exceptions. If flagging down a taxi on the street, check to see that an official phone number is displayed on the side and that the driver's official identity card is displayed. Remain alert and trust your instincts. Unless you've negotiated a flat fee with the driver, be sure the meter is turned on.

■ **TIP→ Few cab drivers speak English, so it's a good idea to have your destination written down to show the driver, in case there's a communication gap.**

TRAIN

Few visitors to Rio travel by rail. The urban network serves the North Zone of the city, which is less visited by tourists, and trains tend to be hot, overcrowded, and uncomfortable. Long-distance trips are generally made by bus or plane. Should you have reason to take a local train, these leave from the central station, Estação Central do Brasil.

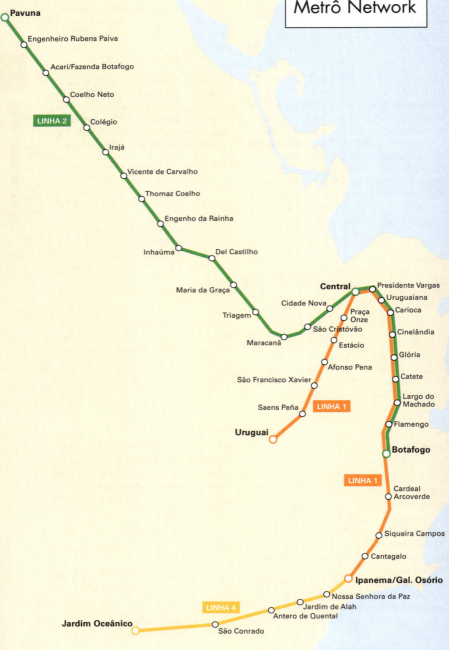

Hotels

Lodgings in Rio de Janeiro are among the most expensive in the world, though the price-to-quality ratio often disappoints. That said, there are some wonderful accommodation options in all price ranges if you know where to look. Copacabana and Ipanema are awash with lodgings and are the best bet for sunseekers, but expect to get more bang for your buck the farther you travel from the famous beaches. Leafy Santa Teresa contains many charming guesthouses and chic boutique hotels, while Centro, Flamengo, and Botafogo have solid options for business travelers.

■ TIP➜ **Note that "motels" are not aimed at tourists. They attract couples looking for privacy and usually rent by the hour.**

Expect to pay a premium for a room with a view. Most hotels include breakfast in the rate, and Brazilian breakfasts are usually a lavish affair involving everything from fresh fruit and juices to cakes, cold meats, and cheeses. If you're traveling during peak periods—from December to March—make reservations as far ahead of your visit as possible.

⇨ *Hotel reviews have been shortened. For full information, visit Fodors.com.*

Nightlife

It's sometimes said that Cariocas would rather expend their energy on the beach and that nighttime is strictly for recharging their batteries and de-sanding their swimsuits. But witnessing the masses swarming into Lapa at 10 pm on a Friday night make this a tricky argument to endorse. New nightclubs and bars continue to sprout up with remarkable regularity, and there are cutting-edge underground rhythms and musical styles competing with samba, choro, and Brazilian pop (MPB) for the locals' hearts.

A much-loved local pastime is drinking a well-chilled *chopp* (draft beer) and enjoying the lively atmosphere of a genuine Rio *botequim* (bar). Every neighborhood has its share of upmarket options (branches of Belmonte and Brewteco are dotted around town), but no less enjoyable are the huge number of hole-in-the-wall spots offering ice-cold bottles of *cerveja* (beer) and the chance to chat with down-to-earth regulars.

Live music is nighttime Rio's raison d'être, with street corners regularly playing host to impromptu renditions. During Carnival the entire city can feel like one giant playground. The electronic music scene is also very much alive, and the underground popularity of funk (the city's own X-rated genre, not to be confused with the James Brown version) is slowly seeping into the mainstream, down from the huge *bailes* or open-air parties held weekly in the city's *favelas*. In addition to samba and MPB, hip-hop, electronica, and rock can be heard in clubs around the city.

Performing Arts

Rio supports a rich variety of cultural activity and cutting-edge nightlife. The classic rhythms of samba can be heard in many clubs and bars, and on street corners, but it's possible to find something to suit every kind of musical taste almost every night of the week. Major theater, opera, ballet, and classical music performances are plentiful, and smaller, more intimate events happen in most neighborhoods. Arts enthusiasts should check the Riotur (the city's tourist board) website for the events schedule. The Portuguese-language newspaper *O Globo* publishes schedules of events in the entertainment supplements of their Thursday editions, which can be found online or printed at newsstands. Finally, *Veja Rio* is the city's most comprehensive entertainment guide, published monthly and available at all newsstands and updated online weekly. Recently, *Time Out* magazine started to issue a local guide about Rio de Janeiro.

Planning Your Time

Rio has more than its fair share of stellar attractions—both natural and manmade—and good planning is key to fitting it all in. It is possible to visit the beaches of Copacabana, Ipanema, and Leblon in one day on foot. From Leblon it's just a short stroll down to Lagoa, home to the city's vast lake set against the mountains.

Set aside another full day to see the historic heart of the city in Downtown, Lapa, Santa Teresa, Glória, and Catete. All are within close walking distance of each other, but the steep hills up to Santa Teresa can be a challenge in the heat, so grab a taxi or bus instead. Do not forget to explore the new Porto Maravilha area, with its museum and historic area. Key attractions such as the Christ statue and Sugarloaf Mountain can be visited as part of a full-day or half-day city tour, which will make whistle-stop visits to other key locations in the city, too.

Restaurants

With nearly a thousand restaurants, Rio's dining choices are broad, from low-key Middle Eastern cafés to elegant contemporary eateries with award-winning kitchens and first-class service. The succulent offerings in the *churrascarias* (restaurants specializing in grilled meats) can be mesmerizing for meat lovers—especially the places that serve *rodízio*-style (grilled meat on skewers is continually brought to your table—until you can eat no more). Hotel restaurants often serve the national dish, feijoada (a hearty stew of black beans and pork), on Saturday—sometimes on Friday, too. Wash it down with a chopp (the local draft beer; pronounced "shop") or a caipirinha (sugarcane rum, lime, and sugar).

⇨ *Prices are per person for a main course at dinner, or if dinner is not served, at lunch. Reviews have been shortened; for full reviews, visit Fodors.com.*

What It Costs in Reais

$	$$	$$$	$$$$
RESTAURANTS			
under R$50	R$50–R$130	R$131–R$200	over R$200
HOTELS			
under R$150	R$150–R$300	R$301–R$500	over R$500

Shopping

Rio shopping is most famous for its incomparable beachwear and gemstone jewelry, both of which are exported globally. Brazil is one of the world's largest suppliers of colored gemstones, with deposits of aquamarines, amethysts, diamonds, emeralds, rubellites, topazes, and tourmalines. If you're planning to go to Minas Gerais, do your jewelry shopping there; otherwise stick with shops that have certificates of authenticity and quality. Other good local buys include shoes, Havaianas flip-flops, arts and crafts, coffee, local music, swimwear, and summer clothing in natural fibers. With lots of low-quality merchandise around, the trick to successful shopping in Rio is knowing where to find high-quality items at reasonable prices. It's helpful to note that most independent shops are shut on Sunday, with some even closed on Saturday afternoon.

Ipanema is Rio's most fashionable shopping district. Its many exclusive boutiques are in arcades, with the majority along Rua Visconde de Pirajá. Leblon's shops, scattered among cafés, restaurants, and newspaper kiosks, are found mainly along Rua Ataulfo da Paiva and in the side streets of Rua Dias Ferreira. Copacabana has souvenir shops, bookstores, and branches of some of Rio's better shops along Avenida Nossa Senhora de Copacabana and connecting streets. For cheap fashion finds and Carnival costumes, head to the maze of shopping streets behind the Uruguaiana metro station known as Saara.

Safety and Precautions

IN THE CITY

As with any city its size, crime occurs in Rio, but taking a few basic precautions should keep you from becoming a victim of it. Crimes involving visitors generally occur in crowded public areas: beaches, busy sidewalks, intersections, and city buses. Pickpockets, usually children, work in groups. One will distract you while another grabs a wallet, bag, or camera. Be particularly wary of children who thrust themselves in front of you and ask for money or offer to shine your shoes. Another member of the gang may strike from behind, grabbing your valuables and disappearing into the crowd. Another tactic is for criminals to approach your car at intersections. Always keep doors locked and windows partially closed. Leave valuables in your hotel safe, don't wear expensive jewelry or watches, and keep cameras hidden except when snapping shots. Avoid walking around after dark, and avoid deserted areas even in broad daylight.

■ **TIP→ Keep large bills and cards in a hidden money belt, carry an inexpensive phone, and have a few notes ready to hand over just in case.**

ON THE BEACH

Don't shun the beaches because of reports of crime, but do take precautions. Leave jewelry, passports, and large sums of cash at your hotel; don't stroll the beaches at night; and be alert if groups

The Cops

Thanks to improved security measures since the 2014 World Cup and 2016 Olympics, Rio is now much less dangerous than it was a few decades ago. Simple changes such as installing lights on the beaches have improved safety. An increased police presence has also helped. In Rio there are three types of police: the gray-uniformed Military Police, the beige-uniformed Municipal Guard, and the black-uniformed special forces called the BOPE (pronounced "boppy"). For a glimpse into Rio's SWAT team, the BOPE, check out the film *Tropa de Elite (Elite Squad)* (2007) and its Oscar-nominated sequel, *Tropa de Elite 2* (2010).

of seemingly friendly youths attempt to engage you in conversation. A big danger is actually the sun. From 10 am to 3 pm the rays are merciless, making heavy-duty sunscreen, hats, cover-ups, and plenty of liquids essential; you can also rent a beach umbrella from vendors on the beach or your hotel.

Vendors stroll the beaches with beverages, food, and trinkets. They can be relentless so say no and mean it if you want them to go away.

Lifeguard stations, with bathrooms and showers, are found every kilometer; there's a fee to use the toilet and shower.

Tours

CITY TOURS
Be a Local
ADVENTURE TOURS | This well-established outfit conducts walking tours of Rocinha that make various stops inside the community, as well as trips to

soccer matches, speedy city tours, and lively nocturnal visits to samba school rehearsals. Accessible prices make it popular with a younger demographic. ✉ *Rua Barata Ribeiro 111, Copacabana* ☎ *21/97973–1442* ⊕ *www.bealocal.com* 🎫 *From R$150.*

Brazil Expedition

ADVENTURE TOURS | This reliable tour company runs a hugely popular city tour—known as the Big Dude tour—which takes a scenic route through Tijuca National Park to the Christ statue before visiting other key Rio landmarks such as Santa Teresa and the Lapa Steps, with an optional visit to Sugarloaf Mountain. Other recommended excursions include trips to samba school rehearsals (August through February) and an interesting street art tour. Language lessons, surf packages, and transfers to Ilha Grande, Cabo Frio, Arraial do Cabo, Búzios, and Paraty are also available. The English-speaking guides are knowledgeable and friendly. ✉ *Rua, Prudente de Moraes 594, Ipanema* ☎ *21/99998–2907* ⊕ *www.brazilexpedition.com* 🎫 *From R$130* Ⓜ *Nossa Senhora da Paz.*

Favela Tour

ADVENTURE TOURS | If you're interested in learning more about the favelas that cling to Rio's mountainsides, Favela Tour is the way to do it. Led by Marcelo Armstrong, this highly respected outfit conducts tours twice daily through Rocinha and Vila Canoas. Marcelo pioneered favela tourism in Rio and offers tours in English, Spanish, French, and Portuguese. Tours are informative but not voyeuristic, and there are opportunities to buy locally produced arts and crafts as you tour the communities. Hotel pickup and drop-off are included in the price. ✉ *Rio de Janeiro* ☎ *21/3322–2727, 21/99989–0074* ⊕ *www.favelatour.com.br* 🎫 *From R$90.*

★ Rio Cultural Secrets

DRIVING TOURS | **FAMILY** | This quality outfit has enthusiastic, knowledgeable English-speaking private guides who whisk visitors around the city in comfortable air-conditioned cars. Popular trips include visits to Tijuca National Park and Rio's Botanical Gardens, soccer games, and city tours that take in major attractions such as Sugarloaf and the Christ statue. Rio Cultural Secrets can also take visitors up to the imperial city of Petropolis, around an hour's drive from Rio. ✉ *Rio de Janeiro* ☎ *21/9949–86622* ⊕ *www.rioculturalsecrets.com* 🎫 *From R$140.*

Rio Free Walking Tour

WALKING TOURS | Expert English-speaking guides lead free tours through Centro, Copacabana, and Rio's downtown dock area each weekday. Rain or shine, the guides will take you on a three-hour morning stroll (tours start between 9:30 and 10:30 am), explaining the history of downtown Rio's major buildings, streets, statues, and monuments. The walk is followed by lunch at a pay-by-weight buffet restaurant. There's no need to book in advance, just look out for the yellow-shirted guides. Although there's no charge, tips are welcomed. ✉ *Rio de Janeiro* ☎ *21/98600–2593* ⊕ *www.riofreewalkingtour.com* 🎫 *Free.*

★ Rio Hiking

ADVENTURE TOURS | **FAMILY** | One of the best ways to explore Rio's top sites, spectacular views, and verdant rainforest is hiking to them. This professional outfit leads two-to-seven-day small group tours and private experiences that combine walking with mountain biking and climbing. The five-day tours include hikes to Ilha Grande's striking Papagaio Peak. All equipment is provided, and guides are bilingual, and there are treks, tours, and adventure trips to suit all levels of experience. ✉ *Copacabana* ☎ *21/2552–9204, 21/99721–0594* ⊕ *riohiking.com.br* 🎫 *From R$650.*

Sou+Carioca

CULTURAL TOURS | This agency seeks to show a Rio de Janeiro beyond the obvious, focusing mainly on Afrotourism and peripheral cultures, such as the North

Zone, *baile charme*. They have a list of guides and most of them are English speakers and specialists in their subjects. ✉ *Rua Moacyr de Almeida 219, Rio de Janeiro* ⊕ *soumaiscarioca.com.br/* 🖃 *R$ 40*.

CULTURAL TOURS
★ Carnival Experience
CULTURAL TOURS | FAMILY | For those visiting Rio outside the party and rehearsals period, this behind-the-scenes tour of a samba school parade will help you understand how the magic happens. The tour begins with a lesson on the origins of samba and the schools, then goes through the development of the parade and includes a special moment for photos. At the end, a toast with the country's typical drink, caipirinha. ✉ *Av. Binário do Porto, Cidade do Samba, Santo Cristo* ☏ *21/96765–9549* ⊕ *carnavalexperience. com.br/* ⊗ *Closed Sun.* ⌨ *Entrance R$ 100* Ⓜ *VLT - Cidade do Samba*.

HELICOPTER TOURS
★ Helisight
ADVENTURE TOURS | With landing pads at Morro da Urca (the smaller peak next to Sugarloaf) and Lagoa, Helisight conducts helicopter tours that pass over the Christ the Redeemer statue, the beaches of the Zona Sul, and other iconic sights. ✉ *Conde de Bernadotte 26, Leblon* ☏ *21/2511–2141 Lagoa, 21/2542–7935 Morro da Urca* ⊕ *www.helisight.com. br* 🖃 *From R$320 (seven-minute flight); from R$1,860 (hour-long trip)*.

Visitor Information

The Rio de Janeiro city tourism department, Riotur (⊕ *riotur.rio/*), operates a tourist information website in English and Portuguese as well as a monthly free magazine with key tourist information and listings. The magazine and city maps can be picked up at Riotur booths at the bus station and airports in Barra, Copacabana, Leblon, Gavea, at Sugarloaf, Lapa, and by Candelaria church in Centro. You can also try contacting Brazil's national tourism board, Embatur, via its Visit Brasil website (⊕ *www.visitbrasil.com*).

When to Go

Rio is a year-round destination, but Carnival, which usually takes place in February, is the best time to soak up the city's party spirit. Arrive a few days before the celebrations begin, or stay a few days after they end to enjoy the museums and other sights that close for the four days of revelry. Prices rise substantially during Carnival season, and accommodations need to be booked several months in advance.

Temperatures in Rio tend to be highest from January to March, when they often soar above 100°F (38°C). The city generally sees the most rain during December, when it might pour for days at a time. To tour the city at a quieter time with gentler temperatures and at lower prices, come in the off-season, from May to October (Brazil's winter). The temperature in the winter tends to be in the upper 70s°F (21°C) during the day and rarely falls below 50°F (10°C) at night.

Centro

What locals generally refer to as Centro is actually several sprawling districts containing the city's oldest neighborhoods, churches, and most enchanting cafés. Rio's beaches, broad boulevards, and modern architecture may be impressive. But its colonial structures, old narrow streets, and alleyways in leafy inland neighborhoods are no less so. The metro stations that serve Centro are Cinelândia, Carioca, Uruguaiana, Presidente Vargas, Central, and Praça Onze. You can also get around the center using the VLT (Light Rail Vehicle), which connects the Gentileza Terminal (next to the Novo Rio Bus Station) and Santos Dumont Airport.

Centro

Sights ▼
1. Beco do Comércio F4
2. Biblioteca Nacional E7
3. Boulevard Olímpico D2
4. Catedral de São Sebastião do Rio de Janeiro C8
5. Centro Cultural Banco do Brasil E4
6. Convento de Santo Antônio D6
7. Igreja de Nossa Senhora da Candelária D4
8. Igreja de São Francisco da Penitência D6
9. Mosteiro de São Bento D2
10. Museu de Arte do Rio C2
11. Museu de Arte Moderna G9
12. Museu do Amanhã D1
13. Museu Histórico Nacional G6
14. Paço Imperial F5
15. Palácio Tiradentes F5
16. Real Gabinete Portugues de Leitura C5
17. Theatro Municipal E7

Restaurants ▼
1. Albamar Restaurante G5
2. Amarelinho E7
3. Bafo da Prainha B3
4. Bistrô do Paço F5
5. Confeitaria Colombo D5
6. Rio Minho F4
7. Santo Scenarium B7

Hotels ▼
1. Windsor Guanabara D4

The ticket costs R$4.30, which must be loaded onto the Rio Card, a transport card that can be purchased at VLT boarding points.

Rio's settlement dates back to 1555. You can experience much of the city's rich history by visiting churches, government buildings, and villas in and around Centro. The metro is a good way to get downtown, but head here early, wear comfortable shoes, and be ready to walk multiple blocks as you explore this historic city center. There are also daily free walking tours with English-speaking guides. If you're not up for a long walk, consider taking an organized bus tour.

Rio city went through many renovations because of the Olympic Games in 2016. One of the areas that had the biggest changes was the Porto area, an extension of Centro. Beyond Praça Mauá, you will find the Olympic Boulevard, with warehouses transformed into exhibition areas, concert halls, and boarding areas for cruise ships.

Sights

Beco do Comércio
PEDESTRIAN MALL | A network of narrow streets and alleys centers on this pedestrian thoroughfare, also called the Travessa do Comércio, whose name translates to Alley of Commerce. The area is flanked by restored 18th-century homes, now converted to offices, shops, and galleries. The best-known sight here is the Arco de Teles, a picturesque archway named in honor of the wealthy Teles de Menezes family, who built many of the street's most handsome buildings. Beco do Comércio is a good place to stop for lunch—the street is lined with everything from simple pay-by-weight buffet spots and casual bars to more upmarket restaurants and cafés. ✉ *Praça 15 de Novembro, Centro* Ⓜ *Uruguaiana/Carioca.*

Biblioteca Nacional
LIBRARY | Corinthian columns adorn the neoclassical National Library (built between 1905 and 1908), the first such establishment in Latin America. Its original archives were brought to Brazil by King João VI in 1808. The library contains roughly 13 million books, including two 15th-century printed Bibles, manuscript New Testaments from the 11th and 12th centuries, and volumes that belonged to Empress Teresa Christina. Also here are first-edition Mozart scores, as well as scores by Carlos Gomes, who adapted the José de Alencar novel about Brazil's Indians, *O Guarani,* into an opera of the same name.

■ **TIP→ Nonmembers can see the library by guided tour only (weekdays 11–4); tours are given in English, Spanish, and Portuguese. Visitors will need photo ID to enter.** ✉ *Av. Rio Branco 219, Centro* ☎ *21/2220–3040* ⊕ *www.gov.br/bn/pt-br* 🎫 *Tours free* Ⓜ *Cinelândia.*

Boulevard Olímpico
PROMENADE | **FAMILY** | The area became known as Olympic Boulevard, due to the events it hosted during the 2016 Olympic games in Rio de Janeiro. Officially, it brings together Porto Maravilha (with the Warehouses and Praça Mauá) and Orla Conde (from Praça Mauá to Praça XV). The boulevard hosts restaurants, exhibition halls, a boarding hall for cruise ships, and museums. One of the highlights is the boldly colored panel *Etinias,* by Brazilian artist Kobra. ✉ *Praça Maua, Centro* Ⓜ *Carioca or Uruguaiana.*

Catedral de São Sebastião do Rio de Janeiro (*Catedral Metropolitana*)
CHURCH | The exterior of this circa-1960 metropolitan cathedral, which looks like a concrete beehive, divides opinion. The daring modern design stands in sharp contrast to the baroque style of other churches in Rio, but don't judge until you've stepped inside. When light floods through the colorful stained-glass windows, it transforms the interior—which is

The Catedral de São Sebastião do Rio de Janeiro was designed based on the pyramid style of Mayan architecture.

80 meters (263 feet) high and 96 meters (315 feet) in diameter—into a warm, serious place of worship that accommodates up to 20,000 people. An 8½-ton granite rock lends considerable weight to the concept of an altar. ✉ *Av. República do Chile 245, Centro* ☏ *21/2240–2669* ⊕ *www.catedral.com.br* 🎫 *Free* Ⓜ *Carioca or Cinelândia.*

★ Centro Cultural Banco do Brasil

ARTS CENTER | FAMILY | What was once the headquarters of Brazil's oldest bank is now an enormous cultural space in downtown Rio. With areas designated for cinema screenings, expositions, music, educational programs, and theater, this is one of the city's best rainy-day options. The 19th-century building, with its ornate domed roof, is impressive in itself, and the visiting exhibitions—which might showcase anything from impressionist masterpieces to the works of São Paulo street artists—rarely disappoint. There are two coffee shops, a restaurant and an arts shop in the building. There is also a children's library on the top floor, and many free activities for all ages.

■ **TIP→ Pre-booked tickets have priority on exhibition entrance. You can book for free at ingressos.ccbb.com.br/cidades** ✉ *Rua Primeiro de Março, 66, Centro* ☏ *21/3808–2020* ⊕ *culturabancodobrasil.com.br/portal/rio-de-janeiro* 🎫 *Free* ☾ *Closed Tues.* Ⓜ *Carioca.*

Convento do Santo Antônio

ABBEY | The Convent of St. Anthony was completed in 1780, but some parts date from 1615, making it one of Rio's oldest structures. Its baroque interior contains priceless colonial art, including wood carvings and wall paintings. The sacristy is covered with traditional Portuguese *azulejos* (ceramic tiles). The church has no bell tower: its bells hang from a double arch on the monastery ceiling. An exterior mausoleum contains the tombs of the offspring of Dom Pedro I and Dom Pedro II. ✉ *Largo da Carioca 5, Centro* ☏ *21/2262–0129* ⊕ *www.conventosantoantonio.org.br* 🎫 *R$10 (guided tour R$20)* ☾ *Closed Sun.* Ⓜ *Carioca.*

Centro Cultural Banco do Brasil is the most-visited cultural center in Brazil and commonly found as a bucket list sight for many people in the world.

Igreja de Nossa Senhora da Candelária

CHURCH | The classic symmetry of Candelária's white dome and bell towers casts an unexpected air of tranquility over the chaos of downtown traffic. The church was built on the site of a chapel founded in 1610. Construction on the present church began in 1775, and although the emperor formally dedicated it in 1811, work on the dome wasn't completed until 1877. The sculpted bronze doors were exhibited at the 1889 World's Fair in Paris. ✉ *Praça Pio X, Centro* ☎ *21/2233–2324* ⊕ *www.candelariorio.org.br/* ✉ *Free* ⊙ *Closed Sat.* ☞ *Check their website for music concerts* Ⓜ *Uruguaiana.*

Igreja de São Francisco da Penitência

CHURCH | This baroque church was completed in 1737, nearly four decades after construction began. Today it's famed for its wooden sculptures and its rich gold-leaf interior. The nave contains a painting of St. Francis, the patron of the church—reportedly the first painting in Brazil done in perspective. ■**TIP**→ **Guided tours are offered weekdays 2–4 pm.** ✉ *Largo da Carioca 5, Centro* ☎ *21/2262–0197* ⊕ *museusacrofranciscano.org.br* ✉ *R$10* ⊙ *Closed Sun.* Ⓜ *Carioca.*

★ Mosteiro de São Bento

ABBEY | Just a glimpse of the Monastery of St. Benedict's main altar can fill you with awe. Layer upon layer of curvaceous wood carvings coated in gold lend the space an opulent air, while spiral columns whirl upward to capitals topped by the chubbiest of cherubs and angels that appear lost in divine thought. Although the Benedictine monks arrived in 1586, work didn't begin on this church and monastery until 1617. It was completed in 1641, but artisans including Mestre Valentim (who designed the silver chandeliers) continued to add details almost to the 19th century. Sunday Mass at 10 am is accompanied by Gregorian chants. ✉ *Rua Dom Gerardo 68, Centro* ☎ *21/2206–8100* ⊕ *www.osb.org.br* ✉ *Free.*

⭐ Museu de Arte do Rio

ART MUSEUM | Rio's once run-down port zone is now the focus of a major investment and regeneration program, and the Museu de Arte do Rio (MAR) has provided a compelling reason for visitors to head to this part of town. The attention-grabbing museum structures—a colonial palace and a modernist former bus station, united visually by a wavelike postmodern form that floats on stilts above them—represent an impressive feat of architectural reimagination. The gallery celebrates depictions of Rio throughout the ages, and the eight gallery spaces inside the buildings contain permanent collections of surrealist, modernist, and *naïf* artworks. Visiting exhibitions tend to be good, and the views from the top floor—looking out to sea and across Rio's port—are impressive. ✉ *Praça Mauá 5, Centro* ☎ *21/3031–2741* ⊕ *www.museudeartedorio.org.br* 🎟 *R$20, free on Tues.* ⊗ *Closed Mon.* ☞ *Ticket office only accepts credit or debit cards* Ⓜ *Uruguaiana.*

Museu de Arte Moderna (MAM)

ART MUSEUM | A great place to take the pulse of the vibrant Brazilian visual-arts scene, the Museum of Modern Art occupies a striking concrete-and-glass modernist building. Augmenting the permanent collection of about 6,400 works by Brazilian and international artists is the slightly larger Gilberto Chateaubriand Collection of modern and contemporary Brazilian art. MAM has earned respect over the years for its bold, often thought-provoking exhibitions, including a vibrant annual street art festival. The venue also hosts events such as music performances and DJ sessions. Its theater screens Brazilian and international independent and art house films. ✉ *Av. Infante Dom Henrique 85, Centro* ☎ *21/2240–4944* ⊕ *www.mamrio.org.br* 🎟 *R$14* Ⓜ *Cinelândia.*

Museu do Amanhã (*Museum of Tomorrow*)

CULTURAL MUSEUM | **FAMILY** | Designed by the Spanish architect Santiago Calatrava, this spectacular sustainability-focused museum juts out into Guanabara Bay from Praca Maúa (restored in honor of the 2016 Olympics) like a spaceship about to take off. The permanent exhibits explore science through the mediums of art and technology, guiding visitors to imagine a new way of living through contemplating the cosmos, the Earth, and our relationship to it all. Don't miss the on-site restaurant Casa do Saulo, with Amazonian cuisine. ✉ *Praça Mauá, 1, Centro* ☎ *21/3812–1812* ⊕ *museudoamanha.org.br* 🎟 *R$20* ⊗ *Closed Mon.*

Museu Histórico Nacional

HISTORY MUSEUM | The building that houses the National History Museum dates from 1762, though some sections—such as the battlements—were erected as early as 1603. It seems appropriate that this colonial structure should exhibit relics that document Brazil's history. Among its treasures are rare papers, Latin American coins, carriages, cannons, and religious art. Always check their social media or website for the temporary exhibitions or events. ✉ *Praça Marechal Ancora s/n, Centro* ✛ *Praça 15 de Novembro* ☎ *21/3299–0324* ⊕ *mhn.museus.gov.br/* 🎟 *Free* ⊗ *Closed Mon. and Tues.* ☞ *Temporary with free entrance, check their website for any change* Ⓜ *Carioca or Cinelândia.*

Paço Imperial

CASTLE/PALACE | This two-story building with thick stone walls and an ornate entrance was built in 1743, and for the next 60 years was the headquarters for Brazil's captains (viceroys), appointed by the Portuguese court in Lisbon. When King João VI arrived, he made it his royal palace. After Brazil's declaration of independence, emperors Dom Pedro I and II called the palace home, and when the monarchy was overthrown, the building became Rio's central post office. Restoration work in the 1980s transformed the palace into a cultural center and concert hall. The building houses a restaurant, a bistro, and a bit of shopping. The square on which the palace sits, Praça 15 de Novembro, known in colonial days as Largo do Paço, has witnessed some of Brazil's most significant historic moments: here two emperors were crowned, slavery was abolished, and Emperor Pedro II was deposed. The square's modern name is a reference to the date of the declaration of the Republic of Brazil: November 15, 1889. Praça 15, as it is widely known, sits in front of Rio's ferry terminal and is at the heart of a major regeneration project aiming to transform Rio's run-down docklands. ✉ *Praça 15 de Novembro 48, Centro* ☎ *21/2215–2093* ⊕ *amigosdopacoimperial.org.br/* 💲 *Free* ⊙ *Closed Mon.* Ⓜ *Carioca.*

Palácio Tiradentes

CASTLE/PALACE | The Tiradentes Palace contains a permanent exhibit describing its history as the seat of the Brazilian parliament before Brasília was built in the late 1950s. Getúlio Vargas, Brazil's president for almost 20 years and by far the biggest force in 20th-century Brazilian politics, used the palace in the 1940s as a nucleus for disseminating propaganda. Free half-hour tours are given in Portuguese, English, and Spanish. ✉ *Rua Primeiro de Março s/n, Centro* ✛ *Praça XV* ☎ *21/2588–1000* ⊕ *www.palaciotiradentes.rj.gov.br/* 💲 *Free* ⚓ *Book beforehand online* Ⓜ *Carioca.*

Real Gabinete Portugues de Leitura

LIBRARY | FAMILY | This evocative library, known as the Royal Reading Room, contains the largest collection of Portuguese literature outside of Portugal and was first established in 1837 as a Portuguese cultural centre during the reign of Portuguese emperor Joao Pedro II. It's a joy to stroll through its soaring Gothic stacks and soak up the Harry Potteresque atmosphere. ✉ *Rua Luis de Camoes 30, Centro* ☎ *21/2221–3138* ⊕ *www.realgabinete.com.br/Visite-o-RGPL/Visiting-RGPL* 💲 *Free* ⊙ *Closed weekends.*

★ Theatro Municipal

NOTABLE BUILDING | If you visit one place in Centro, make it the Municipal Theater, modeled after the Paris Opera House and opened in 1909. Now restored to its sparkling best, the theater boasts Carrara marble, stunning mosaics, glittering chandeliers, bronze and onyx statues, gilded mirrors, German stained-glass windows, and Brazilwood inlay floors. Murals by Brazilian artists Eliseu Visconti and Rodolfo Amoedo further enhance the opulent feel. The main entrance and first two galleries are particularly ornate. As you climb to the upper floors, the decor becomes simpler, a reflection of a time when different classes entered through different doors and sat in separate sections, but also due in part to the exhaustion of funds toward the end of the project. The theater seats 2,357—with outstanding sight lines—for its dance performances and classical music concerts. English-speaking guides are available. ✉ *Rua Marechal Floriano s/n, Centro* ⊕ *www.theatromunicipal.rj.gov.br* 💲 *Tours R$20* Ⓜ *Cinelândia.*

🍴 Restaurants

Albamar Restaurante

$$$ | SEAFOOD | Open since 1933, the Albamar is not hard to spot: this outstanding seafood house is inside a distinctive green octagonal building with 360-degree views of Guanabara Bay (a few minutes walk from Centro's bustling Praça XV square). Chef Rodrigo Costa is behind the array of seafood risottos, fresh fish, and pasta dishes that now draws Centro's business moguls. **Known for:** glistening bay views; iconic architecture; 300-bottle cellar. 💲 *Average main: R$200* ✉ *Praça Marechal Âncora 184, Centro* ☎ *21/3037–1117* ⊕ *www.facebook.com/restaurantealbamar* ⊙ *No dinner* Ⓜ *Carioca.*

Modeled after the Paris Opera House and opened in 1909, the Teatro Municipal is one of the most stunning theaters in South America.

Amarelinho

$ | **BRAZILIAN** | The best spot for city center people-watching, this vast pavement *boteco* overlooking the Biblioteca Nacional and the Theatro Municipal has been a Carioca institution since it opened in 1921. Waitstaffs in bright yellow waistcoats and bow ties flit among the bustling tables delivering reasonably priced Brazilian dishes and ice-cold draft beer to a local after-work crowd. **Known for:** expertly grilled meats; authentic local atmosphere; prawn pastries. $ *Average main: R$65* ✉ *Praça Floriano 55B, Cinelândia, Centro* ☎ *21/3825–0243* ⊕ *www.amarelinhodacinelandia.com.br* Ⓜ *Cinelândia*.

Bafo da Prainha

$ | **BARBECUE** | Listed among the 10 best bars in the world by magazine, this bar is a summary of Rio de Janeiro culture, with tables spread throughout the square, live music, and people from all over. Enjoy your visit to Praça Mauá and finish by tasting the true Carioca barbecue with cold beers. **Known for:** barbecue; Brazilian caipirinhas; live samba. $ *Average main: R$47* ✉ *Largo São Francisco da Prainha 15, Centro* ⊕ *www.instagram.com/bafodaprainha* ⊘ *Closed Mon.* Ⓜ *VLT - Parada dos Museus*.

Bistrô do Paço

$ | **INTERNATIONAL** | Facing the patio at the cool, whitewashed Paço Imperial (The Imperial Palace) and close to the Palacio Tiradentes in the Praça XV square, this charming little bistro is a good option for a light lunch, coffee, or snack for Centro sightseers. European influences abound, and the vegetarian-friendly menu includes salads, quiches, and grilled fish; make sure to leave room for the tempting desserts. **Known for:** intimate views of the Imperial Palace; cozy atmosphere; warm apple strudel. $ *Average main: R$66* ✉ *Praça Quinze de Novembro 48, Centro* ☎ *21/2262–3613* ⊕ *www.bistro.com.br* ⊘ *No dinner* Ⓜ *Uruguaiana*.

★ Confeitaria Colombo

$ | CAFÉ | At the turn of the 20th century, the belle epoque structure that houses Colombo Confectionery was Rio's preeminent café, the site of elaborate balls, afternoon teas for upper-class *senhoras*, and a center of political intrigue and gossip. Now, visitors stop for arguably the most atmospheric coffee, melt-in-the-mouth sweet treats, and tasty *salgados* (savory snacks) in town while admiring the elaborate, Old-World interiors—enormous jacaranda-framed mirrors from Belgium, stained glass from France, and tiles from Portugal are among the art nouveau decor's highlights. **Known for:** a snapshot into Centro's former Golden Age; elaborate interiors; decadent afternoon teas. ⓢ *Average main: R$60* ✉ *Rua Gonçalves Dias 32, Centro* ☎ *21/2505–1500* ⊕ *www.confeitariacolombo.com.br* ⊘ *Closed Sun.; no dinner* Ⓜ *Carioca.*

★ Rio Minho

$$$ | SEAFOOD | The elaborate Portuguese tile work, bow-tied waiters, and first-class seafood dishes make this lunchtime, weekday-only spot one of the top picks for an atmospheric lunch in Rio's downtown. Perch at one of the alfresco barstools for a more informal snack, or head inside to dine in the colonial vestiges of one of the city's oldest restaurants, serving the city's well-to-do since 1884. **Known for:** attentive, friendly service; the sopa leão veloso (a Brazilian bouillabaisse); historical resonance. ⓢ *Average main: R$210* ✉ *Rua do Ouvidor 10, Centro* ☎ *21/2509–2338* ⊘ *Closed weekends. No dinner* Ⓜ *Uruguaiana.*

Santo Scenarium

$ | BRAZILIAN | FAMILY | A smaller, more laid-back neighbor to the long-established samba party at Rio Scenarium, Santo Scenarium shares its parent club's passion for grandiose interiors, and the split-level space here is packed with ornate pillars, carved cherubs, and borderline-kitsch religious artifacts. It's a good option for lunchtime, as the kitchen serves tasty Brazilian classics. **Known for:** fun, kitsch decor; Brazilian cuisine; vibrant local scene. ⓢ *Average main: R$76* ✉ *Rua do Lavradio 36, Lapa* ☎ *21/96550–0034* ⊕ *www.santoscenarium.com.br* ⊘ *No dinner; closed Sun.* Ⓜ *Carioca.*

Favorite Places

Gabriela Godoi: When a friend is visiting Rio, I like to suggest a couple of things and places to help them get to know the city's spirit. Do not forget to include in your travel plans a ride to the North Zone (by subway) and taste the delights from Bar do Momo with a cold beer, see the passion people have for their soccer teams in a match at Maracanã stadium, and dance to the true samba at Barodromo, all located in the Tijuca area.

Hotels

Windsor Guanabara

$$$ | HOTEL | One of the few solid hotel choices right in Centro, the Windsor Guanabara has reasonably sized and tastefully appointed rooms (although some are beginning to show signs of age), and the contemporary rooftop pool area—with white tiles, white trellises, and white patio furnishings—offers a welcome escape from the city swelter and stunning views of Guanabara Bay. The buffet breakfast is good, too, although the evening buffet served in the restaurant is a little steep. **Pros:** good transport links—close to metro and domestic airport; close to downtown attractions and nightlife; good pool with views. **Cons:** far from beaches; Centro is nearly deserted on Sunday; geared toward business travelers. ⓢ *Rooms*

Outdoor markets are a must-see on a trip to Rio de Janeiro, where they sell antique and vintages pieces along with cultural goods to bring home as souvenirs.

from: R$500 ⊠ Av. Presidente Vargas 392, Centro ☎ 21/2195–5000 ⊕ www.windsorhoteis.com.br 🛏 542 rooms 🍴 Free Breakfast Ⓜ Uruguaiana.

🛍 Shopping

BOOKS

Livraria Leonardo da Vinci

BOOKS | One of Rio's best sources for foreign-language titles, this bookstore has a wide selection of titles in English, Spanish, and French. ⊠ Av. Rio Branco 185, Subsolo, Centro ☎ 21/2533–2337 ⊕ www.leonardodavinci.com.br ⊙ Closed Sun. Ⓜ Carioca.

MARKETS

Feira de Antiquários da Praça 15 de Novembro

VINTAGE | This open-air antiques fair held on Saturdays attracts more locals than tourists—it's a good place to pick up vintage clothing, sunglasses, rare vinyl, and antique furniture and jewelry. Arrive early to get the best buys and be prepared to haggle. Serious collectors arrive as early as 6 am, often with an eye to grabbing a bargain and reselling it a few hours later at a higher price. Sellers begin to close up shop by early afternoon. ⊠ Praça 15 de Novembro, Centro ⊙ Closed Sun.–Fri. ☞ Market held on Sat. Ⓜ Carioca.

★ **Feira do Rio Antigo** (*Rio Antiques Fair*)
MARKET | FAMILY | Vendors at this outdoor fair sell antiques, rare books, records, and all types of *objets d'art* every Saturday. New and vintage fashion is also a strong suit, although cheaper fashion has sadly begun to take over. Live samba music and *capoeira* performances create a festival-like atmosphere, and the pavement bars and restaurants buzz with locals and visitors. ⊠ Rua do Lavradio, Centro ☎ 21/2224–6693 ⊕ www.polonovorioantigo.com.br Ⓜ Carioca or Cinelandia.

★ **Feira Nordestina** (*Northeastern Fair*)
SPECIALTY STORE | FAMILY | The crowded, lively Feira de São Cristóvão, better known as the Feira Nordestina, is a social hub for Brazilians from the country's

Northeast who live in Rio. They gather to hear their own distinctive music, eat regional foods, and buy arts, crafts, home furnishings, and clothing. With two stages for live music, the fair takes on a nightclub vibe after dark, and there are some seriously impressive displays of *forro* dancing. This fair is at its busiest and most exciting on the weekends. It's best to take a taxi here. ✉ *Campo de São Cristóvão, Pavilhão de São Cristóvão, 7 km (4½ miles) northwest of Centro, São Cristóvão* ☎ *21/2580–0501, 21/2580–5335* ⊕ *www.feiradesaocristovao.org.br/* ☞ *Cash only for entrance tickets* Ⓜ *São Cristóvão.*

 Performing Arts

OPERA
★ Theatro Municipal
OPERA | Built in 1909, the stunning Municipal Theater at Cinelândia is the city's main performing arts venue, hosting dance, opera, symphony concerts, and theater events for most of the year. The season officially runs from March to December, so don't be surprised to find the theater closed in January and February. The theater also has its own ballet company. ✉ *Praça Floriano, Centro* ☎ *21/2332–9134* ⊕ *www.theatromunicipal.rj.gov.br* Ⓜ *Cinelândia.*

FILM
Centro Cultural Luiz Severiano Ribeiro
FILM | The last remaining movie palace in historic Cinelândia—once the focal point of moviegoing activity in Rio—is one of the most well-preserved and important in the country. The luxurious theater has hosted premieres, exhibits, and events since opening in 1926, and was totally renovated in 2015. Check their program before going, as the movie theater is only open on special occasions nowadays. ✉ *Praça Floriano 7, Cinelândia* ☎ *21/2240–1093* ⊕ *www.kinoplex.com.br/cinema/cine-odeon/.*

Bargaining in Rio

Bargaining in shops is unusual, but you can try your luck and ask if there's a discount for paying in cash, especially if it's a high-priced item. When granted, you can expect a 5% to 10% discount. Market or street vendor shopping is a different story—bargain to your wallet's content.

🏃 Activities

HIKING AND CLIMBING
Centro Excursionista Brasileiro
HIKING & WALKING | The largest and oldest mountaineering organization in Brazil, Centro Excursionista Brasileiro runs climbing courses and leads treks throughout Rio State and as far away as Minas Gerais, providing guides, maps, and all the gear you'll need. ✉ *Av. Almirante Barroso 2, 8th fl., Centro* ☎ *21/2252–9844* ⊕ *www.ceb.org.br.*

Catete and Glória

Though a little rundown, historic, residential Catete and Glória are well worth an afternoon's sightseeing. In addition to its hilltop church, Glória has a lovely marina that's perfect for a picnic or stroll, especially on a Sunday, when the main road is closed to traffic.

Handily located on the metro line between the Zona Sul and Centro, the two neighborhoods' subway stations are just a few minutes' walk from each other. From Ipanema or Copacabana take the 10-minute ride to Catete, and you'll emerge right in front of the Museum of the Republic. Set aside a couple of hours to see the exhibits and enjoy a coffee in the gardens before taking a stroll down

The Palácio do Catete, the presidential palace until the government moved to Brasília, itself warrants at least two hours.

to Glória's marina, taking in the monument to fallen soldiers. The surrounding area can be a little rough, so jump on a metro to Centro or the Zona Sul when you're done sightseeing.

Sights

Igreja de Nossa Senhora da Glória do Outeiro
VIEWPOINT | The aptly named Church of Our Lady of the Glory of the Knoll (Church of Glory for short) sits on top of a hill and is visible from many spots in the city, making it a landmark that's truly cherished by Cariocas. Its location was a strategic point in the city's early days, and the views from church grounds are impressive. Estácio de Sá took this hill from the French in the 1560s and then went on to expand the first settlement and to find a city for the Portuguese. The baroque church, which wasn't built until 1739, is notable for its octagonal floor plan, large dome, ornamental stonework, and vivid tile work. Tours are given by appointment only. As opening hours are sporadic, visitors might choose to arrive shortly before 9 am or 11 am on Sunday, when Mass takes place and the church is open to the public. ✉ *Praça Nossa Senhora da Glória 26, Glória* ☎ *21/2225–2869* ⊕ *www.outeirodagloria.org.br* 🚇 *Free* Ⓜ *Glória.*

Monumento aos Pracinhas
MILITARY SIGHT | The Monument to the Brazilian Dead of World War II—the nation sided with the Allies during the conflict—is actually a combination museum and monument. The museum houses military uniforms, medals, stamps, and documents belonging to soldiers, and two soaring columns flank the tomb of an unknown soldier. The best time to visit is on a Sunday, when the road in front of the monument is closed to traffic, and joggers, dog-walkers, and strolling families fill the area. ✉ *Av. Infante Dom Henrique 75, Glória* ✥ *Parque Brigadeiro Eduardo Gomes - Aterro do Flamengo* ☎ *21/2240–1283* ⊕ *riotur.rio/que_fazer/ monumento-nacional-aos-mortos-da-segunda-guerra-mundial/* 🚇 *Free* Ⓜ *Glória.*

★ Palácio do Catete

GARDEN | FAMILY | Once the villa of a German baron, this elegant, 19th-century granite-and-marble palace became the presidential residence after the 1889 coup overthrew the monarchy and established the Republic of Brazil. Eighteen presidents lived here. Gaze at the palace's gleaming parquet floors and intricate bas-relief ceilings as you wander through its **Museu da República** (Museum of the Republic). The permanent exhibits include a shroud-draped view of the bedroom where President Getúlio Vargas committed suicide in 1954 after the military threatened to overthrow his government. Presidential memorabilia, furniture, and paintings that date from the proclamation of the republic to the end of Brazil's military regime in 1985 are also displayed. The palace gardens are free, and worth a visit in themselves. With their imperial palm trees, water features, chattering monkeys, and strolling geese they are among the most pleasant—and safest, thanks to patrolling guards—parks in the city, and there's a well-equipped children's playground at the far end. ⊠ *Rua do Catete 153, Catete* ☎ *21/3235–3693* ⊕ *museudarepublica.museus.gov.br* R$6 Ⓜ *Catete.*

Activities

BOATING AND SAILING

Saveiro's Tour

BOATING | FAMILY | Take a trip down the coast to Angra or catch one of the two-hour daily cruises around Guanabara Bay—views of Sugarloaf, Botafogo Bay, and the Rio-Niterói Bridge are among the highlights. Saveiro's also hires out speedboats and sailboats by the day.

■ **TIP→** Some of the boats adopt a party vibe with free caipirinhas and loud music, so if this isn't what you seek, double-check in advance. ⊠ *Marina da Glória, Av. Infante Dom Henrique s/n, Lojas 13 e 14, Glória* ☎ *21/2225–6064 (21) 99448–7551* ⊕ *www.saveiros.com.br* From R$55 Ⓜ *Gloria.*

Flamengo and Botafogo

These largely residential neighborhoods connect the southern beach districts and Centro via a series of highways that intersect here. It's easy to reach these neighborhoods by metro. Apartment buildings dominate, but Rio Sul—one of the city's most popular shopping centers—is here, as are some of the city's best museums and public spaces.

The eponymous beach at Flamengo used to be classified as polluted, but after the Olympic Games held in Rio, the water company (Águas do Rio) started to develop cleaning projects and by 2024, people were heading back to the now clean waters. A marina sits on a bay at one end of the beach, which is connected via a busy boulevard to the smaller beach (still polluted) at Botafogo. The city's yacht club is here, and when Rio was Brazil's capital, it was also the site of the city's glittering embassy row. The embassies relocated to Brasília long ago, but the mansions that housed them remain. Among Botafogo's more interesting mansion- and tree-lined streets are Mariana, Sorocaba, Matriz, and Visconde e Silva.

Sights

Futuros Arte e Tecnologia / Musehum Oi Futuro

ARTS CENTER | FAMILY | This slick, ultra-modern exhibition space once housed Rio's Telecommunications Museum. The museum itself delivers a unique multimedia adventure—lots of monitors, blinking lights, and media artifacts. After you've been oriented in the use of the MP3 headsets, a light- and mirror-filled airlock-like room awaits. The sights in this tiny exhibit space will likely mesmerize you, and if you don't speak Portuguese, the English guide will explain what you can't figure out from the visual cues. The building has two different spaces: one focused on the transformation of communications over the years and how this affects our lives, and the other focused on the relationship between technology and arts. ✉ *Rua Dois de Dezembro 63, Flamengo* ☏ *21/3131–3060* ⊕ *www.oifuturo.org.br/en* ⊙ *Closed Mon.* Ⓜ *Largo do Machado or Catete.*

Museu Casa de Rui Barbosa (*The Rui Barbosa House Museum*)
OTHER ATTRACTION | FAMILY | Steps away from Botafogo metro station is a museum in the former home of the 19th-century Brazilian statesman, writer, and scholar Rui Barbosa, a liberal from Bahia State who drafted one of Brazil's early constitutions. The pink mansion, which dates from 1849, is itself worth a visit. Stepping inside instantly transports you to the period when writers and other intellectuals inhabited this street's grand houses. Among the memorabilia and artifacts on display are Barbosa's 1913 car and legal, political, and journalistic works. The extensive libraries are testament to Rui Barbosa's love for literature. The well-tended gardens stretch for 9,000 meters (29,527 feet) and are filled with small pools and fountains, making them a pleasant place to take respite from the rush and crush of the city. There's a good children's library, regular kids' workshops and events, and free live music performances. ✉ *Rua São Clemente 134, Botafogo* ☏ *21/3289–4600* ⊕ *www.casaruibarbosa.gov.br* ⊙ *Closed Mon.* Ⓜ *Botafogo.*

Parque do Flamengo
STATE/PROVINCIAL PARK | FAMILY | The landscape architect Roberto Burle Marx designed this waterfront park that flanks the Baía de Guanabara from the Glória neighborhood to Flamengo. Frequently referred to as "Aterro do Flamengo," the park contains playgrounds and public tennis and basketball courts, and paths used for jogging, walking, and biking wind through it. On weekends the freeway beside the park is closed to traffic and the entire area becomes one enormous public space.

■ **TIP→ For safety reasons, avoid wandering the park after dark and stick to busy sections even in daylight hours.** ✉ *Inland of beach from Glória to Botafogo, Av. Infante Dom Henrique, Flamengo* ⊕ *www.parquedoflamengo.com.br* Ⓜ *Glória.*

🏖 Beaches

Praia do Botafogo
BEACH | Though it's pretty, Botafogo Beach doesn't attract swimmers and sunbathers. Locals joke that the fish here come ready-coated in oil for frying, but don't let that stop you from jogging along the sidewalk if you're staying nearby. Early risers are often rewarded with a stunning sunrise from this shore. **Amenities:** none. **Best for:** sunrise; walking. ✉ *Botafogo* ✢ *between Praça Praia Nova and Praça Marinha do Brasil* ⊕ *praialimpa.net/* Ⓜ *Botafogo.*

Praia do Flamengo
BEACH | This small curved beach with a terrific view of Sugarloaf had a longtime reputation of being better for working out and walking than for swimming. Flamengo beach was restored and is now also popular for swimming. Check the local news for bathing conditions, as they may vary. **Amenities:** food and drink. **Best for:** walking and swimming. ✉ *Rua Praia do Flamengo, Flamengo* ⊕ *praialimpa.net/* Ⓜ *Flamengo.*

🍴 Restaurants

Brewteco
$ | BRAZILIAN | If you want to enjoy a beautiful view of Sugarloaf Mountain and Botafogo Beach, be sure to visit the rooftop of Botafogo Praia Shopping. The Brewteco bar and restaurant offers a variety of beers and draft beers, signature drinks, and the Brazilian classics. **Known for:** draft beer variety; feijoada; the view. 💲 *Average main: R$44* ✉ *Praia*

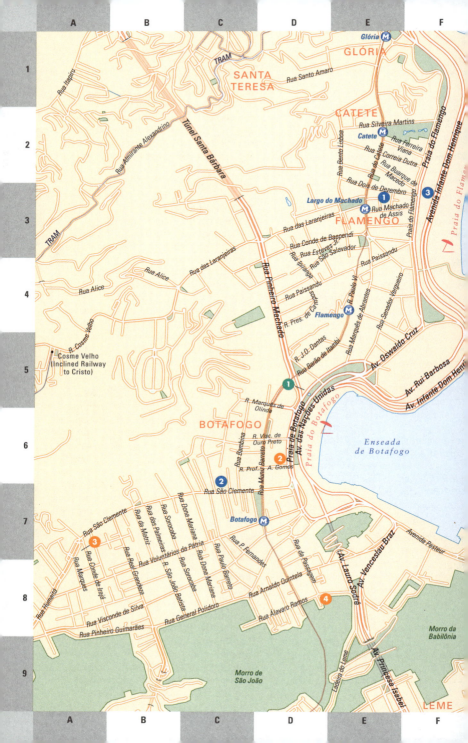

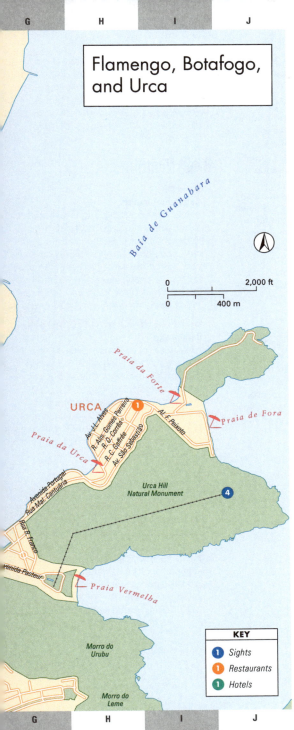

de Botafogo 400, Botafogo ✣ Rooftop of Botafogo Praia Shopping ⊕ brewteco.com.br/brew-botafogo/ Ⓜ Botafogo.

★ Lasai
$$$$ | BRAZILIAN | At Lasai, the gastronomic experience goes beyond simply tasting the ingredients, guided by renowned chef Rafa Costa e Silva. Every guest is seated at a balcony table facing the kitchen, able to follow every step of preparation and observe the constant coming and going of the team. **Known for:** gourmet experience at the forefront of Brazil's culinary scene; expert cocktails; view of the Christ statue from the roof terrace. ⓢ *Average main: R$1,150* ✉ *Largo dos Leões 35, Humaitá* ☎ *21/3449–1854* ⊕ *www.lasai.com.br* ☾ *Closed Sun.–Mon.; no lunch* ☞ *Tasting menu* Ⓜ *Botafogo.*

Miam Miam
$ | ECLECTIC | Blink and you could miss this hip Botafogo eatery housed in a tiny white colonial building and furnished entirely with pieces from the 1950s to the 1970s. The French–Brazilian owners have created a relaxed, casual dining space where they prepare hearty portions of tasty comfort food and award-winning cocktails that draw a bohemian crowd. **Known for:** vegetarian specials such as the lentil ragu with mushrooms and spiced okra; kitsch design; rum-based basil julep. ⓢ *Average main: R$72* ✉ *Rua General Góes Monteiro 34, Botafogo* ☎ *21/2244–0125* ⊕ *www.miammiam.com.br* ☾ *Closed Mon.* Ⓜ *Botafogo.*

 Hotels

Yoo2
$$$ | HOTEL | FAMILY | With a prime location overlooking Botafogo beach and Sugarloaf Mountain, this well-run hotel has become a favorite since opening in 2016. **Pros:** stunning views; great value for the offering; fresh, modern design. **Cons:** rooms can be compact; early check-in is charged; the beach in front of the hotel is polluted and only for exploring by foot. ⓢ *Rooms from: R$1,300* ✉ *Praia de Botafogo 242, Botafogo* ☎ *21/3445–2000* ⊕ *yoo2.com* ⇌ *143 rooms* ⓘ◎ *No Meals* Ⓜ *Flamengo.*

 Nightlife

BARS
Cobal do Humaitá
BARS | FAMILY | Occupying a vast outdoor space under the gaze of Christ the Redeemer, this collection of bars, restaurant, and shops throngs with people after dark, when the air is filled with the tipsy chatter of locals relaxing over dinner and drinks. ✉ *Cobal do Humaitá, Rua Voluntarios Da Patria 446, Loja 3/4 A, Humaitá.*

NIGHTCLUBS AND LIVE MUSIC
Reconvexo
PUB | Rock 'n' roll fans looking for a bar with a good food and drink menu and good music can enjoy this address in Botafogo. From Monday to Saturday, the bar offers specials on beers and drinks, a DJ, and TV for sporting events. ✉ *Rua Henrique de Novais 55, Botafogo* ⊕ *www.instagram.com/reconvexo_bar/* ☾ *Closed Sun.* Ⓜ *Botafogo.*

 Activities

HIKING AND CLIMBING
Rio Adventures
HIKING & WALKING | FAMILY | This professional outfit with English-speaking guides runs a range of adventure sports activities and tours, including stand-up paddleboarding, white water rafting, jungle treks, and climbing trips. ✉ *Av. Lucio Costa, Botafogo* ☎ *21/96423-9366* ⊕ *rioadventures.com* Ⓜ *Botafogo.*

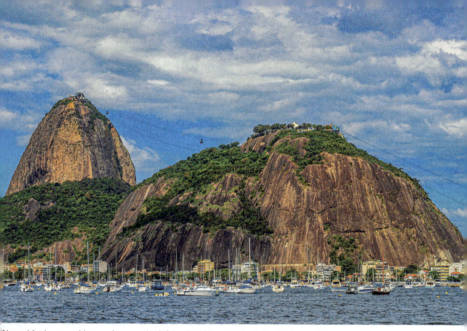

Named for its resemblance of a sugar loaf, Sugarloaf Mountain in Rio is about 600 million years old.

Urca

Tiny sheltered Urca is home to one of Rio's most famous attractions, the *Pão de Açúcar morro* (Sugarloaf Mountain). As tranquil and bucolic as the rest of Rio is fast-paced and frenetic, Urca is a wonderful place for an afternoon's wandering. Fishing boats bob on a bay set against a spectacular view of Christ the Redeemer on his mountaintop perch, and the neighborhood contains some wonderful colonial architecture. The Pão de Açúcar separates Urca's tree-lined streets from Praia Vermelha, its small, coarse-sand beach. This beach is, in turn, blocked by the Urubu and Leme mountains from the 1-km (½-mile) Leme Beach at the start of the Zona Sul.

Urca is a little tricky to reach by public transport, so take a cab from Botafogo metro station. Come here in the morning and spend some time on the beaches. Take the pleasant 30-minute nature walk around the base of Sugarloaf and aim to be at the cable car station late afternoon to appreciate the stunning sunset views from the peak. Round off a perfect day by sipping a caipirinha by the harbor wall at Bar e Restaurante Urca.

◉ Sights

★ **Pão de Açúcar** (*Sugarloaf Mountain*)
MOUNTAIN | FAMILY | The indigenous Tupi people originally called the soaring 396-meter (1,300-foot) granite block at the mouth of Baía de Guanabara *pau-nh-acugua* (high, pointed peak). To the Portuguese the phrase seemed similar to *pão de açúcar,* itself fitting because the rock's shape reminded them of the conical loaves in which refined sugar were sold. Italian-made bubble cars holding 75 passengers each move up the mountain in two stages. The first stop is at Morro da Urca, a smaller, 212-meter (705-foot) mountain; the second is at the summit of Pão de Açúcar. The trip to each level takes three minutes. In high season long lines form for the cable car; the rest of the year the wait is seldom more than 30

minutes. Consider visiting Pão de Açúcar before climbing the considerably higher Corcovado—as breathtaking as the view is, it may seem anticlimactic if experienced second. There are special deals to have breakfast and see the sunrise at the mountain. On the Friday and Saturday sunsets, there is a DJ playing to keep the vibe chilling. ⊠ *Av. Pasteur 520, Urca* ☎ *21/2546–8400* ⊕ *www.bondinho.com.br* 🎫 *R$185*.

Beaches

Praia Vermelha

BEACH | FAMILY | Right at the foot of Sugarloaf, this sheltered, rough-sand beach (the name means "red beach," a reference to the distinctive coarse sand here) is one of the safest places in the city for sunbathing thanks to its location next to a military base. Frequented more by local families than by tourists, and with only a few vendors, Praia Vermelha is a tranquil spot to catch some rays. The water here is calm, but it's often too dirty for swimming. **Amenities:** food and drink. **Best for:** sunset. ⊠ *Praça General Tibúrcio, Urca*.

🍴 Restaurants

Bar e Restaurante Urca

$ | BRAZILIAN | While you can dine indoors in this relaxed spot, make like the locals and enjoy a snack alfresco, propped against the harbor wall across the street: the sea wall doubles as a makeshift table, and waiters run to and fro delivering orders of ice-cold beer and deep-fried *salgadinhos* (seafood snacks). You'll have a stunning backdrop to your light meal—the panorama takes in bobbing boats, framed by a clear view of Christ the Redeemer. **Known for:** fried shrimp pastries; fish soup; bolinhos de bacalhau (salted cod balls). ⑤ *Average main: R$38* ⊠ *Rua Cândido Gaffrée 205, Urca* ☎ *21/2295–8744* ⊕ *www.barurca.com.br* ⊗ *No dinner Sun*.

Copacabana

Copacabana is Rio's most famous tourist neighborhood thanks to its fabulous beach and grande-dame hotels such as the Copacabana Palace. The main thoroughfare is Avenida Nossa Senhora de Copacabana, two blocks inland from the beach. The commercial street is filled with shops, restaurants, and sidewalks crowded with colorful characters. Despite having some of the best hotels in Rio, Copacabana's heyday is over, and the neighborhood is grittier than Ipanema or Leblon. It's no secret to thieves that tourists congregate here, so keep your eyes peeled for shady types when walking around after dark⇨. The beach is the main attraction and is served by three metro stations. Cardeal Arcoverde is the closest to Leme, the quieter, family-oriented end of the beach, Siqueira Campos is right at the center, and Cantagalo is within walking distance of Ipanema. Plan to spend the better part of a day here, buying food and drink from beach vendors or the many kiosks that line the sidewalk.

Sights

Forte de Copacabana and Museu Histórico do Exército

MILITARY SIGHT | FAMILY | Copacabana Fort was built in 1914 as part of Rio's first line of defense, and many original features, such as the thick brick fortification and old Krupp cannons, are still visible. In the '60s and '70s, during Brazil's military dictatorship, political prisoners were kept here. The fort is impressive and the entrance archway perfectly frames a postcard view of Sugarloaf. The best views, however, follow the path to its end and climb the steep stairs to the cannon roof, which juts right out into the ocean and takes in sweeping vistas over the Zona Sul beaches. The on-site military history museum is worth a stop, and there are two good cafés here as well as a gift shop. During the Brazilian summer, violin recitals, classical music performances, and outdoor cinema screenings are held here, many free of charge. ✉ *Praça Coronel Eugênio Franco 1, Copacabana* ☎ *21/2522–4460* ⊕ *www.fortedecopacabana.com* 🎫 *R$6 (free on Tues.)* 🕙 *Closed Mon.* Ⓜ *Cantagalo.*

Beaches

Praia do Leme

BEACH | FAMILY | Leme Beach is a natural extension of Copacabana Beach to the northeast, toward Pão de Açúcar (Sugarloaf). A rock formation juts into the water here, forming a quiet cove that's less crowded than the rest of the beach. This is a top spot for families, and small wading pools can be rented along with the usual beach chairs and sun umbrellas at the many *barracas* (beach tents selling food and drink). Along a sidewalk, at the side of the mountain overlooking Leme, anglers stand elbow to elbow with their lines dangling into the sea. Many locals swim here, but be wary of the strong undertow, and never head into the water when the red flag is displayed on the beach. **Amenities:** food and drink; toilets; showers; lifeguards. **Best for:** walking; sunset. ✉ *From Av. Princesa Isabel to Morro do Leme, Leme* Ⓜ *Cardeal Arcoverde.*

★ Praia de Copacabana

BEACH | Maddening traffic, noise, packed apartment blocks, and a world-famous beach—this is Copacabana, or, Manhattan with bikinis. Walk along the neighborhood's classic crescent to dive headfirst into Rio's beach culture, a cradle-to-grave lifestyle that begins with toddlers accompanying their parents to the water and ends with silver-haired seniors walking hand in hand along the sidewalk. Copacabana hums with activity: you're likely to see athletic men playing volleyball using only their feet and heads, not their hands—a sport Brazilians have dubbed futevôlei. Soccer is also popular, and Copacabana has been a frequent host to the annual world beach soccer championships. You can swim here, although pollution levels and a strong undertow can sometimes be discouraging. Pollution levels change daily and are well publicized; someone at your hotel should be able to get you the information.

Copacabana's privileged live on beachfront Avenida Atlântica, famed for its wide mosaic sidewalks designed by Roberto Burle Marx, and for its grand hotels—including the Copacabana Palace Hotel—and cafés with sidewalk seating. On Sunday two of the avenue's lanes are closed to traffic and are taken over by joggers, rollerbladers, cyclists, and pedestrians. **Amenities:** food and drink; lifeguards; showers; toilets. **Best for:** sunset; walking. ✉ *Av. Princesa Isabel to Rua Francisco Otaviano, Copacabana* Ⓜ *Cardeal Arcoverde, Siqueira Campos, and Cantagalo.*

Praia do Diabo

BEACH | A barely noticeable stretch of sand tucked away between Arpoador and a natural rock wall that extends to Copacabana's fort, Praia do Diabo is popular with local *surfistas* (surfers) but the dangerous waves, which can smash an unskilled surfer into the nearby rocks, leave no mystery as to why this beach is called the Devil's Beach in Portuguese. Take advantage of the exercise bars, and watch the sunrise while from Arpoador rock, but stay out of the water unless you are a very experienced surfer. Toilets and showers can be found at nearby Arpoador and Copacabana. **Amenities:** none. **Best for:** surfing. ✉ *Between Arpoador rock and Copacabana Fort, Copacabana* Ⓜ *Ipanema/General Osório.*

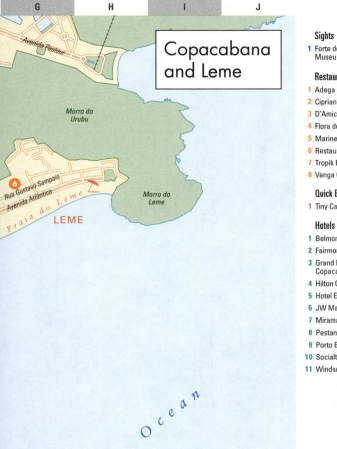

Copacabana and Leme

Sights ▼
1 Forte de Copacabana and Museu Histórico do Exército......C7

Restaurants ▼
1 Adega Pérola......................C3
2 Cipriani............................E4
3 D'Amici............................F3
4 Flora de Copa C6
5 Marine Restô....................C7
6 Restaurante Shirley G3
7 Tropik Beach Club C7
8 Venga Chiringuito.................C7

Quick Bites ▼
1 Tiny Cat Café E3

Hotels ▼
1 Belmond Copacabana Palace E4
2 Fairmont Copacabana.............C7
3 Grand Mercure Rio de Janeiro Copacabana......................C7
4 Hilton Copacabana F3
5 Hotel Emiliano....................C7
6 JW Marriott Rio de Janeiro D5
7 Miramar Hotel by Windsor C6
8 Pestana Rio Atlântica C5
9 Porto Bay Rio Internacional.......E3
10 Socialtel Copacabana.............C6
11 Windsor Excelsior E4

KEY
- Sights
- Restaurants
- Quick Bites
- Hotels

Did You Know?

Copacabana comes from the Quechua word copa caguana, which means "luminous place." The gorgeous beach is dotted with beach kiosks and is close to many of the main sights of Rio de Janeiro.

🍴 Restaurants

Adega Pérola

$ | **PORTUGUESE** | One of the most authentic botequim (traditional bar) experiences in Rio is this hole-in-the-wall kitchen serving up tasty Portuguese-style tapas to shared tables and a long deli-bar where regulars crowd after dark. While the staff's English is limited, the service and general atmosphere—vintage prints and liters of wine lining the walls—is so warm and welcoming that you will barely notice. **Known for:** friendly local atmosphere; strong flavors, including generous helpings of marinated garlic cloves; the calamari. ⑤ *Average main: R$45* ✉ *Rua Siqueira Campos 138, Copacabana* ☎ *21/2255–9425* ⊕ *www.instagram.com/adegaperola/* ⊘ *Closed Sun.* Ⓜ *Siqueira Campos.*

Cipriani

$$$$ | **ITALIAN** | The most lavish of Copacabana Palace's three restaurants is this homage to Northern Italian cooking, set overlooking the enormous swimming pool and replete in soft lighting, velvet chairs, and impeccable staff. This contender for the most formal restaurant in Rio has changed their menu into a tasting menu with a vegan option. **Known for:** homemade gnocchi with lobster; impeccable fine dining contrasted by bikini bathers by the pool; live pianist. ⑤ *Average main: R$575* ✉ *Copacabana Palace Hotel, Av. Atlântica 1702, Copacabana* ☎ *21/2545–8747* ⊕ *www.belmond.com* ⊘ *Closed Sun.; no lunch* Ⓜ *Cardeal Arcoverde.*

★ Marine Restô

$ | **BARBECUE** | French chef Jerome Dardillac was inspired by his travels to Amazonas, Minas Gerais, and Bahia to create a menu that introduces Brazil to an international audience. The portions are generous and can easily be shared, giving you the opportunity to try a little bit of everything. **Known for:** view of Copacabana beach; grilled meat and vegetables (brasserie concept); breakfast open to nonguests. ⑤ *Average main: R$120* ✉ *Av. Atlântica 4240, Copacabana* ⊕ *fairmontrio.com/marine-resto/* Ⓜ *General Osório.*

★ Tropik Beach Club

$ | **MEDITERRANEAN** | The beach club located at Posto 6 on Copacabana beach brings a bit of the Mediterranean atmosphere to Rio de Janeiro. Locals and visitors can enjoy the space that offers all meals, from breakfast to post-beach drinks. **Known for:** roasted fish dumpling with coriander mayonnaise; tropical drinks; skewers—meat, shrimp, chicken, or cheese. ⑤ *Average main: R$50* ✉ *Posto 6, Copacabana* ✛ *close to Rua Rainha Elizabeth* ⊕ *fairmontrio.com/tropik/* Ⓜ *General Osório.*

Venga Chiringuito

$ | **SPANISH** | This contemporary Spanish *chiringuito* is always packed, thanks to its vibrant vibe and prime beachfront location overlooking Copacabana's Posto 5. Opt for one of the alfresco tables and feast on top-quality tapas, plates of high-class charcuterie and rich seafood rices washed down with big jugs of tropical fruit *cleriquot* (a South American

---

Dining Tips

Some restaurants in Rio serve a *couvert* (a little something to nibble), usually bread, olives, or another type of munchie. The couvert is not free. If you don't want to pay for it, just hand it to your waiter. An "artistic" cover charge of around R$20 is usually applied when there's live music. Also, restaurants will include a 10% service charge, only half of which is distributed among the restaurant staff. Feel free to leave a little extra on the table for your server, but this is by no means obligatory.

champagne punch); there are sister locations in Leblon and Ipanema. **Known for:** fun, local atmosphere; the salted dark chocolate mousse; black squid ink rice. $ *Average main: R$50* ⊠ *Av. Atlântica 3880, Copacabana* ☎ *21/3264–9806* ⊕ *www.venga.com.br.*

☕ Coffee and Quick Bites

Tiny Cat Café
$ | **CAFÉ** | **FAMILY** | Cat lovers and coffee lovers will find their meeting point here. Tiny Cat Café has food and drinks on its menu that are reminiscent of feline friends. **Known for:** good place for remote work; cat decoration; coffee blends. $ *Average main: R$35* ⊠ *Av. Nossa Sra. de Copacabana 308, Copacabana* ⊕ *www.tinycatcafe.com.br/* Ⓜ *Cardeal Arcoverde.*

Hotels

Belmond Copacabana Palace
$$$$ | **HOTEL** | Built in 1923 for the visiting king of Belgium and inspired by Nice's Negresco and Cannes's Carlton, Copacabana Palace was the first luxury hotel in South America, and it's still one of the top hotels on the continent. **Pros:** historic landmark; front-facing rooms have spectacular ocean views; great on-site restaurants. **Cons:** area is a little seedy at night; need to take taxis to best bars and restaurants; "city view" rooms have poor views of backstreets. $ *Rooms from: R$4200* ⊠ *Av. Atlântica 1702, Copacabana* ☎ *21/2548–7070* ⊕ *www.copacabanapalace.com.br* ⇌ *245 rooms* ⫞⊙⫝ *Free Breakfast* Ⓜ *Cardeal Arcoverde.*

★ Fairmont Copacabana
$$$$ | **HOTEL** | Located almost on the border between Copacabana and Ipanema, the Fairmont Copacabana is housed in a historic building that has hosted many other luxury hotel brands in the past. **Pros:** view of most of Copacabana beach; walkable to Ipanema; quality of service. **Cons:** location can be crowded in some periods of the year; busy restaurants all day long; some rooms smell moldy. $ *Rooms from: R$2,000* ⊠ *Av. Atlântica 4240, Copacabana* ☎ *21/2525–1232* ⊕ *fairmontrio.com* ⇌ *375 rooms* ⫞⊙⫝ *No Meals* Ⓜ *General Osório.*

Grand Mercure Rio de Janeiro Copacabana
$$$ | **HOTEL** | The excellent location in front of Copacabana Beach is this hotel's main draw. **Pros:** generous breakfast; small but well-equipped gym; rooftop pool. **Cons:** south-facing rooms have poor view; Copacabana isn't the safest area; impersonal feel. $ *Rooms from: R$737* ⊠ *Av. Atlântica 3716, Copacabana* ☎ *21/3545–5400, 21/3545–5445 reservations* ⊕ *www.accorhotels.com* ⇌ *230 rooms* ⫞⊙⫝ *No Meals* Ⓜ *Cantagalo.*

Hilton Copacabana
$$$$ | **HOTEL** | **FAMILY** | With 360° views from the tallest building on Copacabana Beach, since 2017 the Hilton Copacabana has been one of the largest Hilton properties in the region and the company's 100th hotel in Latin America. **Pros:** rooftop view to all Copacabana beach; walking distance to a quieter beach; notable breakfast. **Cons:** not walking distance to subway; can be noisy; rooms are slightly dated. $ *Rooms from: R$1,300* ⊠ *Av. Atlântica 1020, Leme* ☎ *21/3501–8000*

Alternative Housing

Rio has accommodations to suit virtually every taste and wallet. There are plenty of self-catering options for those who value their own space over hotel luxury, and there are agencies that specialize in everything from luxury Ipanema penthouses to pokey Copacabana digs. Airbnb also offers a wide variety of unique, well-priced options for all sizes and budgets.

⊕ *www.hiltoncopacabana.com* ⇌ *545 rooms* ¶⊘ *No Meals* Ⓜ *Cardeal Arcoverde.*

★ Hotel Emiliano

$$$$ | **HOTEL** | **FAMILY** | When this strikingly chic beachfront hotel opened, it quietly raised the bar in Rio's hospitality scene with a level of attentiveness unmatched across the city. **Pros:** impeccable design; personalized service includes room butlers; wonderful spa and great gym. **Cons:** Copacabana location is less sophisticated than Ipanema; striking exterior can be misleading to the level of luxury inside; bathrooms sacrifice some functionality in the name of design. ⓢ *Rooms from: R$3,400* ⊠ *Av. Atlântica 3804, Copacabana* ☎ *21/3503–6600* ⊕ *emiliano.com.br* ⇌ *90 rooms* ¶⊘ *Free Breakfast* Ⓜ *Cantagalo.*

JW Marriott Rio de Janeiro

$$$$ | **HOTEL** | You could be walking into a Marriott anywhere in the world, which is a comfort for some and a curse for others. **Pros:** close to beach; efficient service; bountiful breakfast. **Cons:** expensive extras like Wi-Fi; front-facing rooms can be noisy; tired swimming pool area. ⓢ *Rooms from: R$1,900* ⊠ *Av. Atlântica 2600, Copacabana* ☎ *21/2545–6500* ⊕ *www.marriott.com* ⇌ *245 rooms* ¶⊘ *Free Breakfast* Ⓜ *Siqueira Campos.*

Miramar Hotel by Windsor

$$$ | **HOTEL** | **FAMILY** | With a prime beachfront location, this classic Copacabana hotel underwent a complete face-lift and is now one of the neighborhood's best hotels. **Pros:** great service; beach towels, chairs, and sunshades are free; great on-site restaurant from highly-rated chef Paulo Góes. **Cons:** small pool and gym; can feel busy; windows cannot be opened by guests. ⓢ *Rooms from: R$800* ⊠ *Av. Atlântica 3668, Copacabana* ☎ *21/2195–6200* ⊕ *www.windsorhoteis.com* ⇌ *200 rooms* ¶⊘ *Free Breakfast* Ⓜ *Cantagalo.*

Bar Talk

A few useful Portuguese words under your belt will make the bar experience even more enjoyable and help you feel like a local. Chopp is the ubiquitous draft beer served in small glasses, while *cerveja* is the universal word for bottled beer. A simple *mais uma* will get you "one more," and a *saideira* will get you "one for the road." Finally, ask for *a conta* or "the bill" when you want to settle your tab.

Pestana Rio Atlântica

$$$ | **HOTEL** | This well-located hotel offers friendly service, a solid breakfast, and a good location opposite Copacabana Beach. **Pros:** good value for the area; rooftop pool; good beachfront location. **Cons:** parts of the hotel feel tired; impersonal lobby and communal areas; unrelaxed atmosphere. ⓢ *Rooms from: R$819* ⊠ *Av. Atlântica 2964, Copacabana* ☎ *21/3816–8500* ⊕ *www.pestana.com* ⇌ *214 rooms* ¶⊘ *Free Breakfast* Ⓜ *Cantagalo.*

★ Porto Bay Rio Internacional

$$$ | **HOTEL** | **FAMILY** | One of the stars of Copacabana's midrange hotels, this beachfront property combines beautiful rooms—all have balconies with sea views—with a great rooftop pool and charming, attentive staff. **Pros:** excellent service; good views; great in-house restaurant. **Cons:** some rooms quite small; Copacabana not as safe as Ipanema after dark; small gym. ⓢ *Rooms from: R$848* ⊠ *Av. Atlântica 1500, Copacabana* ☎ *21/2546–8000* ⊕ *www.portobay.com* ⇌ *128 rooms* ¶⊘ *Free Breakfast* Ⓜ *Cardeal Arcoverde.*

Socialtel Copacabana

$$$ | **HOTEL** | **FAMILY** | For those who no longer feel comfortable sharing a room with strangers but would like to meet

other travelers, the Socialtel chain offers a relaxed atmosphere in its facilities, overlooking Copacabana beach. **Pros:** beachfront hotel with a better rate; great way to meet other travelers; WhatsApp list to share events and tips. **Cons:** gets very crowded on dates like Carnival or New Years; the better breakfast place is not included with the fare; can be noisy in high season. ⑤ *Rooms from: R$400* ✉ *Rua Almirante Gonçalves 5, Copacabana* ☎ *21/98194–8941* ⊕ *www.socialtel.com* ⇨ *113 rooms* ⏧ *Free Breakfast* Ⓜ *Cantagalo / Copacabana.*

Windsor Excelsior
$$$ | **HOTEL** | This beachfront hotel may have been built in the 1950s, but its look is sleek and contemporary—from the sparkling marble lobby to the guest room closets paneled in gleaming Brazilian redwood. **Pros:** top-notch service; rooftop pool; expansive buffets for all meals. **Cons:** slightly impersonal chain feel; busy street can be dangerous at night; team not well trained. ⑤ *Rooms from: R$660* ✉ *Av. Atlântica 1800, Copacabana* ☎ *21/2195–5800* ⊕ *www.windsorhoteis.com.br* ⇨ *233 rooms* ⏧ *Free Breakfast* Ⓜ *Cardeal Arcoverde.*

Nightlife

BARS
★ Bip Bip
LIVE MUSIC | Here the *roda de samba*—where musicians sit and play instruments around a central table (in fact the only table in this tiny bar)—is legendary, as is the help-yourself beer policy. The no-nonsense owner makes drink notations and keeps the crowd in check. The standards of the music here are as high as the bar is simple: big-name Brazilian musicians have been known to drop in for a jam session, and on weekend evenings the revelry often spills out onto the street. ✉ *Rua Almirante Gonçalves 50, Copacabana* ☎ *21/2267–9696* ⊕ *www.instagram.com/rodadobip/* ⊗ *Closed Mon. and Sat.* Ⓜ *Cantagalo.*

New Year's Eve in Rio

Rio's New Year's celebration, or *Réveillon* as it's known in Brazil, is a whirling dervish of a party in which an estimated 3 million people truck over to Copacabana for drinks, dancing, and a spectacular fireworks show over the water. A word of warning: stay away from the stage. The area immediately surrounding the temporary stage on the beach becomes packed with people, and you run the risk of getting pickpocketed. Plan your hotel stay months in advance and be prepared to pay more. Prices at least double and rooms fill quickly.

★ Spirit Copa
LOUNGES | Fans of fine cocktails will find a seaside retreat at Spirit Copa, where they can enjoy Brazilian flavors in revisited classic drinks. The food menu includes snacks and tapas to enjoy while enjoying the view. Nonguests can also enjoy the bar inside Fairmont Copacabana hotel but it's better to make a reservation beforehand to secure a table. Some days of the week the bar offers free live music, mostly bossa nova. ✉ *Av. Atlântica 4240, Copacabana* ☎ *21/2525–1232* ⊕ *fairmontrio.com/spirit-copa/* Ⓜ *General Osório.*

NIGHTCLUBS AND LIVE MUSIC
Blue Note Rio
LIVE MUSIC | The iconic Blue Note has opened a branch in one of the most musical cities in the world, the birthplace of bossa nova. Every week, big names in Brazilian and international music perform in concerts. Check the updated schedule on the website before you go. The bar also participates in special events in the city, such as the LGBTQ+ parade and New Year's Eve, selling VIP seats. ✉ *Av.*

Atlantica 1910, Copacabana ⊕ bluenoterio.com.br/ Ⓜ Cardeal Arcoverde.

Shopping

SHOPPING CENTERS AND MALLS
Shopping Center Cassino Atlântico
ANTIQUES & COLLECTIBLES | Antiques shops, jewelry stores, art galleries, and souvenir outlets predominate at this mall. There is also a good flea market on Sunday. ✉ *Av. Atlântica, 4240, Copacabana* ☎ *021/2523–8709* ⊕ *shoppingcassinoatlantico.com.br/* Ⓜ *Ipanema/General Osorio.*

SURF AND EXTREME SPORTS GEAR
Galeria River
SPORTING GOODS | Stores at this youth-focused arcade sell all the clothing and equipment you'll need for a surfing or sporting vacation, as well as gear for climbing, rappelling, and other extreme sports. ✉ *Rua Francisco Otaviano 67, Copacabana* ☎ *21/2267–1709* ⊕ *www.galeriariver.com.br* Ⓜ *Ipanema/General Osório.*

🎬 Performing Arts

SAMBA SHOWS
Roxy Dinner Show
DINNER THEATER | Brazil is well-known by its music and rhythm, and many come to Rio de Janeiro looking for a place to listen to samba and bossa nova. Historical Movie Theater Roxy in Copacabana was restored and turned into a music hall, with music shows and dinner in one package. Tickets include a bossa nova opening act and a main show with a trip around Brazilian musical traditions for four hours. The event finishes by turning into a big party, gathering artists and audience. ✉ *Av. Nossa Senhora de Copacabana 945, Copacabana* ⊕ *www.roxydinnershow.com.br/* 🕙 *Closed Mon. and Tues.* ☞ *Admission from R$580* Ⓜ *Cantagalo.*

Leme

 Restaurants

D'Amici
$$$$ | **ITALIAN** | A world away from the touristy restaurants that line Copacabana's beachfront, this refined Italian restaurant is easily overlooked but well worth seeking out. The menu celebrates Italy's diverse regional cuisines, including wonderful homemade pastas, quality meats, and delicious desserts. **Known for:** fish-stuffed ravioli with saffron and shrimp sauce; delicious desserts like tiramisu; elegant interiors. 💲 *Average main: R$83* ✉ *Rua Antônio Vieira 18, Leme* ☎ *21/2541–4477* ⊕ *damici.com.br/* Ⓜ *Cardeal Arcoverde.*

Restaurante Shirley
$$$$ | **SPANISH** | Traditional Spanish seafood casseroles are a strong suit at this small restaurant on a shady street, which has been attracting locals for more than 70 years. The waiters, clad in white suits, add to the nostalgic 70's atmosphere. **Known for:** seafood paella; friendly, attentive service; traditional atmosphere. 💲 *Average main: R$115.80* ✉ *Rua Gustavo Sampaio 610, Loja A, Leme* ☎ *21/2275–1398* ⊕ *www.instagram.com/restauranteshirley/* Ⓜ *Cardeal Arcoverde.*

Santa Teresa and Lapa

With its cobblestone streets and bohemian atmosphere, Santa Teresa is a delightfully eccentric neighborhood. Gabled Victorian mansions sit beside alpine-style chalets as well as more prosaic dwellings—many hanging at unbelievable angles from the flower-encrusted hills. Cafés, galleries, and antique shops have nudged their way into nooks and crannies between the colorful homes, many of which house artists and their studios. Downhill from Santa Teresa, Lapa has some of the oldest buildings in the city and is home to the imposing Arcos da Lapa (Lapa Aqueduct) and the colorful Escadaria Selarón, also called the Lapa Steps, as well as the city's oldest street, the café-paved Rua do Lavradio. By night, Lapa is transformed into the party heart of Rio, with countless bars and clubs and a notoriously wild weekend street party.

Santa Teresa and Lapa merit a full day's exploring, and Santa Teresa is at its bohemian best from Thursday through Saturday—many bars and restaurants don't open early in the week. Take the metro to Carioca metro station and stroll past the towering cubic Petrobras building to Rua do Lavradio to browse the antiques stores and sidewalk cafés. From here, the Lapa Steps and Lapa Aqueduct are a quick stroll, or take the bone-rattling cab ride up the cobbled steps. Jump off at Largo do Guimaraes and prepare to spend a few hours admiring the architecture, galleries, and museums and enjoying the café culture here. The area is best seen on foot but avoid deserted streets. If it's a weekend or holiday, make a night of it by starting with drinks in one of Santa Teresa's many lively bars before taking a cab or bus down to the Lapa street party around midnight.

 Sights

Arcos da Lapa

TRANSPORTATION | Formerly the Aqueduto da Carioca (Carioca Aqueduct), this structure with 42 massive stone arches was built between 1744 and 1750 to carry water from the Carioca River in the hillside neighborhood of Santa Teresa to Centro. In 1896 the city transportation company converted the aqueduct, by then abandoned, into a viaduct, laying trolley tracks along it. For decades, Santa Teresa's rattling yellow street cars (the *bonde* or *bondinho*) passed over the aqueduct as they carried passengers from Centro up to the hillside neighborhood of Santa Teresa. The historic bonde underwent extensive upgrades to improve its quality and safety in time for the 2016 Olympics. ✉ *Rua Lélio Gama 2, Lapa* ✢ *Estação Carioca* ⊕ *www.rj.gov.br/bondesdesantateresa/* ✉ *R$20* Ⓜ *Carioca*.

★ Escadaria Selarón (*Lapa Steps*)

NOTABLE BUILDING | After traveling the world and living in more than 50 countries, Chilean painter Selarón began working in 1990 on the iconic tile staircase that is now one of the highlights of Lapa. With tiles from around the world, Selarón's staircase is the product of years of dedication, artistic vision, and donations of tiles from places far and near. Sadly, in 2013 Selarón was found murdered at his nearby home. The colorful stairs provide a great photo opportunity—Snoop Dogg and Pharell Williams shot the video for their song "Beautiful" here. ✉ *Escadaria Selarón 24, Lapa*.

Largo do Guimarães (*Guimarães Square*)

PLAZA/SQUARE | Much of the activity in close-knit Santa Teresa takes place around its village-like squares, among them Largo do Guimarães, a social hub that frequently hosts street parties. The informal restaurant Bar do Arnaudo is popular with locals; the neighborhood's main drinking and dining strip spans out from here. On weekends, live music spills out from bars opening onto the square, and street vendors sell beer and caipirinhas. If you follow the tram track 1.2 km (¾ mile) northwest from here you'll come to **Largo das Neves** (Neves Square), with its picturesque, whitewashed church. Families and other locals gather in this square until late at night. ✉ *Rua Paschoal Carlos Magno, Ladeira do Castro, and Rua Almirante Alexandrino, Santa Teresa*.

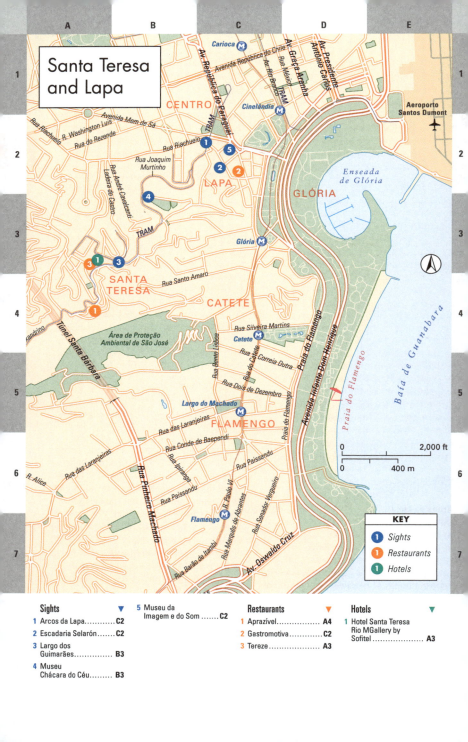

Museu Chácara do Céu

ART MUSEUM | The collection of mostly modern works at this museum was left—along with the hilltop house that contains it—by one of Rio's greatest arts patrons, Raymundo de Castro Maya. Included are originals by 20th-century masters Picasso, Braque, Dalí, Degas, Matisse, Modigliani, and Monet. The Brazilian holdings include priceless 17th- and 18th-century maps and works by leading modernists. The views of the aqueduct, Centro, and the bay are splendid from the museum's grounds. The adjoining Parque das Ruinas (free) is well worth a visit, too, and has some spectacular views from the top floor of a once-abandoned colonial mansion. ✉ *Rua Murtinho Nobre 93, Santa Teresa* ☎ *21/3970–1093* ⊕ *www.museuscastromaya.com.br/chacara.htm* 💵 *R$8; free Wed.* ⊗ *Closed Tues.*

Museu da Imagem e do Som

ARTS CENTER | The first audiovisual museum in Brazil, the Museum of Image and Sound (MIS) was founded to acquire, preserve, and exhibit important collections tied to Rio's cultural history. The museum houses collections of images and sound in a range of mediums, including engravings, drawings, caricatures, musical instruments, photographs, books, discs, recordings, and even antique gramophones, microphones, and musical instruments. The collections highlight the works of many of Rio's lesser-known names of the past, such as the Batista sisters of Brazil's Golden Age of Radio, and Elizeth Cardoso, considered to be one of the greatest female singers of Brazilian popular music. ✉ *Rua Visconde de Maranguape 15, Lapa* ☎ *21/2332–9520* ⊕ *www.mis.rj.gov.br* 💵 *Free* ⊗ *Closed Mon. and Tues.*

🍴 Restaurants

★ Aprazível

$$$$ | **BRAZILIAN** | **FAMILY** | A lantern-lit tropical garden filled with exotic plants, monkeys, and birds is the spectacular setting for this family restaurant serving pan-Brazilian dishes and an exciting selection of Brazilian wines. The owner and chef, Ana Castilha, hails from Minas Gerais but received her formal training at New York City's French Culinary Institute. **Known for:** sustainable dishes with a French twist like grilled palm heart with cashew pesto; the Tangemahall (a mint and tangerine caipirinha); the handful of tables set in private tree houses. 💲 *Average main: R$80* ✉ *Rua Aprazível 62, Santa Teresa* ☎ *21/2508–9174* ⊕ *www.aprazivel.com.br* ⊗ *Closed Mon.; no dinner Sun.*

Gastromotiva

$ | **BRAZILIAN** | Created by chefs Massimo Bottura and David Hertz, the restaurant school aims to train professionals and serve the homeless population in downtown Rio. The lunches prepared by renowned chefs and sold to the general public fund dinners for the homeless. **Known for:** restaurant with a social purpose; renowned chefs; feeds the homeless at night. 💲 *Average main: R$45* ✉ *Rua da Lapa 108, Lapa* ⊕ *www.instagram.com/refettoriogastromotiva/* ⊗ *Closed weekends* ⌖ *No dinner* Ⓜ *Cinelândia.*

★ Tereze

$$$$ | **INTERNATIONAL** | Located in the Santa Teresa MGallery Hotel, the restaurant offers an international menu with a touch of Brazilian cuisine. Chef Luanna Malheiros brings to the menu all her experience in several French and Brazilian restaurants. **Known for:** desserts made with Brazilian fruits; French-Brazilian cuisine. 💲 *Average main: R$130* ✉ *Rua Felicio dos Santos, 15, Santa Teresa* ☎ *21/3380–0259* ⊕ *www.santateresahotelrio.com/pt-br/tereze/* Ⓜ *Carioca.*

Hotels

★ Hotel Santa Teresa Rio MGallery by Sofitel
$$$$ | **HOTEL** | This five-star hotel, located in the historic hilltop neighborhood of Santa Teresa, is housed in a regenerated coffee plantation mansion that pays homage to Brazil's cultures and traditions with folk art and handicrafts from across the nation; the location is an ideal area for travelers keen to discover Rio's artistic side. **Pros:** activities for guests; fabulous jungle pool; close to Santa Teresa's drinking and dining scene. **Cons:** it's a cab ride to the beach; hotel bar sometimes closed for private events; limited access by public transportation. $ *Rooms from: R$1,100* ⊠ *Rua Almirante Alexandrino 660, Santa Teresa* ☎ *21/3380-0204* ⊕ *www.santateresahotelrio.com* ⇌ *43 rooms* ⫟◎⫟ *No Meals.*

 Nightlife

BARS
★ Bar do Gomez
BARS | Officially Armazem São Thiago, this neighborhood institution is universally referred to by its nickname, Bar do Gomez, in honor of the late owner whose family has run the business for close to 100 years. Pictures documenting the bar's history adorn the high wooden walls, and surveying the scene in the present, you get the pleasant impression that little has changed over the years. The draft beer flows like water, locals swap stories at the long wooden bar, and new friendships are forged at the outdoor drinking posts. Favorites among the bar snacks include the giant olives, a pastrami sandwich, and the shrimp plate. Early on a Friday night, this is a good place to strike up a conversation with locals before heading down the hill to Lapa. ⊠ *Rua Aurea 22, Santa Teresa* ☎ *21/2232-0822* ⊕ *armazemsaothiago.com.*

Bar do Mineiro
BARS | The liveliest of Santa Teresa's many drinking dens and the hub of much social activity, this enduringly popular boteco anchors one end of the neighborhood's main drinking and dining strip. Some excellent snacks are served here—the *pasteis de feijão* (fried pastries filled with black beans) being a firm favorite with locals—as well as hearty plates of meat-based *comida mineira* (cuisine from Minas Gerais State). A street party atmosphere prevails on Sunday afternoon, when the bar is standing room only and revelers spill out onto the road outside. ⊠ *Rua Paschoal Carlos Magno 99, Santa Teresa* ☎ *21/2221-9227* ⊕ *www.bardomineiro.net.*

Mangue Seco Cachaçaria
BARS | Specializing in some of Brazil's finest institutions—strong and fine-tasting cachaças (Brazilian rum), mouthwatering *moquecas* (stews), and, of course, live samba—Mangue Seco's location on the popular Rua do Lavradio makes it a perfect place to start a night out. Arrive at sundown, grab one of the sidewalk tables, and watch Lapa life unfold as you sip a caipirinha and browse the menu. ⊠ *Rua do Lavradio 23, Lapa* ☎ *21/3852-1947* ⊕ *www.instagram.com/manguesecocachacaria/* ⊘ *Closed Sun.*

NIGHTCLUBS AND LIVE MUSIC
Beco do Rato
LIVE MUSIC | This little corner of Lapa brings together the city's best samba musicians in groups that go on all night long. Wear comfortable clothes and be prepared to spend hours standing and enjoying the music. Check the website for the monthly schedule and buy your ticket in advance. ⊠ *Rua Joaquim Silva 11, Lapa* ☎ *21/97968-3670* ⊕ *becodorato.com.br/* Ⓜ *Cinelândia.*

★ Carioca da Gema
LIVE MUSIC | A favorite among local *sambistas* (samba musicians) and a great spot to listen to live samba in a comfortable environment, Carioca da Gema is one of

Did You Know?

The 215 steps of Escadaria Selarón are covered with 2,000 tiles from more than 60 countries around the world.

What's Your Beach Style?

To Cariocas, where you hang out on the beach says a lot about you. Each of Rio's beaches has its own style, and the longer stretches of sand are themselves informally divided according to social groupings and lifestyles. There are sections of beach for singles, families, sporty types, and those looking for a quiet time. Cariocas who choose to bronze their bodies at Ipanema are generally considered to be more chic than those who catch their rays at Copacabana, with Ipanema's Posto Nove (lifeguard post 9) the hangout of choice for a young, fashionable crowd. Nearby, a vast rainbow flag in front of Rua Farme do Amoeda marks Ipanema Beach's gay and lesbian section. Families and beachgoers who prefer working on their tans to making new friends, on the other hand, largely populate Leblon Beach.

Wherever you choose to make your beach base, note that bringing along a beach towel constitutes a social faux pas. Women should equip themselves with a colorful sarong, and men are expected to remain either standing or engaged in sporting activity.

Lapa's liveliest spots, with talented musicians performing seven nights a week. By 11 pm, finding a place to stand can be difficult, but regulars still find a way to samba. Call ahead and book a table if you're keener to be a spectator. There's a good pizzeria downstairs.

■ TIP→ **On paying your entrance fee, you're given a white paper card where all food and drinks are noted and your bill's paid at the cashier at the end of the night. Don't lose it; it's your ticket out at the end of the night!**
✉ *Rua Mem de Sá 79, Lapa* ☎ *21/2221–0043* ⊕ *www.barcariocadagema.com.br* ⊙ *Closed Mon.* ☞ *Entrance fee R$ 25–30, but you can also buy tickets with a table included for groups.*

★ Circo Voador

LIVE MUSIC | A great venue in an excellent location right by the Lapa arches, Circo Voador hosts club nights during the week, but it's the varied live shows that really stand out, with a big stage set under a huge open-sided circular tent and room for up to 1,500 people to dance the night away.

■ TIP→ **Check the website for a regular roster of international acts and local stars.**
✉ *Rua dos Arcos s/n, Lapa* ☎ *21/2533–0354* ⊕ *www.circovoador.com.br.*

★ Pedra do Sal

GATHERING PLACE | For one of the most authentic samba experiences in town, head to Monday night's live roda de samba in Pedra do Sal. Located in a residential pocket in the docklands neighborhood of Saúde, crowds of samba-loving locals gather round a central circle of musicians who jam late into the night. The story goes that this spot marks the birthplace of samba in Rio de Janeiro and there is a really tangible sense of living heritage here. Although the vibe is welcoming and friendly and crime is minimal, go without valuables and little in your pockets so you can relax into the experience. Ice-cold beers and caipirinhas can be bought from surrounding bars and vendors. During summer months, this also takes place on Fridays and is a great spot to kick off a night out, with crowds gathering from around 8 pm. The roda is cancelled in the

Pedra do Sal translates to "Salt Stone" and is a pivotal site where African slaves and salt were sold.

event of rain. ✉ *R. Argemiro Bulcão, São Cristóvão* ⊕ *www.instagram.com/pedra-dosaloficial/* Ⓜ *Presidente Vargas.*

★ Rio Scenarium
LIVE MUSIC | Despite the hordes of samba-seeking tourists, Rio Scenarium somehow manages to retain its authenticity and magic. This is partly due to the incredible setting—a former movie props warehouse still crammed to the rafters with old instruments, bikes, furniture, and puppets—but also to the great bands and persevering locals who love to show off their moves and entice novices onto the dance floor. On weekends arrive before 9 pm to avoid the lines, or call ahead and book a table. If you prefer a daytime visit, they offer a feijoada every Saturday at lunchtime with live music. ✉ *Rua, Lavradio 20, Lapa* ☎ *21/3147–9005* ⊕ *www.rioscenarium.com.br* ⊙ *Closed Sun. and Mon.* Ⓜ *Carioca or Cinelandia.*

🎭 Performing Arts
CLASSICAL MUSIC
Centro Cultural Parque Glória Maria (Parque das Ruínas)
MUSIC | FAMILY | With a glorious view of Guanabara Bay and downtown, the Parque das Ruínas houses the remains of a mansion building that was Rio's bohemian epicenter in the first half of the 20th century. Today live music and theater performances are held here, and the panoramic views from the top of the building are stunning. Occasional music and art events take place during the summer. It was recently renamed to Parque Gloria Maria to honor a famous local TV journalist. ✉ *Rua Murtinho Nobre 169, Santa Teresa* ☎ *21/2252–1039.*

Escola de Música da UFRJ
MUSIC | The music school auditorium, inspired by the Salle Gaveau in Paris, has 1,100 seats, and you can listen to chamber music, symphony orchestras,

and opera, all free of charge. There is no regular schedule for performances, so check online or call the venue to confirm programming while you are in town. ✉ *Rua do Passeio 98, Lapa* ☎ *21/2222–1029* ⊕ *www.musica.ufrj.br* Ⓜ *Cinelândia.*

Sala Cecília Meireles

MUSIC | A popular concert venue for classical music in the city, the Sala hosts regular performances in a midsize hall and is known for its excellent acoustics. ✉ *Largo da Lapa 47, Lapa* ☎ *21/2332–9223* ⊕ *salaceciliameireles.inf.br* 🎫 *From R$40* Ⓜ *Cinelândia.*

🛍 Shopping
HANDICRAFTS
La Vereda

CRAFTS | Head to this Santa Teresa arts and crafts store for colorful ceramics, ornate mirrors, and original works by local artists. For the quality and inventiveness of the objects it sells, La Vereda warrants a lengthy browsing session. ✉ *Rua Almirante Alexandrino 428, Santa Teresa* ☎ *21/2507–0317* ⊕ *www.lavereda.com.br* ⊘ *Closed Mon.*

Ipanema and Leblon

Ipanema, Leblon, and the blocks surrounding Lagoa Rodrigo de Freitas are part of Rio's money belt. For an up-close look at the posh apartment buildings, stroll down beachfront Avenida Vieira Souto and its extension, Avenida Delfim Moreira, or drive around the lagoon on Avenida Epitácio Pessoa. The tree-lined streets between Ipanema Beach and the lagoon are as peaceful as they are attractive. The boutiques along Rua Garcia D'Ávila make window-shopping a sophisticated endeavor. Other chic areas near the beach include Praça Nossa Senhora da Paz, which is lined with wonderful restaurants and bars; Rua Vinicius de Moraes; and Rua Farme de Amoedo. Gourmands should make a beeline for Leblon's Rua Dias Ferreira, where top-notch restaurants thrill diners daily. The lively bar scene here encompasses everything from exclusive lounges and wine bars to relaxed post-beach watering holes.

Ipanema is famous for its beach, beautiful people, and boutiques, so sunseekers and shopaholics will want to spend at least a day here. There's a metro station a couple of blocks from the beach. Arrive at the beach early to bag a prime people-watching position and spend a few hours here—beach vendors will keep you refreshed with coconut water, soft drinks, beer, and snacks. In the afternoon head to Visconde de Piraja for shopping, before stopping at one of the many upscale restaurants for early evening food and drinks. Should you choose to make a night of it, there are plenty of lively bars here.

👁 Sights

Museu Flamengo

SPECIALTY MUSEUM | **FAMILY** | The most popular team in Rio de Janeiro created a museum at its headquarters to tell its story and influence on the city's culture. Immerse yourself in this history and learn about Flamengo's participation in world football and other sports. You can buy a special ticket that also includes the tour at Maracanã stadium. ✉ *Av. Borges de Medeiros 997, Leblon* ⊕ *museuflamengo.com/* 🎫 *R$80* Ⓜ *Jardim de Alah/Leblon.*

🏖 Beaches

Praia do Arpoador

BEACH | At the point where Ipanema Beach meets Copacabana, Praia do Arpoador has great waves for surfing. They're so great that nonsurfers tend to avoid the water for fear of getting hit by boards. A giant rock jutting out into the waves provides panoramic views over the beaches and out to sea. Not surprisingly, the rock is a favorite haunt

Footvolley, a combination of football and volleyball, is a popular sport played by Brazilians and can be seen being played on Ipanema Beach.

of romantic couples looking to catch the sunset. With more elbow room and fewer, pushy vendors than Ipanema, this beach is a prime spot for a relaxed sunbathing session. **Amenities:** food and drink; toilets; showers; lifeguards. **Best for:** sunset; surfing. ✉ *Rua Francisco Otaviano, Arpoador* Ⓜ *Ipanema / General Osório or Cantagalo.*

★ Praia de Ipanema

BEACH | FAMILY | As you stroll this world-famous beach you'll encounter a cross section of the city's residents, each favoring a particular stretch. Families predominate in the area near Posto (Post) 10, for instance, and the gay community clusters near Posto 8 by a giant rainbow flag. Throughout the day you'll see groups playing beach volleyball and soccer, and if you're lucky you might even come across the Brazilian Olympic volleyball team practicing here. At kiosks along the boardwalk, you can sample all sorts of food and drink, from the typical coconut water to fried shrimp and sushi. **Amenities:** food and drink; lifeguards; showers; toilets. **Best for:** walking; sunset. ✉ *Av. Viera Souto to Praça do Arpoador, Ipanema* Ⓜ *Ipanema / General Osório.*

Praia do Leblon

BEACH | FAMILY | At the far end of Ipanema lies Praia do Leblon, a stretch of beach usually occupied by families and generally less lively as far as beach sports are concerned. The water tends to be rough, and a strong undertow makes swimming unwise, but this is a nice place for a paddle and a splash. Vendors pass by selling everything from ice-cold beer and coconut water to bikinis and sarongs, so come with a few reais to spend. As you stroll along the beautifully tiled sidewalk, take note of the sprawling Vidigal favela, which perches on the hillside overlooking the area. Continue up the road a bit to one of Leblon's *mirantes,* boardwalk-like areas that offer a great view of the entire beach from Leblon to Arpoador. **Amenities:** food and drink; lifeguards; toilets; showers. **Best for:** walking; sunset. ✉ *Av. Epitácio Pessoa to Praça Escritor Antônio Callado, Leblon* Ⓜ *Jardim de Alah.*

Praia do Vidigal

BEACH | Quiet Vidigal Beach is next to the Sheraton Grand Rio hotel. The small stretch of sand was the playground of residents of the nearby Vidigal favela until the hotel was built in the 1970s. These days it's practically a private beach for hotel guests. The water is calm enough for swimming, but like others in Rio can be dirty after heavy rainfall. **Amenities:** food and drink. **Best for:** swimming. ✉ *Av. Niemeyer at Sheraton, Vidigal.*

 Restaurants

Amazonia Soul

$$ | **BRAZILIAN** | **FAMILY** | While hundreds of places in Rio serve the antioxidant-rich acai berry bowls, few are more authentic than this Amazonian restaurant, which prizes the purity of its superfood pulp that's sourced straight from Para and delivered sugar and additive-free. The ultimate beach snack or light meal, add banana, sprinkle on granola, or go for the full Amazonian set menu to experience an authentic feast of flavors you've likely never tried before. **Known for:** tapioca pancakes; organic acai berries; jambu snappes (guava liquor). ⑤ *Average main: R$30* ✉ *Praça General Osório, Rua Teixeira de Melo 37, Loja B, Ipanema* ☎ *21/2247–1028* ⊕ *www.instagram.com/amazoniasoul/* Ⓜ *General Osório.*

Capricciosa

$$$$ | **ITALIAN** | **FAMILY** | Rio fairly bursts with pizza places, but this upmarket chain's Ipanema branch emerges at the top of the list. Wood-fired, thin-crust pizzas are made with imported Italian flour, and the toppings—from wild mushrooms and handmade buffalo mozzarella to wafer-thin Parma ham and fresh tuna—are of the highest quality. **Known for:** wood-fired oven; prime people-watching location; gluten-free pizzas. ⑤ *Average main: R$65* ✉ *Rua Vinicius de Moraes 134, Ipanema* ☎ *21/2523–3394* ⊕ *www.capricciosa.com.br* Ⓜ *Ipanema / General Osório.*

Casa da Feijoada

$$$$ | **BRAZILIAN** | **FAMILY** | Restaurants traditionally serve feijoada, Brazil's savory national dish, on Saturday, but here the huge pots of the substantial stew simmer every day; it's a great option for groups or when you are particularly hungry. The menu also features options such as baked chicken, shrimp in coconut milk, grilled trout, and filet mignon. **Known for:** the set menu, complete with black bean soup, dessert, and a caipirinha; a quintessential Brazilian dining experience; Romeo and Juliet dessert (guava compote with fresh cheese). ⑤ *Average main: R$145* ✉ *Rua Prudente de Morais 10, Ipanema* ☎ *21/2247–2776* ⊕ *casadafeijoada.com.br/* Ⓜ *Ipanema/ General Osório.*

Celeiro

$$$ | **VEGETARIAN** | One of an increasing number of organic eateries in Rio, Celeiro is a combination café and health-food store that's popular with models and other body-conscious locals. The restaurant operates on a pay-by-weight system, and the expensive buffet features a staggering 50 types of salad, as well as oven-baked pies, whole-wheat pastries, fish and chicken dishes, and low-calorie desserts. **Known for:** delicious homemade breads; pay-by-weight buffet system with 50 types of salads; café and health-food store in one. ⑤ *Average main: R$50* ✉ *Rua Dias Ferreira 199, Leblon* ☎ *21/2274–7843* ⊕ *www.celeiroculinaria.com.br* ⊘ *Closed Sun.; no dinner* Ⓜ *Antero de Quental / Leblon.*

CT Boucherie

$$$$ | **FRENCH** | The city's most celebrated chef—Claude Troisgros—has changed the face of the all-you-can-eat churrascaria with this chic bistro. Unlike at traditional rodizios, where waiters deliver cut after cut of meat, here they dash from table to table with steaming plates of roasted palm hearts, stuffed tomatoes, creamy mashed potatoes, and other meat-free sides to accompany meaty

mains like the substantial prime rib or the more accessibly priced house burger. **Known for:** charming French-style interiors; the banana 'farofa' breadcrumbs; never-ending flow of vegetable plates. $ *Average main: R$90* ✉ *Rua Dias Ferreira 636, Leblon* ☎ *21/2529–2329* ⊕ *www.ctboucherie.com.br* Ⓜ *Antero de Quental.*

Chez Claude

$$$ | BRAZILIAN | Opened in 2017, the latest restaurant from leading Franco-Brazilian chef Claude Troisgros is reliably packed every night of the week with well-to-do locals feasting on gourmet Brazilian dishes in a fun, buzzy atmosphere. Dishes are served tapas-style and come crafted from an open-plan kitchen set smack in the center of the restaurant, so you can watch the chefs at work while you sip the house bubbly. **Known for:** raw scallop ravioli; foie gras duck egg; vibrant see-and-be-seen atmosphere. $ *Average main: R$62* ✉ *Rua Conde de Bernadotte 26, Loja Q & R, Leblon* ☎ *21/3579–1185* ⊕ *chezclaude.com.br/restaurante/* ⊗ *No lunch Mon.–Sat.*

Esplanada Grill

$$$$ | BRAZILIAN | This upmarket churrascaria is famed for the quality of its grilled meats, which are served in a sleek wooden dining room on a quiet tree-lined street in Ipanema. All the grilled dishes come with fried palm hearts, seasoned rice, and a choice of fried, baked, or sautéed potatoes. **Known for:** the T-bone; the picanha (a Brazilian cut of beef with little fat); attentive service. $ *Average main: R$86* ✉ *Rua Barão da Torre 600, Ipanema* ☎ *21/2512–2970* ⊕ *www.esplanadagrill.com.br* Ⓜ *Jardim de Alah.*

Gero Panini Ipanema

$$$$ | ITALIAN | Owned by the Italian Fasano chain, this award-strewn and beautifully appointed restaurant is frequently cited as the best Italian in Rio, although quality like this comes at a cost. The high-ceilinged, wooden-floor building exhibits the clean, contemporary design that is the Fasano hallmark and the menu contains wonderful panini, pastas, and risottos, as well as excellent fish and meat dishes; a second Rio branch operates in Barra da Tijuca. **Known for:** plentiful vegetarian options in a meat-heavy menu; the tiramisu, a perfect blend of creamy, espresso-laced mascarpone; elegant surroundings. $ *Average main: R$110* ✉ *Rua Anibal de Mendonca 157, Ipanema* ☎ *21/2239–8158* ⊕ *www.fasano.com.br.*

Gurume Ipanema

$$$ | JAPANESE | A prime Ipanema location paired with great service and elegant design make this trendy sushi spot a good option for a great meal surrounded by well-dressed locals. Long lines are common, so go early or sip sake in the street while you wait—just don't miss the daily specials or the trio of *nigiri* (thin slices of raw fish over vinegar rice). **Known for:** innovative combinations of sushi and sashimi; extensive sake menu; nigiri (thin slices of raw fish over vinegar rice). $ *Average main: R$83* ✉ *Rua Aníbal de Mendonça 132, Ipanema* ☎ *21/2540–7065* ⊕ *www.japagurume.com.br* Ⓜ *Jardim de Alah.*

Pizza Rio Style

Cariocas love pizza, and they've added some touches of their own to the established formula. As well as sharing the pan-Brazilian penchant for pizza bases covered in chocolate, Rio residents are also known to indulge in unusual topping combinations such as cheese with pepperoni, banana, and cinnamon. In one last break with tradition, many Cariocas eschew the idea of tomato sauce beneath the cheese, in favor of squirting ketchup on the surface.

Margutta

$$$$ | ITALIAN | A block from Ipanema Beach, Margutta has a reputation for outstanding Mediterranean-style seafood, such as shrimp panfried in olive oil, white wine, and garlic; and lobster baked with butter and saffron rice. There's a handful of vegetarian options including mixed-vegetable risotto with truffle oil. **Known for:** oven-baked whole fish; seafood risotto; strong wine list. $ Average main: R$74 ✉ Av. Henrique Dumont 62, Ipanema ☎ 21/2259–3887 ⊕ margutta.com.br/ ⊙ Closed Mon. Ⓜ Ipanema/General Osório.

★ Pabu Izakaya

$$ | JAPANESE | FAMILY | Inspired by Japan's informal izakayas, this intimate spot combines first-class sashimi with more traditional hot Japanese dishes—grab a seat at the bar that loops around the center of the restaurant or the handful of tables outside. Good-value prices, an extensive sake menu, delicious food, and the laid-back vibe make it a reliable neighborhood favorite for just about everyone. **Known for:** langoustine dumplings; soba noodle soup; sashimi. $ Average main: R$30 ✉ Rua Humberto de Campos 827, Loja G, Leblon ☎ 21/3738–0416 ⊕ www.instagram.com/pabuizakayario/.

★ Satyricon

$$$$ | SEAFOOD | A tank of snapping lobsters and a fish counter where you can pick your catch of the day ensures you'll get some of the best seafood in town. And white tablecloths, off-the-boat-fresh fish, and excellent service ensure the quality of the experience is worth the price tag. **Known for:** classic seafood dishes like salt-baked whole fish; trio of fish carpaccio; homemade Italian ice cream. $ Average main: R$90 ✉ Rua Barão da Torre 192, Ipanema ☎ 21/2521–0627 ⊕ www.satyricon.com.br Ⓜ Ipanema / General Osório.

Food on the Go

There's a street snack for every taste in Rio—from low-cal treats such as corn on the cob and chilled pineapple slices to less virtuous, but absolutely delicious, barbecued sticks of grilled cheese served with or without herbs. Tasty bags of roasted and salted peanuts and cashews are found everywhere, as are giant hot dogs, served on a stick and covered in manioc flour. Barbecued chicken heart (*coração*) is not for the fainthearted, and the grilled shrimp at the beach is best avoided unless you want a side order of food poisoning.

★ Spazziano

$$ | VEGETARIAN | FAMILY | Hidden away on the second floor of the unassuming apart-hotel Ipanema Beach Star, this low-key vegan lunch spot and sister spa (Maria Bonita) is a real find, not just for the quality of the all-you-can-eat buffet, but also for the reasonable prices. The daily changing menu is crafted from ingredients sourced from the restaurant's organic farm, while friendly staff deliver complimentary detox juices and digestion shots to your table. **Known for:** shiitake mushroom stew; eggplant lasagna; green detox juice. $ Average main: R$45 ✉ Rua Prudente de Morais 729, Ipanema ☎ 21/2513–4050 ⊕ www.instagram.com/spazziano/ ⊙ No dinner Ⓜ Nossa Senhora da Paz / Ipanema.

★ Teva

$$ | VEGETARIAN | The food at this happening little Ipanema restaurant is so fresh and inventive that you'll barely notice that they only serve plant-based vegan dishes. Its chic industrial design and top-quality cooking make this one of Rio's go-to spots for a relaxed lunch or dinner. **Known for:** vegan dishes like

jackfruit tacos and spicy Manchurian cauliflower; sophisticated cocktails like cucumber-infused sake; interesting wine list that includes biodynamic and organic options. $ *Average main: R$40* ⊠ *Av. Henrique Dumont 110, Loja B, Ipanema* ☎ *21/3253–1355* ⊕ *linklist.bio/Teva* Ⓜ *Jardim de Alah / Leblon.*

Hotels

Fasano Rio
$$$$ | HOTEL | The Italian-owned Fasano Group is renowned for its stylish, elegant hotels and restaurants, and Fasano Rio has the added glamour of having been crafted by the French designer Philippe Starck. **Pros:** stylish design; wonderful views from pool; glamorous clientele. **Cons:** standard rooms lack views; expensive; street noise. $ *Rooms from: R$3,500* ⊠ *Av. Viera Souto 80, Ipanema* ☎ *21/3202–4000* ⊕ *www.fasano.com.br* 🛏 *92 rooms* ⓘ◯ⓘ *No Meals* Ⓜ *Ipanema/General Osório.*

★ Ipanema Inn
$$$ | HOTEL | FAMILY | The pick of the bunch in Ipanema for a midrange option with a great location, this stylish little property was renovated in 2016 by renowned architect Bel Lobo and now combines elegant, breezy design and a vibrant restaurant serving contemporary Brazilian food with comfortable rooms. **Pros:** great location close to bars, clubs, and upmarket shops; good value; friendly, efficient staff. **Cons:** compact rooms; no views; no pool. $ *Rooms from: R$1,400* ⊠ *Rua Maria Quitéria 27, Ipanema* ☎ *21/2523–6092, 21/2529–1000* ⊕ *www.ipanemainn.com.br* 🛏 *56 rooms* ⓘ◯ⓘ *Free Breakfast* Ⓜ *Ipanema/General Osório.*

Janeiro
$$$$ | HOTEL | Formerly known as the Marina All Suites, this intimate beachfront hotel was redesigned in 2018 by eco warrior and founder of fashion brand Osklen as an ode to Carioca style. **Pros:** prime location in front of Leblon's Posto 11; serious style credentials; a fun local scene to tap into. **Cons:** small swimming pool; the beach bar can get busy; open-plan bathrooms offer little privacy. $ *Rooms from: R$1,900* ⊠ *Av. Delfim Moreira 696, Leblon* ☎ *21/2172–1001* ⊕ *www.janeirohotel.rio* 🛏 *53 suites* ⓘ◯ⓘ *Free Breakfast.*

Sheraton Grand Rio Hotel & Resort
$$$$ | RESORT | FAMILY | Between the upmarket neighborhoods of São Conrado and Leblon, this hotel has the most spacious leisure area in the city, with three pools, two tennis courts, and a children's playground; this is the only hotel in Rio with a "private" beach. **Pros:** great for families; wonderful beach; good amenities. **Cons:** some furnishings past their prime; pool area is not clean; location directly in front of the sprawling favela of Vidigal may make some guests uncomfortable. $ *Rooms from: R$2,500* ⊠ *Av. Niemeyer 121, Leblon* ☎ *21/2529–1122* ⊕ *www.sheraton-rio.com* 🛏 *559 rooms* ⓘ◯ⓘ *Free Breakfast.*

Sol Ipanema
$$$$ | HOTEL | FAMILY | Another of Rio's tall, slender hotels, this one has a great location at the eastern end of Ipanema Beach between Rua Vinicius de Moraes and Farme de Amoedo. **Pros:** near lively Ipanema nightlife; large buffet breakfast with lots of variety; decent value for Ipanema. **Cons:** standard facilities; tiny pool; not the best on-site restaurant. $ *Rooms from: R$1,000* ⊠ *Av. Vieira Souto 320, Ipanema* ☎ *21/2525–2020* ⊕ *www.solipanema.com.br* 🛏 *90 rooms* ⓘ◯ⓘ *Free Breakfast* Ⓜ *Ipanema / General Osório.*

Nightlife

BARS
★ Academia da Cachaça
BARS | Not merely the place in Rio to try caipirinhas (made here with a variety of tropical fruits), Academia da Cachaça is a veritable temple to cachaça. The small

bar sells close to 100 brands of cachaça by the glass or bottle, as well as mixing the famous sugarcane rum into dangerously drinkable concoctions such as the *cocada geladinha*—frozen coconut, coconut water, brown sugar, and cachaça. The Northeastern bar snacks here include sun-dried beef, baked palm hearts, and delicious black bean soup. There's now an affiliate in Barra da Tijuca, but it's hard to beat the Leblon original. ✉ *Rua Conde de Bernadotte 26, Leblon* ☎ *21/2239–1542* ⊕ *www.academiadacachaca.com.br* Ⓜ *Jardim de Alah.*

Bracarense
BARS | A trip to Bracarense after a hard day on the beach is what Rio is all about. Crowds spill onto the streets while parked cars double as chairs and the sandy masses gather at sunset for ice-cold chopp (draft tap beer) and some of Leblon's best pork sandwiches, codfish balls, and empanadas. ✉ *Rua José Linhares 85, Leblon* ☎ *21/2294–3549* ⊕ *www.instagram.com/bar_bracarense/* Ⓜ *Antero de Quental.*

Garota de Ipanema
BARS | This is the original Garota (there are branches all over the city), where Tom Jobim and Vinicius de Moraes penned the timeless song "The Girl from Ipanema." The place serves decent food and drink, but it's the historical significance that draws the crowds. Occasional live music events take place in the upstairs lounge. ✉ *Rua Vinicius de Moraes 49, Ipanema* ☎ *21/2523–3787* Ⓜ *Ipanema / General Osório.*

Jobi Bar
BARS | Authentically Carioca and a fine place to experience Rio spirit, the bar at down-to-earth Jobi stays open on weekends until the last customer leaves. Don't be fooled by the unassuming exterior—Jobi serves some of Rio's most delicious bar snacks and is one of the best-loved bars in the Zona Sul. ✉ *Av. Ataulfo de Paiva 1166, Loja B, Leblon* ☎ *21/2274–0547* ⊕ *www.facebook.com/barjobi* Ⓜ *Antero de Quental.*

★ Nosso
BARS | This happening hangout is set on one of Ipanema's prettiest squares. Spread over three floors, it combines a rum bar with a rooftop terrace and vibrant lounge area. The star of the show is mixologist Tai Barbin, who is known for his barrel-aged negronis. Gourmet snacks are available alongside an extensive drinks list and service is reliably attentive. ✉ *Rua Maria Quitéria 91, Ipanema* ☎ *21/99619–0099* ⊕ *www.nossoipanema.com/* ⊘ *Closed Mon.* Ⓜ *Nossa Senhora de Paz.*

>
> # The Real Girl from Ipanema
>
> Have you ever wondered if there really was a girl from Ipanema? The song was inspired by schoolgirl Heloisa Pinheiro, who caught the fancy of songwriter Antônio Carlos (aka Tom) Jobim and his pal, lyricist Vinicius de Moraes, as she walked past the two bohemians sitting in their favorite bar. They then penned one of last century's classics. That was in 1962, and today the bar has been renamed **Bar Garota de Ipanema.**

🛍 Shopping

ART
★ Gam Arte e Molduras
ART GALLERY | A good place to find high-quality modern and contemporary paintings and sculptures, this gallery, which ships items abroad for customers, also sells photographs that can be made to size. ✉ *Rua Garcia D'Ávila 145, Loja C, Ipanema* ☎ *21/98081–0364* ⊕ *www.gamarteemolduras.com.br* Ⓜ *Ipanema/General Osório.*

As the 1,000 favelas in Rio grow and progress, these bright and colorful communities continue to make strides despite the lack of adequate plumbing and electricity systems.

BEACHWEAR

★ Lenny
SWIMWEAR | Upmarket swimwear store Lenny sells sophisticated, exquisitely cut pieces in a range of sizes, and lots of fashionable beach accessories. Prices are high, but the bikinis are particularly creative. ✉ *Rua Garcia d'Avila 149, Loja A, Ipanema* ☎ *21/2227–5537* ⊕ *www.lenny.com.br* Ⓜ *Ipanema / General Osório.*

BEAUTY

Granado
COSMETICS | This upmarket chain's traditional cosmetics make for great souvenirs, with beautifully packaged body creams, soaps, and shampoos crafted from Brazilian ingredients like acai and cashew nuts. The most charming of the stores is located in a renovated pharmacy in Leblon's upmarket Dias Ferreira street. ✉ *Rua Gen. Artigas 470, Loja A, Leblon* ☎ *21/2512–9964* ⊕ *www.granado.com.br/* Ⓜ *Antero de Quental.*

BOOKS

Argumento
BOOKS | Its large selection of books in English has made this bookstore popular with expats and vacationers. There's also a CD section. The cozy Café Severino in the back has coffee, pastries, salads, crepes, and sandwiches. ✉ *Rua Dias Ferreira 417, Leblon* ☎ *21/2239–5294* ⊕ *www.livrariaargumento.com* Ⓜ *Antero de Quental / Leblon.*

CACHAÇA

Academia da Cachaça
WINE/SPIRITS | You can buy close to 100 brands of cachaça here. The bar serves amazing caipirinhas and other cachaça-based drinks. ✉ *Rua Conde Bernadote 26, Loja G, Leblon* ☎ *21/2239–1542* ⊕ *www.academiadacachaca.com.br.*

A Garrafeira
WINE/SPIRITS | The charming liquor store Garrafeira sells a wide range of cachaça, including excellent versions from Minas Gerais State. ✉ *Av. General San Martin 1227, Loja A, Leblon* ☎ *21/2512–3336,*

Favelas

A Bit of History
Named after the flowers that grow on the hills of Rio, the first favela began as a squatter town for homeless soldiers at the end of the 19th century. Later, freed slaves illegally made their homes on these undeveloped government lands. The favelas flourished and expanded in the 1940s as the population in Brazil shifted from a rural-based to an urban-based one. In the 1970s, during the military dictatorship, the government moved favela dwellers into public housing projects.

Rio's Largest Favela
Rocinha is Rio's largest and most developed favela. About 72,154 (around 48,300 people per square meter) people reside in this well-developed community (there are three banks, a nightclub, and many shops and small markets). Brace yourself for a variety of smells, both good and bad: you'll find savory-smelling, grilled *churrasquinho* (meat skewers) sold in the street, and any number of delicious aromas drifting out of nearby restaurants. On the flip side, residents dump their trash on the side of the road (in designated areas) and in some places, raw sewage flows in open canals.

Exploring
The main thoroughfare, the Estrada da Gávea, begins in São Conrado and ends on the other side of Rocinha in Gávea. Anyone can take a stroll up this street, and visitors are likely to hear English being spoken. If you're feeling intrepid and want to explore Rocinha on foot without a guide, be aware of the following: In 2012 police wrested control of Rocinha from the drug faction Amigos dos Amigos (ADA) as part of an ongoing citywide pacification project. Though UPPs (Police Pacification Units) have largely kept the peace since then, shoot-outs between police and faction members are not unheard of. Crime against tourists in the favela is rare, but unguided visitors stand a real chance of getting lost in the maze of streets. By far the safest way to visit Rocinha or other favelas is to take an organized tour.

21/99906–3336 WhatsApp ⊕ www.instagram.com/agarrafeirarj/ ⊘ Closed Sun. Ⓜ *Antero de Quental / Leblon.*

SHOPPING CENTERS AND MALLS
Shopping Leblon

SHOPPING CENTER | International designers and chic local boutiques can be found at this upmarket fashion mall in Leblon. There is some good food to be found in the food court—think fine dining rather than fast food—and the mall has free Wi-Fi and a modern four-screen cineplex. ✉ *Av. Afrânio de Melo Franco 290, Leblon* ☎ *21/2430–5122* ⊕ *www.shoppingleblon.com.br* Ⓜ *Jardim de Alah.*

CLOTHING
Alessa

CLOTHING | For fashion-forward designs, visit Alessa. Pay special attention to Alessa's fabulously fun underwear, which makes for great presents. ✉ *Rua Visconde de Pirajá 580, loja 117, Ipanema* ☎ *21/2287–9939* ⊕ *www.casadaalessa.com.br/* ⊘ *Closed Sun.* Ⓜ *General Osorio.*

Animale

CLOTHING | A favorite among local fashionistas, Animale carries casual wear and formal wear that's both sophisticated and sexy. If you want to make an impression in Rio's social scene, head here for slinky dresses, chic cover-ups, and showstopping shoes and accessories. ✉ *Rua Joana Angelica 116, Ipanema* ☎ *21/99709–0053* ⊕ *www.animale.com.br* ⊙ *Closed Sun.* Ⓜ *Nossa Senhora.*

FARM

CLOTHING | Fun colors and bold patterns make Farm popular with Cariocas. It's a great place to find feminine dresses and cute tops that epitomize Rio's fun-loving beach style. Can be found in the biggest shopping malls in the city, but their concept shop in Lagoa is worth visiting, as it also has a Bibi juice shop by the entrance. ✉ *Av. Epitácio Pessoa 1210, Lagoa* ☎ *21/3813–3817* ⊕ *www.farmrio.com.br* ⊙ *Closed Mon.* Ⓜ *Nossa Senhora da Paz / Ipanema.*

★ Osklen

CLOTHING | The Osklen brand is synonymous with fashionable everyday wear, and all the clothes and accessories are designed to help you look good while remaining functional. A favorite with the city's fashionistas, the brand combines simple T-shirts with evening wear and accessories. ✉ *Rua Maria Quitéria 85, Ipanema* ☎ *21/2227–2911* ⊕ *www.osklen.com.br* Ⓜ *Ipanema / General Osório.*

Richards

CLOTHING | A classic Brazilian clothing store selling tasteful, well-made pieces, Richards was originally just for men but now also carries women's clothing and children's wear. It's the place to go for good-quality linen clothing. ✉ *Rua Maria Quiteria 95, Ipanema* ☎ *21/2522–1245* ⊕ *www.richards.com.br* Ⓜ *Nossa Senhora da Paz / Ipanema.*

FOOD

Armazém do Café

FOOD & DRINK | The "Coffee Store" chain has several branches in Rio, including ones in Ipanema and Leblon where you can enjoy a cappuccino or espresso and a pastry at the café before browsing the coffees and coffee-making devices for sale. ✉ *Rua Visconde de Pirajá 595, Loja 101/102, Ipanema* ☎ *21/3874–2920* ⊕ *www.armazemdocafe.com.br* ⊙ *Closed Sun.* Ⓜ *Ipanema / General Osório.*

★ Casa Aquim

CHOCOLATE | The interior of this intimate chocolate shop is almost as exquisite as their hand-crafted chocolate bars. Produced by the Aquim´s, one of Rio's leading gourmet families, whose mission is to show the world what chocolate can really taste like when cultivated with care and free from over-production and too much sugar. In addition to chocolate bars, there are delectable brownies and gifts wrapped in evocative jungle packaging.

■ **TIP→ Ask the staff for tasters before you buy.** ✉ *Av. Ataulfo de Paiva 1120, Leblon* ☎ *21/2274–1001, 21/99991–7625 WhatsApp* ⊕ *www.chocolateq.com* ⊙ *Closed Sun.* Ⓜ *Antero de Quental.*

Zona Sul

FOOD & DRINK | Branches of this upscale supermarket can be found throughout Rio's South Zone, and they're good

---

The Brazilian Bikini

Urban myth has it that Brazilian model Rose de Primo fashioned the Brazilian string bikini when she hurriedly sewed a bikini for a photo shoot with too little material. Whatever its history, the Tanga (string bikini) provides less than half the coverage of conventional bikinis, and makes the itsy bitsy teeny-weeny yellow polka-dot bikini look rather conservative. If you're looking to buy a Brazilian bikini but want a little more coverage, ask for a "sunkini."

The Seven Wonders of Rio Shopping

Arts and crafts. The hills of Santa Teresa brim with arts and crafts stores selling paintings, colorful wooden animals, and other works by local artists. (R$10 and up)

Brazilian soccer shirt. You just can't leave Brazil without one of the country's most emblematic gifts. (R$35 and up)

Cachaça. While showing your friends your vacation pictures, you can impress them with a caipirinha made with genuine cachaça. (R$10 and up)

Chic swimwear. You can show off your Rio tan back home in a daringly revealing bikini—Lenny has some of the best designs—or a more modest, but still sexy, one-piece suit. (R$90 and up)

Gilson Martins bag. Whatever style or size you buy from the hip designer's stores will make a cool souvenir or gift. (R$30 and up)

Havaianas. The brand's stores in Ipanema and Centro sell its flip-flops at such low prices, how can you not take home a bagful? (R$17 and up)

Mini-Cristo. Sobral makes a colorful miniversion of one of the seven wonders of the modern world. (R$50)

---

places to pick up deli goods, coffee, chocolate, and fresh fruit and vegetables. The promotional prices displayed usually apply only to those holding Zona Sul loyalty cards. ✉ *Prudente de Morais 49, Ipanema* ☎ *21/2267–0361* Ⓜ *Ipanema / General Osório.*

JEWELRY
H.Stern
JEWELRY & WATCHES | The award-winning designers at H.Stern create distinctive contemporary pieces—the inventory runs to about 300,000 items. The shops downstairs sell more affordable pieces and folkloric items. Around the corner at the company's world headquarters, you can see exhibits of rare stones and watch craftspeople transform rough stones into sparkling jewels. ✉ *Rua Garcia D'Ávila 113, Ipanema* ☎ *21/2274–8897* ⊕ *www.hstern.com.br* ⊙ *Closed Sun.* Ⓜ *Ipanema / General Osorio.*

Sobral
JEWELRY & WATCHES | Visit Sobral for chunky, colorful resin jewelry, accessories, and decorative items, including its signature multicolored replicas of the Christ statue. Reclaimed materials are used to make the store's funky goods, and its owners invest in social projects such as jewelry-making classes for young people in disadvantaged communities. ✉ *Forum Ipanema, Rua Visconde de Pirajá 351, Loja 105, Ipanema* ☎ *21/2267–0009* ⊕ *sobraldesign.net/#!home* Ⓜ *Ipanema / General Osório.*

MARKETS
Feira Hippie (*Hippie Fair*)
MARKET | FAMILY | The colorful handicrafts street fair takes place on Sunday between 8 am and 6 pm. Shop for high-quality jewelry, hand-painted dresses, paintings, wood carvings, leather bags and sandals, rag dolls, knickknacks, furniture, and samba percussion instruments, among many other items. It's fun to browse here even if you're not looking to buy anything. ✉ *Praça General Osório, Ipanema* ⊕ *www.feirahippieipanema.net* Ⓜ *Ipanema / General Osório.*

SHOES, BAGS, AND ACCESSORIES
Gilson Martins
HANDBAGS | The shops of one of Brazil's most gifted and acclaimed designers sell

his colorful Rio-inspired bags and accessories at affordable prices. There are two additional locations in Copacabana. ✉ *Rua Visconde de Pirajá 462, Ipanema* ☎ *21/2227–6178* ⊕ *www.gilsonmartins.com.br* ⊗ *Closed Sun.* Ⓜ *Nossa Senhora da Paz / Ipanema.*

Havaianas Store
SHOES | The Ipanema Havaianas store carries the fun and funky flip-flops in all colors, styles, and sizes, for men, women, and kids. The range is staggering, from classic Brazil flag designs to limited-edition gem-encrusted versions. The prices start at R$28 and creep over R$100. Alongside the legendary flops, the store also sells canvas deck shoes and sturdier sandals, as well as opinion-dividing "flip-flop socks." Don't miss their brightly colored plastic wallets—a clever solution to protect your loose change and phone from sand at the beach. Other locations around town include one in Centro. ✉ *Rua Visc. de Pirajá 310, Ipanema* ☎ *21/2247–4713* ⊕ *havaianas.com* Ⓜ *Nossa Senhora da Paz / Ipanema.*

Mr. Cat
SHOES | The stylish Mr. Cat carries handbags and leather shoes for men and women and has stores all over the city. ✉ *Rua Visconde de Pirajá 550, Loja D, Ipanema* ☎ *21/2227–6521* ⊕ *www.mrcat.com.br* ⊗ *Closed Sun.* Ⓜ *Nossa Senhora da Paz / Ipanema.*

Via Mia
SHOES | You'll find a large selection of reasonably priced shoes, bags, and accessories at Via Mia. ✉ *Av. Afranio de Melo Franco 290, Leblon* ☎ *21/3204–4083* ⊕ *www.viamia.com.br* Ⓜ *Jardim de Alah / Leblon.*

SURF AND EXTREME SPORTS GEAR

Centauro
SPORTING GOODS | The massive Centauro store caters to the needs of all sorts of sporting enthusiasts. ✉ *Shopping Leblon,*

Cycle Rio

With its many bike paths, Rio is a great place to explore by bicycle, and Bike Rio, a citywide bicycle-sharing system, has made it easier than ever to do so. Locals and visitors can pick up one of hundreds of bicycles at rental stations along the beachfront and at other bike-friendly locations, returning the bikes to similar stations at journey's end. Daily passes cost R$5 and can be purchased online at the Bike Rio app. Visitors can also hire a bike through car-sharing app Uber.

Av. Afrânio de Melo Franco 290, Loja 106 and 107 A, Leblon ☎ *21/2512–1246* ⊕ *www.centauro.com.br* Ⓜ *Jardim de Alah.*

🏃 Activities

BOATING AND SAILING
Dive Point
BOATING | Schooner tours around the main beaches of Rio and as far afield as Búzios and Arraial do Cabo are offered here, as well as deep-sea and wreck diving. Be sure to ask if prices include all the necessary equipment and training (if required). ✉ *Av. Ataulfo da Paiva 1174, SS 04, Leblon* ☎ *21/2239–5105, 21/96429–0895 WhatsApp* ⊕ *www.divepoint.com.br.*

HANG GLIDING
Rio Hang Gliding
HANG GLIDING & PARAGLIDING | This highly reputable and experienced hang gliding outfit, run by Brazilian champion Konrad Heilmann, who has more than 30 years of experience, will collect you from your hotel, take you through the basics, and then run you off Pedra Bonita mountain into the sky high above Tijuca Forest. The excellent instructors can also film or

The Sítio Roberto Burle Marx is the first modern tropical garden to be a UNESCO World Heritage site.

photograph the experience for an extra charge. Fluent English and German is spoken and there are opportunities for beginners. ✉ *Ipanema* ☎ *21/2422–2411, 21/99843–9006* ⊕ *www.riohanggliding.com* 🚗 *From R$800.*

SPAS
Spa Maria Bonita

SPA | This holistic spa combines a range of beauty treatments, massages, and alternative healing therapies like acupuncture, colonics, and lymphatic massages. ✉ *Rua Prudente de Morais 729, Ipanema* ☎ *21/2513–4050* ⊕ *www.spamariabonita.com.br/* Ⓜ *General Osorio.*

São Conrado and Barra da Tijuca

West of the Zona Sul lie the largely residential (and considerably affluent) neighborhoods of São Conrado and Barra da Tijuca. If you're accustomed to the shop-lined and restaurant-filled streets of Copacabana and Ipanema, you're in for a shock if you head to these neighborhoods, dominated mainly by towering, modern apartment buildings. São Conrado's main attractions are the beach, which serves as a landing point for hang gliders and paragliders, and the chic Fashion Mall. Barra da Tijuca, often likened to Miami because of its wide avenues, towering condos, and sprawling malls, offers ample high-end dining opportunities as well as a white-sand beach that stretches for a staggering 15 km (9 miles). The Olympic Park in Barra da Tijuca is a place to see the legacy of the Rio 2016 games held in the city.

👁 Sights

Museu Casa do Pontal
ART MUSEUM | FAMILY | Brazil's largest folk art museum now has a new address, closer to Barra da Tijuca and easier to reach. One room houses a wonderful mechanical sculpture that represents all of the *escolas de samba* (samba schools) that march in the Carnival parades.

Another mechanical "scene" depicts a circus in action. This is the private collection of French expatriate Jacques Van de Beuque, who collected Brazilian treasures—including religious pieces—from his arrival in the country in 1946 until his death in 2000. ✉ *Av. Célia Ribeiro da Silva Mendes s/n, Barra da Tijuca* ✣ *next to Alphaville condo* ☎ *21/2490–2429* 🌐 *www.museucasadopontal.com.br* 💰 *R$12* 🕒 *Closed Mon.–Wed.* Ⓜ *Santa Mônica Jardins.*

Olympic Park

PLAZA/SQUARE | FAMILY | A legacy of the Rio 2016 Olympic Games, the Rita Lee Olympic Park includes several sports arenas, a skate park, a climbing wall, multisports courts, a seniors' gym, a playground, public restrooms, a bicycle parking area, and a wet square. ✉ *Av. Abelardo Bueno 3.401, Barra da Tijuca* 🌐 *www.instagram.com/parqueritaleerj/* 🕒 *Closed Mon.*

São Conrado

BEACH | The juxtaposition of the "haves" and "have nots" couldn't be starker, or more startling, than it is in São Conrado, where mansions and expensive condos sit right next to sprawling favelas. As you approach the neighborhood heading west from Ipanema, Avenida Niemeyer, blocked by the imposing Dois Irmãos Mountain, snakes along rugged cliffs that offer spectacular sea views on the left. The road returns to sea level again in São Conrado, a natural amphitheater surrounded by forested mountains and the ocean. Development of this upper-class residential area began in the late 1960s with an eye on Rio's high society. A short stretch along the beach includes the condominiums of a former president, the ex-wife of another former president, an ex-governor of Rio de Janeiro State, and a onetime Central Bank president. The towering Pedra da Gávea, a huge flattop granite boulder, marks the western edge of São Conrado. North of the boulder lies Pedra Bonita, the mountain from which gliders depart. ✉ *Just west of Leblon, Rio de Janeiro* Ⓜ *São Conrado.*

★ **Sítio Roberto Burle Marx** (*Roberto Burle Marx Farm*)
GARDEN | FAMILY | Nature lovers and architecture buffs will find it worth making the advance booking required to visit this plantation-turned-museum honoring Roberto Burle Marx, Brazil's legendary landscape architect. Marx, the mind behind Rio's swirling mosaic beachfront walkways and the Aterro do Flamengo, was said to have "painted with plants," and he was the first designer to use Brazilian flora in his projects. More than 3,500 species—including some discovered by and named for Marx, as well as many on the endangered list—flourish at this 100-acre estate. Marx grouped his plants not only according to their soil and light needs but also according to their shape and texture. He also liked to mix the modern with the traditional—a recurring theme throughout the property. The results are both whimsical and elegant. In 1985 he bequeathed the farm to the Brazilian government, though he remained here until his death in 1994. His house is now a cultural center full of his belongings, including collections of folk art, and the beautiful gardens are a tribute to his talents. The grounds also contain his ultramodern studio (he was a painter, too) and a small, restored colonial chapel dedicated to St. Anthony. ✉ *Estrada Roberto Burle Marx 2019, Jardim Piaí* ✣ *At far end of Barra da Tijuca* ☎ *21/2410–1412* 🌐 *sitioburlemarx.org/* 💰 *R$10* 🕒 *Closed Sun.–Mon.* 🗝 *Booking needed.*

🏖 Beaches

If you continue walking west from Recreio, you'll notice that this part of Rio is largely untouched. In fact, you'll see just three things: the mountains on your right, the road ahead, and the beach to your left. Numerous trails maintained by city workers lead to the hidden beaches west of Recreio. You'll see Rio's nude beach, Praia do Abricó, among the many short stretches of sand. Many of these beaches can be reached only on foot or by car, and are practically deserted during the week. Grumari is a favorite with surfers, but there is always lots of room on the sands during the workweek.

Praia da Barra

BEACH | FAMILY | Some Cariocas consider the beach at Barra da Tijuca to be Rio's best, and the 18-km-long (11-mile-long) sweep of sand and jostling waves certainly are dramatic. Pollution isn't generally a problem, and in many spots neither are crowds. Barra's water is cooler and its breezes more refreshing than those at other beaches. The strong waves in some sections attract surfers, windsurfers, and jet skiers, so you should swim with caution. The beach is set slightly below a sidewalk, where cafés and restaurants beckon. Condos have also sprung up here, and the city's largest shopping centers and supermarkets have made inland Barra their home. **Amenities:** food and drink; toilets; showers. **Best for:** walking; surfing. ✉ Av. Sernambetiba to Av. Lúcio Costa, Barra da Tijuca Ⓜ Jardim Oceanico.

★ Praia de Grumari

BEACH | FAMILY | A bit beyond Prainha, off Estrada de Guaratiba, is Grumari, a beach that seems a preview of paradise. What it lacks in amenities—it has only a couple of groupings of thatch-roof huts selling drinks and snacks—it makes up for in natural beauty: the glorious red sands of its quiet cove are backed by low, lush hills. Weekends are extremely crowded—arrive early—but during the week it's blissfully quiet and makes for a great day out from town. Take a lunch break at Restaurante Point de Grumari, which serves excellent fish dishes. If you've ventured this far, you might as well take a slight detour to the Museu Casa do Pontal, Brazil's largest folk art museum, and, for an in-depth look at one of the world's greatest landscape artists, the Sítio Roberto Burle Marx. **Amenities:** food and drink. **Best for:** surfing; sunset. ✉ Av. Estado de Guanabara, Grumari.

Praia de São Conrado

BEACH | West of Leblon, Praia de São Conrado sits empty during the week but is often packed on weekends and holidays. The strand of soft sand attracts both wealthy locals and residents of the nearby Rocinha favela, and it provides a soft landing for hang gliders swooping over the city. Surfers love the crashing waves, but swimmers should be cautious because of the undertow. It's worth remaining until sunset; the pumpkin sun often performs a dazzling show over Pedra da Gávea (Gávea Rock). **Amenities:** food and drink; water sports; lifeguards. **Best for:** sunset; surfing. ✉ Av. Niemeyer, São Conrado Ⓜ Sao Conrado.

Prainha

BEACH | The length of two football fields, Prainha ("Little Beach") is a vest-pocket beach favored by surfers, who take charge of it on weekends. The swimming is good, but watch out for surfboards. On weekdays, especially in the off-season, the beach is almost empty. On weekends, particularly in peak season, the road to and from Prainha and nearby Grumari is so crowded it almost becomes a parking lot. **Amenities:** toilets; showers. **Best for:** swimming; surfing; sunset. ✉ Grumari ✥ 35 km (22 miles) west of Ipanema on coast road; accessible only by car from Av. Lúcio Costa (Av. Sernambetiba).

Recreio dos Bandeirantes

BEACH | FAMILY | At the far end of Barra's beachfront avenue—the name of the street was changed a few years back to Avenida Lúcio Costa, but locals still call it Sernambetiba—is this 1-km (½-mile) stretch of sand anchored by a huge rock that creates a small, protected cove. Recreio's quiet seclusion makes it popular with families. Although busy on weekends, the beach here is wonderfully quiet during the workweek. The calm, pollution-free water, with no waves or currents, is good for bathing. But don't try to swim around the rock—it's bigger than it looks. **Amenities:** food and drink. **Best for:** swimming; walking. ⊠ *Av. Lúcio Costa, Recreio dos Bandeirantes* Ⓜ *Jardim Oceanico (Barra da Tijuca).*

🍴 Restaurants

Barra Grill

$$$ | BRAZILIAN | FAMILY | A nice place to stop after a long day at Barra Beach, this popular steak house serves more than 30 cuts of top-quality meat. Choose from the menu or go whole hog with the impressive all-you-can-eat rodizio buffet, which includes seafood, sushi, and colorful, fresh salads in addition to the succulent grilled cuts; there is a vegetarian option. **Known for:** the picanha steak; the prime rib; the wild boar. ⑤ *Average main: R$165* ⊠ *Av. Ministro Ivan Lins 314, Barra da Tijuca* ☎ *21/2493–6060* ⊕ *www.barragrill.com.br.*

Restaurante Point de Grumari

$$$ | SEAFOOD | Set overlooking the vast Guaratiba flatlands and enveloped in dense forest, the seafood-focused menu at this casual restaurant is best known for its moqueca stew and spectacular sunsets. The colorful flora and glorious vistas give the feeling of being far out of town (you'll need a car to get here), but it's a great place to stop between visits to Grumari beach and Sitio Roberto Burle Marx. **Known for:** nearly flawless passion fruit caipirinhas; sunset views; deep-fried shrimp pastries. ⑤ *Average main: R$62* ⊠ *Estrada do Grumari 2710, Grumari* ☎ *21/2410–1434* ⊕ *www.pointdegrumari.com.br* ⊗ *No dinner.*

🛏 Hotels

★ Grand Hyatt Rio de Janeiro

$$$ | HOTEL | FAMILY | Opened in 2016, this is the first unit of the chain in the state of Rio de Janeiro. The beachfront urban resort combines nature and urban elements, offering a relaxed environment with a pool, spa, and Japanese and Brazilian restaurants. **Pros:** beachfront hotel; good restaurant options inside; spa facilities. **Cons:** away from the subway; away from the main tourist attractions; not all-inclusive resort. ⑤ *Rooms from: R$1,175* ⊠ *Av. Lucio Costa 9600, Barra da Tijuca* ⊕ *www.hyatt.com/grand-hyatt/pt-PT/riogh-grand-hyatt-rio-de-janeiro* ⇌ *436 rooms* ⓄⅠ *No Meals.*

Hilton Barra

$$$ | HOTEL | Contemporary and comfortable, the Hilton Barra began operations in 2014, becoming the first property of the chain in Rio de Janeiro and the second in Brazil. **Pros:** close to Olympic Park; ballroom for events up to 950 guests; wedding packages. **Cons:** not a beachfront location; away from main tourist attractions; delays on room service. ⑤ *Rooms from: R$539* ⊠ *Av. Embaixador Abelardo Bueno 1430, Barra da Tijuca* ⊕ *www.hiltonbarra.com* ⇌ *298 rooms* ⓄⅠ *No Meals* Ⓜ *Jardim Oceânico.*

Lagune Barra Hotel

$$$ | HOTEL | Lagune Barra hotel is located in the heart of Barra da Tijuca, Rio de Janeiro—a perfect blend of comfort and functionality for both leisure and business travelers. **Pros:** wellness area; Inside Riocentro event area; amazing staff. **Cons:** far from the nearest beaches; need private car or taxi to reach the city; dated rooms. ⑤ *Rooms from: R$532* ⊠ *Av. Salvador Allende 6555, Barra da Tijuca* ⊕ *www.lagunebarrahotel.com.br/* ⇌ *306 rooms* ⓄⅠ *Free Breakfast* Ⓜ *Olof Palme.*

La Suite by Dussol

$$$$ | HOTEL | This off-the-beaten-track location amid the secluded mansions of Joatinga—often referred to as "the Beverly Hills of Rio"—gives La Suite an ultra-exclusive feel, and the French owners have imbued their boutique hotel with real Parisian chic. **Pros:** impossibly scenic location; fantastic beach on your doorstep; romantic ambience. **Cons:**

it's a cab ride to bars and restaurants; impractical for extensive sightseeing; on-site prices for food and drink are high. ⑤ *Rooms from: R$1,170* ✉ *Rua Jackson de Figueiredo 501, Joatinga* ☎ *21/2484–1962* ⊕ *bydussol.com/* ⇌ *7 rooms* ⦿ *Free Breakfast.*

Radisson Hotel Barra Rio de Janeiro
$$$ | **HOTEL | FAMILY** | Each of the spacious and comfortable rooms in this mammoth hotel has a balcony overlooking Barra Beach, while facilities include a large heated pool, tennis courts, and a fitness center. **Pros:** good facilities; Barra Beach is quieter than Zona Sul; spacious rooms with balconies. **Cons:** traffic is bad; neighborhood is more like Miami than Rio; guests report average cleanliness. ⑤ *Rooms from: R$770* ✉ *Av. Evandro Lins e Silva 600, Barra da Tijuca* ☎ *21/3139–8000* ⊕ *www.radisson.com* ⇌ *292 rooms* ⦿ *Free Breakfast* Ⓜ *Jardim Oceanico.*

 Nightlife

★ Samba do Trabalhador
LIVE MUSIC | Samba do Trabalhador began as a fun time for musicians who worked on the weekends and met on Mondays at the traditional Renascença club to play together and relax while doing what they love most. The reputation for good music has spread and is bringing more and more people from the south zone to the traditional Tijuca. Don't be surprised to find music stars like Tereza Cristina and Jorge Aragão singing with the band led by Moacyr Luz. Arrive early to get in and buy your ticket in advance if possible. ✉ *Rua Barão de São Francisco 54, Tijuca* ⊕ *www.instagram.com/moacyrluzesambadotrabalhador/* ☞ *Only happens on Mon. from 5–10 pm.*

Performing Arts
CONCERT HALLS
Cidade das Artes
PERFORMANCE VENUES | This enormous cultural complex and live music venue opened in 2013 and is now the largest concert hall in South America, seating 1,780. Designed by French architect Christian de Portzamparc, the Cidade das Artes (City of Arts) complex covers around 90,000 square meters (969,000 square feet) and houses theaters and cinemas, and is home to the Brazilian Symphony Orchestra, and hosts major rock and pop shows. ✉ *Av. das Americas 5300, Barra da Tijuca* ☎ *21/3325–0102* ⊕ *cidadedasartes.rio.rj.gov.br/* Ⓜ *Jardim Oceanico.*

Farmasi Arena
CONCERTS | First built as a venue for the Pan American Games held in 2007, this venue hosts various events like sports or live concerts from national and international artists. ✉ *Av. Embaixador Abelardo Bueno 3401, Barra da Tijuca* ⊕ *farmasiarena.com.br/.*

Qualistage
MUSIC | This huge venue hosts some of the biggest Brazilian and international names playing in Rio, such as Caetano Veloso, Adele, Smashing Pumpkins, and Lady Gaga. ✉ *Via Parque Shopping, Av. Ayrton Senna 3000, Barra da Tijuca* ⊕ *qualistage.com.br/* 🎫 *From R$70.*

 Activities

GOLF
Campo Olímpico de Golfe
GOLF | Created for the Rio 2016 Olympic Games, the 18-hole course remains open for sports enthusiasts to play. There's also a restaurant. Despite being outside the main tourist area, it can be an interesting outing even for those who do not play sports, due to its integration with the local fauna and flora. This is the only

Olympic field in the world. ✉ *Av. General Moiséis Castelo Branco Filho 700, Barra da Tijuca* ⊕ *rioogc.com.br/* 🏷 *R$ 600 - Greens fee 9 holes international.*

Gávea Golf and Country Club
GOLF | With a stunning setting overlooking the ocean and framed by the towering Pedra da Gávea mountain, Gávea Golf and Country Club has an impeccably groomed course. It's members-only on weekends, but nonmembers can play during the week. Clubs are available to rent. ✉ *Estrada da Gávea 800, São Conrado* ☎ *21/3323–6050* ⊕ *www.gaveagolfclub.com.br* 🏷 *R$350 weekdays* ⛳ *18 holes, 5986 yards, par 18* Ⓜ *No metro.*

Golden Green Golf Club
GOLF | **FAMILY** | This small but well-maintained golf course may only have six holes, but given the exclusivity and prices of the alternatives, this could be your best option for getting in a little play in Rio. Nonmembers are welcome every day, but it's a little out of town. There is the option to circle the course three times and play a full 18 holes. ✉ *Av. Prefeito Dulcídio Cardoso 2901, Barra da Tijuca* ☎ *21/2434–0696* 🏷 *R$80 weekdays, R$100 weekends* ⛳ *6 holes, 2637 yards, par 54* 🕙 *Closed Mon.*

SURFING
Kitepoint Rio
SURFING | One of several companies based in beach kiosks along Avenida do Pepê near Posto 7, Kitepoint provides all the equipment and training you'll need to master the sport of kite surfing. Wind conditions have to be just right, though, so patience is a virtue when seeking lessons. ✉ *Av. do Pepê 930, next to Bombeiro / Kiosk 7, Barra da Tijuca* ☎ *21/8859–2112, 21/9200–0418* ⊕ *www.kitepointrio.com.br* 🏷 *From R$150* Ⓜ *Jardim Oceânico.*

 Shopping

SHOPPING CENTERS AND MALLS
São Conrado Fashion Mall
SHOPPING CENTER | The shops at Rio's least-crowded mall sell domestic and international fashions to a clientele that knows how to splurge. High-end Brazilian and international labels can be found here, and there are some very decent restaurants as well as a four-screen movie theater. ✉ *Estrada da Gávea 899, São Conrado* ☎ *21/2111–4444* ⊕ *www.fashionmall.com.br* Ⓜ *Sao Conrado.*

Village Mall
SHOPPING CENTER | **FAMILY** | There are some 600 stores here, ranging from high-street names such as Renner to small and seriously chic boutique fashion, jewelry, and lingerie stores. A branch of the legendary bikini store Lenny Niemeyer is here, and there's a wealth of good dining options and one of the city's most luxurious cinemas. ✉ *Av. das Américas 3900, Barra da Tijuca* ☎ *21/3003–4177* ⊕ *shoppingvillagemall.com.br.*

West of Downtown

Neighborhoods west of downtown are mainly residential. Unless you're a local, it's hard to know which areas are safe and which are not, so you should avoid wandering around. One exception is pleasant Quinta da Boa Vista, which is fine to wander. You can easily get here by metro, but avoid coming after dark.

Few visitors will make their base in the area west of downtown, but one compelling reason to visit is the mighty Maracanã soccer stadium, which is open for tours on nonmatch days. If you want to catch a game it is easiest to go as part of a group trip. Nearby, the city zoo and scenic gardens at Quinta da Boa Vista are worth a visit if you have the time. This area is also known for its culinary and musical hidden gems.

Fans have witnessed many historic sports moments at the Maracanã stadium that hosted the finals of the 1950 and 2014 FIFA World Cups and was the venue where the soccer star Pelé scored his 1,000th goal.

Sights

Bioparque do Rio

ZOO | FAMILY | For children and others with an interest in seeing birds and beasts up close, Rio's city zoo makes for a fun day out. Colorful native birds and a variety of South American monkeys are among the attractions; the "nursery" for baby animals and the reptile house are always popular with younger visitors. The zoo has received criticism for the somewhat small enclosures the larger animals—including lions and bears—endure, but conditions have improved in recent years, and an extensive refurbishment program was completed to improve facilities for animals and visitors alike, turning it into a biopark. ✉ *Parque da Quinta da Boa Vista, São Cristóvão* ☎ *21/3878–4219* ⊕ *bioparquedorio.com.br/* ✉ *R$49.50* Ⓜ *São Cristóvão.*

★ Maracanã

SPORTS VENUE | FAMILY | Now seating 78,838 fans after a major makeover in anticipation of the 2014 World Cup, the stadium hosted key matches during the 2016 Rio Olympics, and big local games are also held here during the seemingly never-ending Brazilian soccer season. The stadium is officially called Estádio Mário Filho, after a famous journalist, but it's best known as Maracanã, the name of the surrounding neighborhood and a nearby river. Guided and nonguided stadium tours can be booked on the official website; on match days the last tour begins three hours before gates open.

■**TIP→ Check local press outlets for match times.** ✉ *Rua Professor Eurico Rabelo, Gate 16, Maracanã* ☎ *21/98341–1949 tours* ⊕ *www.tourmaracana.com.br* ✉ *Match tickets R$80–R$700; tours R$75* Ⓜ *Maracanã.*

Museu Nacional

HISTORIC PARK | FAMILY | A little off Rio's main tourist track, the National Museum is well worth the metro ride to view its exhibits of botanical, anthropological, and animal specimens. With a permanent collection of 20 million objects (give or take a few), the supply is nearly endless. Temporary exhibitions focus on subjects such as meteorites, tribal art, and animal evolution. The opulent museum building—a former imperial palace—itself merits a visit, and the vast grounds are home to Rio's city zoo.

Unfortunately, the museum was damaged by a fire in 2018, closing its exhibitions rooms inside. The open-air exhibition Museu Nacional Vive was installed nearby, with panels and photographs that highlight the history and reconstruction of the institution. The restoration process can be followed on this website. (⊕ *museunacionalvive.org.br/*)

✉ *Quinta da Boa Vista, São Cristóvão* ☎ *21/3938–1100* ⊕ *www.museunacional.ufrj.br* 💲 *free* ⊙ *Closed Mon.* Ⓜ *Estação São Cristóvão.*

Quinta da Boa Vista
CITY PARK | FAMILY | Complete with lakes and marble statuary, this vast public park on a former royal estate's landscaped grounds is a popular spot for family picnics. You can rent boats to pedal on the water, and bicycles to pedal on land. The former imperial palace now houses the Museu Nacional. The city zoo sits adjacent to the park, which often hosts live music events. ✉ *Av. Paulo e Silva at Av. Bartolomeu de Gusmão, São Cristóvão* ⊕ *visit.rio/que_fazer/quinta-da-boa-vista* Ⓜ *São Cristóvão.*

🍴 Restaurants

★ Bar do Momo
$ | BRAZILIAN | The bar is considered a heritage site of the city and it is worth leaving the South Zone to Tijuca to try Toninho Laffargue's creations, which are often listed among the best snacks in the city. Be sure to try the rice balls, filled with cheese and sausage, and the artisanal burgers. **Known for:** salty rice balls; batidas (drinks with vodka and fruit); feijoada. 💲 *Average main: R$35* ✉ *Rua General Espírito Santo Cardoso 50, Tijuca* ⊕ *https://www.instagram.com/bardomomooficial/* ⊙ *Closed Tues.* Ⓜ *Uruguai.*

🍸 Nightlife

Baródromo
LIVE MUSIC | FAMILY | Everything in this themed bar—from the dishes to the decor—is inspired by samba celebrities and memorable parades held at Sambadrome. Don't forget to try dumplings like *martinho* (rice with cod) and the vegetarian *selminha* (cheese, sun-dried tomato, eggplant and zucchini), always accompanied by a cold beer and good live samba. ✉ *Rua, Dona Zulmira 41, Maracanã* ⊕ *www.instagram.com/barodromo/* ⊙ *Closed Mon.* Ⓜ *Saens Pena.*

🎭 Performing Arts

Acadêmicos do Salgueiro
MUSIC | The samba school Salgueiro holds its pre-Carnival rehearsals only on Saturdays from 10 pm. The school also runs other events through the year, like feijoada lunches and cultural fairs, all with live samba music playing all night. Their venue is easily accessed by taxis or rideshare cars, even if you leave late at night. ✉ *Rua Silva Teles 104, Andaraí* ☎ *21/2238–0389* ⊕ *www.salgueiro.com.br* 💲 *From R$30.*

Beija-Flor
MUSIC | The several-times winner of Rio's annual Samba School competition, Beija-Flor holds public rehearsals on Thursdays at 9 pm in the months leading up to Carnival. Since it's far from the usual tourist route, we recommend booking a tour with transport through a travel agency or book a car to go and return. ✉ *Pracinha Wallace Paes Leme 1025, Nilópolis* ☎ *21/2247–4800* ⊕ *www.beija-flor.com.br* 💲 *From R$30.*

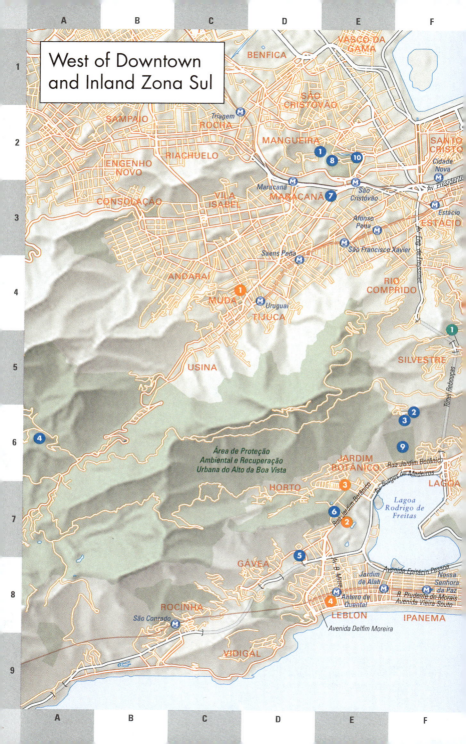

Sights ▼

1. Bioparque do Rio **D2**
2. Christ the Redeemer **F6**
3. Corcovado.......................... **F6**
4. Floresta da Tijuca **A6**
5. Fundação Planetário **D7**
6. Jardim Botânico **E7**
7. Maracanã **E3**
8. Museu Nacional................... **E2**
9. Parque Lage....................... **F6**
10. Quinta da Boa Vista **E2**

Restaurants ▼

1. Bar do Momo...................... **C4**
2. Casa Camolese **E7**
3. La Bicyclette **E7**
4. Oro................................. **E8**

Hotels ▼

1. JO&JOE Rio **F5**

Estação Primeira de Mangueira
MUSIC | One of the most popular schools and always a challenger for the Carnival title, Estação Primeira de Mangueira holds events throughout the year, with emphasis on monthly feijoadas on Saturday afternoons and show rehearsals on Saturday nights. Check the website for the schedule when you are in town. ✉ *Rua Visconde de Niterói 1072, Mangueira* ☎ *21/2567-4637* ⊕ *www.mangueira.com.br* 🖂 *From R$50* Ⓜ *Maracanã.*

Inland Zona Sul

In the western portion of the city north of Leblon, trees and hills dominate the landscape in the neighborhoods of Jardim Botânico, Lagoa, Cosme Velho, and Laranjeiras. In addition to their parks and gardens, these primarily residential neighborhoods have marvelous museums, seductive architecture, and tantalizing restaurants. The architecture is a blend of modern condominiums and colonial houses. These neighborhoods tend to be quieter during the day because they're not on the beachfront, but they do have some of the hippest nightclubs in Rio. You can't say you've seen Rio until you've taken in the view from Corcovado and then strolled through its forested areas or beside its inland Lagoa (Lagoon) Rodrigo de Freitas—hanging out just like a true Carioca.

These picturesque inland neighborhoods lack metro stops, so the best way to visit them all in one day is as part of an organized tour or with a private guide. If you have time to spare, each neighborhood warrants at least half a day's exploring. Be sure to visit Lagoa, which can be reached on foot from Leblon, Ipanema, and Copacabana, and the nearby Botanical Gardens. Cosme Velho is home to impressive mansions as well as the station for trains up to the Christ statue, and it's a pleasant stroll along the main road from here to Laranjeiras, which has some good bars and restaurants as well as pleasant squares and street markets.

Sights

★ Christ the Redeemer
MOUNTAIN | FAMILY | Rio's iconic *Cristo Redentor* (Christ the Redeemer) statue stands arms outstretched atop 690-meter-high (2,300-foot-high) Corcovado mountain. It wasn't until 1921, the centennial of Brazil's independence from Portugal, that someone had the idea of placing a statue atop Corcovado. A team of French artisans headed by sculptor Paul Landowski was assigned the task of erecting a statue of Christ with his arms apart as if embracing the city. (Nowadays, mischievous Cariocas say Christ is getting ready to clap for his favorite escola de samba.) It took 10 years, but on October 12, 1931, Christ the Redeemer was inaugurated by then-president Getúlio Vargas, Brazil's FDR. The sleek, modern figure rises more than 30 meters (100 feet) from a 6-meter (20-foot) pedestal and weighs 700 tons. In the evening a powerful lighting system transforms it into an even more dramatic icon. Access to Rio's most iconic monument is via the Corcovado Mountain. ✉ *Estrada da Redentor, Cosme Velho* ⊕ *visit.rio/en/que_fazer/christtheredeemer* 🖂 *R$97.50 by train; R$56.50 by minibus.*

★ Corcovado
MOUNTAIN | There's an eternal argument about which city view is better, the one from Pão de Açúcar (Sugarloaf) or the one from Corcovado. In our opinion, it's best to visit Sugarloaf before you visit Corcovado, or you may experience Sugarloaf only as an anticlimax. Corcovado has two advantages: it's nearly twice as high, and it offers an excellent view of Pão de Açúcar. The sheer 300-meter (1,000-foot) granite face of Corcovado (the name means "hunchback" and refers to the mountain's shape) has always been a difficult undertaking for climbers. There

are three ways to reach the top: by funicular railway, by official van, or on foot. The train (advance online tickets only) was built in 1885 and provides delightful views of Ipanema and Leblon from an absurd angle of ascent, as well as a close look at thick vegetation and butterflies. Official vans (⊕ www.paineirascorcovado.com.br) are slightly cheaper but not as much fun as the railway. There are boarding points for the vans in Copacabana and Largo do Machado, and at Paineiras inside the national park. After disembarking you can climb up 220 steep, zigzagging steps to the summit, or take an escalator or a panoramic elevator. If you choose the stairs, you pass little cafés and shops selling souvenirs along the way but save your money for Copacabana's night market; you'll pay at least double atop Corcovado. If you hike, keep in mind that it's a short but strenuous journey that's best undertaken with a local guide for safety reasons.

■ TIP→ **Visit Corcovado on a clear day; clouds often obscure the Christ statue and the view of the city. Go as early in the morning as possible, before people start pouring out of tour buses, and before the haze sets in.** ✉ *Cosme Velho Train Station, Rua Cosme Velho 513, Cosme Velho* ☎ *21/2558–1329 train station* ⊕ *www. corcovado.com.br* 🖃 *R$97.50 by train; R$56.50 by minibus.*

Floresta da Tijuca (*Tijuca Forest*)
OTHER ATTRACTION | FAMILY | Surrounding Corcovado is the dense, tropical Tijuca Forest, also known as the Parque Nacional da Tijuca. Once part of a Brazilian nobleman's estate, it's studded with exotic trees and thick jungle vines and has several waterfalls, including the delightful Cascatinha de Taunay (Taunay Waterfall). About 180 meters (200 yards) beyond the waterfall is the small pink-and-purple Capela Mayrink (Mayrink Chapel) with painted panels by the 20th-century Brazilian artist Cândido Portinari.

The views are breathtaking from several points along this national park's 96 km (60 miles) of narrow winding roads. Some of the most spectacular are from Dona Marta, on the way up Corcovado; the Emperor's Table, supposedly where Brazil's last emperor, Pedro II, took his court for picnics; and, farther down the road, the Chinese View, the area where Portuguese king João VI allegedly settled the first Chinese immigrants to Brazil, who came in the early 19th century to develop tea plantations. A great way to see the forest is by Jeep or van. You can arrange tours through several agencies, among them Brazil Expedition (⊕ *www. brazilexpedition.com*) and Jeep Tour (☎ *21/2108–5800* ⊕ *www.jeeptour.com. br*). ✉ *Estrada da Cascatinha 850, Alto da Boa Vista* ☎ *21/2492–2252* ⊕ *parquenacionaldatijuca.rio/.*

Fundação Planetário
OBSERVATORY | FAMILY | Rio's planetarium is a great escape if your vacation gets rained on, or if you simply have a passion for astronomy. The adjoining interactive Museu do Universo (Museum of the Universe) illustrates the history of space exploration and travel in a futuristic exhibition area with lots of hands-on activities for kids. The planetarium frequently updates its programming, which consists of a mixture of fictitious adventures in space (recommended for kids) and nonfiction shows about the constellations and our solar system.
✉ *Rua Vice-Governador Ruben Bernardo 100, Gávea* ☎ *21/2088–0536* ⊕ *planeta. rio/* 🖃 *Museum R$20; museum and planetarium session R$40* ⊗ *Museum closed Mon. and Tues.*

★ **Jardim Botânico**
GARDEN | FAMILY | The 340-acre (0.5 sq miles) Botanical Garden contains more than 5,000 species of tropical and subtropical plants and trees, including 900 varieties of palms (some more than a century old) and more than 140 species of birds. The shady garden, created in

With more than 300,000 visitors per year, the Corcovado mountain is home to the Christ the Redeemer statue and offers excellent views of Sugarloaf Mountain.

1808 by the Portuguese king João VI during his exile in Brazil, offers respite from Rio's sticky heat. In 1842 the garden gained its most impressive adornment, the Avenue of the Royal Palms, a 720-meter (800-yard) double row of 134 soaring royal palms. Elsewhere, the Casa dos Pilões, an old gunpowder factory, has been restored and displays objects pertaining to the nobility and their slaves. Also on the grounds are a museum dedicated to environmental concerns, a library, two small cafés, and a gift shop. ✉ *Rua Jardim Botânico 1008, Jardim Botânico* ☎ *21/3874–1808* ⊕ *jbrj. eleventickets.com* 🎟 *R$73.*

★ Parque Lage

GARDEN | FAMILY | This lush green space down the road from Jardim Botânico was acquired by Antônio Martins Lage Jr., whose grandson, Henrique Lage, fell head over heels in love with the Italian singer Gabriela Bezanzoni. The magnificent palace he had constructed for her was completed in 1922; the impressive mansion and grounds were turned into a public park in 1960. A visual arts school and a café occupy the mansion. On the grounds are small aquariums and a few caves that have stalactites and stalagmites. If you want to tackle Corcovado on foot to make your pilgrimage to see Christ the Redeemer, start in Parque Lage. Trails are clearly marked, but you shouldn't go alone. ✉ *Rua Jardim Botânico 414, Jardim Botânico* ☎ *21/2334–4088* ⊕ *www.eavparquelage.rj.gov.br.*

🍴 Restaurants

La Bicyclette

$$ | BISTRO | FAMILY | Located a stone's throw from Rio's Botanical Gardens, this cozy bakery is a great pit stop for lazy brunches, light lunches, or afternoon snacks pre- or post-stroll through the gardens. French owners are behind the buttery croissants, homemade breads, fresh juices, delicious cakes, organic coffee, and sophisticated sandwiches. **Known for:** desserts like tapioca cake with dulce de leche caramel; La Pascualina spinach quiche; hibiscus iced tea. $ *Average main: R$30* ✉ *Rua Pacheco Leão 320, Loja D,, Jardim Botânico* ☎ *21/3256–9052* ⊕ *www.labicyclette.com.br.*

★ Casa Camolese

$$$ | ITALIAN | Owned by artist Vik Muniz and hospitality guru Cello Camolese, this trendy, split-level industrial-chic converted warehouse combines Italian-fusion dishes with a vibrant cocktail bar, in-house deli, microbrewery, and underground jazz club. Alfresco tables are set overlooking the racetrack, making it an idyllic spot to watch Sunday afternoon races fly by. **Known for:** artisanal microbrewery on the mezzanine level; vibrant, bohemian-chic atmosphere; killer cocktails served round a curved art-deco bar. $ *Average main: R$50* ✉ *Rua Jardim Botânico 983, Jardim Botânico* ☎ *21/99239–4969* ⊕ *casacamolese.com.br.*

Oro

$$$$ | CONTEMPORARY | While rising star Felipe Bronze has long been known for his avant-garde Brazilian tasting menus, his approach has found a welcomed simplicity since he moved fine dining restaurant Oro from its Jardim Botânico location to Leblon in 2016. The two versions of the menu degustation feature a series of small, elaborately prepared dishes, including oysters, pão de queijo and other Brazilians delicacies. **Known for:** pumpkin and shrimp; 14- and 16-course tasting menus; oysters with guava. $ *Average main: R$690* ✉ *Av. Gen. San Martin 889, Leblon* ☎ *21/2540–8768* ⊕ *ororestaurante.com.br/en* ☉ *Closed Sun. and Mon.; no lunch Tues.–Fri.*

🛏 Hotels

★ JO&JOE Rio

$$ | B&B/INN | Located in a restored historic building, this modern boutique hostel offers guests comfort and the opportunity to socialize with other travelers, with several common areas, a bar, restaurant, sports courts, and swimming pools. The hostel also offers a store with basic items, such as snacks, drinks, sunscreen, and beachwear. **Pros:** walking distance to the Christ train station; lively bar with daily attractions; historical site renewed. **Cons:** not beachfront; away from the nearest subway station; no bedside lamp in the private rooms. $ *Rooms from: R$285* ✉ *Largo do Boticário 32, Cosme Velho* ☎ *21/3235–2600* ⊕ *www.joandjoe.com/rio/pt-br/* ⇨ *80 rooms* ⦿| *No Meals* Ⓜ *Largo do Machado.*

 Performing Arts

THEATER

Teatro das Artes

THEATER | FAMILY | Located in a shopping mall in well-heeled Gavea, this theater hosts popular productions. Two smaller theaters are reserved for less-commercial productions. Most productions tend to be in Portuguese. ✉ *Shopping Center da Gávea, Rua Marques de São Vicente 52, Loja 264, Gávea* ☎ *21/2540–6004, 21/2294–1096* ⊕ *www.teatrodasartes.com.br* ⛁ *From R$40.*

Activities

HORSE RACING

★ Jóquei Clube

HORSE RACING | This beautiful old racetrack conjures up a bygone era of grandeur with its impeccably preserved betting hall, 1920s grandstand, and distant beach views framed by Cristo Redentor and the Dois Irmãos mountain. When the big event of the year, the Grande Prêmio, comes around in August, expect the crowds to swell and everyone to be dressed to the nines. Entry is free year-round—race days tend to be Monday, Friday, and Sunday. Dress is smart casual, with no shorts or flip-flops allowed in the main stand. If you're casually dressed, you can sit in the cheap seats at the front. ✉ *Praça Santos Dumont 31, Gávea* ☎ *21/2512–9988* ⊕ *www.jcb.com.br* Ⓜ *No metro.*

SURFING

★ Surf's Up Rio

SURFING | FAMILY | Run by globe-trotting, multilingual surfer Gabriela Pulcherio, this agency offers individual and group surf lessons, as well as stand-up paddle boarding experiences, both on Zona Sul's beaches and as part of day trips out to the natural reserve of Guaratiba. ✆ 21/99214–0797 ⊕ surfsuprio.com ✉ R$90.

Shopping

SHOPPING CENTERS AND MALLS

Shopping da Gávea

GENERAL STORE | The brand-name stores and smaller boutiques at the fashionable Shopping da Gávea mall sell designer fashions, accessories, and swimwear, and there are several good cafés and coffee shops. ✉ Rua Marquês de São Vicente 52, Gávea ✆ 21/2294–1096 ⊕ www.shoppingdagavea.com.br.

CLOTHING

Dona Coisa

CLOTHING | This gorgeous womenswear boutique stocks a selection of Brazil's chicest designers and emerging talents. The friendly stylists will guide you through the range of day and evening wear, as well as the fabulous jewelry and accessories. ✉ Rua Lopes Quintas 153, Jardim Botânico ✆ 21/2249–2336 ⊕ www.donacoisa.com.br ⊙ Closed Sun.

HANDICRAFTS

★ O Sol Artesanato

CRAFTS | Exhibiting Brazilian craftsmanship at its finest, O Sol is a nonprofit, nongovernmental shop promoting and selling the handiwork of artisans from all regions of Brazil. It's one of Rio's best handicraft stores and well worth a visit. ✉ Rua Corcovado 213, Jardim Botânico ✆ 21/2294–6198 ⊕ www.instagram.com/osolartesanato/ ⊙ Closed Sun.

Pé de Boi

CRAFTS | A popular arts and crafts store that carries woodwork pieces, ceramics, weaving, and sculptures created by artists from around Brazil, Pé de Boi specializes in objects from the states of Pernambuco and Minas Gerais. ✉ Rua Ipiranga 55, Laranjeiras ✆ 21/2285–4395 ⊕ www.pedeboi.com.br ⊙ Closed Sun.

MARKETS

★ Babilônia Feira Hype (Babylon Hype Fair)

MARKET | This fair that takes place roughly every couple of months combines fashion, design, art, and gastronomy from independent labels and artisans. The quality of the goods on offer and the experience itself has improved over the years, and since it moved to an alfresco spot overlooking the Lagoa, it's become a highlight in Rio's event calendar. Expect live music, great shopping, and the chance to watch a parade of beautiful people. Location may vary between Clube Monte Líbano and Parque das Figueiras, both in Lagoa Rodrigo de Freitas. ✉ Av. Borges de Medeiros 701, Clube Monte Líbano, Leblon ✆ 21/2267–0066 ⊕ www.babiloniafeirahype.com.br Ⓜ Jardim de Alah / Leblon.

★ Feira da General Glicério

MARKET | FAMILY | Browse for local crafts, enjoy delicious snacks, sip a caipirinha, and listen to the delicate sounds of live *choro* at this laid-back Saturday street market in the leafy residential neighborhood of Laranjeiras. Vendors selling fruit and veggies set up stalls on the streets surrounding a small neighborhood square, but the main focus of attention is on the clothing and crafts stalls on the square, as well as on food and drink sellers and the famous Barraca do Luiz—a tent selling caipirinhas and rare music CDs—as choro bands perform nearby. Come early: the market opens at 10 am and the fun is over by midafternoon. ✉ Rua General Glicério, Laranjeiras Ⓜ No metro.

Chapter 4

SIDE TRIPS FROM RIO

4

Updated by
Luana Ferreira

WELCOME TO SIDE TRIPS FROM RIO

TOP REASONS TO GO

★ **Glamorous Búzios:** Hang out with the young and beautiful on the beach at Búzios in the morning, then enjoy the sunset on Orla Bardot.

★ **Water Sports:** Sail a schooner to a deserted island for some scuba diving, then watch the dolphins play in your wake on the way home.

★ **Mountain Excursions:** Get lost in time at the Imperial Museum in mountainous Petrópolis.

★ **Glorious Ilha Grande:** Take an early-morning hike through the Atlantic rainforests of Ilha Grande.

★ **Historic Paraty:** Stroll the cobbled streets of this colonial town before boarding a sailboat for an island-hopping afternoon.

★ **Fresh Beach Food:** Tuck into freshly caught fish at beach kiosks in Búzios and Arraial do Cabo, washing them down with coconut water sipped straight from the shell.

1 Niterói. Take in breathtaking views of Rio de Janeiro from Niterói's iconic Museum of Contemporary Art, perched over the Guanabara Bay.

2 Arraial do Cabo. Dive into the crystal-clear waters of Arraial do Cabo, famous for its stunning beaches and rich marine life.

3 Búzios. Hang out with the Cariocas on the beach at Búzios in the morning, then explore the city's rich gastronomy.

4 Petrópolis. Get lost in time at the Imperial Museum in mountainous Petrópolis.

5 Angra Dos Reis. Sail between Angra dos Reis' emerald islands, discovering hidden beaches and tropical rainforests.

6 Ilha Grande. Take an early-morning hike through the Atlantic rainforests of Ilha Grande.

7 Paraty. Stroll the cobbled streets of this colonial town before boarding a sailboat for an island-hopping afternoon.

Rio is often the main reason people include Brazil on their bucket list. Yet the state is scattered with secluded islands, historic towns, and charming beach towns that are also popular among Cariocas. You can escape the scorching days and discover the Região Serrana (Mountain Region), boasting charming cities that combine history and romance, such as Petropolis, established as the official summer residence of Emperor Pedro II, and Teresopolis.

The coast is home to hundreds of beaches that are worth the journey. Just a couple of hours' drive east is the fancy beach resort of Búzios, with its 23 beaches, boutiques, and lively nightlife, while to the west is the unspoiled, untamed beauty of Ilha Grande. Nearby lies Paraty, a well-preserved colonial town.

The Região dos Lagos, also known as Costa do Sol (Sun Coast), famed for its beautiful beaches, enjoys more sunny days than anywhere else in Rio de Janeiro State. Here, the hip resort town of Búzios is a playground for Rio de Janeiro's *gente bonita* (beautiful people), who come to relax on the beaches by day and socialize in the stylish bars and clubs by night. En route to Búzios is the quieter beach resort of Arraial do Cabo, an unpretentious fishing town known as the Caribbean of Brazil because of its crystal-clear waters and white-sand beaches.

Sitting west of the city on the verdant Costa Verde (Green Coast), pretty Paraty's pedestrianized historical center has changed little since the 18th century. The vast nature reserve island of Ilha Grande, just off the Green Coast, provides virtually unlimited opportunities for beach hopping, hiking on nature trails, and just relaxing.

MAJOR REGIONS
En route to the gorgeous beaches and scorched mountains of the **Costa do Sol** is the small city of Niterói, whose ancient forts stand in stark contrast to its contemporary Museu de Arte Contemporânea. Farther east is the coastal town of Cabo Frio, one of the country's oldest settlements, and the small village of Arraial do Cabo, whose clear turquoise waters make it one of Brazil's top spots for diving. Nearby Búzios, with its many beaches, year-round sunshine, and vibrant nightlife, is a popular weekend holiday destination

for wealthy *Cariocas* as well as foreign visitors to Rio.

Northeast of Rio de Janeiro lies Petrópolis, whose opulent imperial palace was once the emperor's summer home. A twisting road through majestic mountains takes you to Teresópolis, named for Empress Teresa Christina. Nestled between these two towns is Parque Nacional da Serra dos Órgãos, famous for its curious rock formations and spectacular views.

West of Rio de Janeiro, the **Costa Verde** sees wild jungle tumbling down rocky mountains to a seemingly endless string of beaches. Angra dos Reis is the jumping-off point for 365, mostly uninhabited islands that pepper an extensive emerald bay. The largest, Ilha Grande, is a short boat ride from Angra dos Reis or nearby Conceição de Jacareí. Paraty, a UNESCO World Heritage Site, is a perfectly preserved colonial town farther down the coast whose proximity to secluded beaches makes it one of the region's highlights.

Planning

Getting Here and Around

While most resort towns boast an airport of some kind, the area is small enough that few people fly to destinations within the state. The roads along the coasts and to the towns in the mountains tend to be well-maintained, so most Brazilians travel by car or bus. There are often long traffic jams during the holiday season, especially during Christmas and New Year's Eve. Check weather conditions before heading to the mountains, as heavy rains can cause serious landslides. Along the Green Coast, collective transfer services such as Paraty Tours provide door-to-door services that are a convenient and cost-effective way to travel in the region. At the beach resorts of Búzios, driving from beach to beach in a buggy is great fun, and the cost of renting works out to be a reasonable value. You can also rent a bike or take a taxi boat. Driving within the city of Rio can be a daunting experience, but it's fairly easy to get around outside the city. The roads, especially to the major tourist destinations, are well-signposted. Buses are cheap, comfortable, and efficient, but the vast terminal in Rio can be uncomfortably hot and the surrounding area is a little edgy. It's best to leave plenty of time to buy tickets and locate your boarding point. Don't rely on using the ATMs here as they are frequently out of service, but you can pay for everything using the Pix system by Pag Brasil. Note that nonBrazilians may have problems buying advance tickets online, as a CPF (Brazilian social security number) is usually required. You can avoid that by using platforms like Busbud. At popular times, arranging a group or private transfer or booking through a travel agent may be preferable. ■**TIP**→ **Avoid leaving the city on Friday afternoon when residents flee the city en masse and the traffic is horrific. For the same reason, try to avoid returning on Sunday evening.**

BUS

As a rule, private buses in Rio, such as Autoviacao 1001 (⊕ *www.autoviacao1001.com.br*), Águia Branca, and Costa Verde (⊕ *www.costaverdetransportes.com.br*), tend to be clean, punctual, air-conditioned, and comfortable. Buses leave from the Rodoviária do Rio (⊕ *www.rodoviariadorio.com.br*), and most destinations are within three hours of the city. Expect to catch a taxi or app car (Uber or 99 Taxis) from the bus station to your hotel. Autoviacao 1001 is the principal bus company to travel to Búzios, while Costa Verde will take you through Angra, Paraty, and all the way to São Paulo. Outside the city, local bus service within towns, or districts, tends to be regular and cheap, but buses rarely have air-conditioning and are not well-maintained. There are few routes, and the bus driver will either nod or shake his head if you tell him where you want to go. You can buy your ticket on the bus, but don't use large notes. Bus terminals and stands are easy to spot. Beware of pickpockets if the stand or bus is particularly crowded.

CAR

The roads in Rio de Janeiro State are generally in good condition and well-marked, especially in the areas frequented by holidaymakers. If you plan to travel around and spend a few nights in different towns, it makes sense to rent a car in Rio, although it can be a bit tricky finding your way out of the city. Remember that if you travel to Ilha Grande, you will have to leave your car on the mainland, so be sure to remove all valuables. You also have to pay a toll at certain points. The road that runs the final stretch from Rio to Paraty combines the occasional hairpin turn with fast drivers and single-lane traffic.

■ TIP→ **Car rental prices in resort towns can be exorbitant, so if you plan to rent a car, do it in Rio. In Cabo Frio and Búzios, it is a better value and more fun to rent a beach buggy—numerous agencies offer this service.**

Hotels

There are hotels for all budgets and all tastes, from beachfront *pousadas* offering simple rooms with barely more than a bed and a ceiling fan to boutique hotels with luxurious amenities and on-site spas. Paraty and Petrópolis have gorgeous 18th-century inns, some of which can be a bit drafty in winter.

⇨ *Hotel reviews have been shortened. For full information, visit Fodors.com.*

WHAT IT COSTS in Reais

	$	$$	$$$	$$$$
RESTAURANTS				
	under R$50	R$50–R$130	R$131–R$200	over R$200
HOTELS				
	under R$150	R$150–R$300	R$301–R$500	over R$500

Planning Your Time

The many attractions of Rio de Janeiro fan out in all directions from the city itself, so it makes sense to focus your time on one region, whether it be the mountainous inland, the Sun Coast, or the Emerald Coast. Whichever direction you head, trips along the coast invariably merit a few days, especially since driving times each way average between three to four hours. For remote beaches, wild nature, and limited nightlife, head to the lovely Ilha Grande, although be aware that accommodation options can be more rustic than the mainland and the majority of visitors are often backpackers with endless days to while away.

For a more sophisticated beach destination packed with history and evocative culture, continue a few hours farther down the coast to the colonial town of Paraty. Block off at least three days days to explore the spectacular archipelago by boat, horse ride and hike through jungle trails, and visit nearby deserted beaches. Should rain clouds linger on the horizon, Paraty is invariably a better option than Ilha Grande as there is a far greater choice of things to do and places to dine. While the highlights of this historic town can be seen in one day and night, those who can spare the time may well want to head to the tranquil beach village of Trindade nearby.

A Bit of History

The history of Rio de Janeiro State is as colorful as it is bloody. Portuguese colonizers set foot in the city for the first time in 1502, but the first settlement was established in 1565. It was a period of conflicts, when Portuguese and Indigenous people fought against the French. Rio became the capital of the Portuguese colony in 1763.The city's economy developed slowly, and it revolved around the trade of Pau-Brasil (Brazilwood). The discovery of gold in the state of Minas Gerais in 1695 and the construction of the Caminho do Ouro (Path of Gold) from the mines to Paraty brought prosperity. In its wake came pirates and corsairs who used the islands and bays of Angra dos Reis as cover while they plundered the ships bound for Rio de Janeiro.

The mines gave out in the late 1700s, but the relatively new crop of coffee, introduced to the state around 1727, brought another boom. In the mid-19th century the state produced more than 70% of Brazil's coffee. Sadly, vast tracts of Atlantic rainforest were destroyed to make room for the crop across the interior of the state.In 1808, threatened by Napoléon, King Dom Joáo VI of Portugal moved his court to Rio, initiating a significant urban development in the city. He returned to Portugal in 1821 and left his son, Dom Pedro I, behind as prince regent. The following year Dom Pedro I was called back to Portugal, but he refused to leave. Instead, he declared Brazil an independent state and himself its emperor.

The highlights of Rio's sister city, Niterói, can be seen in a morning or afternoon, and sun lovers will want to set aside at least a couple of nights to visit the beach resorts that lie farther up the coast. The aptly named Costa do Sol is home to some of the best beaches in the state. Make your base in Búzios, where chic accommodation options abound, and set aside at least one full day to take a boat trip to some of Búzios's best beaches, and another to day trip to the beaches of Arraial do Cabo.

The mountainous north is often visited as a day trip from Rio, taking in the imperial town of Petrópolis, but it's also nice to slow down and relax for a few days, soaking up the stunning colonial palaces, hiking through national parks, and scaling the peaks that surround nearby Teresópolis.

Restaurants

The food here is nothing if not eclectic. Expect to find sushi bars, Italian restaurants, and German biergartens alongside restaurants selling typical Brazilian cuisine. At lunchtime, you can try a *prato feito*, a popular Brazilian meal consisting of a set plate with rice, beans, a protein (such as beef, chicken, or fish), salad, and sometimes fries. It is typically served in casual restaurants at an affordable price.

Coastal towns serve a large selection of fresh seafood, and most have a local specialty that's worth trying. Beachfront restaurants, especially the ubiquitous *barracas* (kiosks), can be a pleasant surprise and most will bring food and drink right up to your chosen spot on the sand.

Paraty and Búzios have excellent restaurants serving international cuisine. During high season they fill up beginning at 9 pm. Restaurants in Petrópolis and Teresópolis serve European cuisine and *mineira*, the hearty, meaty fare from Minas Gerais. Generally, dinner starts at seven and restaurants close around midnight.

■ TIP→ **To be on the safe side, don't buy seafood from venders strolling along the beach. Be especially careful about the oysters in Búzios and Cabo Frio, which may not be as fresh as the vendor claims.**

Pousada Defined

Wherever you travel in Brazil, you're likely to stay in a *pousada*. The name translates as "rest stop." A pousada can be an inn, a bed-and-breakfast, or a fancy boutique lodging with a pool and spa. The one thing all pousadas have in common is that they are independently run and managed. Generally smaller than hotels, they tend to offer more personalized service.

Tours

Rio Xtreme
ADVENTURE TOURS | Rio Xtreme offers group and private adventure tours and activities in Rio de Janeiro State. The friendly, English-speaking guides and instructors can take you scuba diving in Cabo Frio or ziplining, hiking, and rafting in the jungle that surrounds Rio.

■ TIP→ **Booking inquiries are best made via the website, email or WhatsApp.** ⊕ *www.rioxtreme.com* ✉ *From R$290.*

When to Go

The towns along the Costa do Sol and Costa Verde are packed on national holidays and between early December and Carnival, so reservations should be made well in advance. The populations of Paraty and Búzios can more than double as families and young people arrive from nearby Rio de Janeiro and São Paulo on the weekend. Paraty books up well ahead of its annual literary festival and Bourbon Festival. The weather along the coast is fairly predictable: summers are hot. During low season, from March to June and September to November, the weather is milder and there is plenty of elbow room on the beach. To top it off, prices can be half of what they are in high season. The Região Serrana (mountainous region), Petrópolis, and Teresópolis provide a refreshing change from the oppressive heat of the coast. The beaches and towns along the Emerald Coast, thus named because of the abundance of tropical vegetation framing the turquoise-green waters, often attract the most rain due to its topography. Check the forecast on the local site, ⊕ *www.climatempo.com.br*, if this is a concern. The highlights of Rio's sister city, Niterói, can be seen in a morning or afternoon, and sun lovers will want to set aside at least a couple of nights to visit the beach resorts that lie farther up the coast. The aptly named Costa do Sol is home to some of the best beaches in the state. Make your base in Búzios, where chic accommodation options abound. Then plan to spend at least one full day on a boat trip to some of Búzios's best beaches, and take another day to visit the beaches of Arraial do Cabo. The mountainous north is often visited as a day trip from Rio, taking in the imperial town of Petrópolis, but it's also nice to slow down and relax for a few days, soaking up the stunning colonial palaces, hiking through national parks, and scaling the peaks that surround nearby Teresópolis.

Niterói

14 km (9 miles) east of Rio de Janeiro.

Cariocas joke that the best thing about Niterói is the view—on a clear day you can see Rio de Janeiro with the Corcovado and Sugarloaf across the bay. The town itself is quiet and considerably sleepier than the buzzing capital across the water. Catch a ferry from Rio's Praça 15 de Novembro and cross the bay in 20 minutes. From the Praça Araribóia or at the Terminal Hidroviário de Charitas, walk along the esplanade to the Forte de Gragoatá and then walk to Museu de Arte Contemporânea, whose Oscar Niemeyer–designed building and views of Rio are more impressive than the art exhibitions, which rarely thrill. Icaraí beach attracts local beach lovers and offers spectacular panoramic views of Rio. If you have time, enjoy a beer on the beach and watch the sunset over Sugarloaf and the Corcovado. There is plenty to do in Niteroi, but if you plan to head up to Costa do Sol to Búzios or Cabo Frio, a half day is enough.

GETTING HERE AND AROUND

The best way to get to Niterói is by passenger ferry from the Praça 15 de Novembro in Rio de Janeiro. The trip takes about 20 minutes with CCR Barcas boats (R$7.70). Don't travel here by car unless somebody is driving for you. The roads in Niterói are even more confusing than in Rio. Mauá's Bus 2100D (R$8.50) departs for Niterói from Avenida Erasmo Braga 299, Centro. It takes approximately 50 minutes, not counting traffic delays, which can be severe during rush hour.

Did You Know?

Often compared to the shape of a UFO, The Museum of Contemporary Art in Niteroi offers views of Guanabara Bay, Rio de Janeiro, and Sugarloaf Mountain.

ESSENTIALS
VISITOR INFORMATION Neltur - Niterói Tourism Office. ✉ *Estrada Leopoldo Fróes 773, Niterói* ☎ *21/3611–3800.*

Sights

Fortaleza de Santa Cruz
MILITARY SIGHT | Built in 1555, the impressive Fortaleza de Santa Cruz was the first fort on Guanabara Bay. The cannons are distributed over two levels, but more impressive are the 17th-century sun clock and Santa Barbara Chapel. The views over Rio de Janeiro span out in all directions, so keep your camera on hand. It takes 15 minutes by taxi to reach the fort from downtown Niterói, and costs about R$10. ✉ *Estrada General Eurico Gaspar Dutra, Jurujuba* ☎ *21/2710–2354* 🎫 *R$10.*

★ Museu de Arte Contemporânea
VIEWPOINT | The Museum of Contemporary Art (MAC) was designed by the late great modernist architect Oscar Niemeyer, known for his futuristic work. The location offers a 360-degree panoramic view of Niterói, which is enough reason to pay a visit. The museum is a five-minute cab ride from Praça Araribóia, by the ferry terminal in downtown Niterói, or take the 47B bus. The on-site bistro is a good spot for lunch. ✉ *Mirante de Boa Viagem s/n, Niterói* ☎ *21/3619–5800* ⊕ *www.macniteroi.com.br* 🎫 *R$16; free Wed.*

Arraial do Cabo

165 km (102 miles) east of Rio.

Nicknamed the Caribbean of Brazil in honor of its translucent white sands and crystal-clear warm waters, Arraial do Cabo is a favorite destination for divers and sunseekers alike and lies just 10 km (6 miles) south of Cabo Frio. Gorgeous beaches and craggy rock formations surround the village—don't miss the Gruta Azul, a 15-meter-tall (49 feet) cave over the blue sea. It's a popular destination for scuba diving and there are many PADI-accredited dive schools here, while skippers wait at the harbor to whisk visitors to the best beaches and vantage points, often stopping for lunch at a floating restaurant. The sunsets over the small beach Prainha Pontal do Atalaia are often quite stunning. There's a handful of pousadas here, but there are cheaper and better options in nearby Búzios, which is a quick bus or cab ride away. While neighboring Cabo Frio is one of the oldest settlements in Brazil and shares the same crystal blue waters, a recent spike in crime and a boost in mass low-level Brazilian tourism have contributed to it becoming a less desirable tourism destination. While Arraial do Cabo is one of the best places in Brazil for snorkeling and scuba diving, as well as having a decent surf and kitesurf scene, it's very low-key in terms of its hospitality infrastructure when compared with other beach towns.

■ **TIP→ There's a handful of good-value pousadas, but if you want a more sophisticated scene, head to Búzios, an hour's drive away.**

GETTING HERE AND AROUND
From Rio de Janeiro, drive across the Rio–Niterói Bridge (officially the President Costa e Silva Bridge) and bear left, following the BR 101. At Rio Bonito take the exit to the Region dos Lagos and follow the signs to Arraial do Cabo. The trip takes approximately three hours—expect to be held up in traffic outside Niterói for some time. Arraial do Cabo–bound Aviação 1001 buses leave the Rodoviária every half hour. The trip takes around four hours and costs R$66.73. Tourist information desks at Arraial do Cabo's bus station can provide maps. Shuttle transfers from Rio hotels and airports can be arranged for around R$220—speak to hotel staff.

Known as part of the "Brazilian Caribbean," Praia do Forno has clear waters that are perfect for spotting fish.

Beaches

★ Praia do Pontal da Atalaia
BEACH | FAMILY | Across the bay from the idyllic Ilha do Farol (Lighthouse Island), the waters on the peninsula are equally spectacular, but easier to access than the island's beaches. Two beaches straddle the point of this peninsula, and when the tide is low, the white sands join to become one. Surprisingly, these beaches are often emptier than those closer to town, but that's probably because of access—you have to drive or take a taxi to the residential condominium Pontal do Atalaia and follow the dirt track until you reach the stairs down to the beach. **Amenities:** food and drink. **Best for:** solitude; snorkeling; swimming. ✥ *5 km from the City Center.*

★ Praia do Forno
BEACH | FAMILY | Stretching for 500 meters, this beach is famous for its turquoise waters that remain cooling year-round. It's surrounded by rock walls, where natural pools are formed during the low tide. The only way to access the beach is by boat (R$10) or hiking on an easy trail (10 minutes). Despite its secluded access, it's often crowded and features many kiosks along the beach. If you want to find a quiet spot, walk towards the end of the beach. **Amenities:** food and drink. **Best for:** snorkeling, swimming ✉ *Praia do Forno, Arraial.*

Hotels

Casa Mar Arraial
$$ | B&B/INN | This charming no-frills pousada stands out for its warm, welcoming staff and excellent location, situated within walking distance of two of the area's best beaches, Praia Grande and Praia Brava. **Pros:** great value; good local recommendations from the staff; complimentary umbrellas and deck chairs. **Cons:** small bathrooms; pool can get crowded; occasional noise in the surrounding area. ⑤ *Rooms from: R$215* ✉ *Rua Júlio de Macedo, 180* ☎ *22/99888–0229* ⊕ *www.casamararraiai.com.br* ⇨ *9 rooms* ⦿ *Free Breakfast.*

Activities

DIVING
★ Master Dive
BOAT TOURS | This PADI-accredited diving school and trip operator offers highly professional service, with modern boats, well-maintained equipment, and friendly staff. They have daily dive trips and you can purchase additional professional underwater pictures. ✉ *Rua Vera Cruz, 1, Praia dos Anjos* ☎ *22/99969–3005* ⊕ *www.masterdive.com.br* 💰 *From R$250.*

Búzios

24 km (15 miles) northeast of Cabo Frio; 176 km (126 miles) northeast of Rio.

Around two hours from Rio de Janeiro, Búzios is a string of beautiful beaches on an 8-km-long (5-mile-long) peninsula. It was the quintessential sleepy fishing village until the 1960s, when the French actress Brigitte Bardot holidayed here to escape the paparazzi and the place almost instantly transformed into a vacation sensation. Búzios has something for everyone. Some hotels cater specifically to families and provide plenty of activities and around-the-clock childcare. Many have spa facilities, and some specialize in weeklong retreats. For outdoor enthusiasts, Búzios offers surfing, windsurfing, kitesurfing, diving, hiking, and mountain biking, as well as leisurely rounds of golf.

GETTING HERE AND AROUND
From Rio de Janeiro, drive across the Rio–Niterói Bridge and bear left, following the BR 101. At Rio Bonito take the exit to the Region dos Lagos. At São Pedro de Aldeia, turn left at the sign for Búzios. The trip takes about three hours, of which at least an hour may be spent caught in traffic around Niterói. Búzios-bound 1001 buses leave from Rio's Novo Rio bus station every half hour. The trip takes around two hours and costs R$72.41. Transfers from Rio hotels can be arranged for around R$130. Speak to hotel staff who should be happy to set this service up for you. Shuttle transfers from Rio's airports are also available for about the same price. In Buzios and Me Leva Buzios are reliable shuttle operators.

ESSENTIALS
VISITOR INFORMATION Búzios Tourism. ☎ *22/2623–4254* ⊕ *www.buziosonline.com.br.*

TOURS
★ Beira Mar Tours Búzios
BOAT TOURS | This well-recommended agency offers several tours, including scuba diving, buggy rides, and boat trips, which are a must-do when in Buzios. The staff is attentive, values safety, and shares details with the group. ✉ *César Augusto São Luís, Centro, Búzios* ☎ *22/98122–8135.*

Malizia Tour
This prominent tourist agency provides collective and private shuttle transfers to Rio de Janeiro, stopping at airports and Zona Sul hotels, as well as sightseeing trips in and around Búzios. They have multiple shops in Buzios and it's also a cambio house. ✉ *Av. José Bento Ribeiro Dantas, 100, Centro* ✢ *Corner with Rua Das Pedras* ☎ *22/98844–4491* ⊕ *www.maliziatour.com.br.*

 ## Beaches

Búzios boasts 23 beautiful beaches, which can be reached by schooner boat trips or speedier taxi boats. There is a taxi boat "terminal" on Orla Bardot, with skippers ready to whisk passengers off to any of the beaches on the island. Prices are per person and start at R$10 to get to the closest beaches, rising to around R$30 for farther-flung sands. There's a minimum two-person fare, but solo travelers can wait for others to come along and bump up the numbers. Schooners depart from the end of a small pier

Búzios gets its Mediterranean feel from Portuguese influences.

nearby and take groups on beach-hopping trips that might last from a couple of hours to a full day. Prices start at around R$70 per person for a two-hour trip, rising to around R$310 for a full-day trip with stops for swimming and snorkeling.

Praia Azeda
BEACH | Two beaches, Praia Azeda and its smaller neighbor, Praia Azedinha, have clear, calm waters and are accessible via a trail from Praia dos Ossos. The famous view as you descend to the beach on foot is breathtaking. Vendors at kiosks on the beach sell coconut water and frozen caipirinhas, and you can rent beach chairs and umbrellas (R$30). During summer, arrive early to secure a good spot—the beaches start to get crowded by 11 am. **Amenities:** food and drink; toilets. **Best for:** swimming. ✉ *João Fernandes.*

★ Praia da Ferradura
BEACH | FAMILY | Located 1.5 km (0.9 miles) from Buzio's center, Praia da Ferradura has calm waters, making it a perfect choice for families with children. The beach adjoins one of Búzios' most exclusive areas, as some mansions back right onto it. On the left side, there are bars with parties, lounges with umbrellas, and barracas (simple makeshift kiosks selling food and drink). On the right, there are secluded spots to enjoy a quiet day. **Amenities:** food and drink; toilets; water sports. **Best for:** swimming; walking. ✉ *Ferradura.*

★ Praia de Geribá
BEACH | This long half-moon of white sand is fashionable with a young crowd, and its breaks and swells make it popular with surfers and windsurfers. The walk from one end to the other takes 30 minutes, so there's plenty of elbow room here even in high season. The relaxed bars and beach kiosks make it easy to while away whole days here. The surrounding Geribá neighborhood makes a great base for beach lovers, with plenty of good pousadas near the sands. **Amenities:** food and drink, water sports, accommodation. **Best for:** walking; surfing. ✉ *Geribá.*

With more than 20 beaches throughout the area, Búzios is a popular surfing respite.

Praia João Fernandes
BEACH | FAMILY | Praia João Fernandes and the smaller adjoining beach, Praia João Fernandinho, are a short taxi boat ride from the center of town; both are beloved for their crystal waters and soft sands. The sounds of live samba music at nearby restaurants and bars can be heard on the beach, and you can bring cocktails out to your chosen spot on the sand if you're not ready to abandon your sun lounger. This beach can get a little busy, but the sunset here is worth it. **Amenities:** food and drink; toilets; water sports. **Best for:** sunset; swimming. ✉ *João Fernandes.*

🍴 Restaurants

Belli Belli Gastrobar
$ | BRAZILIAN | Owner Alfredo and chef Roque welcome locals like old friends at this great-value gastro bar, which specializes in high-class cocktails, pizzas, and tasty tapas. With a beautiful view over Manguinhos beach, it's one of the best spots in town to catch the sunset and stay for a relaxed dinner. **Known for:** crispy shrimps; clericot with fruits; pastéis. ⑤ *Average main: R$49* ✉ *Av. Jose Bento Ribeiro Dantas 2900, Manguinhos* ☎ *22/2623–9033* ⊕ *www.bellibelligastrobar.com* ⊘ *Closed Mon.*

Chez Michou
$ | BELGIAN | FAMILY | A pancake house might seem an unlikely meeting point for partiers, but this Belgian-owned crêperie is indeed the hangout of choice for many hip young things in Búzios. Locals and tourists alike flock to the street-side tables after dark to soak up the scene and listen to live DJ sets while tucking into their choice of over 60 savory and sweet fillings. **Known for:** live performances; happening atmosphere; chocolate crepes. ⑤ *Average main: R$35* ✉ *Rua das Pedras 90, Centro* ☎ *22/22633–9400* ⊕ *www.chezmichou.com.br.*

★ Cigalon
$$$ | FRENCH | Often cited as one of the best restaurants in Búzios, French-inspired Cigalon is an elegant establishment with a veranda overlooking the

beach. Though the waiters are bow-tied and the tables covered with crisp linens and lighted by flickering candles, the place still has an unpretentious feel. **Known for:** charming atmosphere; thyme-infused lamb; decadent profiteroles. $ *Average main: R$120* ✉ *Av. José Bento Ribeiro Dantas 2900, Centro* ☎ *22/2623–5041.*

Estancia Don Juan

$$$ | **ARGENTINE** | **FAMILY** | Take a walk through the center of Búzios and you might think you've suddenly landed in Argentina thanks to the large number of Spanish speakers who have adopted Búzios as their home. Of all the *parillas* serving Argentina's traditional barbecued steak, Don Juan is easily the best, as its perfectly grilled cuts of prime beef can be washed down with a glass of Malbec from the well-stocked cellar while you take in a live tango show. **Known for:** succulent bife de chorizo; well-stocked wine cellar; live tango shows. $ *Average main: R$130* ✉ *Rua das Pedras 178, Centro* ☎ *22/2633–9400.*

Mistico

$$$$ | **MEDITERRANEAN** | With dazzling views over the bay and out across the mountains, the intimate restaurant at boutique hotel Abracadabara offers impeccable service and exquisitely presented dishes. Enjoy the sunset while sipping signature cocktails and dining on gourmet salads and the freshest local seafood. **Known for:** grilled octopus; tropical rum cocktails; tuna ceviche. $ *Average main: R$160* ✉ *Pousada Abracadabara, Alto do Humaitá 13, Centro* ☎ *22/2623–1217* ⊕ *www.abracadabra-pousada.com.br.*

★ Rocka Beach Lounge & Restaurant

$$$$ | **SEAFOOD** | Overlooking beautiful Praia Brava, relaxed but sophisticated Rocka is one of Búzios's gastronomic highlights as it focuses on superbly fresh, locally sourced seafood that's combined with seasonal fruit, vegetables, and herbs to wonderful effect. A favorite with surfers, come well before lunch so you can spend the day lounging on sun beds or arrive just before sunset when locals stop by for cocktails. **Known for:** spectacular seafood including the freshest oysters; boho-chic vibe; lounging on giant white sun beds or raffia mats on the grass lawn that rolls down to the beach. $ *Average main: R$200* ✉ *Praia Brava 13, Brava* ☎ *22/2623–6159* ⊕ *www.rockafish.com.br* ☾ *No dinner.*

★ 74 Restaurant

$$$ | **SEAFOOD** | It was one of the restaurants that consolidated Buzio's reputation as a gastronomic destination and has remained a reference since opening in 2016. Set on the spectacular terrace of the boutique hotel Casas Brancas with sunset views across the bay, expect Michelin-level cooking using the freshest locally sourced ingredients and a curated selection of Brazil's leading vineyards. **Known for:** fresh seafood; passion fruit beurre blanc; baby lobster stew. $ *Average main: R$130* ✉ *Rua Morro do Humaitá 10, Centro* ☎ *22/2623–0303* ⊕ *www.casasbrancas.com.br.*

🛏 Hotels

Be sure to book well in advance if you plan to visit Búzios on a weekend between December and Carnival. You'll find good accommodation options in the center of town—handy for nightlife, shopping, and organized tours—but there's no real beach there. For beachfront lodgings, you'll have to head a little out of town.

★ Abracadabra

$$$$ | **HOTEL** | Rooms at this gorgeous, centrally located boutique hotel are simply but stylishly appointed and have soft white linens and fresh flowers, but the crowning glory is an infinity pool that has stunning views over the bay and out to sea. **Pros:** stunning views; wonderful breakfasts; excellent service. **Cons:** the best beaches are a taxi or boat ride away;

the pousada accepts small children, which can interrupt the overall tranquility; steep steps to access the pousada at night. ⑤ *Rooms from: R$812* ⊠ *Alto do Humaitá 13, Centro* ☏ *22/2623–1217* ⊕ *www.abracadabrapousada.com.br* ⇌ *16 rooms* ⦿*l Free Breakfast*.

Aquabarra Boutique Hotel and Spa

$$$ | B&B/INN | A Zen-like calm pervades the rooms and living spaces at this casual-chic spot just a few minutes walk from Geribá Beach. **Pros:** short stroll to Geribá beach; excellent spa offers massages and beauty treatments; most rooms have lovely views. **Cons:** you need to cab or bus to get to Centro; some rooms offer limited privacy; bathrooms could be cleaner. ⑤ *Rooms from: R$386* ⊠ *Rua Jaime Francisco 16, Centro* ☏ *22/2623–6186* ⊕ *www.aquabarra.com* ⇌ *15 rooms* ⦿*l Free Breakfast*.

★ Casas Brancas

$$$$ | HOTEL | The epitome of Santorini chic, this sparkling gem of a family-run hotel combines an intimate atmosphere with spectacular views over Búzios's fishing-boat-strewn bay, a first-rate spa, and a gourmet restaurant. **Pros:** friendly, multilingual service; pool with stunning views; special touches such as outdoor yoga classes and classic film screenings. **Cons:** taxi ride to the best beaches; small pool can get crowded; high rates. ⑤ *Rooms from: R$1270* ⊠ *Alto do Humaitá 10, Centro* ☏ *22/2018–0382* ⊕ *www.casasbrancas.com.br* ⇌ *33 rooms* ⦿*l Free Breakfast*.

Hotel le Relais de la Borie

$$$$ | HOTEL | An inviting warmth pervades this historic villa, which sits right on the edge of Geribá Beach. **Pros:** on the beach; great restaurant; friendly staff. **Cons:** it's a bus or cab ride from the center; evenings get chilly in winter; inconsistent service. ⑤ *Rooms from: R$1,324* ⊠ *Gerbert Périssé 554, Geribá* ☏ *22/2620– 8504* ⊕ *www.laborie.com.br* ⇌ *41 rooms* ⦿*l Free Breakfast*.

Pousada Barcarola

$$ | B&B/INN | FAMILY | With a large pool and sun terrace, bright and spacious rooms, generous breakfasts, and free parking and Wi-Fi, this family-friendly guesthouse offers excellent value for its price range. **Pros:** spacious rooms; helpful staff; lovely pool and gardens. **Cons:** 10 minutes' walk to the beach or town center; limited breakfast; noisy air-conditioning. ⑤ *Rooms from: R$260* ⊠ *Rua G-5 Lote 14, Ferradura* ☏ *22/98826–6557* ⊕ *www.pousadabarcarola.com* ⇌ *16 rooms* ⦿*l Free Breakfast*.

Pousada Casa Buzios

$$$$ | B&B/INN | This gorgeous six-room pousada is set right on the water, a short walk from Búzios's main street. **Pros:** intimate, stylish atmosphere; value for money; warm, welcoming service. **Cons:** with only six rooms, it's often booked well ahead; no spa; bathrooms could be more spacious. ⑤ *Rooms from: R$780* ⊠ *Rua do Morro de Humaitá, Casa 1, Centro* ☏ *22/2623–4885* ⇌ *6 rooms* ⦿*l Free Breakfast*.

🛍 Shopping

★ Porto da Barra

CLOTHING | This popular shopping area set close to Manguinhos beach combines an interesting selection of stylish boutiques with waterfront bars and restaurants. ⊠ *Av. José Bento Ribeiro Dantas 2900, Manguinhos* ☏ *22/2623–7302*.

Rua das Pedras

CLOTHING | The majority of Búzios's best boutiques are scattered along the cobblestone street of Rua das Pedras, which comes alive at night and makes for a fun-filled browsing experience. Highlights include Brazilian designer Osklen. It's also where people hang out in the evening. ⊠ *Rua das Pedra, Búzios*.

The Dedo de Deus (God's Finger) mountain is visible from Rio de Janeiro and is popular with hikers.

 Activities

BOATING
Babylon Búzios
BOATING | FAMILY | Babylon Búzios runs a number of water-based trips and activities, the most popular of which whisks passengers to the peninsula's best beaches during a two-and-a-half-hour excursion, with stops for swimming and snorkeling (masks provided). A great option for families, the schooner Babylon Búzios is equipped with a splash pool and a waterslide that flows right into the ocean. It departs three times a day from the main pier in Búzios. ✉ *Trav. dos Pescadores 88, Centro* ☎ *22/2623–2350* ⊕ *www.babylonbuzios.com.br* 🖃 *R$60 per person.*

DIVING
The clear waters of Búzios teem with colorful marine life, making the peninsula a thrilling place to dive.

Mares del Sur Brasil
DIVING & SNORKELING | This professional dive outfit has PADI 5-Star accreditation and operates daily dive trips in Búzios as well as nearby Arraial do Cabo, and offers a full range of instruction from diving "baptisms" to advanced courses. Instructors speak English as well as Spanish and Portuguese. Look out for special promotions during the shoulder season. ✉ *Av. José Bento Ribeiro Dantas s/n, Ferradura* ☎ *22/99233–7035* ⊕ *www.mdsmergulho.com.br.*

GOLF
Golfe Clube Aretê Búzios
GOLF | It's considered one of the best courses in Latin America after its inauguration in 2019. This 27-hole course often hosts events for amateurs and professionals, as well as creates a space for learning the sport for both adults and children. ✉ *Estrada Bento Ribeiro Dantas, km 9, Búzios* ☎ *22/99703–5063* ⊕ *www.clubearetebuzios.com.br/golfe* 🖃 *Greens fee: R$280.*

KITE SURFING
Búzios Kitesurf School
HANG GLIDING & PARAGLIDING | The certified instructors here are an upbeat team dedicated to helping you get the most out of your lessons. ✉ *José Bento Ribeiro Dantas 9, Praia Raza* ☎ *22/99834–8029* ⊕ *www.buzioskitesurfschool.com* 💳 *R$670.*

SURFING
Surf schools set up tents along Geribá Beach, and also rent out boards. Expect to pay around R$85 an hour for a private lesson, including board rental, and R$50 to rent a board for an hour.

★ Fresia Surf Class
SURFING | With a kiosk at Geribá Beach, this outfit rents equipment and offers personalized classes for children and adults of all experience levels. They have a large team of instructors and you can expect to notice progress after three or four classes. ✉ *R. do Caboclo 9, Geriba, Búzios* ☎ *22/99915–7645* ⊕ *www.fresiasurfclass.com.br.*

Shark's Surf School
SURFING | With a kiosk at the western end of Geribá Beach, this outfit rents equipment and offers personalized classes for children and adults of all experience levels. The energetic, enthusiastic instructor, Marcio, has years of experience, and the school has International Surfing Association accreditation. ✉ *Praia de Geribá, Geribá* ✛ *At the right-hand corner of the beach as you face the sea* ☎ *22/2623–1134.*

Petrópolis

68 km (42 miles) northeast of Rio.

The highway northeast of Rio de Janeiro rumbles past forests and waterfalls en route to a mountain town so refreshing and picturesque that Dom Pedro II, Brazil's second emperor, moved there with his summer court. From 1889 to 1899, it was the country's year-round seat of government. The famous horse-drawn carriages were replaced by tuk-tuks and electric carriages to reduce the carbon footprint, passing by flowering gardens, shady parks, and imposing pink mansions. Be sure to visit the Crystal Palace and the Gothic cathedral, São Pedro de Alcântara. The city is also home to the Encantada—literally "Enchanted"—the peculiar house created by Santos Dumont, the country's most prolific inventor and early aviator. Fashion-conscious bargain hunters from across Rio de Janeiro State generally make a beeline for Rua Teresa, a hilly street just outside the historic center that's lined with discount clothing stores.

GETTING HERE AND AROUND
From Rio by car, head north along BR 040 to Petrópolis. The scenic drive (once you leave the city) takes about an hour if traffic isn't heavy. Única buses leave every 40 minutes—less often on weekends— from Rio's Rodoviária Novo Rio. The 90-minute journey costs R$33.50. Upon arrival at Rodoviária Petrópolis, the bus station, you'll be several miles from downtown, so you'll need to take a taxi (R$40, depending on traffic), especially if you're loaded with luggage. The easiest and safest way to get to Petrópolis from Rio, though, is to arrange a shuttle at your hotel or take a tour either privately or as part of a group.

ESSENTIALS
BUS CONTACTS Rodoviária Petrópolis. ✉ *BR 40–Rodovia Washington Luiz, km 82.9–Fazenda Inglesa, Petrópolis* ☎ *24/2249–9858.* **Única.** ✉ *Rua Padre Siqueira 419* ☎ *24/2244–1600* ⊕ *www.unica-facil.com.br.*

TAXI CONTACT Ponto de Taxi Duas Pontes. ✉ *Petrópolis* ☎ *24/2242–2005.*

VISITOR INFORMATION Petrópolis Tourism Office. ✉ *Estrada Ayrton Senna, S/N, Petrópolis* ☎ *24/2231–2217.*

The greenhouse-like Crystal Palace was a gift to Princesa Isabel from her consort, the French Count d'Eu.

TOURS

★ Rio Cultural Secrets

PRIVATE GUIDES | FAMILY | The private tours to Petrópolis run by Rio Cultural Secrets are led by knowledgeable English-speaking guides and include door-to-door transport in comfortable air-conditioned cars. Ask for Fabio, who runs the tours with great enthusiasm and knowledge of Petrópolis's history. Trips take around seven hours, including a stop for lunch. ✉ *Rua Bolivar, Copacabana, Rio de Janeiro* ☎ *21/98031–2692* ⊕ *www.rioculturalsecrets.com/* 🍴 *From R$680, excluding entrance fees.*

★ Terra Vertical

ADVENTURE SPORTS | FAMILY | Adventurous types can enjoy white-knuckle activities including ziplining, rappelling, cascading, and hiking in the mountains with this experienced and professional group. There's a strong emphasis on safety, and the team, led by the highly experienced Anderson, has enormous enthusiasm for their high-altitude adventures. Their principal experience in Petrópolis is a three-day hike. ✉ *Rua Dr. Hermogênio Silva 522, Petrópolis* ☎ *24/99957–4466* 🍴 *From R$30.*

Sights

Casa de Santos Dumont

HISTORIC HOME | FAMILY | Known as *encantado* (enchanted), this diminutive cottage wouldn't look out of place in a fairy-tale wood. Santos Dumont, one of the world's first aviators, built the house in 1918 to a scale in keeping with his own tiny size. The eccentric genius's inventions fill the house, including a heated shower he developed before most homes even had running water. The home doesn't have a kitchen because Dumont ordered his food from a nearby hotel—the first documented restaurant delivery service in Brazil. ✉ *Rua do Encantado 22, Petrópolis* ☎ *24/2247–5222* 🍴 *R$10* ⊙ *Closed Mon.*

Catedral São Pedro de Alcântara

CHURCH | The imposing Cathedral of Saint Peter of Alcantara, a fine example of Gothic architecture and the city's most recognizable landmark, sits at the base of a jungle-clad hill. Inside the building, whose construction began in 1884, lie the tombs of Dom Pedro II, his wife, Dona Teresa Cristina, and their daughter, Princesa Isabel. Elegant sculptures and ornate stained-glass windows add to the interior's visual appeal. ✉ *Rua São Pedro de Alcântara 60, Petrópolis* ☎ *24/2242–4300* ⊕ *www.catedraldepetropolis.org.br* ⊘ *Closed Mon.*

★ Museu Imperial

CASTLE/PALACE | FAMILY | The magnificent 44-room palace that was the summer home of Dom Pedro II, emperor of Brazil, and his family in the 19th century is now the Imperial Museum. The colossal structure is filled with polished wooden floors, artworks, and grand chandeliers. You can also see the diamond-encrusted gold crown and scepter of Brazil's last emperor, as well as other royal jewels. Visitors are handed soft slippers on arrival and asked to slip them over their own shoes to avoid damaging the antique floors. (Children will love sliding around on the polished floors in their slippered feet.) ✉ *Rua da Imperatriz 220, Petrópolis* ☎ *61/3521–4455* ⊕ *www.museuimperial.gov.br* 💲 *R$10* ⊘ *Closed Mon.*

★ Palácio de Cristal

CASTLE/PALACE | The Crystal Palace, a stained-glass and iron building made in France and assembled in Brazil, is rather less grand than its name suggests, resembling a large and very ornate greenhouse, but is worth a visit nonetheless. The palace was a wedding present to Princesa Isabel from her consort, the French Count d'Eu. Their marriage was arranged by their parents—Isabel, then 18, learned of Dom Pedro II's choice only a few weeks before her wedding. The count wrote to his sister that his bride-to-be was "ugly," but after a few weeks of marriage decided he rather liked her. During the imperial years, the palace was used as a ballroom: the princess held a celebration dance here after she abolished slavery in Brazil in 1888. Surrounded by pleasant gardens, the Crystal Palace is now open to the public and often hosts live classical music performances. ✉ *Praça da Confluência, Rua Alfredo Pachá s/n, Petrópolis* ☎ *24/2247–3721* 💲 *R$39.*

🍴 Restaurants

Churrascaria Majórica

$$$ | BRAZILIAN | FAMILY | A classic steak house in the heart of Petrópolis's historic center, Majórica has been a huge hit with meat lovers since it opened in 1962. Every cut is cooked to perfection and served with flair by attentive waitstaff, and there are excellent fish dishes and sides, too. **Known for:** classic caipirinhas; salted picanha (rump steak); puffed potato balls. 💲 *Average main: R$90* ✉ *Rua de Emperador 754, Petrópolis* ☎ *24/2242–2498* ⊕ *www.majorica.com.br.*

★ Trutas do Rocio

$$ | SEAFOOD | It's off the beaten track—ask a local for directions—and only open on weekends, but this rustic, riverside restaurant is really something special. *Trutas* (trout) is what you'll find on the menu—trout, trout, and more trout served fresh from the river in many imaginative ways: as appetizers mashed into a pâté or baked in cassava-dough pastry, and as entrées grilled or cooked with a choice of almond, mustard, or orange sauce. **Known for:** reservations only; atmopsheric alfresco setting; unique riverside location. 💲 *Average main: R$60* ✉ *Estrada da Vargem Grande 6333, Rocio* ☎ *24/99926–5623* ⊕ *www.trutas.com.br* ⊟ *No credit cards* ⊘ *Closed Mon.–Fri.; no dinner.*

🛏 Hotels

Locanda della Mimosa

$$$$ | B&B/INN | If you want to feel like a member of the Brazilian imperial family, this place is the place to go. **Pros:** spacious rooms, some with fireplaces and

Jacuzzi tubs; great restaurant; afternoon tea service is included in the rates. **Cons:** need to book well in advance; some suites have traffic noise; Wi-Fi isn't strong in some areas. ⑤ *Rooms from: R$715 ✉ BR 040, Km 71.5, Alameda das Mimosas 30, Vale Florido ☎ 24/2233–5405 ⊕ www.locanda.com.br ⮡ 24 rooms ⦿ Free Breakfast.*

★ Pousada da Alcobaça

$$$$ | **B&B/INN** | **FAMILY** | This family-run inn set just outside of Petrópolis offers one of the most charming and authentic accommodation experiences in the area. **Pros:** tasty food; great views; breakfast can be taken at any hour. **Cons:** need to book far in advance; 15-minute drive from the city; outdated bathrooms. ⑤ *Rooms from: R$700 ✉ Agostinho Goulão 298, Correias ☎ 24/2221–1240 ⊕ www.pousadadaalcobaca.com.br ⮡ 11 rooms ⦿ Free Breakfast.*

Pousada Monte Imperial

$$$ | **B&B/INN** | A 10-minute walk from downtown, this Bavarian-style inn has a lobby with a fireplace, a comfortable restaurant and bar area, and cozy, rustic rooms that have marshmallow-soft beds and a view to the mountains. **Pros:** close to downtown; friendly, attentive staff; great views. **Cons:** chilly in winter; uphill walk from the city; small bathroom. ⑤ *Rooms from: R$300 ✉ Rua José de Alencar 27, Centro, Petrópolis ☎ 24/2237–1664 ⊕ www.pousadamonteimperial.com.br ⮡ 15 rooms ⦿ Free Breakfast.*

★ Solar do Imperio

$$$$ | **HOTEL** | **FAMILY** | Occupying a tastefully restored 1875 neoclassical building and smaller outlying houses amid Petrópolis's historic center, this elegant hotel provides stylish, comfortable accommodations. **Pros:** excellent location; good in-house restaurant and all-day breakfasts; palatial, historic grounds. **Cons:** insects from the gardens occasionally find their way into the rooms; some rooms can be noisy; staff can't always cover the extensive grounds. ⑤ *Rooms from: R$778 ✉ Av. Koeler 376, Petrópolis ☎ 24/2103–3000 ⊕ www.solardoimperio.com.br ⮡ 25 rooms ⦿ Free Breakfast.*

Walking in the Clouds

The Parque Nacional da Serra dos Órgãos, created in 1939 to protect the region's natural wonders, covers more than 101 square km (39 square miles) of mountainous terrain between Petrópolis and Teresópolis. The Petrópolis to Teresópolis trail—a tough three-day hike with spectacular views—is a must for hardcore hikers. Inexperienced hikers should go with a guide, but everyone should check weather forecasts in advance as heavy rainfall in the region has caused mudslides in recent years.

Angra dos Reis

168 km (91 miles) west of Rio.

Angra dos Reis has it all: colonial architecture, beautiful beaches, and clear green waters. Schooners, yachts, and fishing skiffs drift among the bay's 365 islands, one for each day of the year. Indeed, Angra dos Reis's popularity lies in its strategic location near the islands. Some are deserted stretches of sand, others patches of Atlantic rainforest surrounded by emerald waters perfect for swimming or snorkeling. When you are not exploring the beaches and the rainforest, you can quickly discover the town of Angra, home to historical buildings, bars, and restaurants. Yet, the town is used as a jumping-off point to explore the surrounding islands and Ilha Grande, and you should plan to pick up supplies and take out money. If you don't plan to head to Ilha Grande, opt for a pousada or hotel outside the main center for the best experience.

GETTING HERE AND AROUND

Angra dos Reis–bound Costa Verde buses leave Rio every hour. The three-hour trip costs R$72.80. Ferries leave from Vila do Abrãao in Angra dos Reis and the trip can last from 15 to 50 minutes, depending on the boat. The prices range from R$18 to R$60. From Rio by car, get onto the Rio-Santos highway (BR 101) and follow it south for 190 km (118 miles) until you get to Angra dos Reis. Expect the trip to take between two and four hours, depending on traffic.

ESSENTIALS

AIRPORT CONTACTS Aeroporto Municipal. ✉ *Rua Prefeito João Galindo s/n, Japuiba, Angra dos Reis* ☎ *24/3365–8863* ⊕ *www.angraaeroportos.com.br.*

BUS CONTACT Rodoviária Angra dos Reis. ✉ *Av. Almirante Jair Toscano de Brito 110, Vila Balneário Globo* ☎ *24/3377–8121.*

FERRY CONTACT CCR Barcas. ✉ *Cais da Lapa, 15-113 Av. Júlio Maria, Angra dos Reis* ☎ *800/721–1012 toll-free* ⊕ *www.barcas.grupoccr.com.br.*

TAXI CONTACT Táxi Angra. ✉ *Av. Alm. jair Carneiro Toscano Brito, 110, Centro* ☎ *24/99991–2298.*

TOURS

Angra dos Reis Turismo

TRANSPORTATION | FAMILY | This group runs boat tours to the islands around Angra dos Reis, transfers from Angra to Ilha Grande and rents out boats, plus skipper, for up to 18 people. One great tour is to Lopes Mendes, the paradisiacal beach on Ilha Grande. Some boats, in particular the larger schooners, have a reputation for playing loud music. Check before you book if you prefer a tranquil environment. The company also offers two secure parking locations should you be traveling by car and wish to park it before heading out to the islands. ✉ *Av. Julio Maria 92, Centro* ☎ *24/99055–3229* ⊕ *www.angradosreisturismo.com.br* 🛥 *From R$99.*

★ Exped Angra

BOAT TOURS | This reliable outfit sails its schooners, catamarans, and other boats on day trips to the islands around Angra dos Reis with stops for swimming, snorkeling, and sunbathing. They have boats with slides, which adds extra fun, and glass floor, so you can admire the marine life. They are also highly recommended for scuba diving. ✉ *Estr. das Marinas, 91, Angra dos Reis* ☎ *21/99941–7175* ⊕ *www.expedangra.com* 🛥 *from R$110.*

Hotels

Hotel do Bosque

$$$$ | HOTEL | FAMILY | Set on the river inside a private eco-park, this resort hotel is a favorite with families and couples looking to relax with a wealth of services and activities at their disposal. **Pros:** plenty of activities including tennis courts, swimming pools, volleyball courts, fitness center, and sauna; private beach with bar service; spacious rooms. **Cons:** some parts of the hotel are dated; kids only accepted over 4 years old; no private boat rental service available. 💲 *Rooms from: R$500* ✉ *BR 101, km 533, Mambucaba* ☎ *24/3362–3130* ⊕ *www.hoteldobosque.com.br* 🛏 *102 rooms* 🍽 *Free Breakfast.*

Pousada dos Corsarios

$$ | HOTEL | FAMILY | Its location right on the beach at scenic Praia do Bonfim combined with the friendly staff make this simple hotel a great option for its price range. **Pros:** beachfront location; abundant breakfast; friendly service. **Cons:** few frills; a half-hour walk or 10-minute taxi ride to town center; tiny bathrooms. 💲 *Rooms from: R$300* ✉ *Praia do Bonfim 5, Bonfim* ☎ *24/3365-4445* ⊕ *www.corsarios.com.br* 🛏 *10 rooms* 🍽 *Free Breakfast.*

Angra dos Reis is made up of over 350 islands and 2,000 beaches.

★ Pousada Mestre Augusto

$$$$ | B&B/INN | FAMILY | A wonderful spot to relax, this intimate, charming guesthouse is situated on a white-sand beach that has its own pier giving guests unadulterated access to Angra's spectacular tropical islands. **Pros:** warm, personal staff; as equally suited to couples as families with young children; easy access to taxi boats. **Cons:** no full-time restaurant service; beds are too soft; difficult access. ⑤ *Rooms from: R$1,000* ✉ *Estrada Vereador Benedito Adelino 4509, Angra dos Reis* ☎ *24/3364–1156* ⊕ *www.mestreaugusto.com.br* 🛏 *8 rooms* ❙⓪❙ *Free Breakfast.*

Ilha Grande

21 km (13 miles) south of Angra dos Reis or Mangaratiba via 90-minute ferry ride.

Ilha Grande, 90 minutes via ferry or 40 minutes via speedboat from Angra dos Reis, is one of the most popular island destinations in Brazil. It boasts over 100 idyllic beaches, some of which are sandy ribbons with backdrops of tropical foliage, while others are densely wooded coves with waterfalls tumbling down from the forest. Ferries, catamarans, and schooners arrive at Vila do Abraão. As there are no cars, it's wise to take only what you can carry. Men waiting at the pier make a living helping tourists carry luggage for about R$20 per bag, depending on the distance. Take cash out in Angra—there aren't any ATMs on the island, and credit cards aren't always accepted.

GETTING HERE AND AROUND

By far, the simplest and most cost-effective way to get to the island is by a bus and boat transfer service. Easy Transfer's comfortable, air-conditioned vans pick travelers up from their lodgings in Rio (the service covers the South Zone, Centro, and Santa Teresa) and make the two-hour journey to Conceição de Jacareí, where the company's own double-decker schooner boat waits to ship passengers over to Abraão, Ilha Grande's only real town. Traveling with a transfer service works out cheaper (R$160 with Easy Transfer) and is far easier than arranging taxis to the bus station, taking a bus down the coast, and then a boat trip out to the island. Easy Transfer and its competitors offer the same service back to Rio, as well as transfers between Ilha Grande and Paraty. For those who choose to make the trip independently, the quickest route is to go via Conceição de Jacareí. Comfortable coaches leave from Rio's Novo Rio bus station approximately once an hour, a journey of around two hours (up to R$75). Several operators run schooners (40 minutes) and speedier flex boats (15 minutes) to Ilha Grande roughly every hour, with the first crossing at 8 am and the last at 6:30 pm. The fare is R$60 per person. The best way to do this is to arrive at the pier and assess what options are available. Many of the companies that offer prepaid transfers online charge twice as much and leave off-schedule as they have to wait for pre-booked passengers. Most boats used to sail to Ilha Grande from Angra dos Reis, and it's still possible to take this route, although most travelers coming from Rio make the quicker trip via Conceição de Jacareí. Buses from Rio's Novo Rio bus station takes three hours to reach Angra dos Reis's bus station, from where it's a 10-minute cab ride or hot 20-minute walk to the town center and the boat terminal. Flex boats (R$100) start departing at 8:30 am and take 40 to 50 minutes. A daily ferry (R$20.50) also sails from Mangaratiba, but it's slow and inconveniently scheduled at 8 am daily, except on Friday when it leaves at 10 pm.

TOURS

Touch down in the tiny village of Abraão and the number of tour companies offering boat trips around the islands and beaches is almost endless. Prices are usually negotiable depending on how busy the island is, so don't hesitate to ask for a discount. To make the most of Ilha Grande's wild, natural diversity,

Ilha Grande's Sweet Spot

They appear late in the afternoon to tempt you with their sweet aromas and delicate flavors. We're talking about Vila do Abraão's sweet carts, of course. They first appeared in 1998, when a resident of the island started producing baked goods at his home. His success inspired other dessert makers to sell their sweets on the streets of Abraão. The carts stay out late at night, tempting even the most resolute of travelers. You can try the traditional *brigadeiro*, *beijinho*, and *cocadas*.

consider going scuba diving, hiking up the spectacular Papagaio's peak, or booking an excursion with a local ecologist. The island is a natural paradise and well-suited to fitness lovers. Those with mobility issues may find it a challenge.

Aquamarina Mergulho
ECOTOURISM | Located in the center of Abraão village, this highly professional dive school offers PADI certification and scuba diving guided by a team of local experts with nearly three decades experience diving across Angra's archipelago. ✉ *Rua Santana 1-2, Vila do Abraão, Angra dos Reis* ☎ *24/99812–9484* ⊕ *www.aquamarinamergulho.com.br.*

★ Acqua Jungle Ilha Grande Tours
ADVENTURE TOURS | FAMILY | Knowledgeable local guide Mateus offers spearfishing experiences, and hiking and snorkeling tours around Ilha Grande. The theme that pervades these trips is preservation of the island's natural riches. His small agency also offers direct transfers to Rio. ✉ *Rua Francisco Inácio Nascimento 306, Vila do Abraão, Angra dos Reis, Abraão* ☎ *24/99978-4384* ⊕ *www.ilhagrandeadventure.org.*

Sights

Visitors to Ilha Grande can follow well-marked nature trails that lead to isolated beaches and waterfalls and past the ruins of the former prison. Walks may last from 20 minutes to six hours, and there are maps at strategic points. Bring along water and insect repellent, sun protection clothing, and wear lightweight walking shoes. For a less taxing experience, take a schooner or taxi boat out to the unspoiled beaches. Schooners make regular trips out to the most popular beaches and lagoons, with stops for swimming and snorkeling, while the taxi boats whisk passengers to any point on the island.

Blue Lagoon
OTHER ATTRACTION | FAMILY | This natural pool forms at low tide and is home to thousands of brightly colored fish that will literally eat out of your hands. Many tour operators include a stop here as part of their boat trips around the island, and most provide floats for children. Be sure to bring a mask and snorkel, which is also provided by tour operators for an additional cost. ✉ *Lagoa Azul.*

Beaches

Dois Rios
BEACH | With its pristine white sands and turquoise waters, this beautiful, secluded beach starkly contrasts the dark prison ruins behind it. Visitors have the place practically to themselves, as few people make the arduous 7-km (4-mile) trek through the hot jungle to get here. Those who do are rewarded with one of the island's most gorgeous beaches and the sense of achievement that comes with really getting off the beaten track. The prison ruins are worth exploring, but be sure to head back several hours before sundown. **Amenities:** none. **Best for:** solitude. ✉ *Dois Rios.*

★ Lopes Mendes
BEACH | Locals and visitors alike regard Lopes Mendes, a 3-km (2-mile) stretch of dazzling-white sand lapped by emerald waters, as the most beautiful beach on Ilha Grande. It's often cited as one of the most beautiful in all Brazil. Strict environmental protection orders have kept the jungle-fringed beach from being spoiled by development: expect makeshift beach kiosks, not upscale bars. Take a taxi boat from Vila do Abraão (R$30) if you don't feel up to the two-hour hike through the forest, or hike here and take the boat back—the rough jungle trail and sticky heat can tax even the most hearty of ramblers. While here, use plenty of sunblock, as the rays rebounding off the white sand are particularly strong. If you want to avoid the boatloads of day-trippers, go early. **Amenities:** food and drink. **Best for:** swimming; walking.

■ **TIP→ If you want to avoid the boatloads of day-trippers, go early.** ✉ *Lopez Mendes.*

Restaurants

★ Bonito Bar
$$$ | BRAZILIAN | A traditional *pé na areia* **Known for:** rooftop seating; fresh and local ingredients; caipirinhas. ⓢ *Average main: R$95* ✉ *Praia do Abrãozinho, S/N, Ilha Grande* ☎ *24/99907–0307.*

★ Dom Mario
$$$ | ARGENTINE | Don't be mistaken by its humble setting and location: Dom Mario is a favorite among locals and often ranked among the most-recommended places in Ilha Grande. They present generous dishes that can serve up to two people. **Known for:** caipirinhas; salmon with passion fruit sauce; high gastronomy. ⓢ *Average main: R$100* ✉ *Rua Bouganville, Cila do Abraao, Ilha Grande* ☎ *24/3361–5349* ⓧ *Closed Mon.*

Did You Know?

The isolated Lopes Mendes beach is an extremely popular spot for surfing as it's known for having consistent waves year-round.

Lua e Mar

$$$ | SEAFOOD | Expect fresh, well-prepared seafood and weekly live music during high season at this longtime favorite, which is often cited as the best restaurant in the village of Abraão. Stroll straight from the beach still wearing your Havaianas to try Dona Cidinha's specialty, fish with half-ripe bananas, or the famous *moqueca*, which many islanders claim is the best in Rio de Janeiro State. **Known for:** beachfront location; baked fish with banana; dishes to be shared. ⑤ *Average main: R$75* ✉ *Praia do Canto, Abraão* ☎ *24/98136–1896* ⊘ *Closed Wed.*

Pizza na Praça

$ | PIZZA | FAMILY | On the flagstones of Ilha Grande's main square, this simple restaurant serves up more than four dozen types of pies, from simple margheritas to exotic seafood combinations or dessert pies; salads and other dishes are available at lunchtime. Besides the pizzas, they also have a buffet with many options. **Known for:** great people-watching; healthy pizza options; lively atmopshere on the weekends. ⑤ *Average main: R$40* ✉ *Praça São Sebastião, Rua Alice Kuri 21, Abraão* ☎ *24/3361–9566* ▭ *No credit cards.*

🛏 Hotels

★ Aratinga Inn

$$$ | B&B/INN | Cooled by gentle hill breezes and shaded by trees and coconut palms, this peaceful eco-friendly pousada is a short walk from the beachfront and offers comfortable lodgings in elegantly appointed chalets. **Pros:** lovely, lush gardens home to native animals, butterflies, and birds; complimentary afternoon teas; knowledgeable and helpful owner. **Cons:** an uphill walk from the pier; some rooms have no curtains; it is often booked up well in advance. ⑤ *Rooms from: R$424* ✉ *Rua das Flores 232, Abraão* ☎ *24/98836–0400* ⊕ *www.aratingailhagrande.com.br* ⇄ *9 chalets* ⦿ *Free Breakfast.*

Favorite Places

Luana Ferreira: Rio and São Paulo embody contrasting lifestyles, offering the best of both worlds. In Rio, the irresistible Carioca lifestyle takes center stage—lunchtime bike rides along the beach, shopping at street markets, hanging out on the beach until late at night, and enjoying the city's many *rodas de samba* are memories for a lifetime. Rio is a city that makes you never want to leave.

Pousada do Canto

$$$$ | B&B/INN | FAMILY | In a colonial-style house, this family-friendly pousada with a tropical atmosphere faces lovely Praia do Canto and it has a privileged *pé na areia* (right on the beach) location. **Pros:** on the beach; outdoor pool with Jacuzzi and a thatched-roofed poolside bar; spacious rooms. **Cons:** small bathrooms; a bit of a walk to the boat pier, shops, and restaurants; Wi-Fi isn't strong in some areas. ⑤ *Rooms from: R$528* ✉ *Rua da Praia 121, Abraão* ☎ *21/97098–30602* ⊕ *www.pousadadocantoabraao.com.br* ⇄ *11 rooms* ⦿ *Free Breakfast.*

★ Pousada Naturalia

$$$$ | B&B/INN | A beachfront location, excellent service, and sumptuous breakfasts all contribute to the appeal of Pousada Naturalia, which is set in lush tropical gardens visited by colorful birds, monkeys, and squirrels. **Pros:** spacious rooms can sleep more than two; sumptuous breakfasts; sea views. **Cons:** 10-minute walk to the ferry terminal means that you may need to pay a carrier at the harbor around R$20 to transport your luggage; limited Wi-Fi; a bit remote. ⑤ *Rooms from: R$644* ✉ *Rua da Praia 149, Abraão* ☎ *24/92000–3099* ⊕ *www.naturaliapousada.com.br* ⇄ *18 rooms* ⦿ *Free Breakfast.*

The Fazenda Bananal is a UNESCO World Heritage Site and has a restaurant serving farm-to-table meals.

Activities

Elite Dive Center

DIVING & SNORKELING | Ilha Grande is an excellent spot for amateur and experienced scuba divers. This PADI-accredited dive school offers diving classes from beginner to Dive Master level, rents out equipment, and runs daytime and nocturnal diving excursions to numerous places around the island. ✉ *Rua Santana 55, Vila do Abraão, Abraão* ☎ *24/99221–4053* 🌐 *www.elitedivecenter.com.br.*

Paraty

95 km (59 miles) southwest of Angra dos Reis; 248 km (154 miles) southwest of Rio.

This stunning colonial city—also spelled Parati—is one of South America's gems and a must-visit if you have a few days to spare during a visit to Rio. Giant iron chains hang from posts at the beginning of the mazelike grid of cobblestone streets that make up the historic center, closing them to all but pedestrians, horses, and bicycles. Until the 18th century this was an important transit point for gold plucked from the Minas Gerais—a safe harbor protected by a fort. (The cobblestones are the rock ballast brought from Lisbon, then unloaded to make room in the ships for their gold cargoes.) In 1720, however, the colonial powers cut a new trail from the gold mines straight to Rio de Janeiro, bypassing the town and leaving it isolated. It remained that way until contemporary times, when artists, writers, and others "discovered" the small community of fishermen, and UNESCO placed it on its list of World Heritage Sites. Paraty isn't a city peppered with opulent palaces; rather, it has a simple beauty. By the time the sun breaks over glorious Paraty Bay each morning—illuminating the whitewashed, colorfully trimmed buildings—the fishermen have begun spreading out their catch at the outdoor market. The best way to explore is simply to begin walking winding streets banked with centuries-old buildings that hide chic boutique hotels, tiny restaurants, artisan shops, and art galleries.Paraty holds Brazil's largest literary festival, Flip (Festa Literária Internacional de Paraty), often held in the second semester. Other popular festivals include Bourbon Festival, which is dedicated to jazz, and the Festival Gastronômico de Paraty, the city's most awaited gastronomic festival. The Carnival celebrations here are also a spectacle to behold, with costumed partygoers enjoying the *blocos*, popular street parties. Book well in advance if you plan to visit during the festivals.

GETTING HERE AND AROUND

From Rio de Janeiro, it's a four-hour drive along the BR 101 to Paraty. Costa Verde buses leave Rio daily every two hours. The journey costs R$103.56 and buses arrive at the *rodoviária* in the new town, about 20 minutes' walk from the pedestrianized historic center. It pays to travel light as taxis may not be able to take you to your hotel door.

ESSENTIALS

VISITOR INFORMATION Paraty Tourism Office. ✉ *Av. Roberto Silveira, S/N, Centro Histórico* ☎ *24/3371–1222* ⊕ *www. paraty.com.br.*

TOURS

Aventura Turismo

CRUISE EXCURSIONS | This tourism operator conducts six-hour Jeep tours that head into Serra da Bocaina National Park, crossing rivers and visiting fantastic waterfalls, with stops for swimming in natural pools, hiking through rainforest, and even visiting sugarcane rum distilleries (complete with tastings). Aventura Turismo also runs boat trips, adventure sports excursions, and motorbike trips. ✉ *Av. Dom Pedro I, 444, Centro Histórico* ☎ *24/99995–7041* ⊕ *www.agenciaaventuraturismo.com.br* 💲 *From R$100.*

A Potent Brew

One telling has it that *cachaça* was invented around 1540 by enslaved people working on the sugarcane plantations. A liquid called *cagaço* was removed from the sugarcane to make it easier to transport. The slaves noticed that after a few days this liquid would ferment into a potent brew.

👁 Sights

Casa da Cultura

ART MUSEUM | The largest cultural center in Paraty, Casa da Cultura is dedicated to telling the story of the city and its people. Permanent and visiting exhibitions illustrate the area's rich history and its abundant native flora and fauna. There's a pleasant coffee shop and patio, and the gift shop downstairs, one of the best in town, sells crafts made by local artisans. ✉ *Rua Dona Geralda 177, at Rua Dr. Samuel Costa, Centro Histórico* ☎ *24/3371–2800* ⊕ *www.casadaculturaparaty.org* 💲 *Free, but donations are welcome.*

★ Fazenda Bananal

COLLEGE | FAMILY | Drive 15 minutes inland from Paraty to this immaculately restored colonial *fazenda* (farm), where you can feast on delicious farm-to-table food in the light-filled restaurant before exploring the museum, tropical gardens, and working farm. Simple yet evocative, it gives striking insight into the area's history and future potential. The farm welcomes thousands of local children every year to learn about sustainability and agricultural conservation. Any surplus organic food produced on-site is given to employees, the church, and the elderly in the region. ✉ *Estrada Pedra Branca s/n, Paraty* ☎ *24/3371–1666* ⊕ *wwww. fazendabananal.com.br* 💲 *R$60.*

Forte Defensor Perpétuo

MILITARY SIGHT | Paraty's only fort was built in the early 1700s (and rebuilt in 1822) as a defense against pirates. It's a pleasant short climb through jungle to get here and the views from the fort itself are terrific. Visitors can also see heavy British-made cannons, still in their original positions. ✉ *Morro da Vila Velha, Paraty* ☎ *24/98142–0081* 🎟 *Free.*

Igreja de Nossa Senhora dos Remédios

CHURCH | Also known as Igreja Matriz, the neoclassical Church of Our Lady of Remedies was built in 1712 and is one of Paraty's most iconic buildings, with its gray-and-white facade shaded by a towering imperial palm tree. The small art gallery within, Pinacoteca Antônio Marino Gouveia, has paintings by modern artists such as Djanira, Di Cavalcanti, and Anita Malfatti. ✉ *Praça Monsenhor Hélio Píres 18, Centro Histórico* ☎ *24/3371–1467* ⊕ *www.paraty.com.br/igreja_nsremedios.asp* 🎟 *Free.*

Igreja de Santa Rita

CHURCH | The oldest church in Paraty, the simple whitewashed Church of Saint Rita sits on a grassy square with a mountain backdrop and makes for a terrific photo opportunity. The church was built in 1722 by and for freed enslaved people and has a typical Jesuit layout with a bell tower and domed front. Inside, the carved angels and ornate woodwork and ironwork catch the eye, and there are many valuable religious artifacts on display in the church's small religious art museum. ✉ *Largo de Santa Rita, Rua Santa Rita s/n, Centro Histórico* ⊕ *www.paraty.com.br/igreja_santarita.asp* 🎟 *R$4.*

Trindade

TOWN | FAMILY | About 30 km (20 miles) from Paraty, Trindade was once a hippie hangout. Today Trindade's several gorgeous beaches attract everybody from backpackers to Cariocas on vacation, and the natural pools are perfect for children. Regular buses run from the bus station in Paraty. If you're looking to stay overnight, you'll find simple lodgings and campsites near the beaches. ✉ *Trindade.*

Beaches

Praia de Antiguinhos

BEACH | An environmental protection order keeps beautiful Antigos Beach wonderfully unspoiled—you can swim amid rugged nature here. The thick jungle reaches right down to the sands, and the beach is famous for the large rocks that jut into the transparent water, separating Antigos from the adjoining smaller beach, Antiginhos, whose calmer waters are better for swimming. The beach can be reached via a 20-minute walking trail from equally scenic Sono Beach, which can be reached by boat from Paraty. **Amenities:** none. **Best for:** solitude; snorkeling; sunbathing. ✉ *Take trail from Sono Beach, Trindade.*

★ Praia do Cachadaço

BEACH | Famous for its 2 km (1.2 miles) of white sand and natural pools, formed within the volcanic rocks, the beach can be accessed via a short 600-meter trail starting at Praia do Meio. The long stretches of sand give a sense of solitude. Despite Cachadaço's popularity, it's often a quiet place—this perception often disappears when you reach the pools. The path to the pools is an easy and relaxing 30-minute walk and you can refresh yourself along the way with freshwater springs that flow into the beach. This pristine beach doesn't have kiosks, so bring you own food and water. You can also take advantage of restaurants nearby. **Amenities:** none **Best for:** solitude;

pools; swimming; walking. ✉ *Praia do Cachadaço, Trindade, Paraty.*

★ Praia do Sono

BEACH | Secluded Sono Beach is one of the Paraty area's most beautiful strands, with thick jungle framing the crescent of light, soft sand bordering crystal-clear waters teeming with colorful fish. Campers base themselves here during the summer, when there's a relaxed, bohemian air. In the off-season, the beach is virtually deserted—sunbathers bask in what feels like a private tropical paradise. Although Sono is a bit off the beaten track, the gorgeous setting makes it worth the effort to reach it. The best way to access the beach is by boat from Paraty (about R$35); otherwise you must take a one-hour bus ride and then hike for about 40 minutes. **Amenities:** food and drink (summer). **Best for:** solitude; swimming; walking. ✉ *Trindade.*

Restaurants

Banana da Terra

$$$$ | BRAZILIAN | Seafood is always excellent at this long-standing favorite on Paraty's dining scene, and it's a great place to try giant shrimp when they are in season. The bustling restaurant—usually packed with tourists—is in an elegant colonial house decorated with cachaça labels (the caipirinhas here are another strong suit) and 19th-century pictures of the city. **Known for:** grilled fish with plantains; giant shrimp; lovely atmosphere. $ *Average main: R$200* ✉ *Rua Doutor Samuel Costa 198, Centro Histórico* ☎ *24/99328–2688* ⊙ *Closed Tues.*

★ Punto Divino

$$$ | ITALIAN | Carefully prepared Tuscan and Sicilian dishes are at the fore at this charming candlelit spot set off Paraty's main square. Evening live music performances lend a touch of festivity to the proceedings, and the covered outdoor space means that diners can enjoy meals alfresco even when the famously torrential Paraty rains start to pour. **Known for:** fresh and tasty salads; crisp, generously topped pizzas here are the best in town; romantic atmopshere. ⑤ *Average main: R$99* ✉ *Rua Marechal Deodoro 129, Centro Histórico* ☎ *22/3371-1348* ⊙ *No lunch.*

Refúgio

$$$ | **SEAFOOD** | Near the water in a quiet part of town, this Mediterranean–inspired restaurant is a great place for a romantic dinner, with candlelit tables and a good wine list. On chilly days, heat lamps warm the café tables out front, while evenings are enlivened by music from local musicians (which comes with an additional cover charge). **Known for:** attentive service; good cocktails; cheesy rice balls. ⑤ *Average main: R$96* ✉ *Praça da Bandeira, Loja 4, Centro Histórico* ☎ *24/3371-2447.*

★ Thai Brasil

$$$ | **THAI** | **FAMILY** | This trendy, laid-back restaurant charms with its hand-painted interiors, alfresco courtyard, and affordable prices for its generously sized Thai dishes. In the summer months, live music and great cocktails make this a fun place to spend an evening. **Known for:** green papaya salad; pad Thai; Japanese squid with nirá. ⑤ *Average main: R$100* ✉ *Rua do Comercio 308A, Centro Histórico* ☎ *24/3371-2760* ⊕ *www.thaibrasil.com.br* ⊙ *Closed Sun.*

🛏 Hotels

★ Pousada Casa Turquesa

$$$$ | **B&B/INN** | Split between two colonial houses joined by a central plunge pool surrounded by white daybeds, this intimate guesthouse—set in prime position overlooking Paraty's main bay—is like staying in the private home of a very stylish friend. **Pros:** personal experience; stylish, artsy design; fabulous homemade breakfasts. **Cons:** rooms can be small; pricey, but worth it; no on-site restaurant. ⑤ *Rooms from: R$1,930* ✉ *Rua Dr. Pereira 50, Centro Histórico* ☎ *24/3371-1037* ⊕ *www.casaturquesa.com.br* ⇨ *9 rooms* ⦿ *Free Breakfast.*

Pousada do Príncipe

$$$$ | **B&B/INN** | The name means the Prince's pousada and it's really owned by the great-grandson of Emperor Pedro II. **Pros:** good location a short walk from the bus station; nice pool and courtyard; welcoming, attentive staff. **Cons:** small rooms; some rooms need repainting; no on-site parking. ⑤ *Rooms from: R$528* ✉ *Av. Roberto Silveira 801, Centro Histórico* ☎ *24/3371-2266* ⊕ *www.pousadadoprincipe.com.br* ⇨ *35 rooms* ⦿ *Free Breakfast.*

Pousada do Sandi

$$$$ | **B&B/INN** | **FAMILY** | Its central location a block from the main square, interior courtyard complete with swimming pool, and colorful interiors make this colonial pousada a good local base. **Pros:** close to all the main sights; friendly staff; great breakfasts. **Cons:** street noise and creaky building; can feel very busy; parking lot far away. ⑤ *Rooms from: R$800* ✉ *Largo do Rosário 1, Centro Histórico* ☎ *24/2503-0195* ⊕ *www.pousadadosandi.com.br* ⇨ *30 rooms* ⦿ *Free Breakfast.*

★ Pousada Literária de Paraty

$$$$ | **HOTEL** | **FAMILY** | Arguably one of the most enthralling places to stay in Paraty, this spacious, expertly run colonia guesthouse combines exquisite design with a first-class spa, all-day breakfast, and a resplendent library that celebrates Paraty's literary heart. **Pros:** the many sights, restaurants, and bars of Paraty's historic center are right at the doorstep; great heated pool; three spectacular private houses. **Cons:** books up well ahead of July literary festival; streets nearby car flood during rainy season; some rooms can feel airless. ⑤ *Rooms from: R$1,618* ✉ *Rua Domingos Gonçalves de Abreu 254, Centro Histórico* ☎ *24/2770-0237* ⊕ *www.pousadaliteraria.com.br* ⇨ *25 rooms* ⦿ *Free Breakfast.*

Did You Know?

The small beach village of Sono consists of fewer than 400 residents who rely on fishing for their livelihoods.

Pousada Pardieiro

$$$$ | B&B/INN | Expect a rustic, yet relaxing experience at one of Paraty's oldest guesthouses, where high-ceilinged rooms are decorated in 19th-century colonial style and set around an orchid-filled courtyard garden and swimming pool. **Pros:** close to the historic center; great pool and garden; wonderful staff. **Cons:** no TVs in rooms; cold floors in winter; limited breakfast. ⓢ *Rooms from: R$600* ✉ *Rua Aurora 287, Centro Histórico* ☎ *24/3030–7198* ⊕ *www.pousadapardieiro.com.br* ⇌ *29 rooms* ⓘ *Free Breakfast*.

Shopping

Paraty is known countrywide for its fine cachaça, including brands like Santo Grau, Engenho D'Ouro, Paratiana, Pedra Branca, and Maré Alta. It's also a haven for artists, painters, writers, and musicians. Stroll through the cobblestone streets of the Historic Centre in the early evening—when artists throw open the doors to their ateliers—to pick up collectible pieces by local talents.

Atelier Patricia Sada

ART GALLERY | The colorful artwork doesn't go unnoticed when you pass by this atelier downtown. Patricia is recognized for using natural elements such as wood and twigs. The Mexican artist moved to Paraty in the 1980s and since then, she has become a well-established artist in the city, thanks to her striking and modern paintings. ✉ *Rua Dr. Pereira 85, Centro Histórico, Paraty*.

Empório da Cachaça

WINE/SPIRITS | This shop stocks more than 300 brands—both local and national—of sugarcane liquor as well as bottled chili peppers and locally produced preserves. It stays open well into the evening. ✉ *Rua Doutor Samuel Costa 276, Centro Histórico* ☎ *24/99219–2556*.

Chapter 5

SÃO PAULO

Updated by
Leticia Davino

WELCOME TO SÃO PAULO

TOP REASONS TO GO

★ **Around the clock:** São Paulo is a 24/7 city that never stops. It has everything you might need at any time.

★ **Food Lovers:** Brazil is the fourth country in the world with the highest number of Michelin-starred restaurants, with 98 stars just in São Paulo.

★ **As warm as its weather:** Brazilian people will do everything to make sure you're enjoying your stay.

★ **Diversity:** Full of museums, galleries, and art manifestations that you can experience to learn more about the culture of the entire country.

★ **Hopping Nightlife:** Bars of all shapes, styles, and sizes beckon the thirsty traveler—quench your thirst with a cold beer or strong caipirinha.

★ **The Beautiful Game:** Futebol, or soccer, is truly "the beautiful game" in Brazil. São Paulo, with no fewer than three major teams, is a great place to feel the passion.

1 Centro. Historic part of the city that's great to visit during the day, and best avoided at night.

2 Avenida Paulista, Bela Vista, and Bixiga. Avenida Paulista is the symbol of the city, with cinema, theaters, and museums. Bela Vista is a traditional neighborhood. Bixiga is known for its Italian immigrants and famous cantinas.

3 Vila Madalena and Pinheiros. A bohemian and youthful area of the city.

4 Ibirapuera. The most upscale neighborhood in São Paulo.

5 Itaim Bibi. It stands out for its concentration of numerous restaurants.

6 Liberdade. The Japanese region of the city, where the streets are decorated with lanterns, has a lovely street market.

7 Vila Olímpia and Brooklin. Financial and commercial center, very sophisticated.

8 Barra Funda. Alternative and cool neighborhood.

9 Jardins. One of the quietest and most sought-after neighborhoods.

10 Greater São Paulo. Metropolitan Region that covers 39 municipalities and is home to 22 million people.

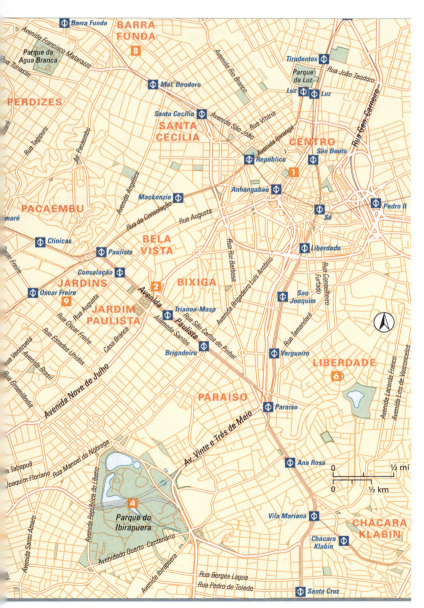

São Paulo WELCOME TO SÃO PAULO

PARQUE IBIRAPUERA

Walking bridge at Ibirapuera Park

Ibirapuera Park is one of the greatest sources of pride for the people of São Paulo. A true treasure amidst the incessant chaos, it is a place of leisure with various activities for all ages and profiles.

You can observe groups practicing yoga, stretching, running, and even hiking, joining together at dog meet-ups (yes, this is a common pastime here), among other activities. *Paulistanos* love to spend Sundays relaxing with their families, strolling with their pets, and exercising, by biking (if you don't have one it's possible to rent), skating, and rollerblading. People sit on the grass with their picnic baskets to enjoy the stunning view of the lake, spend the day in the park's fresh air, relish the sunset, and relax during the weekends.

During the weekdays, the park is also quite busy, with many people practicing their daily physical exercises in a light and pleasant way, taking a break to rehydrate with a coconut water or recharge their energy by enjoying some açaí (a typical Brazilian fruit used to make a creamy, ice cream-like treat that pairs well with fruits, smoothies, and even sweets).

Ibirapuera is São Paulo's Central Park, though it's slightly less than half the size and is often more crowded on sunny weekends than its New York City counterpart. In the 1950s the land, which originally contained the municipal nurseries, was chosen as the site of a public park to commemorate the city's 400th anniversary.

REFUGE

In 1920, then-Mayor of São Paulo, José Pires do Rio, conceived Ibirapuera Park. His inspiration came from places such as Bois de Boulogne in Paris, Hyde Park in London, and Central Park in New York City. In 1927, Manuel Lopes de Oliveira, one of the greatest scientific journalists of the early 20th century and a plant enthusiast, began planting Australian eucalyptus trees to drain the land and eliminate excess moisture. Various proposals from many renowned architects and engineers were considered, but it was Oscar Niemeyer's project (the Brazilian architect who made history worldwide, leaving a legacy of over 600 works) and his team that was ultimately chosen, and their design remains in Ibirapuera Park to this day. The greenest area in São Paulo's concrete jungle, the park serves as a great refuge for those seeking peace amidst the chaos of the big city. In addition to housing many species of fauna and flora in its area, with more than 500 species in total, including various animals, plants, trees, insects, and much more. In October 2020, Urbia Parques took over the management of Ibirapuera Park through a 35-year public concession.

Trees in full bloom in Ibirapuera Park.

HISTORIC HERITAGE OF SÃO PAULO

The space holds very important museums such as the Museum of Modern Art, Afro Brasil, the Planetarium, and the Japanese Pavilion. It receives thousands of visitors every day who are seeking fresh air. Additionally, the park has an auditorium with a capacity for over 800 people, aimed at developing and showcasing cultural activities of all genres.

Within Ibirapuera Park, there are various monuments that represent the culture and history of Brazil. The most well-known and emblematic are:

Ibirapuera Obelisk—a symbol of the 1932 Constitutional Revolution, standing 72 meters tall and made of travertine marble.

Monument to Pedro Álvares Cabral—a 5-meter bronze sculpture inaugurated in commemoration of the 500th anniversary of the Discovery of Brazil.

The Huntress—a considerably stylized female figure resting on the back of an animal.

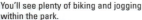

You'll see plenty of biking and jogging within the park.

São Paulo is, with no doubt, one of the most vibrant metropolises in the world and the largest city in Brazil. It is a true cultural and economic epicenter. With a population exceeding 12 million inhabitants, São Paulo is the financial heart of the country, housing the headquarters of numerous national and multinational companies. The city is known for its impressive diversity, the result of a long history of immigration that brought communities from all over the world, contributing to a rich and unique cultural mix. All these characteristics attract more than 2 million tourists every year.

The disposition of Paulistanos (someone who was born in São Paulo) to make the most of every moment is evident. This contagious energy makes São Paulo a place where there is always something new to discover and experience, at any hour of the day or night, making it one of the most dynamic and exciting cities in the world. Paulistanos work tirelessly but also enjoy life to the fullest.

The city offers an internationally renowned gastronomic scene, with award-winning restaurants and a variety of flavors ranging from traditional to contemporary, covering all corners of the world. Additionally, São Paulo is an important center for art and culture, housing prominent museums such as MASP, and hosting major events like the São Paulo Fashion Week. The nightlife is very lively, with bars, concert venues, and clubs ensuring entertainment for all tastes. Finally, urban parks like Ibirapuera offer a green refuge amidst the hustle and bustle, ideal for relaxing and enjoying nature. All these factors make São Paulo an irresistible destination for tourists seeking a rich and multifaceted experience and make the visits of those who come for work very enjoyable.

With exponential growth and construction everywhere, São Paulo is a city extremely rich in every imaginable aspect. Just walking through a few streets reveals its grandiosity: high-standard buildings, a lot of luxury cars circulating, countless designer stores, and the intoxicating energy of its citizens.

Planning

Activities

Maybe it's the environment or maybe the culture, but participating in organized sports isn't usually a huge part of a Paulistano's regime. An exception is soccer, or *futebol,* which you will see being played in most parks, either on full fields, half-size arenas, or even sandy courts, every weekend and on weeknights. Basketball and volleyball also have loyal, if smaller, followings at parks and SESC centers around the city.

SOCCER

São Paulo State has several well-funded teams with some of the country's best players. The four main teams—Corinthians, São Paulo, Palmeiras, and Santos—attract fans from other states. Corinthians and Palmeiras opened new stadiums in 2014. São Paulo's Morumbi and the municipally run Pacaembu, meanwhile, continue to host matchups featuring Brazilian clubs. Covered seats offer the best protection, not only from the elements but also from rowdy spectators.

Buy tickets at the stadiums or online. Regular games usually don't sell out, but finals and classicos between the big four—for which you can buy tickets up to five days in advance—generally do. For a history lesson on the "beautiful game," check out the interactive Soccer Museum at the Pacaembu stadium.

Getting Here and Around

Given that it is a large city, the best choice is to stay in the central area. To get around São Paulo, there are numerous options. Avoid buses, as they are difficult to navigate and usually only take cash. The city offers a large extension of metro and train lines that cover most points of interest and are easy to access but be careful! Pay attention to rush hour as the trains become extremely crowded and almost impossible to use. Traffic is also a problem, so be prepared to spend a few hours of your day getting from one place to another. Uber and taxis are widely used by residents and visitors because they offer a more comfortable way to move around the gigantic city. Renting a car can be a good option if you don't mind driving a lot. Just have a smartphone with Internet access and navigation apps like Waze (most used by Brazilians) and Google Maps. Don't forget to always check the signs when parking; many areas are prohibited or paid, so it may be a good idea to use a parking lot.

AIR

São Paulo is the main gateway for international flights, making it very easy to travel anywhere in Brazil from this city. With over 500 daily flights to destinations all around the world departing from São Paulo, many of them serve as a strategic connection point for thousands of people from various locations.

São Paulo's international airport, Aeroporto Internacional de São Paulo/Guarulhos (GRU) (⊕ *www.infraero.gov.br*), or Cumbica, is in the suburb of Guarulhos, 30 km (19 miles) and a 45-minute drive (longer during rush hour or on rainy days) northeast of Centro. There is another airport in the city, Aeroporto de Congonhas (CGH) (⊕ *www.infraero.gov.br*), 14 km (9 miles) south of Centro (a 15- to 45-minute drive, depending on traffic), which is a very busy airport and only handles regional flights within Brazil.

The Airport Bus Service (⊕ www.airportbusservice.com.br) connects Guarulhos International Airport to Congonhas Airport, covering a distance of 35 kilometers. Managed by the Empresa Metropolitana de Transportes Urbanos de São Paulo (EMTU), this service offers an executive bus line between the two airports. The buses are equipped with air-conditioning, Wi-Fi, bathrooms, and complimentary mineral water. The journey between the airports takes about 1 hour and 20 minutes, with buses operating every 40 minutes. The first bus of the day departs from Guarulhos Airport at 6 am, and the last one at 10:30 pm. From Congonhas, the first bus leaves at 6:20 am and the last one at 10:50 pm. At Congonhas, buses depart from the lower level, while at Guarulhos, they leave from Terminal 3. The fare is R$43.90, and the service also includes routes that serve the Avenida Paulista area, three different bus terminals connected to the metro lines, and Congonhas Airport.

Guarucoop (⊕ www.guarucoop.com.br) is the taxi cooperative in Guarulhos with an exclusive concession from the municipal government to operate at the airport. The services offered have fixed rates and are provided by bilingual drivers and receptionists. The fleet consists of over 650 vehicles, all equipped with air-conditioning. For example, the average cost to go to Paulista Avenue is around R$110, and to Vila Olímpia, it's about R$150. The price tables may vary depending on traffic and the time of day. Congonhas is much closer to the city center and the Zona Sul region, so the cost is typically around R$50 with the radio taxi company Vermelha e Branco. Prices are not fixed before the trip, so fares may vary.

BUS

The three key bus terminals in the city of São Paulo are connected to metro (subway) stations and serve more than 1,100 destinations combined, transporting more than 140,000 people daily. The huge main station—serving all major Brazilian cities (with trips to Rio every 10 minutes during the day and every half hour at night, until 2 am), as well as Argentina, Uruguay, Chile, Peru, and Paraguay—is the Terminal Tietê (⊕ www.terminalrodoviariodotiete.com.br) in the north, on the Marginal Tietê Beltway. Terminal Jabaquara (⊕ www.rodoviariadojabaquara.com.br), near Congonhas Airport, serves coastal towns. Terminal Barra Funda (⊕ www.rodoviariadabarrafunda.com), in the west, near the Memorial da América Latina, has buses to and from western Brazil. Socicam (⊕ www.socicam.com.br), a private company, runs all the bus terminals in the city of São Paulo.

Municipal bus service is frequent and covers the entire city, but regular buses are overcrowded at rush hour and when it rains. If you don't speak Portuguese, it can be hard to figure out the system and the stops. The stops are clearly marked. Buses don't stop at every bus stop, so if you're waiting, you'll have to flag one down. Bus fare is R$4.40. You enter at the front of the bus, pay the *cobrador* (fare collector) in the middle—or the *motorista* (driver), if it's a smaller bus—and exit from the rear of the bus. To pay, you can use either money or a *bilhete único* (rechargeable electronic card). The card allows you to take four buses in three hours for the price of one fare. Cards can be bought and reloaded at special booths at major bus terminals or at lottery shops. For bus numbers and names, routes, and schedules, go to the (Portuguese-language) website of Transporte Público de São Paulo (SPTrans; ⊕ www.sptrans.com.br), the city's public transport agency, or use Google Maps, which is linked to the SPTrans system and shows all bus routes.

CAR

The principal highways leading into São Paulo are: the Dutra, from the northeast (and Rio); Anhangüera and Bandeirantes, from the north; Washington Luis, from the northwest; Raposo Tavares, from the west; Régis Bittencourt, from the south; and Anchieta-Imigrantes, from Santos in the southeast. Driving in the city isn't recommended, however, because of the heavy traffic (nothing moves at rush hour, especially when it rains), daredevil drivers, and inadequate parking. You'll also need to obtain a temporary driver's license from Detran, the State Transit Department, if you plan to stay more than 180 days. Otherwise your drivers license is also valid to drive here.

The high-speed beltways along Rio Pinheiros and Rio Tietê—called Marginal Tietê and Marginal Pinheiros—sandwich the main part of São Paulo. Avenida 23 de Maio runs south from Centro and beneath the Parque do Ibirapuera via the Ayrton Senna Tunnel. Avenida Paulista splits Bela Vista and Jardins with Higienópolis and Vila Mariana as bookends.

You can cut through Itaim en route to Brooklin and Santo Amaro by taking avenidas Brasil and Faria Lima southwest to Avenida Santo Amaro. Avenida João Dias and Viaduto José Bonifácio C. Nogueira cut across the Pinheiros River to Morumbi. The Elevado Costa e Silva, also called Minhocão, is an elevated road that connects Centro with Avenida Francisco Matarazzo in the west.

In most commercial neighborhoods, you must buy hourly tickets (called Cartão Zona Azul) to park on the street during business hours. The only way to buy them is through the app ZONA AZUL-SP. Each one costs R$6.45, and you need to fill it out with the car's license plate and select the area you parked in. After business hours or at any time near major sights, people may offer to watch your car. If you don't pay these "caretakers," there's a chance they'll damage your car (R$2 is enough to keep your car's paint job intact). However, to truly ensure your car's safety, park in a guarded lot, where rates are either flat—from R$10 to R$50 during the day, depending on the neighborhood—or charged by the hour, at anywhere from R$5 to R$20.

Garoa

One of São Paulo's most famous nicknames is *terra da garoa*, which basically means land of drizzling rain. A dearth of sufficient rain in recent years has put an end to that nickname, but especially in the summertime, when afternoon rains wash over the city most days, a lightweight umbrella is a sensible item to carry.

SUBWAY

Six color-coded lines compose the São Paulo Metrô (www.metro.sp.gov.br), known simply as the metro by locals, which interconnects with seven train lines administered by the Companhia Paulista de Trens Metropolitanos (CPTM) to blanket most of São Paulo in rail. The most glaring gaps exist around Morumbi neighborhood, as well as near the airports. You can print maps of the entire network from the metro's English-language website (ticket prices and schedules are also available). You can also download the metro's English-language app to your smartphone, which includes a map of the entire subway and train system, the current status of each line, and an interactive search, where you insert your starting point and final destination to see the best route to get where you're going.

Kiosks at all metro and train stations sell tickets; vendors prefer small bills for payment. You insert the ticket into the turnstile at the platform entrance and, depending on the station, either turn the turnstile yourself or clear sliding doors will open for you. Seniors (65 or older) ride without charge by showing photo IDs at the turnstiles. Transfers within the metro system are free. A single ticket costs R$5. You can also buy a rechargeable bilhete único at metro stations.

TAXI

Taxis in São Paulo are white. Owner-driven taxis are generally well-maintained and reliable, as are radio taxis. Fares start at R$4.10 and run from R$2.70 for each kilometer (½ mile) or R$0.55 for every minute sitting in traffic. After 8 pm and on weekends, fares rise up to 50%. You'll pay a tax if the cab leaves the city, as is the case with trips to Cumbica Airport. Good radio taxi companies, among them Coopertax (⊕ www.coopertax.com.br), Ligue-Taxi (⊕ www.ligue-taxi.com.br), and Radio Taxi Vermelho e Branco (⊕ www.radiotaxivermelhoebranco.com.br), usually accept credit cards. Smartphone apps like Easy Taxi and 99Taxis are popular, reliable, and highly recommended. Some taxi companies also have their own smartphone apps.

Hotels

São Paulo is a vibrant and dynamic city that receives millions of visitors every year, whether they are tourists or business travelers. To meet this demand, the city offers a vast array of hotels that vary in style, price, and quality. From luxurious five-star hotels to more budget-friendly options, São Paulo has accommodations for every taste and budget. Well-known international hotel chains, highly regarded for their quality and service, have multiple hotels in São Paulo.

Luxury hotels like the Unique, Tivoli Mofarrej, and Hotel Fasano are known for their sophisticated facilities, impeccable services, and prime locations. Many of them are situated in the city's most upscale neighborhoods, such as Jardins and Itaim Bibi, offering easy access to major commercial and cultural centers.

In addition to high-end hotels, São Paulo boasts a wide network of midrange hotels that combine comfort and value for money. Well-known chains like Ibis, Mercure, and Novotel offer modern, well-equipped accommodations, ideal for those seeking practicality and convenience during their stay.

What It Costs in Reais			
$	$$	$$$	$$$$
RESTAURANTS			
under R$50	R$50–R$130	R$131–R$200	over R$200
HOTELS			
under R$150	R$150–R$300	R$301–R$500	over R$500

Nightlife

You will certainly be surprised by the number of bars and nightclubs São Paulo has to offer. There are countless options, and the best part is that the styles are extremely varied. It's almost impossible not to find something you like, from simple corner bars perfect for enjoying a really cold beer, to sophisticated venues with live piano music that are ideal for sipping the most exquisite wine you can imagine.

Here, the fun never ends. Bars open early for happy hour and stay open until 1 or 2 in the morning. Think that's it? Think again. There are nightclubs that remain open until 6 or 7 in the morning, and many famous "after-parties" that continue throughout the next day.

Performing Arts

São Paulo, being the cultural and diverse hub that it is, offers an inexhaustible range of activities and artistic performances of various kinds.

To stay informed about schedules, always check the official websites, as

A Bit of History

São Paulo wasn't big and important right from the start. Jesuit priests founded it in 1554 and began converting native Indians to Catholicism. The town was built strategically on a plateau, protected from attack and served by many rivers. It remained unimportant to the Portuguese crown until the 1600s, when it became the departure point for the *bandeira* (literally, "flag") expeditions, whose members set out to look for gemstones and gold, to enslave indigenous peoples, and, later, to capture escaped African enslaved peoples. In the process, these adventurers established roads into vast portions of previously unexplored territory. São Paulo also saw Emperor Dom Pedro I declare independence from Portugal in 1822, by the Rio Ipiranga (Ipiranga River), near the city.

It was only in the late 19th century that São Paulo became a driving force in the country. As the state established itself as one of Brazil's main coffee producers, the city attracted laborers and investors from many countries. Italians, Portuguese, Spanish, Germans, and Japanese put their talents and energies to work. By 1895, 70,000 of the 130,000 residents were immigrants. Their efforts transformed the place from a sleepy mission post into a dynamic financial and cultural hub, with people of all colors and religions living and working together peacefully.

Avenida Paulista was once the site of many a coffee baron's mansion. Money flowed from these private domains into civic and cultural institutions. The arts began to flourish, and by the 1920s São Paulo was promoting such great artists as Mário and Oswald de Andrade, who introduced modern elements into Brazilian art.

In the 1950s the auto industry began to develop and contributed greatly to São Paulo's contemporary wealth—and problems. Over the next 30 years, people from throughout Brazil, especially the Northeast, came seeking jobs, which transformed the city's landscape by increasing *favelas* and poverty. Between the 1950s and today, the city's main revenue has moved from industry to banking and commerce.

Today, like many major European or American hubs, São Paulo struggles to meet its citizens' transportation and housing needs, and goods and services are expensive. Like most of its counterparts elsewhere in the world, it hasn't yet found an answer to these problems.

they provide detailed information about each event scheduled to take place in the coming days, weeks, and months.

The places where free events usually occur include Avenida Paulista, Vale do Anhangabaú, Ibirapuera Park, various Social Service of Commerce (SESC) centers, and the São Paulo Cultural Center, among many others. Some events require reservations through their websites.

Currently, most events allow you to download tickets directly to your phone and present them on the day of the event, without needing a printed copy. These events encompass a variety of types, such as musicals, opera, orchestra performances, art exhibitions, and cultural movements.

For information on free entertainment options, the website Catraca Livre (⊕ *catracalivre.com.br/brasil*) is highly recommended. Additionally, websites like ⊕ *eventbrite.com.br* and ⊕ *sympla.com.br* are great for research, as well as following @agendaculturasp on Instagram for updates. Always pay attention to the type of event, whether it is free or paid.

Planning Your Time

A walk along Avenida Paulista is a good way to ease gently into São Paulo while still soaking up the big-city atmosphere. A long, prominent ridge topped with huge TV and radio antennae, Paulista is a handy geographical reference: you can stroll down into chic, leafy Jardins from here, or grab a cab and head the other way into revitalizing Centro. On Paulista itself, the boxlike MASP art museum has to be seen to be believed, while the little park just opposite, Trianon, is a beautiful scrap of native forest. Centro is where much of the city's remaining historic architecture can be found—don't miss a trip to the foodie-heaven market, the Mercado Municipal, and close to Praça da República, the view from the top of towering Edificio Itália is truly spectacular.

Make sure to enjoy the Liberdade neighborhood on a Saturday, when an entire street is closed off and vendors set up stalls selling food and products, attracting thousands of visitors throughout the day. This vibrant event offers a unique opportunity to experience the cultural and culinary delights of São Paulo's Japanese community, making it a must-visit for both locals and tourists.

Parque do Ibirapuera is a great favorite with Paulistanos, especially on weekends, when a stroll in the park is a chance to see locals of all stripes taking their leisure; while a day spent sauntering around Vila Madalèna is a pleasant, undemanding way to see another side to the city. The neighborhood is packed with boutiques, cafés, restaurants, and bars—but beware the steep hills. Don't miss Beco do Batman, a copiously graffitied pair of alleyways. Finish up at one of the many lovely restaurants here, or in neighboring Pinheiros.

Restaurants

São Paulo boasts over 156,000 bars and restaurants, offering an enormous variety for those who enjoy diverse dining experiences. Whether you have dietary restrictions, a culinary preference, or a budget to stick to, São Paulo provides access to all types of food at any time, with a wide range of prices. Renowned restaurants with Michelin stars and corner bars with homemade food illustrate the city's socio-economic contrasts. You can find elite options costing up to R$1,200 for a tasting menu per person, or enjoy an executive meal for just R$25. In São Paulo, dining is an experience for every taste and budget.

Safety

Despite the city's many police officers, it's always wise to take precautions, as opportunistic thieves are everywhere, waiting for a moment of distraction to strike. Always stay alert and keep your belongings in sight and secure. Avoid wearing flashy jewelry and don't keep your phone in your pocket, as pickpockets can easily take it. Be very careful when withdrawing money from banks and ATMs, and avoid talking on your phone while walking. It's preferable to use a car for transportation at night, especially in neighborhoods that may seem more dangerous; keep your windows closed and doors locked. Avoid using your phone while driving, as the screen's light can attract attention. Be extra vigilant at traffic lights, particularly regarding motorcycles.

Shopping

With no fewer than 54 shopping malls, São Paulo holds the title of Brazil's top consumer city. These establishments attract thousands of visitors daily, whether for shopping, entertainment like movies, dining, or simply strolling—a common hobby among Brazilians. High-end malls, such as Cidade Jardim, boast enviable structures and beautiful views. Other malls cater to the needs of workers in commercial centers and communities in the suburbs, providing entertainment and convenience. From luxurious venues to popular suburban hubs, São Paulo's shopping scene offers something for everyone.

Tours

You can hire a bilingual guide through a travel agency or a hotel concierge for about R$180 for a four-hour tour, or design your own itineraries. The website Visit São Paulo (⊕ *visitesaopaulo.com/blog/*) offers a wide range of programs, places to visit, experiences, and more. The Prefeitura de São Paulo provides the "VAI DE ROTEIRO" program, which features a series of guided tours around the city's strategic tourist spots. Some attractions may charge entrance fees, so check each location in advance. The program aims to highlight São Paulo's most important sites, historical landmarks, and explore the tourist potential of each one.

CONTACTS Check Point. ✉ *São Paulo* ☎ *11/2791–1316 business hours, 11/99187–1393 for after-hours and WhatsApp* ⊕ *www.checkpointtours.com.br.* **Gol Tour Viagens e Turismo.** ☎ *11/3256–2388* ⊕ *www.goltour.com.br.* **SP Free Walking Tours.** ✉ *São Paulo* ⊕ *www.saopaulofreewalkingtour.com.*

Favorite Places

Leticia Davino: São Paulo is the city where I was born, and although I've lived in places like New York and Dublin, I wouldn't trade this city for anything. Here, the energy is unique, the city never stops, and it's always ready to surprise. I am completely addicted to discovering new restaurants, and there's no better place to indulge in this hobby than São Paulo, where the gastronomy is a true journey through the flavors of the world.

Visitor Information

The most helpful contact is the São Paulo Convention and Visitors Bureau (⊕ *www.visitesaopaulo.com*), open weekdays from 9 to 6. Branches of the city-operated São Paulo Turismo are open daily from 9 to 6. The Secretaria de Turismo do Estado de São Paulo (⊕ *www.turismo.sp.gov.br*), open weekdays from 9 to 6, is less helpful, but has maps and information about the city and state of São Paulo. The Secretaria also has a booth at the arrivals terminal in Guarulhos airport; it's open daily from 9 am to 10 pm.

When to Go

Cultural events—film and music festivals, and fashion and art exhibits—usually take place between April and December. In the South American summer (from January through March), the weather is rainy, and floods can disrupt traffic. Between February and March, Carnival happens and attracts people from all over the world. The streets in São Paulo are full of people enjoying the Trio Elétrico, and the official parade takes place in the Sambódromo do Anhembi. During these

The Museu Catavento has four sections within the museum: Universe, Life, Ingenuity, and Society.

high-season periods, always make hotel and beach resort reservations as far in advance as possible, particularly for weekend stays. In winter (June and July), follow the same rule for visits to Campos do Jordão. Summers are hot—35°C (95°F). In winter, temperatures rarely dip below 10°C (50°F).

■ TIP→ **The air pollution might irritate your eyes, especially in July and August (dirty air is held in the city by thermal inversions), so pack eye drops.**

Centro

The downtown area is known as the historic center because it is where many old buildings dating back to the 20th century are located, considered historical landmarks, and meticulously cared for. Lately, the city government of São Paulo has been taking care of the Central Zone, which used to be neglected and had an air of abandonment. Today, it's possible to see clean streets well-monitored by police, which brings a sense of improvement for residents and tourists alike, though it's still advisable to stay alert for pickpockets who might seize an opportunity. It's easy to get here by metro or car.

For an easy glimpse of Centro, start at the Anhangabaú metro station and head northwest along the valley (Vale do Anhangabaú). Pass under the historic Viaduto do Chá and take in the sight of the magnificent, baroque Theatro Municipal to your left. A bit farther along near the São Bento metro station, find your way to the monastery of the same name, uphill to the right. Then continue on over the hill, and make your way downhill, zigzagging through the crowded shopping streets towards Mercado Municipal.

◉ Sights

Catavento Cultural (*Museu Catavento*) **COLLEGE | FAMILY** | Families traveling will find education and entertainment for their children in this interactive and immersive science museum located in the former city hall building. Upon arriving at the museum, the beautiful early 20th-century structure of the building catches the eye, with its inner courtyard alone justifying a visit. It's an incredible space with activities for all ages, where you can learn about science, technology, and history in a very light and enjoyable way. ✉ *Av. Mercúrio s/n, Parque Dom Pedro II, São Paulo* ☎ *11/3315–0051* ⊕ *www.cataventocultural.org.br* 💰 *R$15* ⊗ *Closed Mon.* Ⓜ *Pedro II*.

Catedral da Sé
RELIGIOUS BUILDING | The imposing Sé Cathedral, in neo-Gothic style with 14 towers, occupies São Paulo's official center—known here as the 0 km point. You can enjoy a brunch (costing R$390, a donation with a social approach that helps people in vulnerable situations) on Sundays and take a tour of the cathedral. It houses the tombs of 15 Portuguese and Brazilian bishops who served in the city of São Paulo. ✉ *Praça da Sé s/n, Centro* ☎ *11/98680–7940* ⊕ *www.brunchnacatedral.com.br* 💰 *Tour R$60* Ⓜ *Sé*.

Centro Cultural Banco do Brasil
CONVENTION CENTER | The French-inspired architectural style associated with eclectic ornamentation is evident in the facade of the building and its interiors. There are five floors, plus a tower, constructed with reinforced concrete structure and brick masonry. The building offers spaces for exhibitions, theater, cinema, and music; an auditorium for lectures, debates, and educational workshops; and a cafeteria. ✉ *Rua Álvares Penteado 112, Centro* ☎ *11/4297–0600* ⊕ *www.culturabancodobrasil.com.br/portal/sao-paulo* ⊗ *Closed Tues.* Ⓜ *Sé*.

Convento e Santuário São Francisco
RELIGIOUS BUILDING | One of the city's best-preserved Portuguese colonial buildings, this baroque structure—two churches, one run by Catholic clergy and the other by lay brothers—was built between 1647 and 1790. The image inside of Saint Francis was rescued from a fire in

> ## Centro's Evolution
>
> São Paulo's first inhabitants, Jesuit missionaries and treasure-hunting pioneers, settled in the fledgling city's hilltop and valley areas, particularly Vale do Anhangabaú. Later these areas became Centro (downtown district), a financial and cultural center that's still home to the stock exchange and many banks, and is largely pedestrian-only.

1870. ✉ *Largo São Francisco 133, Centro* ☎ *11/3291–2400* ⊕ *www.franciscanos.org.br* 💰 *Free* Ⓜ *Sé or Anhangabaú*.

Edifício Copan
NOTABLE BUILDING | Originally, COPAN was designed to be a 30-story residential building and another that would house a hotel with 600 apartments, which would be interconnected and also have a cinema, theater, and commerce. However, only the residential project was built in 1950. There are 1,160 apartments with about 5,000 people living there, making it the largest residential complex in the country. ✉ *Av. Ipiranga 200, Centro* ☎ *11/3257–6169, 11/3259–5917* ⊕ *www.copansp.com.br* ⊗ *Closed weekends* Ⓜ *República*.

Edifício Itália
RESTAURANT | The over 500-feet tall skyscraper, Edifício Itália (Italy Building) has a panoramic view of the city. Built by German-Brazilian architect, Franz Heep, was once the tallest building in Sao Paulo. A pleasant but somewhat expensive way to enjoy it is to have lunch or dinner at the Terraço Itália restaurant, a classic and romantic environment, located on the 41st floor of the building. It is also possible to have drinks at the piano bar. If you just want to visit the Terrace, you

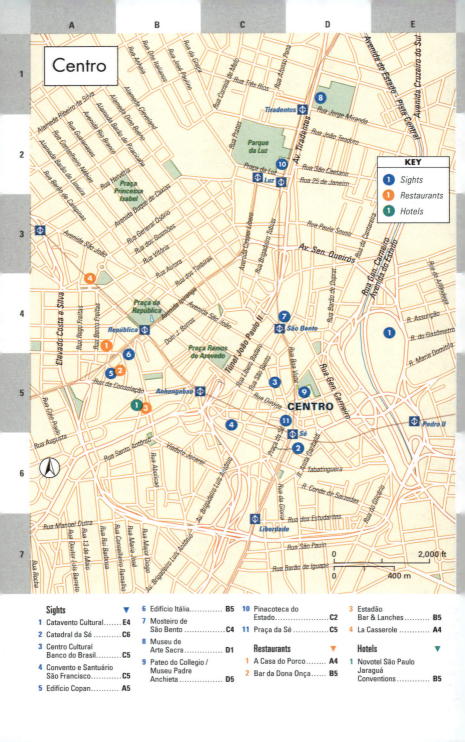

Museu de Arte Sacra (Museum of Sacred Art) is the only 18th-century colonial building left in São Paulo.

need to pay a R$50 fee. ⊠ Av. Ipiranga 344, Centro ☎ 11/2189–2929 restaurant, 11/3256–5574 ⊕ www.edificioitalia.com.br Ⓜ República.

Mosteiro de São Bento
RELIGIOUS BUILDING | The German architect Richard Berndl designed this Norman–Byzantine church that was completed in 1922. Ecclesiastical imagery abounds, and soaring archways extend skyward. The church's enormous organ has some 6,000 pipes, and its Russian image of the Kasperovo Virgin is covered with 6,000 pearls from the Black Sea. On the last Sunday of each month, Paulistanos compete for space at the church's popular brunch (that costs R$357), which also includes a tour and varying performances, from dance to choir; call early to reserve your seat. The don't-miss religious event at Mosterio de São Bento is Sunday Mass at 10 am, when the sound of monks' Gregorian chants echoes throughout the chamber. ⊠ Largo de São Bento 48, Centro ☎ 11/3328–8799, 11/94075–0593 for Sunday brunch (WhatsApp) ⊕ www.mosteirodesaobentosp.com.br ⊠ Free Ⓜ São Bento.

Museu de Arte Sacra (Museum of Sacred Art)
ART MUSEUM | If you can't get to Bahia or Minas Gerais during your stay in Brazil, you can get a taste of the fabulous baroque and rococo art found there at the Museum of Sacred Art. On display are 4,000 wooden and terra-cotta masks, jewelry, and liturgical objects from all over the country (but primarily Minas Gerais and Bahia), dating from the 17th century to the present. The on-site convent was founded in 1774. ⊠ Av. Tiradentes 676, Luz ☎ 11/3326–3336 ⊕ www.museuartesacra.org.br ⊠ R$6, free Sat. ⊘ Closed Mon. Ⓜ Tiradentes.

Pateo do Collegio / Museu Padre Anchieta
RELIGIOUS BUILDING | São Paulo was founded by the Jesuits José de Anchieta and Manoel da Nóbrega in the College Courtyard in 1554. The church was constructed in 1896 in the same style as the chapel built by the Jesuits. In the small museum you can see a fascinating

Did You Know?

The largest Catholic church in São Paulo, Catedral da Sé, was built in a neo-Gothic architecture style with more than 800 tons of rare marble incorporated into its construction.

Take a Walk

The imposing and almost dead-straight Avenida Paulista is a great place to explore on foot. Running from Paraíso (paradise) to Consolação (consolation), two bookending metro stations, the avenue also serves as Paulistanos' tongue-in-cheek comparison to marriage, but many couples of all ages will be found strolling here hand in hand. The Museu de Arte de São Paulo (MASP) has one of Brazil's best collections of fine art. Right across the street is shady Parque Trianon, where locals hang out and eat lunch. Leaving the park, veer right and head for the Centro Cultural FIESP. Here you may be able to catch one of its art shows or performances. A few blocks away is the Instituto Itaú Cultural, a great place to see contemporary Brazilian art. Finally, rest your weary feet in Casa das Rosas, a cultural center and café, with a pretty rose garden attached. On Sundays, the city's famous avenue is closed to car traffic and becomes a large open-air fair, with cultural demonstrations, and people enjoying the weekend with their families and appreciating the city.

relief map of Centro in colonial times and an exhibition of early sacred art and relics. ✉ *Praça Patio do Colegio 2, Centro* ☎ *11/3105–6899 Pateo do Collegio, 11/4704–2654 Museu de Arte Sacra dos Jesuítas* ⊕ *www.pateocollegio.com.br* 🖅 *R$20* ⊘ *Closed Sun and Mon.* ☞ *You must send a message to schedule your visit to the museum.* Ⓜ *Sé*.

Pinacoteca do Estado
ART GALLERY | The highlights of the State Art Gallery's permanent collection include paintings by the renowned Brazilian artists Tarsila do Amaral and Cândido Portinari. The museum occupies a 1905 structure that was renovated in the late 1990s. The exterior recalls a 1950s brick firehouse, while the view through the central courtyard's interior windows evokes the cliffs of Cuenca, Spain. It is now possible to visit the Pinacoteca de São Paulo and its three buildings with a single ticket. The ticket gives access to the exhibitions and installations at Pina Luz, Pina Estação, and Pina Contemporânea.

■ TIP→ **The area is sketchy so stay alert as you go, and don't walk at night.** ✉ *Praça da Luz 2, Centro* ☎ *11/3324–1000* ⊕ *www.pinacoteca.org.br* 🖅 *R$30; free Sat.* ⊘ *Closed Tues.* Ⓜ *Luz*.

Praça da Sé
PLAZA/SQUARE | This large plaza marks the city's geographical center—the 0 km point, as it's called here—and holds the city's main cathedral, the beautiful Catedral da Sé. It can't be missed when you're visiting the rest of the historic downtown, but know that the square has become a place where many of the city's homeless people stay at night and a meeting point for migrants and immigrants new to the area. During the day, just stay alert for pickpockets. The area is well-policed and maintained by the city government.

■ TIP→ **Avoid visiting after dark and be on the lookout for pickpockets.** ✉ *Praça da Sé s/n, Centro* Ⓜ *Sé*.

🍴 Restaurants

A Casa do Porco
$$$ | **BRAZILIAN** | A Casa do Porco reached the seventh position in the *World's 50 Best Restaurants* ranking in 2022, becoming the highest-ranked Brazilian restaurant on the list at the time. This achievement solidified its reputation as

one of the top global dining destinations. **Known for:** great atmosphere; succulent pork belly; wide beer selection. [$] *Average main: R$100* ✉ *Rua Araújo 124, Centro* ☎ *11/3258–2578* ⊕ *www.acasadoporco.com.br* ⊘ *No dinner Sun.* Ⓜ *República.*

Bar da Dona Onça
$$$ | **BRAZILIAN** | Bar da Dona Onça, located in the iconic Copan Building in São Paulo, offers an authentic gastronomic experience with dishes that celebrate Brazilian cuisine. The cozy atmosphere, charming decor, and attentive service make this bar a must-visit spot in the city. **Known for:** cozy and iconic atmosphere; drink rabo de galo; frequented by celebrities. [$] *Average main: R$100* ✉ *Copan Building, Av. Ipiranga 200, CJ 27 e 29, Centro* ☎ *11/3257–2016* ⊕ *www.bardadonaonca.com.br* ⊘ *No dinner Sun.* Ⓜ *República.*

La Casserole
$$$ | **FRENCH** | Facing a little Centro flower market, this romantic Parisian-style bistro has been around for five decades and has witnessed more than its share of wedding proposals. Surrounded by wood-paneled walls decorated with art that nods at famous French artists, you can dine on such delights as *gigot aux soissons* (roast leg of lamb in its own juices, served with white beans), *canard à l'orange* (roast duck in an orange sauce), and a classic *crème brûlée*. **Known for:** French favorites like foie gras; cozy atmosphere; excellent service. [$] *Average main: R$120* ✉ *Largo do Arouche 346, Centro* ☎ *11/3331–6283* ⊕ *www.lacasserole.com.br* ⊘ *Closed Mon.; no dinner Sun.* Ⓜ *República.*

Estadão Bar & Lanches
$ | **SANDWICHES** | Quests for quick, cheap, and good food should start near São Paulo's origins at this greasy spoon that's open 24 hours a day. Estadão's recipe for staying in business for more than four decades is its succulent *pernil* (roast pork) sandwich, a staple of the local street food scene. **Known for:**

> ## Stay Alert
> Pickpocketing can be a problem in Centro, so keep a low profile, don't wear expensive jewelry or watches, and bring only what money you absolutely need. Touring with a guide usually provides some extra security.

eclectic clientele; cheap late-night eats; generous portions. [$] *Average main: R$30* ✉ *Viaduto 9 de Julho 193, Centro* ☎ *11/3257–7121* ⊕ *www.estadaolanches.com.br* Ⓜ *Anhangabaú.*

Hotels

Novotel São Paulo Jaraguá Conventions
$$$ | **HOTEL** | Built in 1951 to be the headquarters of one of the main newspapers in the city, the building that now houses this hotel is a landmark in downtown São Paulo and has hosted Queen Elizabeth II, Fidel Castro, and Errol Flynn. **Pros:** pleasant rooms at average prices; close to many restaurants and sights; 10-minute taxi ride to Paulista. **Cons:** weak water pressure; area can be spooky at night; no pool. [$] *Rooms from: R$480* ✉ *Rua Martins Fontes 71, Centro* ☎ *11/2802–7000* ⊕ *www.novotel.com.br* 🛏 *415 rooms* ❌ *No Meals* Ⓜ *Anhangabaú.*

🎭 Performing Arts

CLASSICAL MUSIC AND OPERA
★ Sala São Paulo
CONCERTS | Despite being housed in a magnificent old train station, Sala São Paulo is one of the most modern concert halls for classical music in Latin America. It's home to the São Paulo Symphony Orchestra. (OSESP). ✉ *Praça Júlio Prestes 16, Centro* ☎ *11/3367–9500* ⊕ *www.salasaopaulo.art.br* ☞ *There are both free and paid concerts. Visit the website to see the tickets.* Ⓜ *Luz.*

CONCERT HALLS

Teatro Cultura Artística
CONCERTS | The theater was closed for many years (since there was a fire in 2008) and experienced an immense and complete renovation and restructuring. It was reopened in August 2024, with an investment of over R$200 million (about $40 million). New programs, educational areas, a restaurant, a café, and a bookstore will keep this important architectural landmark of São Paulo lively all day long. Avoid walking from the metro stop at night. ✉ *Rua Nestor Pestana 196, Consolação* ☎ *011/3256–0223* ⊕ *www.culturaartistica.com.br* Ⓜ *Republica*.

Theatro Municipal
CONCERTS | Inspired by the Paris Opéra, the Municipal Theater was built between 1903 and 1911 with art nouveau elements. *Hamlet* was the first play presented, and the house went on to host such luminaries as Isadora Duncan in 1916 and Anna Pavlova in 1919. Plays and operas are still staged here; local newspapers, as well as the theater's website, have schedules and information on how to get tickets. The auditorium, resplendent with gold leaf, moss-green velvet, marble, and mirrors, has 1,500 seats and is usually open only to those attending cultural events, although prearranged visits are also available. A museum dedicated to the theater's history is located close by at Praça das Artes. Call the theater to arrange a free guided tour in English. You can also enjoy a brunch in the theater's golden hall. ✉ *Praça Ramos de Azevedo s/n, Centro* ☎ *11/3367–7200* ⊕ *www.theatromunicipal.org.br* Ⓜ *Anhangabaú*.

DANCE

Balé da Cidade
BALLET | The City Ballet, São Paulo's official dance company, has performed for many years at the magnificent Theatro Municipal. ✉ *Praça Ramos de Azevedo s/n, Centro* ☎ *11/3053–2053* ⊕ *theatromunicipal.org.br/pt-br/baledacidadedesp/* Ⓜ *República*.

Ballet Stagium
BALLET | The ballet performs contemporary works incorporating Brazilian pop and bossa nova music. Founded in 1971 during Brazil's period of dictatorship, the company made its name performing dances with political and social justice themes. ✉ *Complexo Cultural Funarte SP, Alameda Nothmann 1058, Campos Elíseos* ☎ *11/93482–3704* ⊕ *balletstagium.com.br* Ⓜ *Marechal Deodoro*.

FILM

CineSESC
FILM | Titles already out of other theaters and independent openings show for discounted prices at CineSESC. The screen is visible from the snack bar. ✉ *Rua Augusta 2075, Cerqueira César* ☎ *11/3087–0500* ⊕ *www.sescsp.org.br* Ⓜ *Consolação*.

Espaço Augusta de Cinema
FILM | Brazilian, European, and other nonblockbuster films are shown at the Espaço Augusta, with sessions every day. ✉ *Rua Augusta 1475, Cerqueira César* ☎ *11/3288–6780* ⊕ *www.espacoaugusta.com.br* Ⓜ *Consolação*.

 Nightlife

BARS

Bar Brahma
LIVE MUSIC | First opened in 1948, Bar Brahma used to be the meeting place of artists, intellectuals, and politicians. The decor is a time warp to the mid-20th century, with furniture, lamps, and a piano true to the period. This is one of the best places in São Paulo for live music, with traditional samba and Brazilian pop groups scheduled every week. Caetano Veloso immortalized the intersection of Ipiranga and São João Avenues, where the bar is located, in his 1978 song "Sampa." Cover fees range from R$15 to R$50. ✉ *Av. São João 677, Centro* ☎ *11/94746–2664* ⊕ *www.barbrahmasaopaulo.com.br* Ⓜ *República*.

The Sala São Paulo theater was originally the Julio Prestes Train Station.

DANCE CLUBS
Cine Joia
DANCE CLUB | Cine Joia takes the form of a resurrected vintage cinema, minus the seating but with the added attraction of a top-notch video-mapping system. See the site for live dates, or check out regular club nights like Talco Bells, where you'll hear soul classics. Cover fees average R$60. ✉ *Praça Carlos Gomes 82, Centro* ☎ *11/3231–0705* ⊕ *www.cinejoia.com.br* Ⓜ *Liberdade*.

Tokyo 🎤
KARAOKE | You wouldn't imagine there's a hidden bar inside this old and poorly maintained building, with karaoke rooms that you can reserve for a fun night of singing. There's also a lively rooftop nightclub that attracts people of all styles, especially the young, by playing POP, Brazilian music, hip-hop, and Reggaeton. Snack options available. ✉ *R. Maj. Sertório 110, Centro* ☎ *11/91118–5260* ⊕ *www.tokyo011.com.br* ⊘ *Closed Mon.* ☞ *R$35 up to R$120* Ⓜ *República*.

🛍 Shopping

CHOCOLATE
Brasil Cacau
CHOCOLATE | Brasil Cacau is well-known for its unique combinations of chocolate with fruits and other typical Brazilian ingredients. Highlights include chocolate with açaí, which brings out the bold flavor of the Amazonian fruit. These blends showcase local ingredients, creating innovative and authentic flavor experiences. It's perfect for taking a taste of Brazil home as a souvenir or for gifting others. ✉ *Rua São Bento 534, Centro* ☎ *11/97216–8477* ⊕ *www.brasilcacau.com.br* ⊘ *Closed Sun.* Ⓜ *São Bento*.

BEAUTY
Natura
COSMETICS | Founded in 1969, Natura is known for its sustainability and use of natural ingredients from the Amazon's biodiversity. Its product range includes fragrances, moisturizers, makeup, and skin and hair care, with a strong environmental commitment. Try the

The Mercadão (Big Market) houses about 300 stands.

"Ekos Castanha Body Cream," made with Amazonian Brazil nut oil. ✉ *Shopping Light, Rua Cel. Xavier de Toledo 23, ground floor, São Paulo* ☏ *11/91055–5000* ⊕ *www.natura.com.br* Ⓜ *Anhangabaú.*

O Boticário
SKINCARE | The Brazilian brand O Boticário was founded by dermatologists and pharmacists from Curitiba in the 1970s. The company creates products for men, women, and children, and through its foundation funds ecological projects throughout Brazil. The shops can be found in most neighborhoods and malls in the city. ✉ *Av. Brig. Luis Antonio 282, Centro* ☏ *11/3115–0712* ⊕ *www.oboticario.com.br* Ⓜ *Sé.*

LEATHER GOODS AND LUGGAGE
Inovathi
LEATHER GOODS | A shop you'll find in many malls all over town, Inovathi has leather accessories at good prices. ✉ *Shopping West Plaza, Av. Francisco Matarazzo 408, Água Branca* ☏ *11/3672–4976* ⊕ *www.inovathi.com.br* Ⓜ *Morumbi.*

MARKETS
★ Mercado Municipal (*Mercadão*)
MARKET | The city's first grocery market, this huge 1928 neo-baroque-style building is the quintessential hot spot for gourmets and food lovers. The building, nicknamed Mercadão (Big Market) by locals, houses about 300 stands that sell just about everything edible, including meat, vegetables, cheese, spices, and fish from all over Brazil. It also has restaurants and traditional snack places. The Hocca Bar is justly famous for its *pastel de bacalhau* (salt-cod pastry) and heaping mortadella sandwich. ✉ *Rua da Cantareira 306, Sé, Centro* ☏ *11/4580–1390* ⊕ *www.mercadomunicipalsp.com* Ⓜ *São Bento.*

Praça da República Arts and Crafts Fair
CRAFTS | Vendors sell jewelry, embroidery, leather goods, toys, clothing, paintings, and musical instruments at the Sunday morning arts-and-crafts fair in Praça da República. If you look carefully, you can find reasonably priced, out-of-the-ordinary souvenirs. ✉ *Praça da República, Centro*

☎ 11/98166–8081 ⊕ www.feirapracadarepublica.com.br ⊙ Closed weekdays Ⓜ República.

MUSIC
★ Baratos Afins

MUSIC | Heaven for music collectors, Baratos Afins opened inside the popular Galeria do Rock in 1978 and is also a record label. The company was the brainchild of Arnaldo Baptista, guitar player in the influential 1960s Brazilian rock band Os Mutantes. The store sells all kinds of music, but if you're looking for rare records, ask for the owner, Luiz Calanca. ✉ Galeria do Rock, Av. São João 439, 2nd fl., stores 314/318, Centro ⊕ Second entrance at Rua 24 de Maio 62 ☎ 11/3223–3629 ⊕ www.baratosafins.com.br ⊙ Closed Sun. Ⓜ República.

Avenida Paulista, Bela Vista, and Bixiga

Money once poured into and out of the coffee barons' mansions that lined Avenida Paulista, making it, in a sense, the financial hub. And so it is today, though the money is now centered in the major banks. Like the barons before them, many of these financial institutions generously support the arts. Numerous places have changing exhibitions—often free—in the Paulista neighborhood. Nearby Bixiga, São Paulo's Little Italy, is full of restaurants—Italian, of course.

👁 Sights

Casa das Rosas

HISTORIC HOME | Peek into the Paulista's past at one of the avenue's few remaining early-20th-century buildings, the House of the Roses. A 1935 French-style mansion with gardens inspired by those at Versailles, it seems out of place next to the surrounding skyscrapers. The famous Paulistano architect Ramos de Azevedo designed the home for one of his daughters, and the same family occupied it until 1986, when it was made an official municipal landmark. The site, now a cultural center, hosts classes, workshops, exhibitions, and literary events. Coffee drinks and pastries are served at the café on the terrace. ✉ Av. Paulista 37, Bela Vista/Bixiga ☎ 11/3285–6986 ⊕ www.casadasrosas.org.br 🆓 Free ⊙ Closed Mon. Ⓜ Brigadeiro.

Feira do Bixiga

MARKET | Strolling through this flea market is a favorite Sunday activity for Paulistanos. Crafts, antiques, and furniture are among the wares. Walk up the São José staircase to see **Rua dos Ingleses**, a typical and well-preserved fin-de-siècle Bixiga street. ✉ Praça Dom Orione s/n, Bixiga ⊕ www.portaldobixiga.com.br 🆓 Free ⊙ Closed Mon.–Sat.

Itaú Cultural

OTHER ATTRACTION | Maintained by Itaú, one of Brazil's largest private banks, this cultural institute has art shows as well as lectures, workshops, and films. It also maintains an archive with a photographic history of São Paulo, a library that specializes in works on Brazilian art and culture, and a permanent exhibition tracing the formation of Brazil. ✉ Av. Paulista 149, Paraíso ☎ 11/2168–1777 ⊕ www.itaucultural.org.br 🆓 Free ⊙ Closed Mon. Ⓜ Brigadeiro.

★ Museu de Arte de São Paulo (MASP)

NOTABLE BUILDING | A striking low-rise building elevated on two massive concrete pillars holds one of the city's premier fine arts collections. The highlights include works by Van Gogh, Renoir, Delacroix, Cézanne, Monet, Rembrandt, Picasso, and Degas. The baroque sculptor Aleijadinho, the expressionist painter Lasar Segall, and the expressionist/surrealist painter Cândido Portinari are three of the many Brazilian artists represented. The huge open area beneath the museum is often used for cultural events and protests, and is the site of a charming Sunday antiques fair. ✉ Av. Paulista

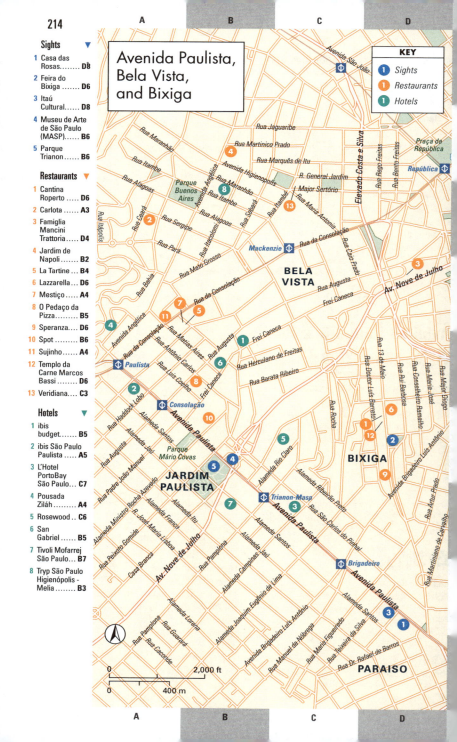

The Museu de Arte de São Paulo (MASP) displays a large range of art, with perfect views of Ibirapuera Park.

1578, Bela Vista/Bixiga ☎ 11/3149–5959 ⊕ masp.org.br 🎫 R$70; free Tues. 🕙 Closed Mon. Ⓜ Trianon-MASP.

Parque Trianon

CITY PARK | Created in 1892 as a showcase for local vegetation, the park was renovated in 1968 by Roberto Burle Marx, the Brazilian landscaper famed for Rio's mosaic-tile beachfront sidewalks. You can escape the noise of the street and admire the flora and the 300-year-old trees while seated on one of the benches sculpted to look like chairs. ✉ Rua Peixoto Gomide 949, Cerqueira César ☎ 11/3289–2160, 🎫 Free Ⓜ Trianon-MASP.

🍴 Restaurants

Cantina Roperto

$$$ | **ITALIAN** | Wine casks and bottles adorn the walls at this typical Bixiga cantina, located on a street so charmingly human-scaled you'll hardly believe you're still in São Paulo. You won't be alone if you order the ever-popular fusilli—either *ao sugo* (with tomato sauce) or *ao frutos do mar* (with seafood)—or the traditional baby goat's leg with potatoes and tomatoes. **Known for:** fresh, handmade pasta; superb service; traditional Italian music played by duos weaving around the dining room tables. 💲 *Average main: R$90* ✉ Rua 13 de Maio 634, Bixiga ☎ 11/3288–2573, 11/3284–2987 ⊕ www.cantinaroperto.com.br.

Carlota

$$$ | **CONTEMPORARY** | TV host, author, and chef Carla Pernambuco introduces Brazilian elements to a multicultural array of recipes at her popular restaurant. The restaurant has a seasonal menu, which may vary according to the time of year. **Known for:** sophisticated decor; signature guava jam soufflé with melted-cheese sauce; older clientele. 💲 *Average main: R$105* ✉ Rua Sergipe 753, Higienópolis ☎ 11/3663–0911, 11/3661–9465 ⊕ www.carlapernambuco.com 🕙 No dinner Sun. Closed Mon.

★ Famiglia Mancini Trattoria

$$$$ | **ITALIAN** | This traditional cantina catches the eye with a decoration full of knickknacks that give the place its charm. An abundance of wonderful wines to choose from, along with a menu of mouth-watering options, including homemade artisanal pastas, is on offer. **Known for:** generous dishes that serve more than two; incredible buffet with cheeses, olives, sausages, and much more; traditional family-style Italian decor. ⑤ *Average main: R$150* ✉ *Rua Avanhandava 81, Bela Vista/Bixiga* ☎ *11/3256-4320* ⊕ *www.famigliamancini.com.br* Ⓜ *Anhangabaú*.

Frevo

$ | **BRAZILIAN** | Paulistanos of all types and ages flock to this luncheonette on the stylish Rua Oscar Freire for its *beirute* sandwiches, filled with ham and cheese, tuna, or chicken, and for its draft beer and fruit juices in flavors such as *acerola* (Antilles cherry), passion fruit, and papaya. **Known for:** whimsical decor; rabo de peixe (ice cold draft beer); capricho (ice cream with farofa and chocolate sauce). ⑤ *Average main: R$30* ✉ *Rua Oscar Freire 588, Jardim Paulista* ☎ *11/3082-3434* ⊕ *www.frevinho.com.br* Ⓜ *Oscar Freire*.

Jardim de Napoli

$$$ | **ITALIAN** | The classic neon sign that adorns this restaurant's exterior cues diners about what to expect inside: traditional Italian cuisine. No surprises here, but dishes such as the unchanging and unmatchable *polpettone alla parmigiana*, a huge meatball with mozzarella and tomato sauce, inspire devotion among the local clientele. **Known for:** Italian pasta and meat dishes; wide selection of pizzas; warm, family atmosphere. ⑤ *Average main: R$85* ✉ *Rua Doutor Martinico Prado 463, Higienópolis* ☎ *11/3668-8383* ⊕ *www.jardimdenapoli.com.br*.

La Tartine

$$$ | **FRENCH** | An ideal place for an intimate meal, this small bistro has a good wine selection and an upstairs bar furnished with mismatched sofas and armchairs. The menu changes daily; a favorite is the classic coq au vin, but you can also fill up on entrées such as beef tenderloin, pasta, soups, and quiches. **Known for:** Moroccan couscous; frogs' legs that taste like Tangier-style chicken wings; trendy crowd. ⑤ *Average main: R$100* ✉ *Rua Fernando de Albuquerque 267, Consolação* ☎ *11/94260-5120* ⊙ *No lunch Mon.* Ⓜ *Consolação*.

Lazzarella

$$ | **ITALIAN** | Generous portions at reasonable prices and live music—that's the Lazzarella way. The cantina, a classic Italian joint founded in 1970, is hardly extravagant, but the rich flavors of a meal here and the Neapolitan stylings of the crooners circling among the red-and-white checkered tabletops are memorable. **Known for:** dishes for two; traditional lasagna; excellent service. ⑤ *Average main: R$70* ✉ *Rua 13 de Maio 589, Bixiga* ☎ *11/95487-1273* ⊕ *lazzarella.menulegal.app*.

Mestiço

$$$ | **ECLECTIC** | Even the fabulous people have to hang at the bar before being shown to a table in this large, sleek dining room; but especially for vegetarians, dishes such as the tofu and vegetable curry make the wait worthwhile. The decidedly eclectic menu includes Italian, Brazilian, Bahian, and even Thai cuisine. **Known for:** free-range chicken and other ecologically responsible ingredients; terrace bar; lunch-specific menu. ⑤ *Average main: R$110* ✉ *Rua Fernando de Albuquerque 277, Consolação* ☎ *11/3256-3165, 11/2532-9452* ⊕ *www.mestico.com.br* Ⓜ *Consolação*.

O Pedaço da Pizza

$ | **PIZZA** | At one of São Paulo's few pizzerias where you can order by the slice, the options for toppings range from pepperoni and other traditional favorites to shimeji mushrooms, kale, and other innovative ingredients. **Known**

for: late-night 4 am closing times on Friday and Saturday; dessert pizzas, like chocolate with strawberries, bananas, or coconut; pizza by the slice. $ *Average main: R$30* ✉ *Rua Augusta 1463, Bela Vista/Bixiga* ☎ *11/99351–7276* ⊕ *www.opedacodapizza.com.br* Ⓜ *Paulista.*

Speranza
$$$ | **ITALIAN** | One of the most traditional pizzerias in São Paulo, this restaurant is famous for its margherita pie. In 2010, Speranza became the first pizzeria in Latin America to win recognition from the Italian pizza quality-control board Associazione Verace Pizza Napoletana. **Known for:** crunchy pão de linguiça (sausage bread) appetizer; true Italian pizza; classic margherita. $ *Average main: R$100* ✉ *Rua 13 de Maio 1004, Bixiga* ☎ *11/3288–8502, 11/3288–3515* ⊕ *www.pizzaria.com.br* ⊙ *No lunch.*

Spot
$$ | **ECLECTIC** | A few blocks west of MASP, this quaint yet futuristic glass-encased diner occupies a lonely single-story building tucked between government skyscrapers. Entrées—Argentine beef is a favorite—don't come with sides, so you'll have to order a dish such as rice with broccoli to fill the plate. **Known for:** extensive drink menu; modern architecture and design; hot spot for those working in the arts. $ *Average main: R$70* ✉ *Alameda Rocha Azevedo 72, Bela Vista/Bixiga* ☎ *11/3283–0946* ⊕ *www.restaurantespot.com.br* Ⓜ *Consolação or Trianon-Masp.*

Sujinho
| **BRAZILIAN** | Occupying corners on both sides of the street, the modest Sujinho honors its roots as an informal bar by serving churrasco without any frills. This is the perfect place for diners craving a gorgeous piece of meat to down with a cold bottle of beer. **Known for:** Jurassic portion sizes that can easily feed two; staying open until 5 am for the post-bar crowd; its famous pork chops. $ *Average main: R$50* ✉ *Rua da Consolação 2063, 2068 and 2078, Consolação* ☎ *11/3154–5207, 11/99656–1747* ⊕ *www.cafeteriasujinho.com.br* ⊟ *No credit cards* Ⓜ *Consolação or Paulista.*

Templo da Carne Marcos Bassi
$$$ | **BRAZILIAN** | The brainchild of the late Marcos Bassi, a former butcher turned restaurateur and radio host, Templo da Carne (Temple of Meat) makes no bones about its specialty. *Contrafilé* (sirloin) and famed Brazilian *picanha* (rump cap) are among the highlights. **Known for:** à la carte meat dishes; chic decor; wines and other items served in the restaurant available at its emporium. $ *Average main: R$150* ✉ *Rua 13 de Maio 668, Bela Vista/Bixiga* ☎ *11/3289–8070* ⊕ *www.templodacarne.com.br* ⊙ *Closed Mon. No dinner Sun.*

★ Veridiana
$$$ | **PIZZA** | Owner Roberto Loscalzo transformed a 1903 mansion into a remarkable dining space; expansive yet intimate, grandiose yet welcoming. At one end of the room chefs pull Napoli-style pizzas from the three mouths of a two-story brick oven that looms over diners like a cathedral organ. **Known for:** Napoli in Beirut (goat cheese and za'atar); Napoli in Brasile (sun-dried meat and Catupiry, a creamy Brazilian cheese); sister branches in the Jardins and Perdizes neighborhoods. $ *Average main: R$110* ✉ *Rua Dona Veridiana 661, Higienópolis* ☎ *11/3801–9000* ⊕ *www.veridiana.com.br* ⊙ *No lunch* Ⓜ *Santa Cecilia.*

🛏 Hotels

Ibis Budget
$$ | **HOTEL** | With hotels at both ends of Paulista and other properties in Jardins, Morumbi, and the city center, the Ibis Budget (formerly the Formule 1) is a great choice if you value location and price over luxury. **Pros:** close to metro and convenience stores; perfect for travelers who plan to be out and about; good for travelers on a budget. **Cons:**

The Tivoli Mofarrej hotel has a rooftop restaurant overlooking Avenida Paulista.

unspectacular breakfast; often fully booked; no pool. *$ Rooms from: R$230 ✉ Rua da Consolação 2303, Consolação ☎ 11/3123–7755 ⊕ ibis.accorhotels.com ⇌ 399 rooms ❙◯❙ No Meals Ⓜ Paulista.*

Ibis São Paulo Paulista

$$$ | HOTEL | One of the best bargains on Avenida Paulista, all rooms at this large hotel feature queen-size beds and contemporary decor, with the focus on function, not beauty. **Pros:** a nonaffiliated airport shuttle bus has a stop next door; close to major thoroughfares; right next to the Consolação/Paulista metro station (green and yellow lines). **Cons:** heavy traffic all day long; Av. Paulista is closed to vehicles on Sunday; breakfast is an additional fee. *$ Rooms from: R$330 ✉ Av. Paulista 2355, Bela Vista/Bixiga ☎ 11/3523–3000 ⊕ www.ibis.com ⇌ 236 rooms ❙◯❙ No Meals Ⓜ Consolação or Paulista.*

Pousada Ziláh

$$ | B&B/INN | Marvelously located in the retail-heavy part of the Jardins district and easily navigable both to and from, Pousada Ziláh is quite cheap—it might be a more affordable alternative if you're seeking to momentarily escape the skyscraper experience. **Pros:** close to Oscar Freire shopping; excellent breakfast in skylighted café; eco-friendly and sustainable. **Cons:** can be noisy; no mini-fridge; sometimes the reception area is left unoccupied. *$ Rooms from: R$490 ✉ Rua Minas Gerais 112, Higienópolis ☎ 11/3062–1444 ⊕ www.zilah.com ⇌ 14 rooms ❙◯❙ Free Breakfast Ⓜ Paulista.*

Rosewood

$$$$ | HOTEL | The old Matarazzo hospital is one of the most famous landmarks in São Paulo and has become the city's newest luxury hotel, inaugurated in 2022. **Pros:** great spa; extremely new; well-attended. **Cons:** super expensive; nothing close by; gets crowded because of the restaurants. *$ Rooms from: R$2.200 ✉ Rua Itapeva 435, Bela Vista/Bixiga ☎ 11/3797–0500 ⊕ www.rosewood-hotels.com/en/sao-paulo ⇌ 160 suites Ⓜ Higienópolis Mackenzie.*

San Gabriel

| **HOTEL** | Expect no frills at this budget hotel in a lively neighborhood close to Avenida Paulista—rooms are small (though there are some larger suites), but have all the basics and are clean, and the rates are unbeatable for this part of town. **Pros:** close to malls, bars, and restaurants; in-house convenience store; near the metro. **Cons:** surrounding area isn't well-lit; room rate doesn't include breakfast; no Internet. ⑤ *Rooms from: R$350* ✉ *Rua Frei Caneca 1006, Cerqueira César* ☎ *11/3253–2279* ⊕ *www.sangabriel.com.br* ⇌ *134 rooms* ⓞ *No Meals* Ⓜ *Consolação.*

★ Tivoli Mofarrej São Paulo

$$$ | **HOTEL** | The five-star Tivoli Mofarrej is home to Latin America's largest residential suite, which costs almost $30,000 per night and counts the king of Sweden and the king of pop Michael Jackson among past patrons. **Pros:** chance of meeting a prince or princess (literally); Thai spa's Rainmist Steam Bath; steps from Avenida Paulista. **Cons:** small pool; extremely expensive; walls are thin. ⑤ *Rooms from: R$1,400* ✉ *Alameda Santos 1437, Cerqueira César* ☎ *11/3146–5900* ⊕ *www.tivolihotels.com* ⇌ *218 rooms* ⓞ *No Meals* Ⓜ *Trianon-MASP.*

Tryp São Paulo Higienópolis - Melia

$$$ | **HOTEL** | Tucked imperceptibly among stately apartment buildings in one of the city's oldest and most attractive residential neighborhoods, this hotel built in 2000 has bright and spacious rooms with contemporary light-wood furnishings. **Pros:** cool half-indoor, half-outdoor pool; breakfast menu in Braille; 10-minute taxi ride from Centro. **Cons:** small bathrooms; boring furniture; lines can be long to check in and out. ⑤ *Rooms from: R$580* ✉ *Rua Maranhão 371, Higienópolis* ☎ *11/3665–8200* ⊕ *www.melia.com* ⇌ *195 rooms* ⓞ *No Meals* Ⓜ *Paulista.*

Performing Arts

FILM

Centro Cultural São Paulo

PERFORMANCE VENUES | The space features a collection of libraries (the second largest in the city), along with a program of visual arts, exhibitions, cinema, dance, literature, music, and theater. It also offers educational activities, open studios, courses and workshops, lectures, and debates. Major renovations finished in 2013 added new projection and sound equipment and saw improvements in the lighting and acoustics. Admission is free or low-price for some events. ✉ *Rua Vergueiro 1000, Paraíso* ☎ *11/3397–4000* ⊕ *www.centrocultural.sp.gov.br* ⊙ *Closed Mon.* Ⓜ *Vergueiro.*

Reserva Cultural

FILM | The complex contains four movie theaters, a small library, and a deck-style restaurant from which you can see—and be seen by—pedestrians on Paulista Avenue. ✉ *Av. Paulista 900, Jardim Paulista* ☎ *11/3287–3529* ⊕ *www.reservacultural.com.br* Ⓜ *Trianon-MASP.*

Shopping

ART GALLERIES

Galeria Luisa Strina

ART GALLERY | One of the city's oldest and best-established galleries, Luisa Strina is a serious player in the international art world, representing artists of the stature of Cildo Meireles and Anna Maria Maiolino, as well as a stable of young stars such as Renata Lucas, Clarissa Tossin, and Fernanda Gomes. ✉ *Rua Padre João Manuel 755, Cerqueira César* ☎ *11/3088–2471* ⊕ *www.galerialuisastrina.com.br.*

ANTIQUES

Juliana Benfatti

ANTIQUES & COLLECTIBLES | The antiques shop run by Juliana Benfatti and her two sons has inventory that dates back to the 18th century. The buyers have a discerning eye for what was unique and special

King Neymar

Brazilians are so passionate about futebol (soccer) that popular wisdom says there are three subjects—soccer, women, and religion—not to be discussed at a bar table among friends, to avoid quarrels. Of these, soccer is surely the most important. The sport, which arrived in Brazil in 1894 with immigrant British railroad workers, is as central to Brazilian culture as samba and the beach.

Soccer is the national passion in no small part thanks to Brazil's world-champion status in 1958, 1962, 1970, 1994, and 2002. The greatest Brazilian soccer players—such as "King" Pelé, as he was called in the 1960s and 1970s—are seen as gods and are treated like royalty.

The king of the ball in Brazil today is Ronaldo Neymar, known simply as Neymar, who came to fame leading Pelé's former team Santos Futebol Club back to prominence. Since signing with Santos at age 13, Neymar has won multiple state, national, and international titles. His showmanship, penchant for scoring (his 100th professional goal came on his 20th birthday), and shared affiliations have drawn comparisons to Pelé. Neymar also has carved out a style all his own with hairstyles, including an emblematic mohawk—as imitated among young Brazilians as his fancy dribbling.

Many lesser stars bring Brazilians to tears and shouts of joy every Sunday afternoon in thrilling games that can be watched live in the fields or on TV. And though soccer reigns supreme in Brazil, you don't have to be royalty to afford a game—admission to one of São Paulo's or nearby Santos's stadiums costs less than US$10.

---

in many lands over many generations. ✉ *Rua Sampaio Vidal 786, Jardim Paulista* ☎ *11/3083-7858* ⊕ *www.julianabenfatti.com.br* Ⓜ *Fradique Coutinho*.

BEACHWEAR
Cia. Marítima

SWIMWEAR | The Brazilian beachwear brand known for its bikinis and swimsuits has a presence in this and many other high-class malls. ✉ *Shopping Pátio Higienópolis, Av. Higienópolis 618, Higienópolis* ☎ *11/3661-7602* ⊕ *www.ciamaritima.com.br*.

CLOTHING
FARM Rio

CLOTHING | Farm Rio is a Brazilian brand founded in 1997, known for featuring tropical prints and designs that celebrate Rio de Janeiro's culture. With a strong appeal to a colorful and laid-back lifestyle, the brand has become an icon of fashion in Brazil and abroad. ✉ *Rua Cincinato Braga 106, Bela Vista/Bixiga* ☎ *11/97871-1126* ⊕ *www.farmrio.com.br* Ⓜ *Vergueiro*

SHOPPING CENTERS AND MALLS
Iguatemi São Paulo

MALL | This may be the city's oldest mall, but it has the latest in fashion and fast food. The Cinemark movie theaters often show films in English with Portuguese subtitles. The Gero Caffé, built in the middle of the main hall, has a fine menu. If you're in São Paulo at Christmas time, the North Pole–theme displays here are well worth a detour. ✉ *Av. Brigadeiro Faria Lima 2232, Jardim Paulista* ☎ *11/3048-7394* ⊕ *www.iguatemisaopaulo.com.br*.

Shopping Pátio Higienópolis

MALL | One of the most upscale shopping malls in São Paulo, Shopping Pátio

Higienópolis is a mixture of old and new architecture styles. It has plenty of shops and restaurants, as well as six screens in the Cinemark movie theater. ✉ *Av. Higienópolis 618, Higienópolis* ☎ *11/4040-2004, 11/3823-2300* ⊕ *www.patiohigienopolis.com.br* Ⓜ *No metro.*

JEWELRY
Antonio Bernardo
JEWELRY & WATCHES | *Carioca* Antonio Bernardo is one of the most famous jewelry designers in Brazil. He creates custom pieces with gold, silver, and other precious metals and stones. ✉ *Rua Bela Cintra 2063, Consolação* ☎ *11/3083-5622* ⊕ *www.antoniobernardo.com.br* ⊙ *Closed Sun.* Ⓜ *Oscar Freire.*

LEATHER GOODS AND LUGGAGE
Arezzo
LEATHER GOODS | This is an old and traditional Brazilian brand, known for its excellent quality products. Stores are spread throughout the city, where you can buy high-quality leather items such as bags, wallets, and shoes. ✉ *Shopping Pátio Paulista, Rua 13 de Maio 1947, Bela Vista/Bixiga* ☎ *11/3289-7448* ⊕ *www.arezzo.com.br.*

🏃 Activities

SOCCER
Pacaembu (*Estádio Municipal Paulo Machado de Carvalho*)
SOCCER | The first games of the 1950 World Cup were played at this stadium. The plaza it inhabits is named for the Englishman who introduced Brazil to soccer. While it isn't used by any team in particular, it does host games occasionally and still houses the Museu de Futebol (soccer museum). ✉ *Praça Charles Miller s/n, Pacaembu* ☎ *11/3664-4650* ⊕ *www.mercadolivrearenapacaembu.com* Ⓜ *Clínicas.*

Vila Madalena and Pinheiros

Vila Madalena, the bohemian hub of Brazil's biggest city, is bustling with a variety of bars, galleries, and live music and is the epicenter of the city's world-renowned street art scene. Don't be surprised to find crowds spilling out onto the sidewalks and streets on the weekend and during happy hour.

One of the most sophisticated areas in São Paulo, Pinheiros was named after the city's famous river and is buzzing with cultural and gastronomical activity over the weekend.

Sights

Instituto Tomie Ohtake
ART MUSEUM | The futuristic green, pink, and purple exterior of this contemporary art museum designed by Ruy Ohtake makes it one of the city's most recognizable buildings. The institute, named for Ohtake's mother, a renowned painter who emigrated from Japan to Brazil, mounts interesting photography and design-related exhibitions. It also houses the independently operated Brazilian restaurant Santinho, which has a popular Sunday brunch. ✉ *Rua Coropés 88, Pinheiros* ☎ *11/2245-1900* ⊕ *www.institutotomieohtake.org.br* 🎟 *Free* ⊙ *Closed Mon.* Ⓜ *Faria Lima.*

🍴 Restaurants

★ Consulado Mineiro
$$$ | **BRAZILIAN** | During and after the Saturday crafts and antiques fair in Praça Benedito Calixto, it may take an hour to get a table at this homey restaurant. Among the shareable, traditional *mineiro* (from Minas Gerais State) dishes are the *mandioca com carne de sol* (cassava with salted meat) appetizer and the *tutu*

Did You Know?

The Instituto Tomie Ohtake, named for Ohtake's mother, a renowned painter who emigrated from Japan to Brazil, shows the strong influence that Japanese immigrants have over the culture of São Paulo.

(pork loin with beans, pasta, cabbage, and rice) entrée. **Known for:** an extensive cachaça menu with rare, premium, and homemade brands; excellent service; feijoada served every day. $ *Average main: R$150* ✉ *Praça Benedito Calixto 74, Pinheiros* ☎ *11/3898–3241, 11/98889–5529* ⊕ *www.consuladomineiro.com.br* ⊗ *Closed Mon.–Wed. No dinner.*

Degas

$$ | **ITALIAN | FAMILY** | Humble-looking Degas owes its more than 50 years in existence to word of mouth among the residents of São Paulo's western neighborhoods. Its famed filet mignon Parmigiana has gained near-legendary status, attracting foodies from across the city. **Known for:** dishes that easily feed two (or more); pizzas at dinnertime; business crowds at lunch, families in the evening. $ *Average main: R$50* ✉ *Rua Teodoro Sampaio 568, Pinheiros* ☎ *11/3062–1276, 11/3085–3545* ⊕ *www.degasrestaurante.com.br* Ⓜ *Clinicas.*

★ Jun Sakamoto

$$$$ | **JAPANESE** | Arguably the best Japanese restaurant in a town famous for them, Jun Sakamoto stands out for serving fish of the highest quality and for employing the most skillful of sushi chefs to slice them, with a Michelin Star. Waiters wearing futuristic earpieces will guide you through the *omakase*, a sushi chef–curated menu. **Known for:** haute gastronomy; the freshest ingredients; top-notch service. $ *Average main: R$500* ✉ *Rua Lisboa 55, Pinheiros* ☎ *11/3088–6019* ⊕ *www.junsakamoto.com.br* ⊗ *No lunch. Closed Sun.*

Oficina de Pizzas

$$$ | **PIZZA** | This restaurant looks like something Spanish architect Gaudí might have designed had he spent his later years in the tropics, but the pizzas couldn't be more Italian and straightforward. Try a pie with mozzarella and toasted garlic. **Known for:** excellent wine menu; special rotating dishes on Thursday, including fettuccine al pesto and bruschetta napolitana; pizza-making courses. $ *Average main: R$60* ✉ *Rua Purpurina 507/517, Vila Madalena* ☎ *11/3816–3749, 11/96581–5081* ⊕ *www.oficinadepizzas.com.br* ⊗ *No lunch.*

Pé de Manga

$$ | **BRAZILIAN** | Pé de Manga's name and charm come from the massive mango tree surrounded by tables on the shaded patio, where appetizers like mini *acarajé* and main dishes named after celebrities—think Mel Gibson and Will Smith—are served. A two-story covered seating area lends the whole affair a Robinson Crusoe touch. **Known for:** feijoada buffet on Saturday; popular for business lunches; shimeji and shiitake mushroom bruschetta. $ *Average main: R$60* ✉ *Rua Arapiraca 152, Vila Madalena* ☎ *11/3032–6068* ⊕ *www.pedemanga.com.br.*

Più Pinheiros

$$$ | **ITALIAN** | The restaurant boasts a chic and minimalist decor with warm tones and sleek design, creating a sophisticated-yet-cozy dining atmosphere. The linguine alla carbonara is a standout dish, perfectly creamy and rich. **Known for:** seasonal and fresh ingredients; homemade pasta; elegant minimalist design. $ *Average main: R$110* ✉ *Rua Ferreira de Araújo 314, Pinheiros* ☎ *11/3360–7718* ⊕ *www.piurestaurante.com.br* Ⓜ *No metro.*

Japanese Fruit

Along with the famous Japanese cuisine, which can be found just about everywhere in São Paulo, Brazil's Japanese immigrants are credited with introducing persimmons, azaleas, tangerines, and kiwis to Brazil.

224

Sights ▼
1. Instituto Tomie Ohtake **A3**

Restaurants ▼
1. Consulado Mineiro **D3**
2. Degas **D2**
3. Jun Sakamoto ... **D4**
4. Oficina de Pizzas **B2**
5. Pé de Manga **A2**
6. Più Pinheiros.... **A3**

Hotels ▼
1. Golden Tower Hotel **B4**

Vila Madalena and Pinheiros

KEY
- ● Sights
- ● Restaurants
- ● Hotels

🛏 Hotels

Golden Tower Hotel
$$$ | HOTEL | Vila Madalena and Pinheiros are not strategic points for accommodation; the hotel options in these areas are few. **Pros:** close to Marginal Pinheiros; quiet neighborhood; views from the terrace and top floors. **Cons:** far from Centro; Wi-Fi signal can be weak; outdated furniture. Ⓢ *Rooms from: R$500* ✉ *Rua Deputado Lacerda Franco 148, Pinheiros* ☎ *11/3094–2200, 11/3094–2202 for WhatsApp* ⊕ *www.goldentowerhotel.com.br* ⇌ *104 rooms* ⑩ *Free Breakfast* Ⓜ *Faria Lima.*

🍸 Nightlife

BARS

Astor
BARS | The 1960s and 1970s bohemian-chic decor here sends you back in time. The quality draft beer and tasty snacks and meals mean that Astor is always hopping—the menu is full of specialties from classic bars in Brazil. Don't miss the *picadinho*: beef stew with rice and black beans, poached eggs, banana, *farofa*, and beef *pastel* (a type of dumpling). To finish up, head downstairs, where SubAstor, a speakeasy-style sister bar, serves the kind of cocktails that inspire you to attempt knockoffs at your next house party. ✉ *Rua Delfina 163, Vila Madalena* ☎ *11/5555–2351* ⊕ *www.barastor.com.br.*

Boteco São Bento
BARS | This is one of the busiest spots in Vila Madalena, always crowded, serving extremely cold draft beer. The famous bean soup is a must, and to accompany it, order the carefully seasoned and roasted beef ribs (that have cooked for 12 hours on a barbecue), along with *cassava* cooked in butter. ✉ *Rua Mourato Coelho 1060, Vila Madalena* ☎ *11/3167–7774* ⊕ *botecosaobento.com.br* Ⓜ *Faria Lima.*

O Pasquim - Bar e Prosa
LIVE MUSIC | In addition to live music every day, the bar offers great caipirinhas in various flavors, such as cashew, to accompany a delicious *dadinho de tapioca*—tapioca dices with *coalho*cheese, baked or fried, served with pepper jam, in a lively, Brazilian-style environment. ✉ *Rua aspicuelta 524, Vila Madalena* ☎ *11/99919–7767* ⊕ *www.opasquimbar.com.br.*

Posto 6
BARS | One of four comparable and fashionable bars at the corner of Mourato Coelho and Aspicuelta streets, Posto 6 pays homage to Rio de Janeiro and its Botafogo soccer club. The bar gets gold stars for its chopp and *escondidinho de camarão* (a lasagna-type dish with shrimp). ✉ *Rua Aspicuelta 644, Vila Madalena* ☎ *11/3812–4342, 11/97690–2637* ⊕ *www.barposto6.com* ⊙ *Closed Mon. No lunch Tues.–Fri.*

SubAstor Bar do Cofre
COCKTAIL BARS | A decommissioned bank vault inside the Altino Arantes Building, inspired by the Empire State Building in New York, has been transformed into an incredible and sophisticated bar offering excellent drinks and appetizers, making it perfect for a happy hour. One of the most striking features is the walls lined with 1,995 drawers that once held the valuables of the former *Banespa*bank's account holders. ✉ *Farol Santander, Rua João Brícola 24, Vila Madalena*

Meal Time

Eating out in São Paulo can be an all-night affair, so most restaurants open late and close even later. The majority will officially throw their doors open around 6 pm but will only get busy after 9 pm, regardless of what day it is. Try a bar that has a good happy hour if you want to eat earlier.

☎ *11/5555–0578* ⊕ *www.subastor.com.br* ⊙ *Closed Mon.* ☞ *Reservations are strongly recommended* Ⓜ *São Bento.*

DANCE CLUBS
Ó do Borogodó
DANCE CLUB | Extremely rustic and humble, with live samba and MPB music every night, this packed little club is a local favorite and provides a reliably good time, every time for those looking for good Brazilian music. ✉ *Rua Horácio Lane 21, Pinheiros* ☎ *11/3813–5898* ⊙ *Closed Mon.* ☞ *R$30 cover fee.*

MUSIC CLUBS
Canto da Ema
DANCE CLUB | At what's widely considered the best place in town to dance *forró* (music/dance from Brazil's Northeast), you'll find people of different ages and styles coming together on the dance floor. *Xiboquinha* is the official forró drink, made with cachaça (a Brazilian sugarcane-based alcohol), lemon, honey, cinnamon, and ginger. The doors open at 8:30 pm Wednesday and Thursday, and 10:30 pm Friday and Saturday; the hours on Sunday are from 7 pm to midnight. ✉ *Av. Brigadeiro Faria Lima 364, Pinheiros* ☎ *11/3813–4708, 11/2503–2915* ⊕ *www.cantodaema.com.br* Ⓜ *Faria Lima.*

Carioca Club

LIVE MUSIC | Cariocas are people from Rio de Janeiro, and Carioca Club has the decor of old-style Rio clubs. Its large dance floor attracts an eclectic mix of up to 1,200 college students, couples, and professional dancers who move to samba, *gafieira*, and *pagode* from Thursday through Saturday starting at varying times. Cover fees average R$70. ✉ *Rua Cardeal Arcoverde 2899, Pinheiros* ☎ *11/3813–8598* ⊕ *www.cariocaclub.com.br* Ⓜ *Faria Lima*.

★ Madeleine

LIVE MUSIC | The riffs heard at Madeleine place it in an exclusive stratum of São Paulo music clubs. But it's the mix of music, food, drinks, and atmosphere that lends the bar its comprehensive appeal. Jazz ensembles play in the exposed-brick lounge, which has clear sightlines from the mezzanine. Better for chatting are the candlelit tables in the well-stocked wine cellar, and the seats on the veranda, with its panoramic views of Vila Madalena. Wherever you sit, the gourmet pizzas go great with the craft beers poured here. ✉ *Rua Aspicuelta 201, Vila Madalena* ☎ *11/2936–0616* ⊕ *www.madeleine.com.br* ⊙ *Closed Sun. and Mon.*

🛍 Shopping

CLOTHING

Uma

CLOTHING | Women of all ages lust after the simple elegance of Uma's swimsuits, dresses, shorts, shirts, and pants—they're not cheap, but they're good. ✉ *Rua Girassol 273, Vila Madalena* ☎ *11/3813–5559* ⊕ *www.uma.com.br*.

Parque Ibirapuera

Architect Oscar Niemeyer and landscape architect Roberto Burle Marx joined the team of professionals assigned to the project of Ibirapuera Park. The park was inaugurated in 1954, and some pavilions

People's Park

One of the city's all-too-few parks, Parque Ibirapuera is a great place to find a bit of peace and quiet during the week, and for people-watching on weekends, when the packed park plays host to Paulistanos of every background. Stalls selling coconut water are easily found, as well as some restaurants and snack bars scattered throughout the park.

used for the opening festivities still sit amid its 160 hectares (395 acres). It has jogging and biking paths, a lake, and rolling lawns. You can rent bicycles near some of the park entrances for about R$15 an hour.

👁 Sights

Auditório Ibirapuera

NOTABLE BUILDING | The final building in Oscar Niemeyer's design for the park, the Auditório opened in 2005. It has since become one of São Paulo's trademark sights, with what looks like a giant red lightning bolt striking a massive white daredevil ramp. Seating up to 800, the concert hall regularly welcomes leading Brazilian and international musical acts. Its back wall can be retracted to reveal the stage to thousands more on the lawn outside. ✉ *Portão 2, Av. Pedro Álvares Cabral s/n, Parque Ibirapuera* ☎ *11/3889–3000* ⊕ *www.parquedoibirapuera.org/auditorio-ibirapuera/* ⊙ *Closed Mon.–Thurs.*

Museu Afro Brasil

CULTURAL MUSEUM | Among Parque Ibirapuera's various attractions, natural and architectural, this museum might easily pass unnoticed. But in terms of its content—a thorough if sometimes patchily organized survey of Brazil's profoundly important but underreported black history—it's highly recommended. English

Although it is smaller than Central Park, Parque Ibirapuera is one of the largest parks in South America.

tours are available only to download as audio, so bring your headphones. ✉ *Av. Pedro Álvares Cabral, Portão 10, Parque Ibirapuera* 📞 *11/3320–8900* 🌐 *www.museuafrobrasil.org.br* 💰 *R$15; free Wed.* 🕙 *Closed Mon.*

Museu de Arte Contemporânea (MAC)
ART MUSEUM | The Museum of Contemporary Art expanded its Ibirapuera presence in 2012 by renovating and moving into the eight-floor former Department of Transportation building. Now shorn of its bureaucratic coldness, the space ranks among Parque Ibirapuera's architectural highlights (even though it is just over the road, rather than inside the park). The museum houses the MAC's entire 10,000-piece collection, including works by Picasso, Modigliani, and Chagall. ✉ *Av. Pedro Álvares Cabral 1301, Parque Ibirapuera* 📞 *11/2648–0254* 🌐 *www.mac.usp.br* 💰 *Free* 🕙 *Closed Mon.*

Museu de Arte Moderna (MAM)
ART MUSEUM | More than 4,500 paintings, installations, sculptures, and other works from modern and contemporary artists such as Alfredo Volpi and Lygia Clark are part of the Museum of Modern Art's permanent collection. Temporary exhibits often feature works by new local artists. The giant wall of glass, designed by Brazilian architect Lina Bo Bardi, serves as a window beckoning you to glimpse inside; an exterior mural painted in 2010 by Os Gêmeos, São Paulo twin brothers famous for their graffiti art, shows a little of MAM's inner appeal to the outside world. ✉ *Av. Pedro Álvares Cabral s/n, Portão 3, Parque Ibirapuera* 📞 *11/5085–1300* 🌐 *www.mam.org.br* 💰 *R$30; free Sun.* 🕙 *Closed Mon.*

Pavilhão da Bienal
NOTABLE BUILDING | In even-numbered years this pavilion hosts the *Bienal* (Biennial), an exhibition that presents the works of artists from more than 60 countries. The first such event was held in 1951 in Parque Trianon and drew artists from 21 countries. After Ibirapuera Park's inauguration in 1954, the Bienal was moved to this Oscar Niemeyer–designed building that's noteworthy for its large

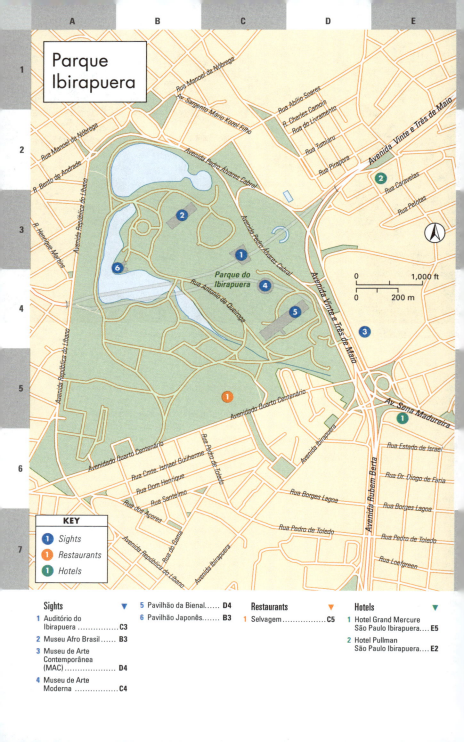

open spaces and floors connected by circular slopes. ✉ *Av. Pedro Álvares Cabral, Portão 3, Pavilhão Ciccillo Matarazzo, Parque Ibirapuera* ☎ *11/5576–7600, 011/5576–7641* ⊕ *www.bienal.org.br.*

Pavilhão Japonês

NOTABLE BUILDING | An exact replica of the Katsura Imperial Palace in Kyoto, Japan, the Japanese Pavilion is one of the structures built for the Parque Ibirapuera's inauguration. Designed by professor Sutemi Horiguti of the University of Tokyo, it was built in Japan and reassembled here beside the man-made lake in the Japanese-style garden. The main building displays samurai clothing, pottery, and sculpture from several dynasties; rooms upstairs are used for traditional tea ceremonies. ✉ *Av. Pedro Álvares Cabral s/n, Portões 3 and 10, Parque Ibirapuera* ☎ *11/99538–1927* ⊕ *www.bunkyo.org.br/br/pavilhao-japones* 💲 *R$16* ⊙ *Closed Mon., Tues., Thurs.*

🍴 Restaurants

Selvagem

$$$ | **BRAZILIAN** | After a nice walk around the park, why not stop by Selvagem for lunch? It offers contemporary Brazilian cuisine with a creative twist, utilizing local ingredients for a unique dining experience. **Known for:** rustic and cozy atmosphere; the best restaurant inside Ibirapuera Park; great selection of meats. 💲 *Average main: R$120* ✉ *Ibirapuera Park, Av. Quarto Centenário 454, Portão 5, Ibirapuera* ☎ *11/5198–0844* ⊕ *www.selvagemibirapuera.com.br* ⊙ *No dinner Sun.–Mon.*

🛏 Hotels

Hotel Grand Mercure São Paulo Ibirapuera

$$$ | **HOTEL** | Fully renovated in 2024, near the Congonhas Airport and Ibirapuera Park, the Hotel Grand Mercure São Paulo Ibirapuera is a modern, luxury hotel noted for its French style. **Pros:** many amenities; convenient helipad for millionaires; park views. **Cons:** afternoon traffic; far from business centers; bathrooms can be a bit small. 💲 *Rooms from: R$999* ✉ *Rua Sena Madureira 1355, Bloco 1, Vila Mariana* ☎ *11/3201–0800, 11/5575–4544* ⊕ *www.accorhotels.com.br* ⇌ *217 rooms* 🍽 *No Meals.*

Hotel Pullman São Paulo Ibirapuera

$$$ | **HOTEL** | With three floors completely renovated in 2024, Hotel Pullman São Paulo Ibirapuera brings contemporary design and reasonable prices considering the Ibirapuera area. **Pros:** near Ibirapuera Park, Avenida Paulista, and museums; affordable; courteous staff. **Cons:** considerable ride from main business and nightlife districts; small pool; spa is not of the same quality as the hotel. 💲 *Rooms from: R$750* ✉ *Rua Joinville 515, Vila Mariana* ☎ *11/5088–4000* ⊕ *www.pullmanhotels.com* ⇌ *380 rooms* 🍽 *No Meals* Ⓜ *Paraíso.*

 # Nightlife

BARS
★ Veloso

BARS | Tables here are as disputed as a parking spot in front of a downtown apartment. An intimate corner bar on a quiet cobblestone plaza, Veloso dispenses some of São Paulo's best caipirinhas, including exotic versions such as tangerine with red pepper, and *coxinhas* (fried balls of chicken with cheese). ✉ *Rua Conceição Veloso 54, Vila Mariana* ⊕ *www.velosobar.com.br* ⊙ *Closed Mon.* Ⓜ *Ana Rosa.*

 # Shopping

ART
Galeria Jacques Ardies

ART GALLERY | If you like *art naïf*—as the name suggests, the art is simple, with a primitive and handcrafted look—Galeria Jacques Ardies is a must. ✉ *Rua Morgado de Mateus 579, Vila Mariana* ☎ *11/96815–0887* ⊕ *www.ardies.com* ⊙ *Closed Sun. and Mon.* Ⓜ *Paraíso.*

Activities

CYCLING AND JOGGING
Parque Ibirapuera
BIKING | Going for a ride or a run in one of São Paulo's parks is a good choice if you want a little exercise. For cyclists there are usually plenty of rental options (from R$15 per hour) available and special lanes just for riders. Parque Ibirapuera gets busy on the weekends, but it's still worth coming here. ✉ *Av. Pedro Álvares Cabral s/n, Parque Ibirapuera* ☎ *11/5574–5045*.

Itaim Bibi

The working crowd in this modern business district spills out into a multitude of restaurants, bars, and nightclubs, while daytime visitors stroll around its shops and cafés.

 Restaurants

Bar do Juarez
$$ | BRAZILIAN | With the look of an old-style saloon, Bar do Juarez has won awards for its draft beers and buffet of *petiscos* (small tapas-like dishes), but *picanha* (rump cap of beef) is this gastropub's calling card. Served raw on a minigrill, the platter is perfect for small groups and gives individuals direct control over how their meat is done. **Known for:** waiters with bow ties; A-plus attentive service; sister locations in Moema, Pinheiros, and Brooklin neighborhoods. ⑤ *Average main: R$60* ✉ *Av. Pres. Juscelino Kubitschek 1164, Itaim Bibi* ☎ *11/3078–3458* ⊕ *www.bardojuarez.com.br*.

Cantaloup
$$$$ | EUROPEAN | Cantaloup's converted warehouse has two dining areas: oversize photos decorate the walls of the slightly formal room, while a fountain and plants make the second area feel more casual and nice to have a meal.

Gay Pride Parade

São Paulo hosts one of the world's biggest and most famous gay parades each year on the Sunday of the Corpus Christi holiday, which generally falls at the end of May or in early June. The Gay Pride Parade, which was first held in 1997, runs along Avenida Paulista and attracts more than 3 million people.

Try the low-temperature roasted pork ribs, pumpkin puree, asparagus and lemongrass sauce or the shrimp with curry, jasmine coconut rice, and mango chutney. **Known for:** merengata with wild berries and strawberry; white chocolate and cheese mousse ball with guava sorbet and syrup; top-notch service. ⑤ *Average main: R$190* ✉ *Rua Manoel Guedes 474, Itaim Bibi* ☎ *11/3165–3445, 11/97220–0124* ⊕ *www.cantaloup.com.br* ⊘ *No dinner Sun*.

Freddy
$$$$ | FRENCH | A pioneer in bringing French cuisine to São Paulo, Freddy opened originally in 1935. Despite moving from its original location, Freddy has managed to retain the feel of an upscale Parisian bistro, thanks to a number of small touches as well as some larger ones, like the grand chandeliers hanging from its ceiling, and traditional French dishes such as escalopes *Foie Gras au Porto*. **Known for:** duck with Madeira sauce and apple puree; upscale Parisian decor; cassoulet with white beans, lamb, duck, and garlic sausage. ⑤ *Average main: R$200* ✉ *Rua Pedroso Alvarenga 1170, Itaim Bibi* ☎ *11/3167–0977* ⊕ *www.restaurantefreddy.com.br* ⊘ *No dinner Sun*. ☞ *Reservations are encouraged*.

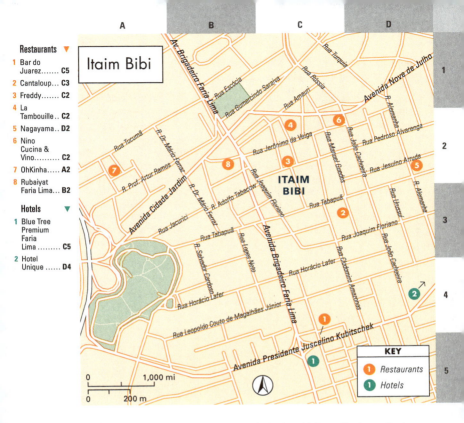

Restaurants ▼
1. Bar do Juarez....... **C5**
2. Cantaloup... **C3**
3. Freddy....... **C2**
4. La Tambouille.. **C2**
5. Nagayama.. **D2**
6. Nino Cucina & Vino.......... **C2**
7. OhKinha..... **A2**
8. Rubaiyat Faria Lima... **B2**

Hotels ▼
1. Blue Tree Premium Faria Lima **C5**
2. Hotel Unique **D4**

La Tambouille

$$$$ | ECLECTIC | This Italo-French restaurant with a partially enclosed garden isn't just a place for businesspeople and impresarios to see and be seen. It also has some of the best food in town and is one of the most classic restaurants around. **Known for:** piano bar; decor in the style of an Italian villa; excellent service. ⑤ *Average main: R$200* ✉ *Av. 9 de Julho 5925, Itaim Bibi* ☎ *11/3079–6277, 11/3079–6276* ⊕ *www.tambouille.com.br* ⊘ *Closed Mon.*

Nagayama

$$$$ | JAPANESE | Low-key, dependable, and well-loved, Nagayama consistently serves excellent sushi and sashimi. The chefs like to experiment: the California *uramaki* Philadelphia has rice, cream cheese, grilled salmon, roe, cucumber, and spring onions rolled together. **Known for:** sleek design; high-quality ingredients; excellent service. ⑤ *Average main: R$190* ✉ *Rua Bandeira Paulista 369, Itaim Bibi* ☎ *11/3079–7553* ⊕ *www.nagayama.com.br* ⊘ *Closed Sun.*

Nino Cucina & Vino

$$$ | ITALIAN | Nino Cucina, located in one of the busiest areas of Jardins in São Paulo, is a charming Italian restaurant with a cozy and sophisticated decor. The menu, inspired by traditional Italian cuisine, features dishes like gnocchi alla bolognese and burrata with prosciutto, with all pasta made in-house to ensure top quality. **Known for:** great selection of wine; charming, intimate ambiance; tiramisu. ⑤ *Average main: R$140* ✉ *Rua Jerônimo da Veiga 30, Itaim Bibi* ☎ *11/3368–6863* ⊕ *www.alifenino.com.br/restaurante-nino.*

OhKinha

$$$ | SUSHI | OhKinha stands out with the "Special Combo," featuring a varied selection of salmon, white fish, and tuna sushi and sashimi, perfect for sampling different flavors in one meal. To accompany your meal, try the *Sakerinha*, a caipirinha made with sake instead of cachaça. **Known for:** fresh, flavorful tuna tartare; innovative sushi creations; excellent service. $ *Average main: R$150* ✉ *Rua Sabuji 40, Jardins* ☎ *11/3031–8272* 🌐 *www.ohka.com.br* ⊙ *Closed Sun.*

Rubaiyat Faria Lima

$$$$ | BRAZILIAN | The family that owns and runs this restaurant serves meat from its ranch in Mato Grosso do Sul State. Charcoal-grilled fare— steak, chicken, salmon, and more—is served at the buffet, and options abound at the salad bar. **Known for:** sensational steaks; exceptional dessert buffet; top-notch service. $ *Average main: R$150* ✉ *Av. Brigadeiro Faria Lima 2954, Itaim Bibi* ☎ *11/3165–8888* 🌐 *www.rubaiyat.com.br* Ⓜ *Faria Lima.*

Hotels

Blue Tree Premium Faria Lima

$$$ | HOTEL | Techno beats enliven the lobby of this chic business hotel halfway between Paulista and Brooklin, whose rooms have clean lines and dark-wood furnishings that contrast with the bright-white walls and fabrics. **Pros:** courteous staff; on major thoroughfare close to many multinationals; close to restaurants. **Cons:** taxi needed to visit sights; heavy rush hour; can be noisy. $ *Rooms from: R$590* ✉ *Av. Brigadeiro Faria Lima 3989, Itaim Bibi* ☎ *11/3896–7544, 11/3018–1848 general line for reservations at all Blue Tree hotels* 🌐 *www.bluetree.com.br* ⇌ *338 rooms* ⎸◎⎹ *Free Breakfast* Ⓜ *Faria Lima.*

Motels and Pousadas

If you check into a reasonably priced motel with the hope of a humble-but-cheap lodging alternative, you may be surprised to find a heart-shape bed and strategically placed mirrors. Yes, motels in Brazil are specifically set aside for romantic rendezvous. The market is large because most unmarried people live with their parents until well into their 20s or 30s, not to mention the soap-opera lives that many Brazilians lead. If you're looking for a bed that doesn't vibrate, the term for what you seek is *pousada*.

★ Hotel Unique

$$$$ | HOTEL | The hotel's unique and bold design catches the eye. **Pros:** steps from Ibirapuera Park and a taxi ride to many top restaurants; attractive, modern design; spectacular rooftop restaurant and lobby bar. **Cons:** expensive; no metro station nearby; rooftop pool is too cold. $ *Rooms from: R$2000* ✉ *Av. Brigadeiro Luís Antônio 4700, Jardins* ☎ *11/3055–4700* 🌐 *www.unique.com.br* ⇌ *87 rooms* ⎸◎⎹ *No Meals.*

Nightlife

BARS

Tatu Bola

LIVE MUSIC | For a great Saturday afternoon into the evening in the bohemian city of São Paulo, Tatu Bola is an excellent choice. With its laid-back atmosphere, live music, ice-cold caipirinhas, and delicious snacks, you'll have a blast dancing to various Brazilian styles like pagode, MPB, and *sertanejo*. Tatu Bola boasts five different locations around São Paulo, making it easy to find a spot

The boat shaped Unique Hotel has a large rooftop pool and restaurant.

to enjoy its vibrant atmosphere. ✉ *Rua Clodomiro Amazonas, 260, Itaim Bibi* ☎ *11/5990–2359* ⊕ *www.alifenino.com.br/bar-tatu-bola*.

MUSIC CLUBS

Kia Ora Pub

LIVE MUSIC | Rock and pop cover bands perform at this Down Under–themed pub. Seven international draft beers and happy hour specials make Kia Ora popular after businesses close. Cover fees average R$60. ✉ *Rua Dr. Eduardo de Souza Aranha 377, Itaim Bibi* ☎ *11/98416–0330* ⊕ *www.kiaora.com.br* ☺ *Closed Mon.*

Liberdade

The red-porticoed entryway to Liberdade (which means "Freedom") is south of Praça da Sé, behind the cathedral. The neighborhood is home to many first-, second-, and third-generation Nippo-Brazilians, as well as to more recent Chinese and Korean immigrants. Clustered around Avenida Liberdade are shops with everything from imported bubble gum to miniature robots and Kabuki face paint.

The best time to visit Liberdade is on Sunday during the street fair at Praça da Liberdade, where Asian food, crafts, and souvenirs are sold. The fair is usually crowded, so keep your wits about you and do not wander around at night.

 Sights

Museu Histórico da Imigração Japonesa no Brasil

HISTORY MUSEUM | The three-floor Museum of Japanese Immigration has exhibits about Nippo-Brazilian culture and farm life, and about Japanese contributions to Brazilian horticulture. There are also World War II memorials. Relics and life-size re-creations of scenes from the Japanese diaspora line the walls, and paintings hang from the ceiling like wind chimes. ✉ *Rua São Joaquim 381, Liberdade* ☎ *11/3208–1755* ⊕ *www.museubunkyo.org.br* 🎫 *R$16* ☺ *Closed Mon.* Ⓜ *São Joaquim*.

Liberdade is home to the largest Japanese population outside of Japan.

Praça da Liberdade
MARKET | To experience the eclectic cultural mix that keeps São Paulo pulsing, visit Praça da Liberdade on a weekend, when the square hosts a sprawling Asian food and crafts fair. You might see Afro-Brazilians dressed in colorful kimonos hawking grilled shrimp on a stick, or perhaps a religious celebration such as April's Hanamatsuri, commemorating the birth of the Buddha. Many Japanese shops and restaurants worth a stop can be found near the square. ✉ *Av. da Liberdade and Rua dos Estudantes, Liberdade* Ⓜ *Liberdade.*

🍴 Restaurants

Hello Kitty and Friends 2D
$$ | **ASIAN FUSION** | This is a unique whimsical café in São Paulo. The 2D hand-drawn black-and-white decor makes you feel like you're stepping into a comic book. **Known for:** whimsical and fun decor; creative, themed menu items; unique Hello Kitty theme. 💲 *Average main: R$60* ✉ *Rua Américo de Campos 118, Liberdade* ☎ *11/3399–5609* 🌐 *www.eatasia.com.br* Ⓜ *Japão-Liberdade.*

★ Restaurante Migá
$$$ | **KOREAN BARBECUE** | São Paulo's latest foray in Korean barbecue, Migá has grills built into its tables and waitstaff well-versed in how to use them, in case it's your first time. Try the popular *bulgogi*: beef marinated in soy sauce and spices served with a variety of sides. **Known for:** Korean barbecue that's true to the original; excellent service; a wide variety of delicious sides. 💲 *Average main: R$80* ✉ *Rua Americo de Campos 128, Liberdade* 🕙 *Closed Mon.* Ⓜ *Liberdade.*

Vila Olímpia and Brooklin

Multinational companies like Google, Yahoo!, and Unilever all have their offices here, which makes Vila Olímpia one of the most desirable addresses in the city and an expat haven.

Named after New York's iconic neighborhood, Brooklin is now split into two parts—the newer side boasts modern Brazilian architecture and serves as a business center, while the other remains residential.

Restaurants

★ Bráz

$$$ | PIZZA | This restaurant's name comes from one of the most traditional Italian neighborhoods in São Paulo, and no one argues that Bráz doesn't have the right. Each of the nearly 20 varieties of pies is delicious, from the traditional margherita to the house specialty, pizza *Bráz,* with tomato sauce, zucchini, and mozzarella and Parmesan cheeses. **Known for:** pizzas with medium thickness and high, bubbly crusts; good chopp (draft beer); traditional and specialized pizzas, including Castelões, with mozzarella and its exclusive calabresa. $ *Average main: R$80* ✉ *Rua Graúna 125, Moema* ☎ *11/5561–1736* ⊕ *www.brazpizzaria.com.br* ✆ *No lunch.*

Don Pepe Di Napoli

$$$$ | ITALIAN | Good and simple Italian food is what you'll find at this traditional spot. Choose from a great variety of pastas, salads, and meat dishes. **Known for:** talharina a Don Pepe (pasta with meat, broccoli, and garlic); several types of bruschetta, from traditional tomato to Gorgonzola; top-notch service. $ *Average main: R$90* ✉ *Alameda dos Arapanés 955, Moema* ☎ *11/5055–6626* ⊕ *www.donpepedinapoli.com.br.*

Purple Power

Açai, an antioxidant-rich super fruit, has made its way to juice bars around the world. Don't miss your chance to get it close to the source, where it's cheaper and purer than the versions you'll find back home. Always frozen, scoops of it are blended together with syrup of the energy-filled guaraná berry. The most popular way to get it is *na tigela*, in a glass bowl with bananas and granola, though juice stands dedicated to the fruit should serve up a pure milk-shake-thick *suco* (juice) as well.

Dona Lucinha

$$ | BRAZILIAN | Mineiro dishes are the specialties at this modest eatery with plain wooden tables. The classic cuisine is served as a buffet only: more than 50 stone pots hold dishes like *feijão tropeiro* (beans with manioc flour) and *frango com quiabo* (chicken with okra). **Known for:** regional decor from Minas Gerais; family-friendly; post-lunch coffee with cinnamon and rapadura, a brown sugar sweet. $ *Average main: R$60* ✉ *Av. Bem-te-vi 312, Moema* ☎ *11/98226–2438* ✆ *No dinner Sun.*

Enoteca Saint VinSaint

$$$$ | WINE BAR | A snug bistro on as secluded a street as you're apt to find in São Paulo's hip southern neighborhoods, Enoteca triples as a wineshop, restaurant, and live-music venue. The kitchen's specialty is a risotto with wine-braised beef, whose plain appearance belies its exceptional flavor. **Known for:** a wide array of wines from places like France, Spain, and Italy; live tango, jazz, and flamenco music Wednesday–Saturday nights; seasonal dishes made with organic ingredients. $ *Average main: R$100* ✉ *Rua Professor Atílio Innocenti 811, Moema*

☎ 11/3846-0384 ⊕ www.saintvinsaint.com.br ⊟ No credit cards ⊗ Closed Sun. No lunch. ⌒ Brunch on Saturdays.

★ Kinoshita
$$$$ | **JAPANESE** | Contemporary Japanese plates with international influences are the draw at Kinoshita, where foie gras might accompany a Kobe beef hamburger or truffles might enliven salmon roe and shellfish. The freshness of the ingredients available on any given day determines the suggestions of chef. **Known for:** geishas serve guests in the Krug Room (available only for groups of 6 to 12); omakase (tasting menus) of seven or nine courses, plus dessert; Krug Room, one of the few in the world that serves its namesake French champagne. ⑤ Average main: R$140 ⊠ Rua Jacques Félix 405, Moema ☎ 11/3849-6940 ⊕ www.restaurantekinoshita.com.br ⊗ Closed Sun.

La Piadina Cucina Italiana
$$ | **ITALIAN** | After several years in Italy, the founders of La Piadinha Cucina decided to open a restaurant, which has now been a success for over 14 years in São Paulo. Known for its authentic Italian flavors, the *Piadina di Parma*, featuring Parma ham, arugula, and stracchino cheese, is a popular choice among diners. **Known for:** delicious prosciutto di parma; authentic Italian piadinas; great service. ⑤ Average main: R$70 ⊠ Rua Prof. Atílio Innocenti 911, Vila Olímpia ☎ 11/4750-1920 ⊕ www.lapiadina.com.br ⊗ No dinner Sun.–Tues.

Hotels

Hilton São Paulo Morumbi
$$$$ | **HOTEL** | The brightest star in Brooklin and the hot spot of the São Paulo business world, this venue is one of three skyscrapers that form an office park loaded with Fortune 500 companies. **Pros:** attached by tunnel to D&D Shopping mall; art exhibits at Canvas Bar; spa uses treatments from the Amazon. **Cons:** far from anything cultural or historical; charge for Internet access; high traffic area on weekdays and severe gridlock at rush hour. ⑤ Rooms from: R$1,200 ⊠ Av. das Nações Unidas 12901, Torre Leste (World Trade Center), Brooklin ☎ 11/2845-0000, 11/2845-0001 ⊕ www.hiltonmorumbi.com.br ⟿ 516 rooms.

Nightlife

BARS
Bar Do Arnesto
COCKTAIL BARS | More than 500 types of the rum-like liquor cachaça—the main ingredient in caipirinhas, Brazil's national cocktail—line a huge wall at this traditional Brazilian *botequim*. These casual bars generally specialize in cold bottled beer, snack foods, and caipirinhas. ⊠ Rua Ministro Jesuíno Cardoso 207, Vila Olímpia ☎ 11/94998-8539 ⊗ Closed Mon.

Eu Tu Eles Bar
BARS | The bar offers a relaxed and welcoming atmosphere, perfect for a lively night out with friends. The snacks, such as the feijoada balls, are tasty and well-prepared, while drinks like a good caipirinha enhance the experience. Live music, ranging from samba to MPB, adds a vibrant and festive touch. ⊠ Rua Gomes de Carvalho 1575, Vila Olímpia ☎ 11/5990-2359 ⊕ www.alifenino.com.br/bar-eu-tu-eles ⊗ Closed Sun.

MUSIC CLUBS
All of Jazz
LIVE MUSIC | People come here to listen quietly to good jazz and bossa nova in an intimate environment—there's even a CD store upstairs with more than 3,000 discs. Local musicians jam from 10 pm. The club gets crowded on weekends, when it's best to reserve a table. ⊠ Rua João Cachoeira 1366, Vila Olímpia ☎ 11/3849-1345 ⊕ www.allofjazz.com.br ⊗ Closed Sun.–Mon.

Bourbon Street

LIVE MUSIC | With a name right out of New Orleans, it's no wonder that Bourbon Street is where the best jazz and blues bands, Brazilian and international, play. Most performances start at midnight, but Sunday shows tend to start earlier. Cover fees start at R$45. ✉ *Rua dos Chanés 127, Moema* ☎ *11/5095–6100, 11/97060–0113* ⊕ *www.bourbonstreet.com.br* Ⓜ *Eucaliptos*.

 Shopping

CLOTHING
Fil du Fil

CLOTHING | The women's clothing brand Fil du Fil maintains three locations across Moema and Vila Olímpia. Looks are casual with colorful blouses and dresses featuring prominently. ✉ *Av. Miruna 265, Moema* ☎ *11/99401–9955* ⊕ *www.fildufil.com.br* ☾ *Closed Sun*.

Richards

CLOTHING | The collections at Richards include casualwear for men, women, and kids. ✉ *JK Iguatemi, Av. Presidente Juscelino Kubitschek 2041, Vila Olímpia* ☎ *11/3073–1332* ⊕ *www.richards.com.br*.

SHOPPING CENTERS AND MALLS
JK Iguatemi

MALL | Natural light illuminates the atrium and walkways of this luxury mall for the elite, where international brands from Gucci, Dior, Chanel, and others, to Zara mix it up with national brands like Animale and Carlos Miele. If scheduled beforehand, the mall will supply you with a personal shopper. There are plenty of fancy dining spots, too. ✉ *Av. Presidente Juscelino Kubitschek, 2041, Vila Olímpia* ☎ *11/4933–2216* ⊕ *iguatemi.com.br/jkiguatemi*.

Barra Funda

 Sights

Memorial da América Latina
NOTABLE BUILDING | The memorial's massive concrete hand sculpture, its fingers reaching toward the São Paulo sky, is one of the city's signature images. Part of a 20-acre park filled with Oscar Niemeyer–designed structures, the Memorial da América Latina was inaugurated in 1989 in homage to regional unity and its greatest champions, among them Simón Bolívar and José Martí. Aside from the monument, the grounds' highlights include works by Cândido Portinari and an auditorium dedicated to musical and theatrical performances. ✉ *Av. Mario de Andrade 664, Barra Funda* ☎ *11/3823–4600* ⊕ *www.memorial.org.br* 🎟 *Free* ☾ *Closed Mon.* Ⓜ *Barra Funda*.

 Nightlife

DANCE CLUBS
D.Edge

DANCE CLUB | Electronic music is the main attraction at this popular club with a Death Star–meets–Studio 54 appeal. As many as nine DJs, often including internationally renowned turntablists, spin music several nights a week. The terrace here has views of a park of Oscar Niemeyer design. Cover charges starts at R$20 but sometimes exceed R$100.

■ **TIP→ Put your name on the list ahead of time or arrive early to pay a discounted rate, depending on the event.** ✉ *Av. Mário de Andrade, 141, Barra Funda* ☎ *11/3665–9500* ⊕ *www.d-edge.com.br* ☾ *Closed Mon.–Wed.* Ⓜ *Barra Funda*.

Villa Country

DANCE CLUB | This is *the* place to dance to American country music and sertanejo , Brazilian country music. The huge club has a restaurant, bars, shops, game

Brazilian architect Oscar Niemeyer designed the Memorial da América Latina along with many other structures around São Paulo.

rooms, and a big dance floor. The decor is strictly Old West. Cover fees range from R$40 (women) to more than R$100 for special events. ✉ *Av. Francisco Matarazzo 774, Água Branca* ☎ *11/3868–5858* ⊕ *www.villacountry.com.br* ⊙ *Closed Mon., Tues., Thurs.* Ⓜ *Barra Funda.*

GAY AND LESBIAN BARS AND CLUBS
Blue Space
DANCE CLUB | In a huge colonial blue house in an old industrial neighborhood, Blue Space is one of the largest gay nightclubs in São Paulo. Every Saturday and Sunday, two dance floors and four bars, along with lounge and private rooms, fill with a large crowd, mostly 40 and over, interested in the house DJs and go-go boy and drag shows. Cover charges average R$30. ✉ *Rua Brigadeiro Galvão 723, Barra Funda* ☎ *11/3666–1616, 11/99629–9274 for WhatsApp* ⊙ *Closed Mon.–Thurs.* Ⓜ *Marechal Deodoro.*

Performing Arts
CLASSICAL MUSIC AND OPERA
Theatro São Pedro
CONCERTS | Built in the neoclassical style in 1917, São Paulo's second-oldest theater is one of its best venues for chamber concerts and operas. Free morning events take place on Sunday and Wednesday. ✉ *Rua Barra Funda 171, Barra Funda* ☎ *11/3221–7326* ⊕ *www.theatrosaopedro.org.br* Ⓜ *Marechal Deodoro.*

CONCERT HALLS
SESC Pompéia
PERFORMANCE VENUES | Part of a chain of cultural centers throughout the city, SESC Pompéia incorporates a former factory into its design. There are multiple performance spaces, but the *choperia* (beer hall) and theater host the most prominent Brazilian and international musical acts—from jazz and soul to rock and hip-hop. ✉ *Rua Clélia 93, Pompéia* ☎ *11/3871–7700* ⊕ *www.sescsp.org.br* ⊙ *Closed Mon.*

SAMBA SHOWS

Mocidade Alegre

MUSIC | Up to 3,000 people at a time attend rehearsals at Mocidade Alegre just before Carnival. Check the website to see if there's availability. ✉ *Rua Samaritá 1020, Limão* ☎ *11/3857-7525* ⊕ *www.mocidadealegre.com.br.*

 Shopping

ART

Fortes D'Aloia & Gabriel

ART GALLERY | This fine gallery is one of the city's big hitters and always worth a look. ✉ *Rua James Holland 71, Barra Funda* ☎ *11/3032-7066* ⊕ *www.fdag.com.br.*

BEACHWEAR

Havaianas

SHOES | Havaianas, founded in 1962, are an iconic Brazilian sandal brand known for its simple, colorful design inspired by traditional Japanese sandals. Comfortable and affordable, they are worn by people of all ages in Brazil and around the world. Havaianas make a great gift or souvenir for foreigners, offering a touch of relaxed Brazilian style. ✉ *Bourbon Shopping, Rua Turiassu 2100, 3rd floor, Barra Funda* ☎ *11/3868-3823* ⊕ *www.havaianas.com.br.*

Líquido Store

SWIMWEAR | Líquido is a Brazilian swimwear and fitness brand, founded in 2001 and known for its high-quality bikinis and vibrant prints. With a focus on comfort and style, the brand stands out for its versatile and contemporary designs. ✉ *Rua José Paulino 516, Bom Retiro* ☎ *11/3333-5644* ⊕ *www.liquido.com.br* ⊙ *Closed Sun.* Ⓜ *Luz.*

Jardins

 Restaurants

Almanara

$$$ | LEBANESE | Part of a chain of Lebanese semifast-food outlets, Almanara is perfect for a quick lunch of hummus, tabbouleh, grilled chicken, and rice. A full-blown restaurant also on the premises offers up Lebanese specialties *rodízio* style, meaning you're served continuously until you can ingest no more. **Known for:** food that is quick and delicious; Lebanese favorites, like falafel, and chicken with rice and almonds; artisanal ingredients. ⑤ *Average main: R$80* ✉ *Rua Oscar Freire 523, Jardins* ☎ *11/3085-6916* ⊕ *www.almanara.com.br.*

Amadeus

$$$$ | SEAFOOD | Because São Paulo isn't on the ocean, most restaurants here don't base their reputations on seafood, but Amadeus is an exception. Appetizers such as fresh oysters and salmon and endive with mustard, and entrées like shrimp in cognac sauce make it a challenge to find better fruits of the sea elsewhere in town. **Known for:** a good option for a business lunch; excellent selection of wines; a wide variety of shrimp dishes. ⑤ *Average main: R$100* ✉ *Rua Haddock Lobo 807, Jardins* ☎ *11/3061-2859, 11/3088-1792* ⊕ *www.restauranteamadeus.com.br* ⊙ *No dinner Sun.* Ⓜ *Consolação.*

Arábia

$$ | LEBANESE | For almost 20 years Arábia has served traditional Lebanese cuisine at this beautiful high-ceilinged restaurant. Simple dishes such as hummus and stuffed grape leaves are executed with aplomb, and the lamb melts in your mouth. **Known for:** dishes you can share, like meat-stuffed artichokes; executive lunch menu (an appetizer, cold dish, meat dish, drink, dessert, and coffee); ataife (a type of crepe filled with pistachios or

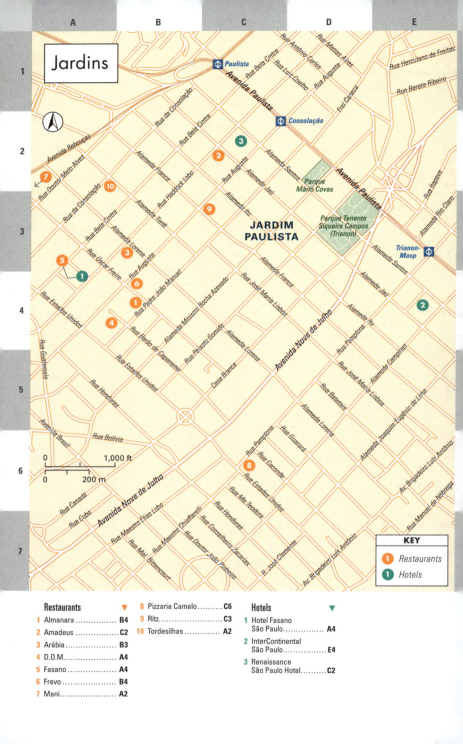

cream). *Average main: R$70* ✉ *Rua Haddock Lobo 1397, Jardins* ☎ *11/3061–3234* ⊕ *www.arabia.com.br.*

D.O.M.

$$$$ | **CONTEMPORARY** | Regularly named among the best restaurants in South America and the world, celebrity chef Alex Atala's D.O.M. is synonymous with exclusivity in São Paulo's gastronomic circles—its popularity is limited only by a self-imposed cap on the number of customers served. The focus is on Brazilian fare with added flair, such as *filhote* (Amazonian catfish) with tapioca in *tucupi* (manioc root) sauce and sweet potato in a Béarnaise made from maté, a South American tea. **Known for:** sky-high prices; tasting menu (12 courses); spectacular plating. *Average main: R$760* ✉ *Rua Barão de Capanema 549, Jardins* ☎ *11/3088–0761, 11/3081–4599* ⊕ *www.domrestaurante.com.br* ⊗ *Closed Sun. No lunch Sat.*

Fasano

$$$$ | **ITALIAN** | A family-owned Northern Italian classic tucked away behind the elegantly modern lobby of the hotel of the same name, this restaurant is as famous for its superior cuisine as for its exorbitant prices. In the kitchen, a 20-strong brigade of chefs, butchers, and bakers commanded by Luca Gozzani sends out exquisite, sinfully rich dishes like agnollottis of Angola chicken on heart-of-mozzarella cream. **Known for:** luxurious decor (marble, mahogany, mirrors, and a breathtaking skylight); tasting menu, including five classic pastas from different regions of Italy; high-quality service. *Average main: R$200* ✉ *Rua Vittorio Fasano 88, Jardins* ☎ *11/3896–4000* ⊕ *www.fasano.com.br* ⊗ *Closed Sun.; no lunch.*

★ Maní

$$$ | **CONTEMPORARY** | With world-class chef-proprietor Helena Rizzo at the helm, Maní has made its way to the top of the restaurant charts in São Paulo. A sophisticated take on Brazilian country cuisine meshed with modern cooking techniques, dishes like chicken and rice with okra might not sound like much, but one bite will be enough to explain why local and visiting foodies beat a path to Maní's door. **Known for:** tasting menu; beautifully colorful dishes; simple, seasonal ingredients from small local farms. *Average main: R$100* ✉ *Rua Joaquim Antunes 210, Jardins* ☎ *11/97473–8994* ⊕ *www.manimanioca.com.br* ⊗ *Closed Mon.; no dinner Sun.* Ⓜ *Faria Lima.*

Pizzaria Camelo

$ | **PIZZA** | Though it's neither fancy nor beautiful, Pizzaria Camelo has kept Paulistanos enthralled for ages with its many thin-crust pies. The *chopp* (draft beer) is great, too. **Known for:** long wait on Sunday; dessert pizzas; thin crusts on a long list of pizzas. *Average main: R$50* ✉ *Rua Pamplona 1873, Jardins* ☎ *11/3887–0702* ⊕ *www.pizzariacamelo.com.br.*

★ Ritz

$$$ | **ECLECTIC** | An animated, gay-friendly crowd chatters at this restaurant with Italian, Brazilian, French, and mixed cuisine, as contemporary pop music plays in the background. Although Ritz serves some of the best hamburgers in the city, another popular dish is *bife à milanesa* (breaded beef cutlet) with creamed spinach and French fries or salad. **Known for:** bolinho de arroz (rice croquettes) with relish made in-house; warm and welcoming atmosphere; top-notch service. *Average main: R$80* ✉ *Alameda Franca 1088, Jardins* ☎ *11/3062–5830* ⊕ *www.restauranteritz.com.br* Ⓜ *Consolação.*

Tordesilhas

$$$ | **BRAZILIAN** | Typically Brazilian from its decor to its daily specials, rustic-elegant Tordesilhas prides itself on spotlighting recipes from across the republic. Feijoada takes center stage on Wednesday and Saturday, while a Brazilian tasting menu is served Tuesday through Saturday.

Known for: northern Brazil's tacacá (shrimp soup); moqueca (fish and shrimp stew); large selection of cachaças. ⑤ *Average main: R$80* ✉ *Alameda Tietê 489, Jardins* ☎ *11/3107–7444* ⊕ *www.tordesilhas.com* ⊘ *Closed Mon.; no lunch weekdays; no dinner Sun.* Ⓜ *Paulista.*

Hotels

★ Hotel Fasano São Paulo
$$$$ | HOTEL | With a decor that hints at 1940s modern but is undeniably 21st-century chic, the Hotel Fasano caters to those for whom money is a mere detail. **Pros:** attentive, knowledgeable staff; top-floor pool with stunning view; central location that's still quiet. **Cons:** extremely expensive; R$185 for breakfast; it could use a renovation. ⑤ *Rooms from: R$3,200* ✉ *Rua Vittorio Fasano 88, Jardins* ☎ *11/3896–4000* ⊕ *www.fasano.com.br* ⇌ *60 rooms* ⑪ *No Meals.*

L'Hotel PortoBay São Paulo
$$$$ | HOTEL | Compared to the top-of-the line chain hotels on Paulista, L'Hotel PortoBay São Paulo stands out as a truly special experience. **Pros:** small number of rooms makes for personalized service; L'Occitane bath products; close to some of the city's best restaurants, bars, museums, and shopping. **Cons:** expensive; pool can be crowded; room service a bit slow. ⑤ *Rooms from: R$1,210* ✉ *Alameda Campinas 266, Jardins* ☎ *11/2183–0500* ⊕ *www.portobay.com* ⇌ *86 rooms* ⑪ *Free Breakfast* Ⓜ *Trianon-MASP.*

InterContinental São Paulo
$$$$ | HOTEL | The InterContinental consistently receives rave reviews because of the attention paid to every detail, including the pillows (guests choose among six different types). **Pros:** Japanese breakfast; gym with personal trainers; great service. **Cons:** suites aren't much bigger than regular rooms; breakfast not included; needs a makeover. ⑤ *Rooms from: R$1,400* ✉ *Alameda Santos 1123, Jardins* ☎ *11/3179–2600* ⊕ *www.intercontinental.com* ⇌ *233 rooms* ⑪ *No Meals* Ⓜ *Trianon-MASP.*

Renaissance São Paulo Hotel
$$$$ | HOTEL | In case the rooftop helipad doesn't say it all, the striking lines of the red-and-black granite lobby announce one serious business hotel. **Pros:** you never have to leave hotel; professional staff; great spa. **Cons:** breakfast isn't included; uninspired decor; expensive. ⑤ *Rooms from: R$1,500* ✉ *Alameda Santos 2233, Jardins* ☎ *011/3069–2233* ⊕ *www.renaissancehotels.com* ⇌ *444 rooms* ⑪ *No Meals* Ⓜ *Consolação.*

Nightlife

BARS
O'Malley's
LIVE MUSIC | A self-proclaimed "gringo" hangout, this is a good place to catch international sporting events, perhaps that major one back home it's killing you to miss. O'Malley's has three bars, a game room, and more than a dozen TVs spread across two floors. Seven beers are on tap, along with more than four dozen by the bottle. Bands play nightly, so there's always a cover after happy hour ends. Cover fee averages R$20. ✉ *Alameda Itú 1529, Jardins*

A Taste of Lebanon

While in São Paulo, be sure to try a *beirute*, a Lebanese sandwich served hot on toasted Syrian bread and filled with roast beef, cheese, lettuce, and tomato. Another quick bite from Lebanon that has established itself in the city is *esfiha*, an open-faced pastry topped with cheese or spiced meat. Fast-food restaurants serving these snacks are scattered around the city.

Known for its luxurious stores, museums, and hotels, the affluent Jardins area attracts big spenders and curious browsers, especially along the famous Rua Oscar Freire.

☎ *11/3086–0780* ⊕ *www.omalleysbar.net* Ⓜ *Consolação.*

🛍 Shopping

ANTIQUES

Legado

ANTIQUES & COLLECTIBLES | At this antiques showroom that holds monthly auctions you'll find plenty of heirlooms looking for new homes—Baccarat bowls and vases, art nouveau and art deco sideboards, and a slew of silver trays and tea sets among them. Past oddities include the helmet of the late race car legend Ayrton Senna. ✉ *Alameda Lorena 882, Jardins* ☎ *11/3063–3400* ⊙ *Closed Sun.*

ART GALLERIES

Arte Aplicada

ART GALLERY | A respected Jardins gallery, Arte Aplicada is known for its high-quality Brazilian paintings, sculptures, and prints. ✉ *Alameda Lorena 1100, Jardins* ☎ *11/98304–8989* ⊕ *www.arteaplicada.com.br.*

Bel Galeria

ART GALLERY | Paintings and sculptures from Brazilian and international artists go up for auction at Bel Galeria. ✉ *Rua Doutor Sampaio Ferraz 57, Jardim Paulista* ☎ *11/3663–6100* ⊕ *www.belgaleriadearte.com.br* ⊙ *Closed Sun.*

Dan Galeria

ART GALLERY | Specializing in 20th-century Brazilian art, this gallery is a must for serious art lovers and monied collectors, and educational for interested amateurs. Look out for works by modernist stars such as Tarsila do Amaral and di Cavalcanti. ✉ *Rua Estados Unidos 1638, Jardins* ☎ *11/3083–4600* ⊕ *www.dangaleria.com.br* ⊙ *Closed Sun.*

BEAUTY

Granado

COSMETICS | As with the other locations of this Brazilian beauty supply chain that dates back to 1870, the Jardins shop maintains the old-time appearance of an apothecary. ✉ *Rua Haddock Lobo*

1626, Jardins ☎ 11/3198–8235 ⊕ www.granado.com.br.

BEACHWEAR
Track & Field
CLOTHING | This brand's shops, which you'll find in nearly every mall in São Paulo, are good places to buy beachwear and sports clothing. ✉ Rua Oscar Freire 959, Jardins ☎ 11/3062–4457 ⊕ www.tf.com.br.

CLOTHING
Animale
CLOTHING | With a deft line in cool, sophisticated fashion, Animale has long been a go-to brand for hip young Brazilian women. Known for its striking prints and sultry-yet-wearable garments, Animale isn't cheap—but these are clothes you'll be slipping into for years. ✉ Rua Gaivota 1207, Ibirapuera ☎ 11/94395–3019 ⊕ www.animale.com.br.

BO.BÔ
CLOTHING | Brazilian models and soap opera stars wear this brand, which blends bohemian and bourgeois (coincidentally, the type of bank account needed to shop here). ✉ Rua Oscar Freire 1039, Jardins ☎ 11/5026–3514 ⊕ www.bobo.com.br.

Le Lis Blanc
CLOTHING | This chain is Brazil's exclusive purveyor of the French brand Vertigo. Look for party dresses in velvet and sheer fabrics. ✉ Rua Oscar Freire 995, Jardins ☎ 11/94595–1862 ⊕ www.lelis.com.br.

Reinaldo Lourenço
CLOTHING | Sophisticated, high-quality women's clothing is Reinaldo Lourenço's calling card. ✉ Rua Bela Cintra 2167, Jardins ☎ 11/3085–8150 ⊕ www.reinaldolourenco.com ☾ Closed Sun.

HANDICRAFTS
Galeria de Arte Brasileira
CRAFTS | Since 1920 Galeria de Arte Brasileira has specialized in art and handicrafts from all over Brazil. Look for objects made of *pau-brasil* (brazilwood), hammocks, jewelry, T-shirts, *marajoara* pottery (from the Amazon), and lace. ✉ Alameda Lorena 2163, Jardins ☎ 11/3085–8769, 11/3062–9452 ⊕ www.galeriaartebrasileira.com.br ☾ Closed Sun.

JEWELRY
H.Stern
JEWELRY & WATCHES | An internationally known Brazilian brand for jewelry, especially featuring precious Brazilian gems, H.Stern has shops in more than 30 countries. This one has designs made especially for the Brazilian stores. ✉ Rua Oscar Freire 652, Jardins ☎ 11/3068–8082 ⊕ www.hstern.com.br.

LEATHER GOODS AND LUGGAGE
Le Postiche
LEATHER GOODS | One of the biggest brands for luggage and leather goods in Brazil, Le Postiche has more than 200 shops around the country. You can find one in almost any mall in São Paulo. ✉ Av. Indianopolis 1111, Indianópolis ☎ 11/3205–0166 ⊕ www.lepostiche.com.br.

Schutz
SHOES | Boots, sandals, wedges, stilettos—if you can't find a pair of shoes you

---

Wok this Way

In a street food scene dominated by hamburgers and hot dogs, Yakisoba stands out—keep an eye peeled for the spectacle of stir-fried noodles tossed over an open flame in the middle of the crowded sidewalk. Another delicious option is homemade *espetinhos* or churrascos, wooden kebabs of beef, chicken, or pork whose juices send towers of fragrant smoke into the air. A calmer alternative is the corn cart. Rather than on the cob, try *pamonha*, steam-cooked sweetened cornmeal wrapped in a husk, or *curau*, sweet creamed corn.

like at Schutz, you're probably not looking properly. This flagship store carries a huge variety of fashion footwear, from statement heels to fun prints on sneakers. ✉ *Rua Oscar Freire 944, Jardins* ☎ *11/99226–1762* ⊕ *www.schutz.com.br* Ⓜ *Consolacão*.

Greater São Paulo

Several far-flung sights are worth a taxi ride to see. West of Centro is the Universidade de São Paulo (USP), which has two interesting museums: a branch of the Museu de Arte Contemporânea and the Instituto Butantan, with its collection of creatures that slither and crawl. Close by, Parque Villa-Lobos is a smaller but still significant alternative to Ibirapuera for sporty locals. Head southwest of Centro to the Fundação Maria Luisa e Oscar Americano, a museum with a forest and garden in the residential neighborhood of Morumbi. In the Parque do Estado, southeast of Centro, are the Jardim Botânico and the Parque Zoológico de São Paulo.

 Sights

Fundação Maria Luisa e Oscar Americano
HISTORIC HOME | A beautiful, quiet, private wooded estate is the setting for the Maria Luisa and Oscar Americano Foundation. Paintings, furniture, sacred art, silver, porcelain, engravings, tapestries, sculptures, and personal possessions of the Brazilian royal family are among the 1,500 objects from the Portuguese colonial and imperial periods on display here, and there are some modern pieces as well. Having afternoon high tea here is an event, albeit an expensive one, and Sunday concerts take place in the auditorium. ✉ *Av. Morumbi 4077, Morumbi* ☎ *11/3742–0077* ⊕ *www.fundacaooscaramericano.org.br* 🎟 *R$30; free Tue.* ⊙ *Closed Mon.*

Starchitect

World-famous Paulistano landscape architect Roberto Burle Marx (1909–94) is responsible for the design of many of São Paulo's top sites, including a host of contemplative gardens and parks. Also an artist, ecologist, and naturalist, Burle Marx has been honored by the naming of a beautiful park in the Morumbi region southwest of the city: Parque Burle Marx features a number of weaving tracks among thick Atlantic Forest as well some fine examples of his design work.

Instituto Butantan
OTHER ATTRACTION | FAMILY | In 1888 a Brazilian scientist, with the aid of the state government, turned a farmhouse into a center for the production of snake serum. Today the Instituto Butantan has more than 70,000 snakes, spiders, scorpions, and lizards in its five museums. It still extracts venom and processes it into serum that's made available to victims of poisonous bites throughout Latin America. Besides that, the Butantan Institute currently produces seven vaccines and 13 serums, such as vaccines for Covid-19. ✉ *Av. Vital Brasil 1500, Butantã* ☎ *11/2627–9536* ⊕ *www.butantan.gov.br* 🎟 *R$10* ⊙ *Closed Mon.* Ⓜ *Butantã*.

Jardim Botânico
GARDEN | FAMILY | A great spot for a midday picnic, the Botanical Gardens contain about 3,000 plants belonging to more than 340 native species. Orchids, aquatic plants, and Atlantic rainforest species thrive in the gardens' greenhouses. The hundred-plus bird species that have been observed at Jardim Botânico make it a favorite stopover for São Paulo birders. ✉ *Av. Miguel Stéfano 3031, Água Funda, Parque do Estado* ⊕ *jardimbotanico.com.br* 🎟 *R$25*.

Museu do Ipiranga

HISTORY MUSEUM | The oldest museum in town, Museu Paulista da Universidade de São Paulo, or Museu do Ipiranga, was closed for 9 years (between 2013 and 2022) and underwent a complete renovation and restructuring, with many new features and spaces that were not previously open to the public, reopening its doors in September 2022. It occupies an 1890 building constructed to honor Brazil's independence from Portugal, declared in the Ipiranga area in 1822 by then-emperor Dom Pedro I. The huge Pedro Américo oil painting depicting this very moment hangs in the main room of this French-inspired eclectic palace, whose famous gardens were patterned after those of Versailles. Dom Pedro's tomb lies under one of the museum's monuments. ✉ *Parque da Independência, Ipiranga* ☎ *011/2065–8000* ⊕ *museudoipiranga.org.br* 🎟 *R$30. Free Wed.* ⊘ *Closed Mon.*

Parque Zoológico de São Paulo

ZOO | **FAMILY** | The 200-acre São Paulo Zoo has more than 3,200 animals, and many of its 410 species—such as the *mico-leão-dourado* (golden lion tamarin monkey)—are endangered. If you visit the zoo, don't miss the monkey houses, built on small islands in the park's lake, and the Casa do Sangue Frio (Cold-Blooded House), with reptilian and amphibious creatures. ✉ *Av. Miguel Stéfano 4241, Água Funda, Parque do Estado* ☎ *11/5073–0811* ⊕ *www.zoologico.com.br* 🎟 *R$79.*

 Restaurants

Esplanada Grill

$$ | **BRAZILIAN** | The beautiful people hang out in the bar of this highly regarded churrascaria. The thinly sliced picanha (rump steak) is excellent; it goes well with a house salad (hearts of palm and shredded, fried potatoes), onion rings, and creamed spinach. **Known for:** its version of the traditional pão de queijo (cheese bread); birobiro rice, with bacon and chives; a wide variety of cuts of meat. 💲 *Average main: R$100* ✉ *Morumbi Shopping Center, Av. Roque Petroni Jr. 1089, Morumbi* ☎ *11/5181–8156.*

 Performing Arts

CONCERT HALLS
Teatro Alfa

CONCERTS | International musicals and ballet, as well as occasional musical performances, are held at Teatro Alfa, which seats more than a thousand people. The sound and lighting technology are top of the line. Tickets can be bought by phone and through Ingresso Rápido, then picked up a half hour before the performance. ✉ *Rua Bento Branco de Andrade Filho 722, Santo Amaro* ☎ *11/5693–4000, 300/789–3377* ⊕ *www.teatroalfa.com.br.*

Vibra São Paulo

CONCERTS | One of the biggest theaters in São Paulo, Credicard Hall can accommodate up to 7,000 people. The venue frequently hosts concerts by famous Brazilian and international artists. Tickets can be bought by phone, at the box office, or online. Get your tickets through Uhu website (⊕ *www.uhu.com*). ✉ *Av. das Nações Unidas 17955, Santo Amaro* ⊕ *vibrasaopaulo.com.*

SAMBA SHOWS

Escolas de samba or samba schools are the heart and soul of many communities. Most people only associate them with the dancing groups that perform during Carnival, but they keep busy all year round. In addition to samba lessons, they organize a range of community services, especially education and health outreach programs. Check them out anytime, but from November to February they're gearing up for Carnival, and often open their rehearsals to the public.

Rosas de Ouro

MUSIC | One of the most popular rehearsals takes place at Rosas de Ouro, with an average of 5,000 people

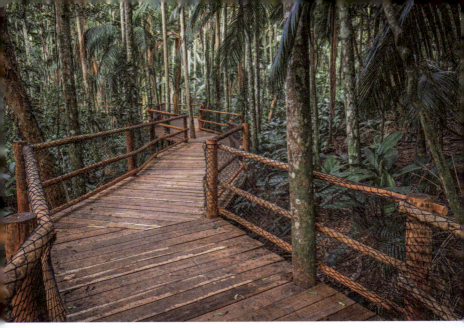

The Jardim Botânico was created in 1928 by botanist Frederico Carlos Hoehne.

attending its rehearsals. ✉ *Rua Coronel Euclides Machado 1066, Freguesia do O* ☏ *11/3931–4555* ⊕ *www.sociedaderosasdeouro.com.br.*

🛍 Shopping

SHOPPING CENTERS AND MALLS
MorumbiShopping

MALL | Though it's taken a back seat to newer malls Cidade Jardim and JK Iguatemi, MorumbiShopping is still a slice of São Paulo's upper crust, seasoned with swank boutiques, record stores, bookstores, and restaurants. The atrium hosts art exhibits. ✉ *Av. Roque Petroni Jr. 1089, Morumbi* ☏ *11/5189–4805* ⊕ *www.morumbishopping.com.br.*

Shopping Cidade Jardim

MALL | The feeling here is almost as though archaeologists have uncovered a lost jungle city's ancient temples—only they're to upscale shopping and gourmet dining, not deities and potentates. Trees outside sprout three stories high, and a bevy of plants inside shrouds boutiques with names like Valentino, Rolex, and Louis Vuitton. For resting, there's a huge open garden with splendid city views. If you get hungry, head to the Argentine steak house Pobre Juan for a hearty meal or, for lighter fare, drop in at Il Barista . ✉ *Av. Magalhães de Castro 12000, Morumbi* ☏ *11/3552–1000* ⊕ *www.shoppingcidadejardim.com.*

Activities

AUTO RACING
Brazilian Grand Prix

AUTO RACING | Racing fans from all over the world come to São Paulo in November for the Brazilian Grand Prix, a Formula 1 race that attracts massive national attention, especially when a Brazilian driver is in the mix. The race is held at Autódromo de Interlagos, which at other times hosts auto races on weekends. ✉ *Autódromo de Interlagos, Av. Senador Teotônio Vilela 261, Interlagos* ☏ *11/5666–8822 Autódromo de Interlagos* ⊕ *www.gpbrasil.com.br.*

CYCLING AND JOGGING
Parque Villa-Lobos
BIKING | It may have fewer trees and less of a history than Parque do Ibirapuera, but Parque Villa-Lobos is big and has plenty of winding pathways wide enough to accommodate cyclists and runners. There are bike rental stands inside the park (from R$12 per hour), as well as a few soccer pitches and a big, concrete square with basketball half-courts. There are some food-and-drink options, too. ✉ *Av. Professor Fonseca Rodrigues 2001, Alto de Pinheiros* ☏ *11/2683–6302* ⊕ *www.parquevillalobos.com.br.*

SOCCER
Allianz Parque (*Nova Arena*)
SOCCER | This new arena opened in 2014 and is configured to seat about 46,000 people for soccer and other events. The home team, Palmeiras, plays here. ✉ *Av. Francisco Matarazzo 1705, Água Branca* ☏ *11/4800–6670* ⊕ *www.allianzparque.com.br* Ⓜ *Palmeiras-Barra Funda.*

Canindé
SOCCER | The home team, Portuguesa, is the main attraction here, though the *bolinhos de bacalhau* (salt-cod fritters), popular among the Portuguese immigrants filling the stadium's 21,000 seats, run a close second. ✉ *Rua Comendador Nestor Pereira 33, Canindé* ☏ *11/2125–9400* ⊕ *www.portuguesa.com.br.*

Estádio Conde Rodolfo Crespi (*Estádio Conde Rodolfo Crespi*)
SOCCER | The 4,000-seat Estádio Rua Javari, also known as Estádio Conde Rodolfo Crespi, is where third-division Juventus plays. It's an ideal place to soak up some Italian atmosphere—Moóca is an Italian neighborhood—and eat a cannoli while cheering for the home team. ✉ *Rua Javari 117, Moóca* ☏ *11/2271–2000* ⊕ *www.juventus.com.br* Ⓜ *Moóca.*

Morumbi Stadium (*Cícero Pompeu de Toledo Stadium*)
SOCCER | The home stadium of São Paulo Futebol Clube seats 67,000 people. When soccer isn't being played here, other events take place, including concerts by stars such as Lady Gaga. ✉ *Praça Roberto Gomes Pedrosa 1, Morumbi* ☏ *11/3749–8000* ⊕ *www.estadiodomorumbi.com.br.*

Neoquimica Arena
SOCCER | The home of Corinthians soccer club hosted the opening of the 2014 World Cup. It holds 48,000 spectators. ✉ *Av. Miguel Ignácio Curi 111, São Paulo* ☏ *11/3152–4001* ⊕ *www.neoquimicaarena.com.br* Ⓜ *Corinthians-Itaquera.*

Chapter 6

SIDE TRIPS FROM SÃO PAULO

Updated by
Leticia Davino

WELCOME TO SIDE TRIPS FROM SÃO PAULO

TOP REASONS TO GO

★ **Escape from the Big City:** Fast highways zip you away from the hustle and bustle of São Paulo to spa towns and beach resorts.

★ **Beach Paradises:** Bask on a range of beautiful beaches, from surfer paradises in Ubatuba to coastal islands and sandy rainforest coves on Ilhabela.

★ **Rich History:** Witness Brazil's colonial and rural history in Embu and Santana de Parnaíba.

★ **Great Nightlife:** Dance until dawn with a seaside view at Maresias, São Sebastião.

★ **Gorgeous Landscapes:** Luxurious forests in Campos do Jordão combine with impressive wildlife and bodies of water in Águas de São Pedro and Serra Negra.

★ **Scrumptious Food:** Sample a variety of local dishes made with the freshest ingredients, including artisanal sausages and locally brewed beer.

You will definitely be pleasantly surprised by the beauty and amenities that the coast of São Paulo has to offer, with its paradisiacal beaches, vibrant nightlife, and a wide variety of water sports like surfing and diving. It's also worth visiting the state's interior, which offers charming historic towns, renowned wineries, and incredible natural attractions such as waterfalls and national parks. Both destinations provide the opportunity to savor authentic local cuisine and connect with nature. Exploring these regions is a unique experience, balancing relaxation and adventure, and ensuring an unforgettable trip.

1 Santos. The city combines coastal charm with vibrant culture. It's perfect for those seeking leisure and history in one place.

2 São Sebastião. With its 36 uniquely beautiful beaches, this place offers everything from tranquil coves to prime surfing spots.

3 Ilhabela. Known for its exceptional hiking trails through tropical forests, beautiful waterfalls, and colorful marine life.

4 Ubatuba. Renowned for its stunning coastline, featuring over 100 pristine beaches and lush Atlantic rainforest. The town offers excellent opportunities for surfing, snorkeling, and exploring its rich biodiversity.

5 Águas de São Pedro. A charming town known for its therapeutic mineral waters. With medicinal springs, high-quality spas, and a pleasant climate, ideal to relax.

6 Campos do Jordão. Its scenic land landscapes are ideal for hiking and mountain biking, while cozy cafés add to the town's charm.

7 Serra Negra. A serene mountain town renowned for its therapeutic mineral waters and rich coffee production history.

8 Embu. A lively town celebrated for its arts and crafts scene, with a weekend market brimming with local handmade treasures.

9 Santana de Parnaíba. Historic town known for its well-preserved colonial architecture and cobblestone streets, picturesque buildings, museums, and cultural events that highlight its past.

For a quick getaway from São Paulo, you have amazing options both inland and along the coast, with travel times ranging from 30 minutes to four hours. Head inland to explore charming towns like Campos do Jordão, where you can enjoy romantic days with a European feel, or Serra Negra, known for its mineral waters and rich coffee history. For a touch of relaxation, unwind in the excellent spas of Águas de São Pedro, where the therapeutic springs promise a rejuvenating experience.

If you prefer the beach, the coastal trips are equally captivating. Access is easy with well-maintained highways leading to destinations like Santos, with its long sandy stretch and vibrant cultural scene. Alternatively, head to Ilhabela (meaning "beautiful island"), where you can adventure through scenic trails in the Atlantic Forest and dive into crystal-clear waters. Whether by car or bus, the roads are well-kept, ensuring a smooth, relaxing, and discovery-filled journey. You won't regret hitting the road to uncover what these nearby destinations have to offer.

After exploring the city of São Paulo and experiencing its relentless hustle and countless activities, take a break and dive into the surrounding areas of this charming city. Discover how a single destination can offer so many fascinating facets: beach, mountain, city, excitement, tranquility, and adventure.

Unlike what you may know about beaches around the world, in Brazil, you don't need to prepare much for a day by the sea. Everything you need is right there! With extensive sandy stretches, if there are no restaurants on the boardwalk, you'll definitely find kiosks and street vendors offering everything from drinks and snacks to swimwear, toys for kids, and, of course, beach umbrellas and loungers. This way, you can relax while enjoying a breaded shrimp and a refreshing caipirinha (traditional Brazilian cocktail made with *cachaça* and fruits).

The countryside also holds its own charm, with picturesque towns where you can find many handcrafted souvenirs There, you can enjoy breathtaking mountain views, embark on thrilling quad bike adventures, and take long hikes through trails. Admire local springs and waterfalls and enjoy unique sunsets, making every moment a memorable experience.

Planning

Getting Here and Around

Bus travel to and from the towns around São Paulo can be a time-consuming affair because of heavy traffic to and from the big city to commuter towns along the coast and inland, particularly on weekends. It can take a few hours to reach your destination. (*Paulistanos* love to take these trips, leaving on Friday night and returning on Sunday after lunch or in the late afternoon). It is also possible to rent a car or take a taxi, particularly as roads are good and traffic isn't too chaotic once you're out of the city. Reaching many of the destinations around São Paulo is feasible by taxi, but expect to pay upwards of R$250 for one-way trips, even for relatively nearby destinations such as Embu das Artes and Santana de Parnaíba. Your taxi driver might agree to a flat fee over turning on the meter. Another well-used alternative is to opt for ride hailing services like Uber and 99app, which offer great prices.

AIR

There are no airports near the coastal cities. The airports serving the region are in the capital: São Paulo/Congonhas Airport—Deputado Freitas Nobre and São Paulo/Guarulhos International Airport—Governor André Franco Montoro. In the countryside, we have the Viracopos-Campinas International Airport.

The city of São Paulo holds the record for the highest number of helicopter operations in the world. There are about 2,300 landings and takeoffs per day, and believe it or not, it's very common for the wealthy part of São Paulo's population to use this mode of transportation to travel from the city to the coast, known as the famous air taxis.

BUS

As São Paulo has many bus lines and three main bus terminals (Terminal Barra Funda, Terminal Tietê, and Terminal Jabaquara), there are schedule options for cities in the countryside and on the coast every day and at all times, with prices starting at R$40 and reaching over R$200.

CAR

If you don't mind driving and dealing with some traffic, going by car is the most comfortable and practical option. Use the Waze app for navigation and stay alert to speed cameras along the highways, always respecting speed limits and being cautious with the numerous winding curves on the road. To reach the coast or the countryside, you will also encounter many tolls, so it is advisable to arrange for an electronic toll system with your rental company or carry cash to pay them.

TAXI

Taxis are not commonly used for this type of trip as they can be quite expensive, and not all taxi drivers are willing to accept such fares since finding passengers for the return trip can be difficult. However, it is possible to arrange with a taxi driver to both drop off and pick up. Alternatively, using ride-hailing apps like Uber and 99app, which typically offer lower and more attractive rates, can be a good option.

Hotels

São Paulo has by far the best accommodations in the state, with numerous options. In other places, you can typically find basic inns (bed-and-breakfast types), with occasional gems like TW Guaimbê in Ilhabela and Shangri-Lá in Serra Negra (these better, boutique options tend to book up quickly, even though they are much more expensive). Coastal cities become crowded in the summer (December to March), and it is almost impossible to find anything without advance reservations. The same applies to Campos do Jordão and Serra Negra in the winter (June to September).

⇨ *Hotel reviews have been shortened. For full information, visit Fodors.com. Restaurant prices are the average cost of a main course at dinner or, if dinner is not served, at lunch. Hotel prices are the lowest cost of a standard double room in high season, excluding tax.*

WHAT IT COSTS in Reais			
$	$$	$$$	$$$$
RESTAURANTS			
Under R$50	R$50–R$130	R$131–R$200	Over R$200
HOTELS			
Under R$150	R$151–R$300	R$301–R$500	Over R$500

Restaurants

Restaurants in coastal cities tend to be rustic beach cafés and predictably serve a lot of seafood. For a change of taste, visit Ubatuba and these three neighborhoods in or near São Sebastião—Maresias, Boiçucanga, and Camburi—where you can find good pizzerias, steak houses, and Japanese restaurants. In Campos do Jordão, a popular mountain retreat for São Paulo residents, you can find a Brazilian version of Swiss fondue (there are options with chocolate, cheese, and meat, all varieties are delicious) and many bars with great food and generous meat portions. In Serra Negra, you will find typical countryside fare, including plenty of fresh meat and agricultural products, as well as a wide range of local sweets like the famous *doce de leite*, craft beers, and wine.

Favorite Places

 Leticia Davino: What fascinates me the most is the possibility of having so many amazing places to visit just a short distance from São Paulo. I love going to the beach! Since childhood, I've cherished unforgettable memories of these family moments. It's when we gather, have fun, and share the joy of being together. Between the warmth of the sun, the sea breeze, and the laughter, I always find time to relax, appreciate the view, and savor every moment.

Tours

For those visiting any of these cities for the first time, taking a tour is highly recommended. This way, you can explore the area more deeply with guides who know the region like the back of their hand, uncovering its unique features and discovering all the interesting things to explore.

Santos

70 km (43 miles) south of São Paulo.

Santos is the largest city on the São Paulo coast and home to the largest container port in South America. At the turn of the 20th century, the local economy focused on coffee exports, which contributed significantly to the city's wealth and development. The tourist cruises that travel around Brazil depart from here, as well as those heading to Europe. The historic center, lined with neoclassical buildings and cobblestone streets, is compact enough to explore on foot. However, the main attraction is the coastline, a full 7 km (4½ miles) long, adorned with

Santos is home to the largest container port in South America.

a large beachfront garden. It's best to visit on weekdays or Saturday. Returning to São Paulo on Sunday afternoon can be a nightmare, especially when the sun is shining, and Paulistanos have flocked en masse to the nearest beach, trying to make the most of every last minute of the day.

GETTING HERE AND AROUND

The city of São Paulo rests on a plateau 72 km (46 miles) inland. If you can avoid traffic, getaways to the South Shore are fairly quick on the parallel Imigrantes (SP 160) or Anchieta (SP 150) highways, both of which can become one-way on weekends and holidays due to high demand. Buses to Santos depart every 30–60 minutes from São Paulo's Jabaquara Terminal, located at the south end of Line 1 (Blue) of the subway. The journey takes just over an hour, but depending on traffic, it can take up to three hours, offering views of the spectacular Serra do Mar mountain range. Santos's bus station is centrally located, a 10-minute walk from the Museu do Café in the historic center and the Museu Pelé in Valongo. A 15-minute cab ride will take you to Gonzaga and José Menino Beaches, where most of the hotels, bars, and restaurants are situated.

ESSENTIALS
BUS CONTACTS Terminal Rodoviário de Santos. ✉ *Praça dos Andradas 45, Centro, Centro* ☎ *13/3213–2290.*

VISITOR INFORMATION Tourist Information. ✉ *Largo Marquês de Monte Alegre 2, Estação do Valongo, Centro, Centro* ☎ *13/3201–8000* ⊕ *www.turismosantos.com.br.*

TOURS
Bonde Turístico de Santos
GUIDED TOURS | FAMILY | This delightful tour is onboard a restored 1920s tram, which stops at all the main points of interest in the historic center. It's a hop-on, hop-off service, which allows you to jump off, have a look around, and get on the next tram when you're ready to move on. ✉ *Largo Marquês de Monte Alegre 2, Valongo, Centro* ☎ *800/881–3887*

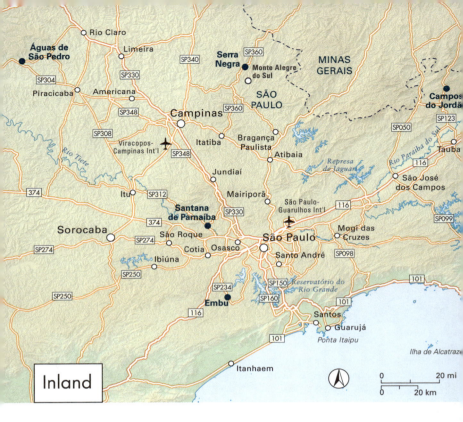

www.turismosantos.com.br/?q=pt-br/node/72 R$7.

Sights

Museu do Café (*Coffee Museum*)
HISTORY MUSEUM | FAMILY | The grand neo-classical Palácio da Bolsa Oficial de Café, where the Coffee Museum is located, was home to the coffee exchange up to 1957. Rosewood chairs are set out for traders in the trading hall, whose walls are hung with panels painted by Brazilian Benedito Calixto. Upstairs are exhibits related to the world of coffee. Visitors can also sample the drink at the museum's cafeteria. The last major renovation of the Museu do Café in Santos was completed in 2017. The restoration and modernization aimed to preserve the historic building and enhance the visitor experience, including upgrades to the facilities and exhibits. *Rua Quinze de Novembro 95, Centro* 13/3213–1750 *www.museudocafe.org.br* R$10 Closed Mon.

★ **Museu Pelé**
HISTORY MUSEUM | Edson Arantes do Nascimento's, better known as Pelé's, self-assessment—"I was born for soccer just as Beethoven was born for music."—may seem a tad self-important, but to many soccer fans, who regard him as one of the world's greatest footballers, it is not far from the truth. Housed in a 19th-century mansion and opened during the 2014 World Cup, Museu Pelé honors Santos's most famous son through displays of his personal items and trophies, plus photos, videos, and documents concerning the footballer. *Largo Marquês de Monte Alegre 1, Valongo* 0800/173–887, 13/3233–9670 *www.*

Soccer fans will love a visit to the the Museu Pelé in Valongo.

turismosantos.com.br/?q=pt-br/node/77
R$10; R$5 on Sun.

Beaches

Praia do Santos
BEACH | The massive, 7-km (4½-mile) strip of sand along Santos's shoreline is made up of a series of lively beaches. The city is crossed by seven channels, which act as borders between districts and separate the beaches. The busiest beaches—José Menino, Gonzaga, and Boqueirão—are between channels 1 and 4, where you'll find the greatest concentration of hotels and restaurants. The sea conditions do not differ greatly from one beach to another, but at José Menino (channels 1 to 2) the waves are a bit stronger and better for surfing. Partiers gather at Gonzaga Beach (channels 2 to 3), where open-air concerts often take place. Boqueirão (channels 3 to 4) has Santos's best infrastructure with ATMs, toilets, and showers, as well as a crafts fair on the weekend. Embaré Beach (channels 4 to 5) has many kiosks and bars and is a magnet for the younger set. Aparecida Beach (channels 5 to 6) is the meeting point for families with children, as well as seniors, and the location of the biggest beachfront garden in the world. The calm, almost flat sea at Ponta da Praia (channels 6 to 7) is suitable for water sports such as sailing, windsurfing, and jet skiing. **Amenities:** food and drink; lifeguards; showers; toilets. **Best for:** partiers; walking. *From Av. Presidente Wilsom 1900 (José Menino beach) to Av. Saldanha da Gama (Ponta da Praia).*

Restaurants

Madê Cozinha Autoral
$$$ | **SEAFOOD** | The restaurant combines a relaxed atmosphere with a creative menu that showcases local ingredients. The dishes, such as their signature slow-roasted pork belly, are flavorful and expertly prepared. **Known for:** creative use of local ingredients; signature slow-roasted pork belly; relaxed, stylish dining environment. *Average main:*

R$120 ✉ Rua Minas Gerais 93, Boqueirão ☎ 13/3288–2434 ⊙ Closed Mon.

Hotels

Parque Balneário Hotel Santos
$$$ | HOTEL | The hotel offers a prime location in Santos, just steps from the beach and shopping areas. **Pros:** nice rooftop; great location; good price. **Cons:** parking can be challenging; limited on-site dining options; elevator service can be slow. ⑤ *Rooms from: R$739* ✉ *Avenida Ana Costa 555, Gonzaga* ☎ *0800/799–9925* ⊕ *www.castelodeitaipavahoteis.com.br/hotel/parque-balneario-santos* ⇌ *278 rooms* ⁍⁜ *Free Breakfast.*

São Sebastião

São Sebastião, located on the northern coast of São Paulo (204 km or 127 miles), is a destination that blends beautiful beaches with rich history and culture. With 100 km (62 miles) of coastline, the city features renowned beaches such as Juquehy, perfect for surfing and leisure, as well as trails in the Atlantic Forest for ecotourism enthusiasts. The historic center, with its colonial architecture, houses churches, museums, and cultural events, and provides a comprehensive experience for visitors. The beaches attract everyone from the youngsters who flock to Maresias and Camburi to the families who favor Barra do Sahy and Camburizinho. The "beautiful island" of Ilhabela⇨ is a 15-minute ferry ride away from downtown São Sebastião.

GETTING HERE AND AROUND

Pássaro Marron buses travel several times a day to São Sebastião (to the ferry dock) from São Paulo's Tietê terminal, close to the international airport of Guarulhos, and take about four hours.

The drive from São Paulo to São Sebastião is about three hours if it is not raining. Some of the North Shore's most beautiful houses line the Rio-Santos Highway (SP 055) on the approach to Maresias. However, extra care is required when driving along the 055, as the road conditions and lighting are precarious, particularly past Maresias. To reach the 055, take the Ayrton Senna (SP 070) highway, followed by Mogi-Bertioga (SP 098). Alternatively if you want to get straight to the center of São Sebastião where the Ilhabela ferry docks, take Rodovia Ayrton Senna–Carvalho Pinto (SP 070), followed by Rodovia Tamoios (SP 099) to Caraguatatuba, and then follow the signs.

ESSENTIALS
BUS CONTACTS Pássaro Marron.
☎ *0800/285–3047* ⊕ *www.passaromarron.com.br.* **Terminal Rodoviário.** ✉ *Rua Minas Gerais 221, Centro.*

VISITOR INFORMATION Turismo São Sebastião. ✉ *Rua Expedicionário Brasileiro, 181, Centro* ☎ *12/3892–2620* ⊕ *www.turismosaosebastiao.com.br.*

Beaches

Barra do Sahy
BEACH | FAMILY | Families with young children favor small, quiet Barra do Sahy. Its narrow strip of sand (with a bay and a river on one side and rocks on the other) is steep but smooth, and the water is clean and calm. Kayakers paddle about, and divers are drawn to the nearby Ilha das Couves. Area restaurants serve mostly basic fish dishes with rice and salad, as well as sharing platters of snacks, seafood, and fries. Note that Barra do Sahy's entrance is atop a slope and appears suddenly—be on the lookout around marker km 174. **Amenities:** food and drink; lifeguards; limited parking (no fee). **Best for:** snorkeling; sunrise. ✉ *Rio-Santos Hwy. SP 055* ✢ *157 km (97 miles) southeast of São Paulo.*

Camburizinho and Camburi
BEACH | While Camburizinho is more secluded and also where the families head to, the latter, on the other side of

The North Coast

the river Camburi, is where the action is, with night owls heading here to play guitar by the moonlight. At the center of the beaches is a cluster of cafés, ice-cream shops, bars, and restaurants. The two beaches are located just north of Barra do Sahy. If you're coming from the south, take the second entrance, which is usually in better shape than the first entrance at km 166. **Amenities:** food and drink; lifeguards; parking (fee). **Best for:** partiers; sunset; surfing. ✉ *Rio-Santos Hwy. SP 055* ✣ *162 km (100 miles) southeast of São Paulo.*

Maresias

BEACH | Maresias is a 4-km (2-mile) stretch of white and soft sand with clean, green waters that are good for swimming and surfing. Maresias is popular with a young crowd and compared with the others along the North Coast, its beach village is large and has a good infrastructure, with banks, supermarkets, and a wide choice of nightlife entertainment. **Amenities:** food and drink; lifeguards; parking (fee); toilets. **Best for:** partiers; surfing; windsurfing. ✉ *Rio-Santos Hwy., Km 151, SP 055* ✣ *177 km (109 miles) southeast of São Paulo.*

🍴 Restaurants

Candeeiro Pizza e Crepe

$$ | **PIZZA** | On the main street of Camburi, Candeeiro serves delicious Neapolitan-style pizza, as well as crepes. The little gallery where it is located has a very good ice-cream shop, Gelateria Parmalat, tucked at the back, so save room for dessert. **Known for:** quick and excellent service; square pizza served hot and crispy on an iron plate; a wide variety of pizza toppings available. ⑤ *Average*

Wealthy Paulistanos flock to Camburizinho and Camburi to sunbathe, surf, and party.

main: R$50 ✉ Al Antonio José Marques 81, Camburi ☎ 12/3865–3626 ⊕ www.pizzariacandeeiro.com.br ⊙ No lunch.

Hotels

Amora Hotel Maresias

$$$$ | **HOTEL** | Right on Maresias beachfront, with easy access to the town center, this hotel has cozy rooms and a heated outdoor pool, hot tub, and sauna, perfect for days when agitated seas make the beach less appealing. **Pros:** beach service; comfortable rooms; heated outdoor pool. **Cons:** limited and expensive food options; few rainy day activities nearby; some rooms with views of the beach blocked by lifeguards. ⑤ *Rooms from: R$1,000* ✉ *Av. Dr. Francisco Loup 1285, Maresias* ☎ *12/3865–7109, 12/3865–7397* ⊕ *www.amorahotel.com.br* ⇌ *27 suites* ⦿ *Free Breakfast.*

★ Hotel Spa Nau Royal

$$$$ | **HOTEL** | Tucked away from the main cluster of Camburi's bars and all the noise of weekend partiers, this very special boutique hotel is the perfect choice for couples looking for peace and quiet. **Pros:** unparalleled service; excellent restaurant; direct access to the sand and beach service. **Cons:** suites near reception area can be noisy; too secluded for some tastes; extremely expensive. ⑤ *Rooms from: R$3,259* ✉ *Alameda Patriarca Antônio José Marques 1533, Camburi* ✥ *When using GPS, use address Av. Deble Luiza Derani 1533* ☎ *12/2626–9662, 11/93772–2001 WhatsApp* ⊕ *www.nauroyal.com.br* ⊙ *Closed June* ⇌ *15 suites* ⦿ *Free Breakfast.*

Pousada Porto Mare

$$ | **B&B/INN** | **FAMILY** | On the main street just a stone's throw from the town's clubs and bars, Pousada Porto Mare is a great choice for those who like to be close to the action, with plenty of amenities thrown in—a nice pool and sauna facilities, and beach service, too. **Pros:** excellent breakfast; beach service; great price. **Cons:** rooms near the breakfast area can be noisy; check in at

pm; neighboring hostel can be noisy on the weekends. $ Rooms from: R$289 ⊠ Rua Sebastião Romão César 400 ☏ 12/98137–1250 ⊕ www.pousadaporomare.com.br ⇌ 28 rooms ⊚ Free Breakfast.

Villa Bebek

$$$ | B&B/INN | The owners of this chic hotel sought inspiration from Bali to create the beautiful gardens inlaid with pebbles, sculptures, and tropical plants surrounding the pool and sauna areas. **Pros:** beautiful decor; good service; spa with massages, saunas, and other treatments and activities. **Cons:** fewer options at breakfast during low season; a five-minute stroll from Camburi Beach, but there is beach service (parasols, chairs, and transportation); restaurant is a bit pricey. $ Rooms from: R$1,100 ⊠ Rua Pezito 251, Camburi ☏ 12/3865–3320, 12/99704–8089 for WhatsApp ⊕ www.villabebek.com.br ⊙ Closed June ⇌ 15 rooms ⊚ Free Breakfast.

🍸 Nightlife

Santo Gole

LIVE MUSIC | Santo Gole is an informal beach-style bar run by three friends that attracts a younger crowd and stays open until dawn. Come here for live rock music, draft beer, and light snacks. Check the schedule on the website. ⊠ Rua Sebastião Romão César 477, Maresias ☏ 12/3865–5044 ⊕ www.santogolemaresias.com.br ⊐ Check the website for special events.

Sirena

LIVE MUSIC | Wealthy, sun-kissed Paulistanos head to Sirena to see and be seen, sip cocktails, and dance the night away, watching the sun rise from the external dance floor. The house serves as a venue for many parties featuring international DJs, attracting crowds during end-of-year celebrations. ⊠ Rua Sebastião Romão César 418, Maresias.

Ilhabela

7 km (5 miles)/15-minute by ferry from São Sebastião.

Ilhabela is favored by those who like beach and water sports. Indeed, many sailing competitions are held here as well as scuba diving. This is the biggest sea island in the country, with 22 calm beaches along its western shore, which faces the mainland. The hotels are mostly at the north end, though the best sandy stretches are the 13 to the south, which face the open sea. Eighty percent of the island is in a state park area, with some parts accessible by car and others by boat only.

There are two small towns on the island: one is where the locals live; the other is where most visitors stay because of its hotels, restaurants, and stores. During the winter months most businesses that cater to tourists, including restaurants, are open only on weekends.

Scuba divers have several 19th- and early-20th-century wrecks to explore—this region has the most wrecks of any area off Brazil's coast—and hikers can set off on the numerous inland trails, many of which lead to a waterfall. Locals say that there is a waterfall for each day of the year, totaling 365.

■ **TIP→ Mosquitoes are a problem; bring plenty of insect repellent.**

GETTING HERE AND AROUND

Balsas (ferries) from São Sebastião to Ilhabela run every 30 minutes from 5:30 am to 11:30 pm and hourly during the night. The São Sebastião Balsa transports vehicles as well as passengers. Pedestrians and cyclists travel for free, while fares for motorcycles, cars, and trucks vary by type of vehicle and whether or not you'll be traveling on a weekday or a weekend. Passenger cars pay R$19 during the week and R$28.50 on weekends

Divers in Ilhabela get a close-up look at some of the most beautiful marine life.

and holidays. To get to the ferry dock in São Sebastião, take Avenida São Sebastião from town to the coast. Make advance ferry reservations, particularly December through February. On rainy days, it is worth checking whether ferries are operating at all.

The best way to get around Ilhabela is by car. There are no rental agencies on the island (or connecting bridges) so be sure to make arrangements beforehand. Public buses also cross the island from north to south daily.

ESSENTIALS
FERRY INFORMATION São Sebastião Balsa (Ferry). ✉ *Av. Antônio Januário do Nascimento s/n* ☎ *12/3892–1268* ⊕ *www.ilhabela.com.br/balsa.*

VISITOR AND TOUR INFORMATION Ilhabela Secretaria de Turismo. ✉ *Rua Prefeito Mariano Procópio de Araújo Carvalho 86, Ilhabela* ☎ *12/3896–9200* ⊕ *www.ilhabela.sp.gov.br.*

TOURS
Maremar Turismo
GUIDED TOURS | Maremar Turismo offers a range of scuba diving, horseback riding, Jeep, and hiking tours around Ilhabela's most popular areas, as well as some off-the-beaten track tours and speedboat rental. There is also a kiosk on the Perequê Pier. ✉ *Av. São João 548, Perequê* ☎ *12/3896–1783 kiosk, 12/3896–3679 WhatsApp* ⊕ *www.maremar.tur.br.*

Beaches

Praia da Armação
BEACH | The long strip of white sand and calm sea attract sailing, windsurfing, and kitesurfing aficionados. Busy during most of the year, Praia da Armação has an excellent infrastructure, with bars, restaurants, and kiosks serving food and drinks and renting parasols and beach chairs. Bathrooms, baby changing facilities, and parking bays are available. There is a church on-site, which is said to be one of the oldest buildings on the island, that hosts beachside weddings. The

beach was also once the site of a factory for processing blubber and other resources from whales caught in the waters around Ilhabela. **Amenities:** food and drink; lifeguards; parking (fee); toilets; water sports. **Best for:** snorkeling; sunset; walking; windsurfing. ✉ *Ilhabela ✈ 12 km (7.5 miles) from the ferry dock* ⊕ *www.ilhabela.com.br/praias/praia-da-armacao.*

Praia do Curral

BEACH | Curral is one of the most famous beaches on Ilhabela, and is popular with tourists as well as young people. It has clear and slightly rough waters and also a large green area, which serves as a refuge for those needing a break from sunbathing. The local vendors provide tables and chairs, fresh showers with clean water, bathrooms, and parking. At night people gather at the many restaurants and bars—some with live music—and there are places to camp. The wreck of the ship *Aymoré* (1921) can be found off the coast of this beach, near Ponta do Ribeirão, where you can also look for a waterfall trail. **Amenities:** food and drink; lifeguards; showers; toilets. **Best for:** partiers; sunset. ✉ *6 km (4 miles) south of Praia Grande, Ilhabela* ⊕ *www.ilhabela.com.br/praias/praia-do-curral.*

Praia Grande

BEACH | It's busy, but some of the best infrastructure in Ilhabela can be found here: the kiosks have tables in the shade; you can rent a chair from most vendors along the long sandy strip; showers are available free of charge; and there's even a chapel. The beach is popular for windsurfing, diving, and surfing. The sandy strip is rather inclined, with a tumble in the central part. The sands are thick and yellowish. On the far left there is a small river that ends in the sea. **Amenities:** food and drink; lifeguards; showers; toilets. **Best for:** partiers; surfing; walking; windsurfing. ✉ *Ilhabela ✈ 6.5 km (4 miles) south of ferry dock* ⊕ *www.ilhabela.com.br/praias/praia-grande.*

🍴 Restaurants

Ilha Sul

$$$$ | **SEAFOOD** | The best option on the menu at Ilha Sul is the grilled shrimp with vegetables. Fish and other seafood are also available. **Known for:** excellent fresh seafood; top-notch service; cozy atmosphere. ⑤ *Average main: R$120* ✉ *Av. Riachuelo 287, Praia da Feiticeira* ☎ *12/3894–9426, 12/3894–1536* ⊕ *www.restauranteilhasul.com.br* ⊗ *Closed Feb.–Nov. Mon.–Thurs.*

Viana

$$$$ | **SEAFOOD | FAMILY** | *Camarão* (shrimp) is prepared in various ways at this traditional, petite restaurant with just a few tables. It's popular among locals, who come here to eat and enjoy the gorgeous view and sunsets. **Known for:** a variety of shrimp and other seafood dishes; sitting on the beachfront; excellent service. ⑤ *Average main: R$110* ✉ *Av. Leonardo Reale 2301, Ilhabela* ☎ *12/99101–5473 WhatsApp* ⊕ *www.viana.com.br* ⊗ *No dinner.*

Hotels

★ DPNY Beach Hotel & Spa

$$$$ | **HOTEL** | This luxury hotel with direct access to Praia do Curral is geared toward couples looking for romance and relaxation, with modern, cozy and comfortable rooms and access to one of Ilhabela's most famous beaches. **Pros:** luxuriously comfortable rooms; excellent food; perfect for poolside relaxation. **Cons:** service can be slow at busy times; mattresses are too soft; not for families. ⑤ *Rooms from: R$1,200* ✉ *Av. Jose Pacheco do Nascimento 7668, Ilhabela* ☎ *12/3894–3000* ⊕ *www.dpny.com.br* ⤴ *79 suites* ⧖ *Free Breakfast.*

Hotel Porto Pacuíba

$$$ | **HOTEL** | Peaceful and family-friendly, Porto Pacuíba is close to a beach (just across the street) and has easy access to good hikes nearby. **Pros:** excellent

The TW Guaimbê Exclusive Suites in Ilhabela has an infinity pool looking over the nearby beach.

service; good restaurant; well-decorated rooms. **Cons:** far from the town center and ferry dock; small rooms; lots of stairs. ⓢ *Rooms from: R$899* ✉ *Av. Leonardo Reale 2392, Ilhabela* ☎ *12/99175–9159 also WhatsApp* ⊕ *www.portopacuiba.com.br* ⇌ *29 suites* ⑩ *Free Breakfast.*

Maison Joly
$$$ | **HOTEL** | The former guests of this exclusive hotel atop Morro do Cantagalo range from Swedish royalty to the Rolling Stones. **Pros:** spectacular views; excellent restaurant; top-notch service. **Cons:** service a little erratic in busy seasons; a lot of stairs; old air-conditioning. ⓢ *Rooms from: R$499* ✉ *R. Anibal Telles Correa 772, Ilhabela* ☎ *12/98114–2289* ⊕ *www.maisonjoly.com.br* ⇌ *9 rooms* ⑩ *No Meals.*

TW Guaimbê Exclusive Suites
$$$$ | **HOTEL** | TW Guaimbê stands out as one of the few beachfront hotels in the area, offering direct access to the sand and sea. **Pros:** very exclusive; direct access to the beach; unique sunset. **Cons:** extremely expensive; you will get thousands of bites from bugs; limited dining options on-site. ⓢ *Rooms from: R$2,300* ✉ *Av. Riachuelo 5360, Ilhabela* ☎ *12/99745–3484* ⊕ *www.twguaimbe.com.br* ⇌ *16 suites* ⑩ *Free Breakfast.*

Activities

BOATING AND SAILING
Ilhabela is a prime destination for boating and sailing enthusiasts, with its calm waters and picturesque coastline. The island offers numerous marinas and anchorages, making it ideal for exploring by sea. Sailors can enjoy both leisurely cruises and adventurous regattas in this stunning tropical setting.

SCUBA DIVING
Diving is a popular activity for those visiting Ilhabela. In the calm transparent waters, you can explore the marine wildlife as well as discover the mysteries surrounding the island's various shipwrecks. It is said that Ilhabela has more than 100 close to its shore. These vessels have formed huge submerged artificial reefs,

nd are now home to a wide variety of quatic species such as turtles, octo- uses, and the like. It is still possible to ctually see the ships. Beginning divers hould aim for the most popular wrecks, uch as the *Aymoré* (1914; Curral Beach; –7 meters) and the *Darth* (1894; Itaboca Beach; 5–15 meters). There are numer- us diving schools along nearly every each, which also rent equipment if you re happy to go solo.

olonial Diver

CUBA DIVING | You can rent equipment, ke diving classes, and arrange for a ve boat trip through Colonial Diver. ourses include equipment for the class- s, course material, and an international ertificate. ✉ *Av. Brasil, 1751, Ilhabela* 🕿 *12/3894–9459* 🌐 *www.colonialdiver. om.br.*

Ilha das Cabras

CUBA DIVING | The main attractions of is little piece of paradise—besides the hite sand and clear water—are the tiny ars that serve delicious, fresh seafood nd the Ecological Sanctuary of Ilha das abras. The park, created in 1992, is a ecluded reserve around the island and is so a great diving and fish-watching site. hile most "baptisms" of diving begin- ers take place here, seasoned divers ead off to their underwater adventures the diving/snorkeling sanctuary off e shore of the isle, where a statue of eptune can be found at the 22-foot epth. ✉ *Ilhabela* ✚ *in front of Praia das edras Miúdas, 2 km (1 mile) from the rry dock* 🌐 *www.ilhabela.com.br/praias/ a-das-cabras.*

Ilha de Búzios

CUBA DIVING | A nearly two-hour boat trip eparates Ilhabela from Ilha de Búzios, t the effort is totally worthwhile. ecause it is located far from the coast, e water is very transparent, mean- g divers will be able to see plenty of olorful fish and other underwater fauna ıch as rays and sea turtles. The main ars, however, are the dolphins, which fearlessly approach boats. ✉ *15 km (9 miles) offshore; take boat from São Sebastião, Ilhabela* 🌐 *www.ilhabela.com. br/praias/ilha-dos-buzios.*

SURFING

One of the best beaches to surf in Ilhabela is Baía de Castelhanos, which is located 22 km (14 miles) east of the ferry dock. To get there you'll need a four- wheel-drive vehicle, and if it rains even this won't be enough. Consider arriving by sailboat, which demands a 1.5 to 3.5- hour trip that can be arranged through local tour operators. If you're lucky, you might spot a dolphin off the shore of this 2-km (1¼-mile) beach—the largest on the island. Pacuíba, which is located 20 km (12 miles) north of the ferry dock, also has decent wave action. The main beaches on the island are busy most of the year; the months of July and August are colder and much quieter. Boards can be rented in surf shops, ever-present on most beaches.

Ubatuba

234 km (145 miles) southeast of São Paulo.

Many of the more than 70 beaches around Ubatuba are more than beautiful enough to merit the long drive from São Paulo. Young people, surfers, and couples with and without children hang out in the 90-km (56-mile) area, where waterfalls, boat rides, aquariums, diving, and trek- king in the wild are major attractions. The city is also known for its frequent rain, so be sure to check the weather before hitting the road.

GETTING HERE AND AROUND

Pássaro Marron buses travel eight times a day to Ubatuba from São Paulo. The journey takes almost five hours. By car from São Paulo, take Rodovia Ayrton Sen- na–Carvalho Pinto (SP 070), followed by Rodovia Tamoios (SP 099) to Caraguatatu- ba. Turn right and head north on SP 055.

ESSENTIALS

BUS CONTACTS Litorânea. ☎ 0800/285–3047 ⊕ https://www.passaromarron.com.br. **Terminal Rodoviária de Ubatuba.** ✉ Rua Maria Vitória Jean 381, Ubatuba.

Beaches

Praia Grande

BEACH | For those seeking a party atmosphere, Praia Grande is a great option. It has bars and restaurants by the sea, with local samba and country music playing all day. Chairs and parasols can be hired from beach vendors. The waters here are clean and green, and the hard sands are ideal for football, volleyball, and racquetball; it's also a great place for hiking. Praia Grande is a major surf spot in Ubatuba, with consistent, perfect waves. **Amenities:** food and drink; lifeguards; parking (fee). **Best for:** partiers; surfing; walking. ✉ Off Tamoios (SP 099) and Rio-Santos intersection, Ubatuba.

Praia do Prumirim

BEACH | Surrounded by rainforest and lined with summer holiday mansions, Prumirim is a small beach of coarse sands and turquoise calm waters. Despite its exuberant natural beauty, Prumirim is not very busy. There's good surfing, but the waves are generally smaller than those at Praia Grande. About a kilometer out to sea, Prumirim Island also has magnificent scenery and is a great place for diving. To reach the island you can pay one of the local fishermen to ferry you out there or, if you're particularly fit, you could even swim. The access to Praia do Prumirim is near km 29 of SP 055, past the entrance to a private condominium. A beautiful waterfall with a natural pool can also be accessed nearby off the highway. **Amenities:** food and drink. **Best for:** snorkeling; solitude; sunrise; walking. ✉ Near Km 29 of BR 101 (Rio-Santos), Ubatuba.

 Restaurants

Padaria Integrale

$ | **BAKERY** | **FAMILY** | This popular, centrally located *padaria* (bakery) offers a range of healthy sandwiches and drinks, as well as an excellent deli selection. You can either have your breakfast or light meal here, or take it away like many locals do. **Known for:** wide variety of artisanal breads; quick service; fresh ingredients. ⑤ Average main: R$25 ✉ Rua Dr. Esteve da Silva 360, Ubatuba ☎ 12/3836–1836.

Hotels

★ Pousada Picinguaba

$$$$ | **HOTEL** | A luxury *pousada* in the beautiful, unspoiled fishing village of Picinguaba, this place is ideal for couples looking for peace and quiet. **Pros:** bird and wildlife watching for early risers; excellent food; unparalleled service. **Cons:** the pousada is up a steep hill; small rooms; lots of mosquitoes because of the forest location. ⑤ Rooms from: R$2,000 ✉ Rua G Picinguaba 130, Picinguaba, Ubatuba ☎ 12/99637–7173 ⊕ wearenature.com/picinguaba/hotel ⇌ 10 suites ⑩ Free Breakfast.

Pousada Torre del Mar

$$ | **B&B/INN** | **FAMILY** | A simple but comfortable and very clean pousada, Torre del Mar is just a stone's throw from the town's main attractions, beaches, and restaurants. **Pros:** comfortable beds; excellent homemade breakfast; central location. **Cons:** rooms facing the street can be noisy; rooms can be quite small; parking is tight. ⑤ Rooms from: R$349 ✉ Av. Milton de Holanda Maia 210, Praia do Itaguá, Ubatuba ☎ 12/3832–2751, 12/98208–6761 ⊕ www.torredelmar.com.br ⇌ 18 suites ⑩ Free Breakfast.

Did You Know?

Even skilled surfers know that Praia do Prumirim has strong waves, so be careful while exploring the beautiful beach with golden sands and striking sunsets.

Águas de São Pedro

180 km (112 miles) northwest of São Paulo.

Although Águas de São Pedro is one of the smallest cities in Brazil, at a mere 3.9 square km (1.5 square miles), its sulfurous waters made it famous countrywide in the 1940s and '50s. The healing hot springs were discovered by chance in the 1920s when technicians were drilling for oil.

You can access the springs at the Balneário Publico (public bathhouse) or through some hotels. Though a number of illnesses respond to the water, most visitors are just healthy tourists soaking in relaxation. Águas de São Pedro is compact, so it's easy to get around on foot.

GETTING HERE AND AROUND

Águas de São Pedro is about a two-and-a-half-hour drive north of São Paulo on Anhangüera-Bandeirantes (SP 330/SP 348) and then SP 304.

Sights

Balneário Municipal Dr. Octávio Moura Andrade

HOT SPRING | Want immersion baths in sulfurous spring water? You can swim in the pool or sweat in the sauna while you wait for your private soak, massage, or beauty treatment. A snack bar and a gift shop round out the spa services. The surrounding forested grounds are perfect for a leisurely stroll or a ride on horseback. The park is free and open to the public in the morning on weekdays and all day on weekends. ✉ *Av. Carlos Mauro 213, Águas de São Pedro* ☎ *19/3482-4273 to book services at the SPA Thermal* 💲 *Baths start at R$30; other services start at R$100.*

Hotels

Avenida Charme Hotel

$$$ | HOTEL | This hotel, resembling a large ranch house, has an arcaded veranda and well-maintained, but rather dated, rooms. **Pros:** excellent breakfast; friendly service; good pool area. **Cons:** rooms need updating; air conditioners can be noisy; need to contact the property to make a reservation. 💲 *Rooms from: R$700* ✉ *Av. Carlos Mauro 246, Águas de São Pedro* ☎ *19/3482-7900, 19/99754-8598 for WhatsApp* ⊕ *www.avenidacharmehotel.com.br* ⇨ *53 rooms* 🍴 *All-Inclusive* ⇨ *Drinks not included; meals only.*

★ Grande Hotel São Pedro

$$$$ | HOTEL | In the middle of a 300,000-square-meter (3.2 million-square-foot) park with more than 1 million trees and local wildlife, this hotel is in a beautiful art deco building that was a casino during the 1940s. **Pros:** beautiful location; excellent service; great food and kids' menu. **Cons:** requires booking months in advance, especially during the winter season; there can be long lines to check in and out during high seasons; drinks not included, just meals. 💲 *Rooms from: R$1,490* ✉ *Parque Dr. Octávio de Moura Andrade, s/n, Águas de São Pedro* ☎ *19/3482-7600* ⊕ *grandehotelsenac.com.br* ⇨ *112 rooms* 🍴 *All-Inclusive.*

Campos do Jordão

184 km (114 miles) northeast of São Paulo.

In the Serra da Mantiqueira at an altitude of 5,525 feet, Campos do Jordão and its fresh mountain air are Paulistanos' favorite winter attractions. In July temperatures drop as low as 32°F (0°C), though it never snows.

In the past some people came for their health (the town was once a tuberculosis treatment area), others for inspiration—including such Brazilian artists as writer

Os Bandeirantes

In the 16th and 17th centuries, groups called *bandeiras* (literally meaning "flags" but also an archaic term for an assault force) set out on expeditions from São Paulo. Their objectives were far from noble. Their initial goal was to enslave Native Americans. Later, they were hired to capture escaped African slaves and destroy *quilombos* (communities the slaves created deep in the interior). By heading inland at a time when most colonies were close to the shore, the *bandeirantes* (bandeira members) inadvertently did Brazil a great service.

A fierce breed, bandeirantes often adopted indigenous customs and voyaged for years at a time. Some went as far as the Amazon River; others, only to what is today Minas Gerais, where gold and precious gems were found. In their travels they ignored the 1494 Treaty of Tordesilhas, which established a boundary between Spanish and Portuguese lands. (The boundary was a vague north–south line roughly 1,600 km [1,000 miles] west of the Cape Verde islands.) Other Brazilians followed the bandeirantes, and towns were founded, often in what was technically Spanish territory. These colonists eventually claimed full possession of the lands they settled, and thus Brazil's borders were greatly expanded.

Near Parque Ibirapuera in the city of São Paulo, there's a monument, inaugurated in 1953, to honor the bandeirantes. It's a huge granite sculpture created by Victor Brecheret, a famous Brazilian artist. A major São Paulo highway is named Bandeirantes, and several roads across the state are named after these men who were considered brave and honorable. Protests are occasionally staged at the Ibirapuera statue by those who don't believe the bandeirantes deserve any kind of monument whatsoever.

Monteiro Lobato, dramatist Nelson Rodrigues, and painter Lasar Segall. Nowadays the arts continue to thrive, especially during July's Festival de Inverno (Winter Festival), which draws classical musicians from around the world.

Exploring Campos do Jordão without a car is difficult, as attractions are far-flung. The neighborhood of Vila Capivary is where most restaurants and cafés are located.

GETTING HERE AND AROUND
Seven Passaro Marron buses leave São Paulo for Campos do Jordão daily. The journey takes three hours and 20 minutes and costs R$82.65. To reach Campos do Jordão from São Paulo (a two-and-a-half-hour drive), take Rodovia Carvalho Pinto (SP 070) and SP 123.

ESSENTIALS
BUS CONTACTS Passaro Marron. ☎ *0800/285–3047* ⊕ *www.passaromarron.com.br.* **Terminal Rodoviário.** ✉ *Rua Benedito Lourenço 285, Campos do Jordão.*

VISITOR INFORMATION Campos do Jordão Tourist Office. ✉ *At entrance to town, Campos do Jordão* ☎ *12/3664–4422* ⊕ *www.visitecamposdojordao.org.br.*

Sights

Estação Ferroviária Emílio Ribas
TRAIN/TRAIN STATION | FAMILY | A wonderful little train departs from Estação Ferroviária Emílio Ribas for tours of the city and its environs. There are three different routes available for the train tour

in Campos do Jordão, ranging from 4 km to 7 km (3-5 miles) in distance within the city. The tours last between 30 and 45 minutes, offering visitors a charming way to explore the local scenery and attractions. ✉ Av. Dr. Emílio Ribas 2, Campos do Jordão ⊕ www.stm.sp.gov.br/horarios-e-tarifas 🖃 R$23.

Morro do Elefante (Elephant Hill)
VIEWPOINT | Outside town a chairlift ride to the top of Morro do Elefante is a good way to enjoy the view from a 5,850-foot height. ✉ Rua Ype, Jardim Elizabete, Campos do Jordão ☎ 12/3663–6463 ⊕ tickets.parquecapivari.com.br 🖃 R$69 round-trip.

Palácio Boa Vista
NOTABLE BUILDING | Palácio Boa Vista, the official winter residence of the state's governor, has paintings by such famous Brazilian modernists as Di Cavalcanti, Portinari, Volpi, Tarsila do Amaral, and Anita Malfatti. On the same property, the Capela de São Pedro (São Pedro Chapel) has sacred art from the 17th and 18th centuries.

■ **TIP→ Tours need to be booked in advance.** ✉ Av. Dr. Adhemar de Barros 3001, Campos do Jordão ☎ 12/3662–2033, 11/2193–8452 ⊕ www.saopaulo.sp.gov.br/palacioboavista/#/home 🖃 Free ⊗ Closed Mon., Tues., Thurs.

Parque Amantikir
GARDEN | FAMILY | Open 365 days a year, the Parque Amantikir consists of 26 gardens that are home to 700 different plant species. On the grounds you can find a cafeteria and a learning center, where there are courses on gardening. ✉ Rua Simplício de Toledo Neto 2200, Bairro Gavião Gonzaga, Campos do Jordão ☎ 12/99634–6784 ⊕ www.parqueamantikir.com.br 🖃 R$80.

Parque Estadual Campos do Jordão (Horto Florestal)
CITY PARK | Horto Florestal is a natural playground for macacos-prego (nail monkeys), squirrels, and parrots, as well as people. The park has a trout-filled river, waterfalls, and trails—all set among trees from around the world and one of the last araucária (Brazilian pine) forests in the state. ✉ Av. Pedro Paulo, s/n, Campos do Jordão ☎ 12/99607–0501 ⊕ ingressos.parquecamposdojordao.com.br 🖃 R$25.

 Restaurants

★ Baden-Baden
$$$ | GERMAN | One of the specialties at this charming German restaurant and choperia in the heart of town is sauerkraut garni (sour cabbage with German sausages). The typical dish serves two and is almost as popular as Baden-Baden's cold draft beer from the attached brewery. **Known for:** its adjacent brewery; traditional German dishes, like sauerkraut garni; outstanding service. ⑤ Average main: R$90 ✉ Rua Djalma Forjaz 93, Loja 10, Campos do Jordão ☎ 12/3663–3610, 12/99176–4680 ⊕ www.obadenbaden.com.br.

Chocolates Montanhês
$ | CAFÉ | A well-known chocolate shop and café, Chocolates Montanhês is the perfect stop after a meal, or to stock up on chocolate lollipops and slabs. Don't forget to try the extra-creamy hot chocolate. **Known for:** chocolate in all shapes and sizes, like cell phones, tools, pandas, and snowmen; chocolate-covered bananas and orange slices; a wide variety of chocolate truffles. ⑤ Average main: R$20 ✉ Praça São Benedito 5, Campos do Jordão ☎ 12/3663–1979 ⊕ www.chocolatemontanhes.com.br.

🛏 Hotels

★ Grande Hotel Campos do Jordão
$$$$ | RESORT | FAMILY | A former 1940s casino—just like its sister hotel in Águas de São Pedro—the Grande Hotel is a teaching hotel that boasts extensive grounds with beautiful gardens and plenty of outdoor activities. **Pros:**

Did You Know?

The Morro do Elefante is now completely renovated with a bar, restaurant, and public facilities while taking in the views of Campos do Jordão.

Did You Know?

While strolling through Horto Florestal, make sure to check out the Forestry Museum, where they hold the largest collection of wood types in Latin America.

excellent food; unparalled service; plenty of activities for adults and children. **Cons:** few dining options for vegetarians and others with dietary restrictions; drinks not included, only meals; could be better value for price. ⓢ *Rooms from: R$1,690* ✉ *Av. Frei Orestes Girardi 3549, Vila Capivary, Campos do Jordão* ☎ *012/3668–6000* ⊕ *www.grandehotelsenac.com.br/br/campos-do-jordao* ⤵ *95 suites* ❙◯❙ *All-Inclusive.*

Pousada Villa Capivary

$$$$ | HOTEL | A stay at this cozy guesthouse puts you in the gastronomic and commercial center of Campos. **Pros:** friendly, helpful, and efficient staff; central location; wonderful breakfast. **Cons:** booking well in advance required, particularly in the winter months; rooms facing town can be noisy; small bathrooms. ⓢ *Rooms from: R$900* ✉ *Av. Victor Godinho 131, Campos do Jordão* ☎ *012/3663–1736* ⊕ *www.capivari.com.br* ⤵ *15 rooms* ❙◯❙ *Free Breakfast.*

Shopping

Boulevard Geneve

MALL | FAMILY | This mall in the busy Vila Capivari district is lined with cafés, bars, and restaurants, making it a nightlife hub. You can also find plenty of clothing stores and candy shops selling chocolate, the town's specialty. ✉ *Rua Djalma Forjas 93, Vila Capivari, Campos do Jordão* ☎ *12/3663–5060.*

Serra Negra

142 km (88 miles) northeast of São Paulo.

At 4,265 feet above sea level in the Serra da Mantiqueira, Serra Negra attracts hordes of Paulistanos and cruising motorbike fans looking for a bucolic weekend break in the mountains. In addition to various mineral water fountains, there is the Coffee Route, where you can drive through thousands of acres of coffee fields until you reach Cachoeira dos Sonhos (Dreams Waterfall), where it's possible to swim and have a snack. You can also head over to Alto da Serra, the town's highest point, where paragliding aficionados gather on the weekends. To get there, follow the signs from Avenida João Gerosa and drive up Rua 14 de Julho all the way past Hotel São Mateus, until you reach an unpaved road on the left that will lead to the top. The main shopping street in Serra Negra is Rua Coronel Pedro Penteado, where you can find plenty of knitwear, leather bags, and clothing, as well as sweets and cheeses of all kinds. The town center is small enough to be explored by foot, visit the replica of the famous Fontana di Trevi that was inaugurated in 2023 to boost tourism and pay homage to Italian culture. Located in the city's central square, the fountain has become a popular meeting spot for both locals and tourists. In addition to its architectural beauty, the fountain is surrounded by beautiful gardens and spaces for relaxation.

GETTING HERE AND AROUND

Six Fênix buses leave São Paulo's Tietê bus terminal for Serra Negra daily. The journey takes three hours and costs R$96. To reach Serra Negra from São Paulo (a two-and-a-half-hour drive), take Rodovia Fernão Dias (SP 381) to Atibaia, Rodovia Dom Pedro I (SP 065) toward Itatiba, then the SP 360.

ESSENTIALS

BUS CONTACTS Rápido Fênix. ✉ *Serra Negra* ☎ *19/96497–9861* ⊕ *www.rapidofenix.com.br.*

VISITOR INFORMATION Serra Negra Tourist Office. ✉ *Nossa Senhora do Rosário 630, Serra Negra* ✣ *Behind the bus station and next to chairlift.*

Monte Alegre do Sul is a small, vibrant town of fewer than 10,000 residents.

👁 Sights

Monte Alegre do Sul

TOWN | If you have more than a day to spare and are driving, pay a quick visit to the delightful little town of Monte Alegre do Sul, just 6 km (4 miles) from Serra Negra and known for its September strawberry festival. The buildings of the historic center, including the town's church, Santuario Bom Jesus, date from the 19th century. Check out the shop of local artisan group Associarte, as well as the traditional sweet shop Peschiera nearby. At the old train station, a steam engine used for transporting coffee waits at a decommissioned platform. ✉ *Monte Alegre do Sul, Serra Negra* ⊕ *www.montealegredosul.com.br.*

🍴 Restaurants

★ Café Boteco

$$ | **BRAZILIAN** | **FAMILY** | Located by João Zelante Square in what was once a department store, Café Boteco incorporates elements of the traditional Brazilian *boteco* (dive bar) in some of its recipes and decor, but the comparisons end there: smartly dressed, friendly waiters serve excellent *picanha* (rump steak) and *costelinha com polenta* (pork ribs with polenta chips), as well as salad and pasta dishes with a local twist. The owners also run a small shop next door selling souvenirs, fine wines, and cold cuts. **Known for:** central location; live music in the square; local beers. [$] *Average main: R$80* ✉ *Travessa Tenente Mário Dallari 20 (Praça João Zelante), Serra Negra* ☎ *19/3892–3481* ⊕ *www.cafeboteco.com.br* ⊙ *No dinner Mon.–Tues.*

Gelato Donato

$ | **CAFÉ** | **FAMILY** | A small ice-cream parlor, Gelato Donato is a good destination for dessert and a coffee after a meal. The ice cream is made in Serra Negra using locally sourced ingredients, and the typically Brazilian flavors, such as the strange-sounding but delicious guava and cheese, change often. **Known for:** Brazilian flavors like guava and cheese; eat in or take a container home; lactose-free options. ⑤ *Average main: R$10* ✉ *Rua Cel. Pedro Penteado 373, Serra Negra* ☎ *19/3892–7794* ⊕ *www.gelatodonato.com* ⊟ *No credit cards.*

Padaria e Confeitaria Serrana
$ | **BRAZILIAN** | **FAMILY** | Located at the heart of Serra Negra, Serrana is a bakery that serves breakfast, light snacks, and also meals, as well as sharing platters. Grab a *pao na chapa com saida de requeijão* (grilled bread with Brazilian cream cheese) and coffee for breakfast here on a Sunday morning and sit at one of the tables outside to watch the hordes of motorcycling aficionados—they flock to Serra Negra on weekends from other cities on their amazing touring bikes. **Known for:** bolinhos de bacalhau (cod fritters); local draft beer Ecobier; empada de palmito (mini heart-of-palm pies). ⑤ *Average main: R$25* ✉ *Praça Prefeito João Zelante 2, Serra Negra* ☎ *19/3892–2289*.

Hotels

★ Hotel Firenze
$$$ | **HOTEL** | **FAMILY** | The Firenze hotel in Serra Negra offers a great deal. **Pros:** excellent breakfast; comfortable rooms; unparalled service. **Cons:** the bar and games room close early; months in advance to book a weekend. ⑤ *Rooms from: R$490* ✉ *Rua Sete de Setembro 118, Serra Negra* ☎ *19/3842–9400, 19/3892–2220, 19/99985–3118 WhatsApp* ⊕ *www.hotelfirenzeserranegra.com.br* ⇌ *76 suites* ❖ *Free Breakfast.*

Shangri-la Hotel Pousada
$$$ | **B&B/INN** | At the edge of town, 3,600 feet above sea level, this little gem offers a wonderful pool area open 24 hours and gazebos with breathtaking views of the mountains. **Pros:** amazing views; good restaurant; comfortable beds. **Cons:** need to drive to reach the town center; slightly outdated rooms; not very accessible. ⑤ *Rooms from: R$723* ✉ *Estrada das Tabaranas, Km 4 at the end of Av. Juca Preto, Serra Negra* ☎ *19/3892–3765* ⊕ *www.shangrila.com.br* ⇌ *19 suites* ❖ *Free Breakfast.*

Embu

27 km (17 miles) west of São Paulo.

Founded in 1554, Embu, or Embu das Artes, is a tiny Portuguese colonial town of whitewashed houses, old churches, wood-carvers' studios, and antiques shops. It has a downtown handicrafts fair every weekend. On Sunday the streets sometimes get so crowded you can barely walk, so it's worth arriving early. Embu also has many stores that sell handicrafts and wooden furniture; most of these are close to where the street fair takes place.

GETTING HERE AND AROUND
EMTU runs an *executivo* (executive or first-class) bus from São Paulo to Embu–Engenho Velho, which departs from Anhangabaú, and another that departs from Av. Cruzeira do Sul, next to Rodoviária Tietê. Regular (intermunicipal) buses travel more often—line 033 leaves from Clínicas to Embu, line 065 leaves from Campo Limpo, and line 002 leaves from Capão Redondo. The ride is less comfortable and takes about an hour and 15 minutes, though: you might have to stand up.

To make the 30-minute drive from São Paulo to Embu, drive from Avenida Professor Francisco Morato to Rodovia Régis Bittencourt (BR 116) and then follow the signs.

ESSENTIALS
BUS CONTACTS EMTU. ✉ *São Paulo* ☎ *0800/724–0555* ⊕ *www.emtu.sp.gov.br.*

VISITOR INFORMATION Tourist Information. ✉ *Largo 21 de Abril 139, Embu* ☎ *11/4704–6565* ⊕ *www.cidadeembudasartes.sp.gov.br/embu/portal.* **Gol**

Arts and crafts are easy to find and buy along the streets of Embu.

Tour Viagens e Turismo. ✉ *São Paulo* ☏ *11/94016–0988, 11/94014–5651 for calls or WhatsApp* ⊕ *www.goltour.com.br*.

👁 Sights

Igreja Nossa Senhora do Rosário
CHURCH | Igreja Nossa Senhora do Rosário was built in 1690 and it's worth seeking out if you won't have a chance to visit the historic cities of Minas Gerais. The church contains baroque images of saints and is next to a 1730 monastery now turned into a museum of sacred art. ✉ *Rua da Matriz 11, Embu* ☏ *11/4704–2792* 💲 *Free* ⊗ *Closed Mon.*

🍴 Restaurants

O Garimpo
$$$ | ECLECTIC | Sit in either the beautiful garden or the dining room with a fireplace at Embu's most famous restaurant, and then choose between Brazilian regional dishes such as the house specialty, *moqueca de badejo* (spicy fish-and-coconut-milk stew), and German classics such as *eisbein* (pickled and roasted pork shank). There is live music on weekends, but note that it stops at 10:30 on the dot, regardless of how much patrons might be enjoying themselves. **Known for:** moqueca de badejo (spicy fish-and-coconut-milk stew); beautiful garden views; excellent service. 💲 *Average main: R$80* ✉ *Rua da Matriz 136, Embu* ☏ *11/4785–1400 reservations only by phone* ⊕ *www.ogarimpoembu.com.br* ⊗ *No dinner Mon.–Wed.*

Os Girassóis Restaurante
$ | BRAZILIAN | A great variety of dishes is served at this downtown restaurant next to an art gallery and at the center of the weekend hustle and bustle of the artisan fair. The *picanha brasileira* (barbecued steak) with fries and *farofa* is recommended. **Known for:** central location; Brazilian favorites; Sunday pasta and salad buffet. 💲 *Average main: R$30* ✉ *Largo dos Jesuítas 169, Embu* ☏ *11/4781–6671* ⊕ *www.osgirassois.com.br* ⊗ *Closed Mon.*

Shopping

Associação Casa dos Artesãos de Embu das Artes
CRAFTS | Maintained by the artisan association of Embu das Artes, this shop has a mix of locally produced crafts, with some occasional gems. Many of the artisans help run the shop and are on hand to answer questions about the work. ✉ *Rua Siqueira Campos 100, Embu* ☎ *11/4704–3820.*

Guarani Artesanato
CRAFTS | Check out the handicrafts made of wood and stone, including sculptures carved from *pau-brasil* (brazilwood). Guarani Artesanato was the first craft store in the city, founded in 1986. ✉ *Largo dos Jesuítas 60, Embu* ☎ *11/4704–3200, 11/99941–6799 WhatsApp* ⊕ *www.guaraniartesanatos.com.br.*

Santana de Parnaíba

42 km (26 miles) northwest of São Paulo.

With more than 200 preserved houses from the 18th and 19th centuries, Santana de Parnaíba is considered the "Ouro Preto from São Paulo"—a town rich with history and colonial architecture. Santana was founded in 1580; by 1625 it was the most important point of departure for the bandeirantes.

In 1901, the first hydroelectric power station in South America was built here. Throughout the 20th century, Santana managed to retain its houses and charm while preserving a local tradition: a rural type of samba called "de bumbo," in which the pacing is marked by the *zabumba* (an instrument usually associated with rhythms from the northeastern states of Brazil). The proximity to a couple of São Paulo's finest suburbs explains the region's fine dining. Outdoors lovers feel at home with the canopy-walking and trekking options.

GETTING HERE AND AROUND
EMTU's *executivo* (executive or first-class) bus from Barra Funda in São Paulo to Pirapora do Bom Jesus (Line 385) stops in Santana de Parnaíba daily and takes one hour.

To reach Santana de Parnaíba from São Paulo—a 40-minute drive—take the express lane of Rodovia Castelo Branco (SP 280) and pay attention to the road signs. On weekends parking is scarce in Santana de Parnaíba, and parking lots can be expensive.

ESSENTIALS
BUS CONTACTS EMTU. ✉ *São Paulo* ☎ *0800/724–0555.*

VISITOR INFORMATION Santana de Parnaíba Secretaria de Cultura e Turismo. ✉ *Largo da Matriz 19, Santana de Parnaíba* ☎ *11/4154–1874* ⊕ *www.santanadeparnaiba.sp.gov.br.*

 ## Sights

Centro Histórico
NEIGHBORHOOD | The best place to begin your trip to Santana de Parnaíba is in the Centro Histórico, where you'll be able to appreciate numerous examples of 17th- and 18th-century colonial architecture. The more than 200 well-preserved houses are concentrated around three streets: Suzana Dias, André Fernandes, and Bartolomeu Bueno—two of which are named after famous bandeirantes. ✉ *Estrada dos romeiros, Santana de Parnaíba.*

Igreja Matriz de Santa Ana
CHURCH | Baroque Igreja Matriz de Santa Ana was built in 1610 and restored in 1892. It has terra-cotta sculptures and an altar with gold-plated details. ✉ *Largo da Matriz s/n, Santana de Parnaíba* ☎ *11/4154–2401* 💲 *Free.*

Museu Casa do Anhanguera
HISTORY MUSEUM | Museu Casa do Anhanguera provides a sharp picture

The Igreja Matriz Santa Ana (Saint Anne Church) is known as one of the oldest churches in Brazil.

of the bandeirantes era. In a 1600 house (the second-oldest in the state) where Bartolomeu Bueno—nicknamed Anhanguera, or "old devil," by indigenous people—was born, the museum displays objects and furniture from the past four centuries. ✉ *Largo da Matriz 9, Santana de Parnaíba* ☎ *11/4154–2700* 💲 *Free.*

🍴 Restaurants

Bartolomeu

$$$ | BRAZILIAN | FAMILY | In a 1905 house, this restaurant serves regional specialties like feijoada and *picadinho* (steak stew served with rice and beans, farofa, fried banana, and fried egg). Salmon and boar ribs are some additional choices. **Known for:** location in Centro Histórico; views of the square and Igreja Matriz de Santa Ana; moqueca de peixe. 💲 *Average main: R$90* ✉ *Praça 14 de Novembro 101, Santana de Parnaíba* ☎ *11/4154–1370* 🌐 *www.bartolomeurestaurante.com.br.*

São Paulo Antigo

$$$ | BRAZILIAN | In a century-old ranch-style house, a hearty buffet lunch is served with dishes such as *feijão tropeiro* (beans with bacon, calabresa sausage, eggs, and farofa), *dobradinha com feijão branco* (intestines and white-bean stew), or *galinha atolada* (rural-style hen stew). **Known for:** homemade Brazilian classics; location in the Centro Histórico; excellent service. 💲 *Average main: R$57* ✉ *Rua Álvaro Luiz do Vale 66, Santana de Parnaíba* ☎ *11/4154–2726* 🌐 *www.saopauloantigo.com.br* 🕐 *No dinner* 🍴 *R$57 weekdays and R$90 on weekends.*

Index

A

A Casa do Porco ✕, *208–209*
Abracadabra 🛏, *169–170*
Academia da Cachaça, *131–132*
Açaí, *23, 235*
Acqua Jungle Ilha Grande Tours, *178*
Adega Pérola ✕, *112*
Águas de São Pedro, *268*
Air travel, *42–43, 79–80, 195–196, 253*
Albamar Restaurante ✕, *94*
Alcohol, *49, 133–134, 188*
Almanara ✕, *239*
Amadeus ✕, *239*
Amarelinho ✕, *95*
Amazonia Soul ✕, *128*
Amora Hotel Maresias 🛏, *260*
Angra dos Reis, *175–177*
Antique shops, *116, 219–220, 243*
Apartment buildings, *203*
Aprazível ✕, *119*
Aquabarra Boutique Hotel and Spa 🛏, *170*
Arábia ✕, *239, 241*
Aratinga Inn 🛏, *181*
Arches, *34, 117*
Arpoador, *26*
Arraial do Cabo, *164–166*
Art galleries, *132, 188, 208, 219, 229, 239, 243*
ArtRio, *71*
Arts centers, *33, 91, 100–101, 203, 213*
Auditório Ibirapuera, *59, 226*
Auto racing, *247*
Avenida Charme Hotel 🛏, *268*
Avenida Paulista, *56, 208, 213–221*

B

Babylon Hype Fair, *152*
Baden-Baden ✕, *270*
Bafo da Prainha ✕, *95*
Bakeries, *150–151, 266, 276*
Ballet, *59, 140*
Balneário Municipal Dr. Octávio Moura Andrade, *268*
Banana da Terra ✕, *185*
Bandeirantes, *269, 278–279*
Bar da Dona Onça ✕, *209*
Bar do Gomez, *120*
Bar do Juarez ✕, *230*
Bar do Momo ✕, *145*
Bar e Restaurante Urca ✕, *106*
Bar Garota de Ipanema, *132*
Baratos Afins, *213*
Bargaining, *98*
Barra da Tijuca, *26, 138–143*
Barra do Sahy, *258*
Barra Funda, *237–239*
Barra Grill ✕, *141*

Bars and lounges
  Portuguese vocabulary for, *114*
  Rio de Janeiro, *83, 104, 115, 120, 131–132, 145*
  São Paulo, *198, 210, 224–225, 229, 236, 242–243*
Bartolomeo ✕, *279*
Beaches, *85, 122*
  Ilhabela, *29, 262–263*
  Rio de Janeiro, *26, 85, 101, 106, 107, 122, 124–125, 128, 139–141*
  Rio de Janeiro State, *165, 166–168, 179, 185*
  Santos, *257*
  São Paulo, *28–29*
  São Sebastião, *28–29, 258–259*
  Ubatuba, *29, 266*
Beco do Comércio, *90*
Beira Mar Tours Búzios, *166*
Beirute, *242*
Bel Vista, *213–221*
Belli Belli Gastrobar ✕, *168*
Belmond Copacabana Palace 🛏, *113*
Biblioteca Nacional, *90*
Bienal, *227, 229*
Bienal do Livro, *70–71*
Biking and bike tours, *63, 137, 230, 248*
Bikinis, Brazilian, *135*
Bioparque do Rio, *144*
Bip Bip, *115*
Bistrô do Paço ✕, *95*
Bixiga, *213–221*
Blue Lagoon, *179*
Blue Tree Premium Faria Lima 🛏, *232*
Boating, *100, 137, 171, 264*
Bonito Bar ✕, *179*
Books, *36–37*
Bookstores, *97, 133*
Botafogo, *56, 100–101, 104*
Boulevard Olímpico, *90*
Bráz ✕, *235*
Brazil
  activities, *47*
  addresses, *47*
  communications, *40, 60–61*
  country descriptions, *3*
  culture, *20*
  dining, *47–49, 112*
  economy, *20–21*
  etiquette, *41*
  festivals and events, *40–41, 70*
  health, *40, 50, 53, 59*
  language, *64–65*
  lodging, *54–55*
  money, *55, 57*
  passports and visas, *40, 58*
  politics, *20*
  religion, *21*
  safety, *41, 50–52*
  seasons and weather, *40*
  sports, *21, 47*
  taxes, *20*
  tipping, *61*
  tourist traps, *41*
  transportation, *41, 42–46*
  visitor information, *61–62*
Brewteco ✕, *101, 104*

Brooklin, *235–237*
Burl Marx, Roberto, *245*
Bus travel, *41, 43–44, 63, 80, 157–158, 196, 253*
Búzios, *166–172*

C

Café Boteco ✕, *275*
Cafés, *96, 113, 208, 270, 275–276*
Camburi Beach, *258–259*
Camburizinho Beach, *258–259*
Campos do Jordão, *268–270, 274*
Candeeiro Pizza e Crepe ✕, *259–260*
Cantaloup ✕, *230*
Cantina Roperto ✕, *215*
Capricciosa ✕, *128*
Car guardians, *52*
Car travel and rentals, *44–46, 52, 59*
  Rio de Janeiro, *80–81, 86*
  Rio de Janeiro side trips, *158*
  São Paulo, *196–197*
  São Paulo side trips, *253*
Carioca da Gema, *120, 122*
Carlota ✕, *215*
Carnival, *40–41, 70, 76–77, 87*
Carnival Experience, *87*
Casa Aquim, *135*
Casa Camolese ✕, *151*
Casa da Cultura, *183*
Casa da Feijoada ✕, *128*
Casa das Rosas, *208*
Casa de Santos Dumont, *173*
Casa Mar Arraial 🛏, *165*
Casadas Rosas, *213*
Casas Brancas 🛏, *170*
Catavento Cultural, *202–203*
Catedral da Sé, *203*
Catedral de São Sebastião do Rio de Janeiro, *90–91*
Catedral São Pedro de Alcântara, *173–174*
Catete, *98–100*
Celeiro ✕, *128*
Cemeteries, *35*
Centro Cultural Banco do Brasil (Rio de Janeiro), *33, 91*
Centro Cultural Banco do Brasil (São Paulo), *203, 208*
Centro Histórico (Santana de Parnaíba), *278*
Centro (Rio de Janeiro), *87–98*
Centro (São Paulo), *202–213*
Chez Claude ✕, *129*
Chez Michou ✕, *168*
Chocolate shops, *211, 270*
Chocolates Montanhês, *270*
Christ the Redeemer, *148*
Churches
  Campos do Jordão, *270*
  Embu, *277*
  Paraty, *184*
  Petrópolis, *173–174*
  Rio de Janeiro, *90–91, 92, 99*
  Santana de Parnaíba, *278*
  São Paulo, *203, 205, 208*

Churrascaria Majórica ✕, *174*
Cidade das Artes, *59*
Cigalon ✕, *168–169*
Cipriani ✕, *112*
Circo Voador, *122*
Climbing, *98, 104*
Clothing and dress, *49, 58*
Coffee and quick bites, *113*
Coffee Museum, *256*
Colleges, *35, 183, 202–203*
Comida di Buteco, *70*
Concerts, *142, 209–210, 238, 246*
Confeitaria Colombo ✕, *96*
Consulado Mineiro ✕, *221, 223*
Consulates, *49–50*
Convento do Santo Antônio, *91*
Convento e Santuário São Francisco, *203*
Copacabana, *56, 106–116*
Copacabana Fort, *33, 106*
Corcovado, *148–149*
Costa do Sol, *156–157*
Costa Verde, *157*
COVID-19, *40*
Crafts shops, *124, 152, 244, 278*
CT Boucherie ✕, *128–129*
Cuisine, *22–23, 47–48*
 Rio de Janeiro, 22–23, 84, 129, 130
 Rio de Janeiro State, 159–160
 São Paulo, 22–23, 223, 242, 244
Cultural centers, *208*

D

D'Amici ✕, *116*
Dance clubs, *211, 225, 237–238*
Deborah Coker Dance Company, *59*
Degas ✕, *223*
Dining, *47–49, 112.* ⇨ *See also Restaurants*
Dois Rios, *179*
D.O.M. ✕, *241*
Dom Mario ✕, *179*
Don Pepe Di Napoli ✕, *235*
Dona Lucinha ✕, *235*
DPNY Beach Hotel & Spa 🛏, *263*
Drinks, *24–25, 49*

E

Ecotourism, *178*
Edifício Copan, *203*
Edifício Itália, *203, 205*
Elephant Hill, *270*
Embassies, *49–50*
Embu, *276–278*
Enoteca Saint VinSaint ✕, *235–236*
Esplanada Grill (Rio de Janeiro) ✕, *129*
Esplanada Grill (São Paulo) ✕, *246*
Estação Ferroviária Emílio Ribas, *269–270*
Estadão Bar & Lanches ✕, *209*
Estancia Don Juan ✕, *169*
Exped Angra, *176*
Experimental Theater, *60*

F

Fairmont Copacabana 🛏, *113*
Famiglia Mancini Trattoria ✕, *216*
Farms, *54, 139, 183*
Fasano Rio 🛏, *131*
Fasano ✕, *241*
Favelas, *86, 134*
Fazenda Bananal, *183*
Fazendas, *54, 183*
Feira da General Clicério, *152*
Feira do Bixiga, *213*
Félix Beach, *29*
Festival de Literatura de Paraty, *71*
Festivals and events, *40–41, 70–71, 76–77, 115, 227–228, 230*
Film, *37, 71, 98, 210, 219*
Flamengo, *56, 100–104*
Forests, *149*
Fortaleza de Santa Cruz, *1564*
Forte Defensor Perpétuo, *184*
Forts, *33, 106, 164, 184*
Freddy ✕, *230*
Fresia Surf Class, *172*
Frevo ✕, *216*
Fundação Planetário, *149*
Futuros Arte e Tecnologia, *100–101*

G

Gam Arte e Molduras, *132*
Gardens, *100, 139, 149–150, 245, 270*
Gastromotiva ✕, *119*
Gay Pride Parade, The, *230*
Gelato Donato ✕, *275–276*
Gero Panini Ipanema ✕, *129*
"Girl from Ipanema" (song), *132*
Glória, *98–100*
Golden Tower Hotel 🛏, *224*
Golf, *142–143, 171*
Governor's winter residence, *270*
Grand Hyatt Rio de Janeiro 🛏, *141*
Grand Mercure Rio de Janeiro Copacabana 🛏, *113*
Grande Hotel Campos do Jordão 🛏, *270, 274*
Grande Hotel São Pedro 🛏, *268*
Guimarães Square, *117*
Gurume Ipanema ✕, *129*

H

Hang gliding, *137–138*
Health, *40, 53, 59*
Helisight (helicopter tours), *87*
Hello Kitty and Friends 2D ✕, *234*
Hiking, *98, 104, 173, 175*
Hilton Barra 🛏, *141*
Hilton Copacabana 🛏, *113–114*
Hilton São Paulo Morumbi 🛏, *236*
Historic homes, *173, 213, 245*
Historical Museum of the Army, *33, 106–107*
History, *34–35, 193, 199, 203, 269*
Horse racing, *151*
Hot springs, *268*

Hotel do Bosque 🛏, *176*
Hotel Emiliano 🛏, *114*
Hotel Fasano São Paulo 🛏, *242*
Hotel Firenze 🛏, *276*
Hotel Grand Mercure São Paulo Ibirapuerta 🛏, *229*
Hotel le Relais de la Borie 🛏, *170*
Hotel Porto Pacuíba 🛏, *263–264*
Hotel Pullman São Paulo Ibirapuerta 🛏, *229*
Hotel Santa Teresa Rio MGallery by Sofitel 🛏, *120*
Hotel Spa Nau Royal 🛏, *260*
Hotel Unique 🛏, *232*
Hotels
 Águas de São Pedro, 268
 Campos do Jordão, 254, 270, 274
 Ilhabela, 253, 263–264
 Rio de Janeiro, 54–55, 56, 83, 96–97, 104, 113–115, 120, 131, 141–142, 151
 Rio de Janeiro State, 158, 165, 169–170, 174–175, 176–177, 181, 186, 188
 Santos, 258
 São Paulo, 54–55, 56, 198, 209, 217–219, 224, 229, 232, 236, 242
 São Sebastião, 260–261
 Serra Negra, 253, 276
 Ubatuba, 266
Huntress, The, *193*

I

Ibirapuera Obelisk, *193*
Ibis Budget 🛏, *217–218*
Ibis São Paulo Paulista 🛏, *218*
Ice cream shops, *259, 275–276*
Igreja de Nossa Senhora da Candelária, *92*
Igreja de Nossa Senhora da Glória do Outeiro, *99*
Igreja de Nossa Senhora dos Remédios, *184*
Igreja de Santa Rita, *184*
Igreja de São Francisco da Penitência, *92*
Igreja Matriz de Santa Ana, *278*
Igreja Nossa Senhora do Rosário, *277*
Ilha das Cabras, *265*
Ilha das Couves, *29*
Ilha de Búzios, *265*
Ilha Grande, *177–182*
Ilha Sul ✕, *263*
Ilhabela, *29, 261–265*
Imperial Palace, *34*
Inland Zona Sul, *148–152*
Instituto Butantan, *245*
Instituto Tomie Ohtake, *221*
InterContinental São Paulo 🛏, *242*
Internet, *61*
Ipanema, *84, 124–138*
Ipanema Inn 🛏, *131*
Itaim Bibi, *56, 230–233*
Itaú Cultural, *213*
Itineraries, *66–69, 84, 158–159, 200*

J

Janeiro, *131*
Jardim Botânico (Rio de Janeiro), *149–150*
Jardim Botânico (São Paulo), *245*
Jardim de Napoli ✕, *216*
Jardins, *56, 239–245*
Jogging, *230*
JO&JOE Rio, *151*
Jóquei Clube, *151*
Jun Sakamoto ✕, *223*
Juquehy Beach, *28*
JW Marriott Rio de Janeiro, *114*

K

Kinoshita ✕, *236*
Kite surfing, *79, 172*

L

La Bicyclette ✕, *150–151*
La Casserole ✕, *209*
La Piadina Cucina Italiana ✕, *236*
La Suite by Dussol, *141–142*
La Tambouille ✕, *231*
La Tartine ✕, *216*
Lagune Barra Hotel, *141*
Lapa, *116–124*
Lapa Arches, *34, 117*
Lapa Steps, *117*
Lasai ✕, *104*
Lazzarella ✕, *216*
Leblon, *56, 124-137*
Leme, *116*
Lenny, *133*
LGBTQI+, *70, 230, 238*
L'Hotel PortoBay São Paulo, *242*
Liberdade, *233–234*
Libraries, *34, 90, 94*
Locallnda della Mimosa, *174–175*
Lodging, *54–55, 113, 232*. *See also Hotels; Pousadas*
Lollapalooza São Paulo, *70*
Lopes Mendes, *179*
Lua e Mar ✕, *181*
Luz Station, *35*

M

Madê Cozinha Autoral ✕, *257–258*
Madeleine, *226*
Maison Joly, *264*
Maní ✕, *241*
Maracanã, *144*
Maresia, *28*
Maresias, *259*
Margutta ✕, *130*
Marine Restô ✕, *112*
Markets, *97–98, 136, 152, 212–213, 234*
Memorial da América Latina, *237*
Mercado Municipal, *212*
Mestiço ✕, *216*
Miam Miam ✕, *104*
Miramar Hotel by Windsor, *114*
Mistico ✕, *169*
Monasteries, *92, 205*
Monte Legre do Sul, *275*
Monument to Pedro Álvares Cabral, *193*
Monumento aos Pracinhas, *99*
Monuments and memorials, *99, 193, 237, 269*
Mosteiro de São Bento (Rio de Janeiro), *92*
Mosteiro de São Bento (São Paulo), *205*
Mostra Internacional de Cinema de São Paulo, *71*
Mountains, *105–106, 148–149*
Museum Oi Futuro, *100–101*
Museu Afro Brasil, *226–227*
Museu Carmen Miranda, *33*
Museu Casa do Anhanguera, *278–279*
Museu Casa do Pontal, *138–139*
Museu Chácara do Céu, *119*
Museu da Arte de São Paulo, *32, 213, 215*
Museu da Imagem e do Som, *119*
Museu de Arte Contemporânea (Niterói), *164*
Museu de Arte Contemporânea (São Paulo), *227*
Museu de Arte de São Paulo, *213, 215*
Museu de Arte do Rio, *93*
Museu de Arte Moderna (Rio de Janeiro), *93*
Museu de Arte Moderna (São Paulo), *227*
Museu do Futebol, *32*
Museu do Ipiranga, *35, 246*
Museu Flamengo, *124*
Museu Histórico da Imigração Japonesa no Brasil, *233*
Museu Histórico do Exército, *33, 106–107*
Museu Histórico Nacional, *93*
Museu Imperial, *174*
Museu Nacional, *144–145*
Museu Padre Anchieta, *205, 208*
Museu Pelé, *256–257*
Museum of Japanese Immigration, *32*
Museum of Sacred Art, *205*
Museum of the Portuguese Language, *32*
Museum of the Republic, *100*
Museum of Tomorrow, *32, 93*
Museums
  Rio de Janeiro, *32–33, 93, 100–101, 106–107, 119, 124, 138–139, 144–145*
  Rio de Janeiro State, *164, 183*
  Santana de Parnaíba, *278–279*
  Santos, *256–257*
  São Paulo, *32–33, 35, 205, 208, 213, 215, 221, 226–227, 229, 233, 245, 246*
Music clubs
  Rio de Janeiro, *115–116, 120, 122–123, 142, 145*
  São Paulo, *210, 225, 226, 232–233, 236–237*
  São Sebastião, *261*

N

Nagayama ✕, *231*
National Historical Museum, *34*
Nature preserves, *175*
Neves Square, *117*
New Year's Eve, *115*
Neymar, Ronaldo, *220*
Nightlife
  Rio de Janeiro, *57, 83, 104, 115–116, 120, 122–123, 131–132, 142, 145, 148, 151*
  São Paulo, *57–58, 198, 210–211, 224–226, 229, 232–233, 236–238, 242–243*
  São Sebastião, *261*
Nino Cucina & Vino ✕, *231*
Niterói, *161–164*
Northeastern Fair, *97–98*
Nosso, *132*
Novotel São Paulo Jaraguá Conventions, *209*

O

O Garimpo ✕, *277*
O Pedaço da Pizza ✕, *216–217*
O Sol Artesanato, *152*
Observatories, *149*
Oficina de Pizzas ✕, *223*
OhKinha ✕, *232*
Olympic Park, *139*
Opera, *98*
Oro ✕, *151*
Os Girassóis Restaurante ✕, *277*
Osklen, *135*

P

Pabu Izakaya ✕, *130*
Packing, *58*
Paço Imperial, *93–94*
Padaria e Confeitaria Serrana ✕, *276*
Padaria Integrale ✕, *266*
Paddleboarding, *104*
Palaces, *34, 93–94, 100, 174, 270*
Palácio do Catete, *100*
Palácio Boa Vista, *270*
Palácio de Cristal, *174*
Palácio Tiradentes, *94*
Paraty, *182–188*
Parks
  Campos do Jordão, *270*
  Morumbi, *245*
  Rio de Janeiro, *35, 101, 144–145, 149*
  São Paulo, *192–193, 215, 226–230*
Parque Amantikir, *270*
Parque Balneário Hotel Santos, *258*
Parque Burle Marx, *245*
Parque do Flamengo, *101*
Parque Estadual Campos do Jordão, *270*
Parque Ibirapuera, *192–193, 226–230*
Parque Lage, *150*
Parque Nacional da Serra dos Órgãos, *175*

Parque Trianon, *215*
Parque Zoológico de São Paulo, *246*
Passports, *58, 59*
Pateo do Collegio, *205, 208*
Pátio do Colégio, *35*
Pavilhão da Bienal, *227, 229*
Pavilhão Japonês, *229*
Pé de Manga ✕, *223*
Pedra do Sal, *59, 122–123*
Pelé (Edson Arantes do Nascimento), *220, 256–257*
Performance venues
Rio de Janeiro, *77, 123–124, 142, 145, 148*
São Paulo, *219, 238*
Performing arts
Rio de Janeiro, *59, 83–84, 98, 116, 123–124, 142, 145, 148, 151*
São Paulo, *59–60, 198–200, 209–210, 219, 238–239, 246–247*
Pestana Rio Atlântica 🏨, *114*
Petrópolis, *172–175*
Pinacoteca do Estado de São Paulo, *32, 208*
Pinheiros, *221–226*
Più Pinheiros ✕, *223*
Pizaria Camelo ✕, *241*
Pizza na Praça ✕, *181*
Pizzas, *129*
Plazas and squares, *117, 139, 208*
Police, *85*
Pools, *179*
Porto Bay Rio Internacional 🏨, *114*
Porto da Barra, *170*
Portuguese language, *40, 64–65, 114*
Pousada Barcarola 🏨, *170*
Pousada Casa Turquesa 🏨, *186*
Pousada da Alcobaça 🏨, *175*
Pousada do Canto 🏨, *181*
Pousada do Príncipe 🏨, *186*
Pousada do Sandi 🏨, *186*
Pousada dos Corsarios 🏨, *176*
Pousada Literária de Paraty 🏨, *186*
Pousada Mestre Augusto, *177*
Pousada Monte Imperial 🏨, *175*
Pousada Naturalia 🏨, *181*
Pousada Pardieiro 🏨, *188*
Pousada Picinguaba 🏨, *266*
Pousada Porto Mare 🏨, *260–261*
Pousada Torre del Mar 🏨, *266*
Pousada Villa Capivary 🏨, *274*
Pousada Ziláh 🏨, *218*
Pousadas, *54–55, 160*
Campos do Jordão, *274*
Rio de Janeiro State, *170, 175, 176–177, 181, 186, 188*
São Paulo, *218, 232*
São Sebastião, *260–261*
Serra Negra, *276*
Ubatuba, *266*
Praça da Liberdade, *234*
Praça da Sé, *208*
Praia Azeda, *167*
Praia da Armação, *262–263*
Praia da Barra, *140*
Praia da Ferradura, *167*

Praia de Antiguinhos, *185*
Praia de Castelhanos, *29*
Praia de Copacabana, *107*
Praia de Geribá, *167*
Praia de Grumari, *140*
Praia de Ipanema, *125*
Praia de São Conrado, *140*
Praia do Arpoador, *124–125*
Praia do Botafogo, *101*
Praia do Cachadaço, *185*
Praia do Curral, *263*
Praia do Diabo, *107*
Praia do Flamengo, *101*
Praia do Forno, *165*
Praia do Leblon, *125*
Praia do Leme, *107*
Praia do Pontal da Atalaia, *165*
Praia do Prumirim, *266*
Praia do Santos, *257*
Praia do Sono, *185*
Praia do Vidigal, *128*
Praia Grande (Ilhabela), *263*
Praia Grande (Ubatuba), *266*
Praia João Fernandes, *168*
Praia Vermelha, *106*
Prainha, *140*
Prices, *55, 57, 84, 198, 254*
Promenades, *90*
Punto Divino ✕, *185–186*

Q

Quinta da Boa Vista, *145*

R

Radisson Hotel Barra Rio de Janeiro 🏨, *142*
Rafting, *104*
Real Gabinete Portugues de Leitura, *34–35, 94*
Recife, *50*
Recreio dos Bandeirantes, *140–141*
Refúgio ✕, *186*
Renaissance São Paulo Hotel 🏨, *242*
Reserva, *26*
Restaurante Migá ✕, *234*
Restaurante Point de Grumari ✕, *141*
Restaurante Shirley ✕, *116*
Restaurants, *47–49, 112*
Campos do Jordão, *270*
Embu, *277*
Ilhabela, *263*
Rio de Janeiro, *84, 94–96, 101, 104, 106, 112–113, 116, 119, 128–131, 141, 145, 150–151*
Rio de Janeiro State, *159–160, 168–169, 174, 179, 181, 185–186*
Santana de Parnaíba, *279*
Santos, *257–258*
São Paulo, *200, 208–209, 215–217, 221, 223–224, 225, 229, 230–232, 234, 235–236, 239, 241–242, 246*
São Paulo side trips, *254*
São Sebastião, *259–260*
Serra Negra, *275–276*

Ubatuba, *266*
Ride-sharing, *41*
Rio Antiques Fair, *97*
Rio Cultural Secrets, *86, 173*
Rio de Janeiro
activities, *79, 98, 100, 137–138, 142–143, 151–152*
beaches, *26, 101, 106, 107, 124–125, 128, 139–141*
city descriptions, *3, 78*
coffee and quick bites, *113*
cuisine, *22–23*
drinks, *24–25*
embassies and consulates, *49*
favelas, *134*
festivals and events, *70, 71, 76–77, 115*
history, *34–35*
itineraries, *66–67, 84*
lodging, *54–55, 56, 83, 96–97, 104, 113–115, 120, 131, 141–142, 151*
neighborhoods, *56, 87, 90, 98–99, 100, 105, 106, 116–117, 124, 134, 138, 143, 148*
nightlife, *57, 83, 104, 115–116, 120, 122–123, 131–132, 142, 145, 148, 151*
packing, *58*
performing arts, *59, 83–84, 98, 116, 123–124, 142, 145, 148, 151*
police, *84*
prices, *55*
restaurants, *84, 94–96, 101, 104, 106, 112–113, 116, 119, 128–131, 141, 145, 150–151*
safety, *85*
shopping, *30–31, 84–85, 97–98, 116, 124, 132–137, 143, 152*
side trips from, *153–188*
sights, *32–33, 34–34, 90–94, 99–101, 105–106, 117, 119, 124, 138–139, 144–145, 148–150*
top reasons to go, *74*
tours, *63, 85–87*
transportation, *42–46, 79–82*
travel seasons, *62, 87*
visitor information, *87*
Rio de Janeiro International Film Festival, *71*
Rio de Janeiro State. ⇨ See also Rio de Janeiro
activities, *166, 171–172, 182*
area descriptions, *156–157*
beaches, *165, 166–168, 179, 185*
cities and towns, *161, 164, 166, 172, 175–176, 177, 182–183, 185*
history, *159*
hotels, *158, 165, 169–170, 174–175, 176–177, 181, 186, 188*
itineraries, *158–159*
restaurants, *159–160, 168–169, 174, 179, 181, 185–186*
shopping, *170, 188*
sights, *164, 173–174, 179, 183–185*
top reasons to go, *154*
tours, *160, 166, 173, 176, 178, 183*
transportation, *157–158*
travel seasons, *160*
Rio Hiking, *86*
Rio Minho ✕, *96*
Rio Museum of Art, *33*
Rio Scenarium, *123*
Ritz ✕, *241*

Roberto Burle Marz Farm, *139*
Rocinha, *134*
Rock in Rio, *71*
Rocka Beach Lounge & Restaurant ✕, *169*
Rosewood 🛏, *218*
Rubaiyat Faria Lima ✕, *232*
Rui Barbosa House Museum, The, *101*

S

Safety, *85, 200, 209*
Sailing, *100, 137*
Sala São Paulo, *60, 209*
Samba, *59, 116, 142, 145, 239, 246–247*
Samba do Trabalhador, *142*
Samba Schools, *59*
Sambadrome, *77*
San Gabriel 🛏, *219*
Santa Teresa, *116–124*
Santana de Parnaíba, *278–279*
Santo Scenarium ✕, *96*
Santos, *254–258*
São Conrado, *138–143*
São João Batista Cemetery, *35*
São Paulo
  activities, *195, 221, 230, 247–248*
  beaches outside, *28–29*
  city descriptions, *3, 194–195*
  cuisine, *22–23*
  drinks, *24–25*
  embassies and consulates, *49*
  festivals and events, *70–71, 227, 229, 230*
  greater, *245–248*
  history, *34–35, 193, 199, 203, 269*
  itineraries, *67–69, 200*
  lodging, *54–55, 56, 198, 209, 217–219, 224, 229, 232, 236, 242*
  neighborhoods, *56, 202, 213, 221, 230, 233, 237*
  nicknames, *197*
  nightlife, *57–58, 198, 210–211, 224–226, 229, 232–233, 236–238, 242–243*
  packing, *58*
  performing arts, *59–60, 198–200, 209–210, 219, 238–239, 246–247*
  prices, *55*
  restaurants, *200, 208–209, 215–217, 221, 223–224, 225, 229, 230–232, 234, 235–236, 239, 241–242, 246*
  safety, *200*
  shopping, *30–31, 60, 201, 211–213, 219–221, 226, 229, 237, 239, 243–245, 247*
  side trips from, *249–279*
  sights, *32–33, 35, 192–193, 202–203, 205, 208, 213, 215, 221, 226–227, 229, 233–234, 237, 245–246*
  top reasons to go, *190*
  tours, *63, 201*
  transportation, *42–46, 195–198*
  travel seasons, *62, 201–202*
  visitor information, *201*
  weather, *197*
São Paulo Antigo ✕, *279*
São Paulo Dance Company, *59*

São Paulo Grand Prix, *71*
São Paulo LGBTQI+ Parade, *70*
São Pedro Chapel, *270*
São Sebastião, *28–29, 258–261*
Satyricon ✕, *130*
Scuba diving, *52–53, 166, 171, 182, 264–265*
Selvagem ✕, *229*
Serra Negra, *274–276*
Serum production, *245*
SESC São Paulo, *59*
74 Restaurant ✕, *169*
Shangri-la Hotel Pousada 🛏, *276*
Sheraton Grand Rio Hotel & Resort 🛏, *131*
Shopping, *30–31, 98*
  Campos do Jordão, *274*
  Embu, *278*
  Rio de Janeiro, *30–31, 84–85, 97–98, 116, 124, 132–137, 143, 152*
  Rio de Janeiro State, *170, 188*
  São Paulo, *30–31, 60, 201, 211–213, 219–221, 226, 229, 237, 239, 243–245, 247*
Skyscrapers, *203, 205*
Snorkeling, *182*
Soccer, *195, 220, 221, 248*
Socialtel Copacabana 🛏, *114–115*
Sol Ipanema 🛏, *131*
Solar do Imperio 🛏, *175*
Spas, *138*
Spazziano ✕, *130*
Speranza ✕, *217*
Spirit Copa, *115*
Sports, *79, 195, 220, 221, 248*
Sports venues, *144, 221, 248*
Spot ✕, *217*
Staircases, *117*
Subways, *46, 81–82, 197–198*
Sugarloaf Mountain, *105–106*
Sujinho ✕, *217*
Surfing, *79, 143, 152, 172, 265*
Surf's Up Rio, *152*

T

Tanga, *135*
Taxes, *59, 60*
Taxis, *41, 55, 81, 198, 253*
Teatro Municipal de São Paulo, *35*
Templo da Carne Marcos Bassi ✕, *217*
Tereze ✕, *119*
Terra Vertical, *173*
Teva ✕, *130–131*
Thai Brasil ✕, *186*
Theater(s)
  Rio de Janeiro, *59, 94, 98, 141*
  São Paulo, *35, 59, 60, 210*
Theatro Municipal de Rio de Janeiro, *59, 94, 98*
Theatro Municipal de São Paulo, *59*
Tijuca Forest, *149*
Tiny Cat Café ✕, *113*
Tivoli Mofarrej São Paulo 🛏, *219*

Tombs, *35, 91, 203*
Topik Beach Club ✕, *112*
Tordesilhas ✕, *241–242*
Tours
  Campos do Jordão, *269–270*
  Embu, *277*
  Ilhabela, *262*
  Rio de Janeiro, *63, 85–87, 100, 104*
  Rio de Janeiro State, *160, 166, 173, 176, 178, 183*
  Santos, *255–256*
  São Paulo, *63, 201*
  São Paulo side trips, *254*
Trains and train stations, *35, 46, 81–82, 269–270*
Transportation, *42–46. ⇨ See also specific locations*
Travel seasons, *62, 87, 160, 201–202*
Tridade, *185*
Trutas do Rocio ✕, *174*
Tryp São Paulo Higienópolis - Melia 🛏, *219*
TW Guaimbê Exclusive Suites 🛏, *264*

U

Ubatuba, *29, 265–266*
Urca, *105–106*

V

Vaccinations, *40, 59, 245*
Veloso, *229*
Venga Chiringuito ✕, *112–113*
Veridiana ✕, *217*
Viana ✕, *263*
Vidigal, *128*
Viewpoints, *99, 148–149, 270*
Vila Madalena, *56, 221–226*
Vila Mariana, *56, 197, 229*
Vila Olímpia, *235–237*
Villa Bebek 🛏, *261*
Virada Cultural, *70*
Visas, *40, 58–59*
Visitor information, *87, 201*

W

Walking tours, *63, 85–86, 208*
Weather, *40, 197*
West of Downtown* (Rio de Janeiro), *143–148*
Windsor Excelsior 🛏, *115*
Windsor Guanabara 🛏, *96–97*

Y

Yakisoba, *244*
Yoo2 🛏, *104*

Z

Ziplining, *173*
Zoos, *144, 246*

Photo Credits

Front Cover: Wsfurlan/Getty Images [Descr.:Aerial view of the famous cable stayed bridge located at Sao Paulo city. The name of this bridge is "Octavio Frias de Oliveira ". This is a famous image of the most important city of Brazil. The bridge is over Pinheiros River and Marginal Pinheiros.] **Back cover, from left to right:** Ale Curtinhas/Shutterstock. ADVTP/Shutterstock. Catarina Belova/Shutterstock. **Spine:** Sebastian Forero/Shutterstock. **Interior, from left to right:** Celso Pupo/Shutterstock (1). Caio acquesta/GettyImages (2-3). Arkadij Schell/Shutterstock (6). MKSuzuki/Shutterstock (7). **Chapter 1: Experience Rio de Janeiro and São Paulo:** Ranimiro Lotufo Neto/iStockphoto (8-9). Marianna Ianovska/Shutterstock (10-11). Catarina Belova/Shutterstock (11). Celso Pupo/Shutterstock (11). Donatas Dabravolskas/Shutterstock (12). PeopleImages.com - Yuri A/Shutterstock (12). Eduardo Ortega/MASP (12). Delmiro Junior/Shutterstock (12). Vitormarigo/Shutterstock (13). Catarina Belova/Shutterstock (13). R.M. Nunes/Shutterstock (14). Alf Ribeiro/Shutterstock (14). Fred S. Pinheiro/Shutterstock (14). F de Jesus/Shutterstock (14). Shipsony/Dreamstime (15). Gavergani/Dreamstime (16). Bildagentur Zoonar GmbH/Shutterstock (16). Diego Grandi/Shutterstock (16). MKSuzuki/Shutterstock (16). Catarina Belova/Shutterstock (17). Focus Pix/Shutterstock (17).Dabldy/Dreamstime (17). BW Press/Shutterstock (17). ailsonSantos/Shutterstock (22). Gabriel Gabino/Shutterstock (22). Turpentyne/Shutterstock (22). Hans Elmo/Shutterstock (22). Vinicius Bacarin/Shutterstock (22). Patrick Carvalho/Shutterstock (23). RHJ/iStockphoto (23). T hotography/Shutterstock (23). TMP - An Instant of Time/Shutterstock (23). Ppy2010ha/Dreamstime (23). RHJPhotos/Shutterstock (24). P Photos Brazil/Shutterstock (24). Uilson Junqueira/iStockphoto (24). RHJ/iStockphoto (24). FG Trade/GettyImages (25). Diego Grandi/Shutterstock (26). Catarina Belova/Shutterstock (27). Ranimiro Lotufo Neto/Shutterstock (28). Fred S. Pinheiro/Shutterstock (29). Joaosamam/Shutterstock (30). Stock-boris/Shutterstock (30). Aleksandar Todorovic/Shutterstock (30). Jorge Maricato/Alamy (31). Marcelo.mg.photos/Shutterstock (31). Wagner Santos de Almeida/Shutterstock (32). Samuel Ericksen/Shutterstock (32). Wilfredor/WikimediaCommons (32).Henri Trajan/Shutterstock (33). Renatopmeireles/Shutterstock (33). **Chapter 3: Rio de Janeiro:** Marchello74/Shutterstock (73). Celso Pupo/Shutterstock (76). A.Paes/Shutterstock (77). Andre Luiz Moreira/Shutterstock (77). Davslens - davslens.com/Shutterstock (91). Rafa Barcelos/Shutterstock (92). Catarina Belova/Shutterstock (95). Cesar Lima/Shutterstock (97). Donatas Dabravolskas/Shutterstock (99). Arkadij Schell/Shutterstock (105). Cesar Vieira/iStockphoto (110-111). GiordanoCipriani/GettyImages (121). Roberto Machado Noa/GettyImages (123). Catarina Belova/Shutterstock (125). Skreidzeleu/Shutterstock (133). Halley Pacheco de Oliveira/WikimediaCommons (138). Dabldy/iStockphoto (144). Vitor Marigo/GettyImages (150). **Chapter 4: Side Trips from Rio:** SvetlanaTestova/Shutterstock (153). Renatopmeireles/Shutterstock (162-163). Andre ato/Shutterstock (165). Catarina Belova/Shutterstock (167). Alex Photo Stock/Shutterstock (168).Eduardo onseca Arraes/GettyImages (171). Fabricio Araujo/Shutterstock (173). Luis Inacio P Prado/Shutterstock (177). Arkadij Schell/Shutterstock (180). Stefan Lambauer/Shutterstock (182). Isabella Xisto/500px/GettyImages (187). **Chapter 5: São Paulo:** FerreiraSilva/GettyImages (189). Lucianospagnolribeiro/Shutterstock (192). Fabianomr/Shutterstock (193). Lucianospagnolribeiro/Shutterstock (193). Patricia Hikari/Shutterstock (202). Rafael Elias Henrique/Shutterstock (205). Zigres/Shutterstock (206-207). Aguina/Dreamstim (211). Davslens/Shutterstock 212). Maarten Zeehandelaar/Shutterstock (215). Daniellebra/Shutterstock (218). Afagundes/Dreamstime (222). Reginaldo Bianco/Shutterstock (227). ESB Professional/Shutterstock (233).Vinicius Bacarin/Shutterstock (234). Thiago Leite/Shutterstock (238). MkSuzuki/Shutterstock (243). Sonny Vermeer/Shutterstock (247). **Chapter 6: Side Trips from São Paulo:** Wtondossantos/Shutterstock (249). Lorenzo Costa/Shutterstock (255). Stefan Lambauer/Shutterstock (257). RaquelGomes/Shutterstock (260).Gustavoferretti/GettyImages (262). Erika Cristina Manno/Shutterstock (264). Dancorreaphoto/Shutterstock (267). Mateus Fiuza/Shutterstock (271). Alexandre Nelvis Klanovichs/GettyImages (272-273) Andrea Cirillo Lopes/Shutterstock (275). Renbrins/Shutterstock (277). Luiz Barrionuevo/Shutterstock (279). **About Our Writers:** All photos are courtesy of the writers.

Every effort has been made to trace the copyright holders, and we apologize in advance for any accidental errors. We would be happy to apply the corrections in the following edition of this publication.

Notes

Notes

Fodor's RIO DE JANEIRO & SÃO PAULO

Publisher: Stephen Horowitz, *General Manager*

Editorial: Douglas Stallings, *Editorial Director;* Jill Fergus, Alexis Kelly, Amanda Sadlowski, *Senior Editors;* Brian Eschrich, *Editor;* Angelique Kennedy-Chavannes, Yoojin Shin, *Associate Editors*

Design: Tina Malaney, *Director of Design and Production;* Jessica Gonzalez, *Senior Designer;* Jaimee Shaye, *Graphic Design Associate*

Production: Jennifer DePrima, *Editorial Production Manager;* Elyse Rozelle, *Senior Production Editor;* Carol Seigler, *Production Editor*

Maps: Rebecca Baer, *Map Director;* Mark Stroud (Moon Street Cartography), *Cartographer*

Photography: Viviane Teles, *Director of Photography;* Namrata Aggarwal, Neha Gupta, Payal Gupta, Ashok Kumar, *Photo Editors;* Jade Rodgers, Shanelle Jacobs, *Photo Production Intern*

Business and Operations: Chuck Hoover, *Chief Marketing Officer;* Robert Ames, *Group General Manager*

Public Relations and Marketing: Joe Ewaskiw, *Senior Director of Communications and Public Relations*

Fodors.com: Jeremy Tarr, *Editorial Director;* Rachael Levitt, *Managing Editor*

Technology: Jon Atkinson, *Executive Director of Technology;* Rudresh Teotia, *Associate Director of Technology;* Alison Lieu, *Project Manager*

Writers: Leticia Davino, Luana Ferreira, Gabriela Godoi

Editor: Angelique Kennedy-Chavannes

Production Editor: Jennifer DePrima

Copyright © 2025 by Fodor's Travel, a division of MH Sub I, LLC, dba Internet Brands.

Fodor's is a registered trademark of Internet Brands, Inc. All rights reserved. Published in the United States by Fodor's Travel, a division of Internet Brands, Inc. No maps, illustrations, or other portions of this book may be reproduced in any form without written permission from the publisher.

5th Edition

ISBN 978-1-64097-783-9

ISSN 1941-0239

All details in this book are based on information supplied to us at press time. Always confirm information when it matters, especially if you're making a detour to visit a specific place. Fodor's expressly disclaims any liability, loss, or risk, personal or otherwise, that is incurred as a consequence of the use of any of the contents of this book.

SPECIAL SALES

This book is available at special discounts for bulk purchases for sales promotions or premiums. For more information, e-mail SpecialMarkets@fodors.com.

PRINTED IN CANADA

10 9 8 7 6 5 4 3 2 1